Career Explorations

Cover Credits: greenbutterfly/Shutterstock

mheducation.com/prek-12

Copyright © 2024 McGraw Hill

All rights reserved. No part of this publication may be reproduced or distributed in any form or by any means, or stored in a database or retrieval system, without the prior written consent of McGraw Hill, including, but not limited to, network storage or transmission, or broadcast for distance learning.

Send all inquiries to:
McGraw-Hill
8787 Orion Place
Columbus, OH 43240

ISBN: 978-1-26-543976-7
MHID: 1-26-543976-1

1 2 3 4 5 6 7 8 9 LWI 28 27 26 25 24 23

To the Student

Career Explorations

This book introduces you to the various industries and the variety of opportunities that exist in them. It will show you the steps you need to take to build a career in a field you are passionate about. It will also provide the opportunity to practice the skills that will help you succeed once you begin your career journey. These skills are needed in almost every job and are often called transferable skills, professional skills, employability skills, or soft skills.

Finding a job that interests you is the first step in managing your career. You will need to explore many job and career possibilities. What if your goals change? What if a shift in the labor market or the economy occurs? You may need, or want, to change jobs or even careers. By improving your transferable skills, such as speaking, writing, organizing, planning, and problem-solving, you will make yourself a more valuable employee and be able to cope with changes in the labor market. The more transferable skills you develop, the greater your chance of success at any job.

When considering a career, it is important to understand the realities of the industry. Which jobs have the strongest growth? Which offer good opportunities for advancement? Which jobs align most closely with your own abilities and interests? Are many jobs available in your area?

Keep these questions in mind as you read each chapter in this book. When you have finished, refer to them again to see how many you can answer. Do your answers make you more or less likely to want to work in a particular industry? If you feel an industry may be right for you, go to the online course to access more practice questions. Using real-world situations, they will help you begin preparing for any career in the industry you desire.

Table of Contents

Chapter 1: Exploring Your Future
Lesson 1-1 Introducing Your Future ... 2
Lesson 1-2 Building a Career ... 5
Lesson 1-3 Education and Training ... 6
Lesson 1-4 Trends ... 9

Chapter 2: Science, Technology, Engineering, & Mathematics (STEM)
Lesson 2-1 STEM Today ... 11
Lesson 2-2 STEM Jobs ... 19
Lesson 2-3 Building a Career in STEM ... 27
Lesson 2-4 Education and Training for STEM Opportunities ... 29
Lesson 2-5 Working Conditions in the STEM Industry ... 36
Lesson 2-6 Trends in STEM ... 40

Chapter 3: Manufacturing
Lesson 3-1 Manufacturing Today ... 45
Lesson 3-2 Manufacturing Jobs ... 52
Lesson 3-3 Building a Career in Manufacturing ... 58
Lesson 3-4 Education and Training for Manufacturing Opportunities ... 60
Lesson 3-5 Working Conditions in the Manufacturing Industry ... 66
Lesson 3-6 Trends in Manufacturing ... 70

Chapter 4: Information Technology (IT)
Lesson 4-1 IT Today ... 75
Lesson 4-2 IT Jobs ... 82
Lesson 4-3 Building a Career in IT ... 89
Lesson 4-4 Education and Training for IT Opportunities ... 91
Lesson 4-5 Working Conditions in the IT Industry ... 95
Lesson 4-6 Trends in IT ... 100

Chapter 5: Arts & Media
Lesson 5-1 Arts & Media Today ... 105
Lesson 5-2 Arts & Media Jobs ... 112
Lesson 5-3 Building a Career in Arts & Media ... 120
Lesson 5-4 Education and Training for Arts & Media Opportunities ... 122
Lesson 5-5 Working Conditions in the Arts & Media Industry ... 129
Lesson 5-6 Trends in Arts & Media ... 132

Chapter 6: Architecture & Construction

- **Lesson 6-1** Architecture & Construction Today ... 137
- **Lesson 6-2** Architecture & Construction Jobs ... 145
- **Lesson 6-3** Building a Career in Architecture & Construction ... 151
- **Lesson 6-4** Education and Training for Architecture & Construction Opportunities ... 154
- **Lesson 6-5** Working Conditions in the Architecture & Construction Industry ... 161
- **Lesson 6-6** Trends in Architecture & Construction ... 165

Chapter 7: Agriculture, Food, & Natural Resources

- **Lesson 7-1** Agriculture, Food, & Natural Resources Today ... 170
- **Lesson 7-2** Agriculture, Food, & Natural Resources Jobs ... 178
- **Lesson 7-3** Building a Career in Agricultural, Food, & Natural Resources ... 186
- **Lesson 7-4** Education and Training for Agriculture, Food, & Natural Resources Opportunities ... 189
- **Lesson 7-5** Working Conditions in the Agriculture, Food, & Natural Resources Industry ... 196
- **Lesson 7-6** Trends in Agriculture, Food, & Natural Resources ... 201

Chapter 8: Government & Public Administration

- **Lesson 8-1** Government & Public Administration Today ... 208
- **Lesson 8-2** Government & Public Administration Jobs ... 216
- **Lesson 8-3** Building a Career in Government & Public Administration ... 224
- **Lesson 8-4** Education and Training for Government & Public Administration Opportunities ... 226
- **Lesson 8-5** Working Conditions in the Government & Public Administration Industry ... 232
- **Lesson 8-6** Trends in Government & Public Administration ... 235

Chapter 9: Business Management & Administration

- **Lesson 9-1** Business Management & Administration Today ... 240
- **Lesson 9-2** Business Management & Administration Jobs ... 247
- **Lesson 9-3** Building a Career in Business Management & Administration ... 255
- **Lesson 9-4** Education and Training for Business Management & Administration Opportunities ... 258
- **Lesson 9-5** Working Conditions in the Business Management & Administration Industry ... 264
- **Lesson 9-6** Trends in Business Management & Administration ... 267

Chapter 10: Finance

- **Lesson 10-1** Finance Today ... 272
- **Lesson 10-2** Finance Jobs ... 279
- **Lesson 10-3** Building a Career in Finance ... 287
- **Lesson 10-4** Education and Training for Finance Opportunities ... 290
- **Lesson 10-5** Working Conditions in the Finance Industry ... 297
- **Lesson 10-6** Trends in Finance ... 301

Chapter 11: Marketing

Lesson 11-1 Marketing Today ... 307
Lesson 11-2 Marketing Jobs ... 314
Lesson 11-3 Building a Career in Marketing ... 323
Lesson 11-4 Education and Training for Marketing Opportunities ... 326
Lesson 11-5 Working Conditions in the Marketing Industry ... 333
Lesson 11-6 Trends in Marketing ... 336

Chapter 12: Transportation, Distribution, & Logistics

Lesson 12-1 Transportation, Distribution, & Logistics Today ... 342
Lesson 12-2 Transportation, Distribution, & Logistics Jobs ... 349
Lesson 12-3 Building a Career in Transportation, Distribution, & Logistics ... 356
Lesson 12-4 Education and Training ... 359
Lesson 12-5 Working in the Transportation, Distribution, & Logistics Industry ... 366
Lesson 12-6 Trends in Transportation, Distribution, & Logistics ... 368

Chapter 13: Hospitality & Tourism

Lesson 13-1 Hospitality & Tourism Today ... 375
Lesson 13-2 Hospitality & Tourism Jobs ... 382
Lesson 13-3 Building a Career in Hospitality & Tourism ... 390
Lesson 13-4 Education and Training for Hospitality & Tourism Opportunities ... 393
Lesson 13-5 Working Conditions in the Hospitality & Tourism Industry ... 401
Lesson 13-6 Trends in Hospitality & Tourism ... 405

Chapter 14: Health Science

Lesson 14-1 Health Science Today ... 410
Lesson 14-2 Health Science Jobs ... 417
Lesson 14-3 Building a Career in Health Science ... 425
Lesson 14-4 Education and Training for Health Science Opportunities ... 428
Lesson 14-5 Working Conditions in the Health Science Industry ... 436
Lesson 14-6 Trends in Health Science ... 439

Chapter 15: Human Services

Lesson 15-1 Human Services Today ... 445
Lesson 15-2 Human Services Jobs ... 452
Lesson 15-3 Building a Career in Human Services ... 460
Lesson 15-4 Education and Training for Human Services Opportunities ... 463
Lesson 15-5 Working Conditions in the Human Services Industry ... 471
Lesson 15-6 Trends in Human Services ... 474

Chapter 16: Education & Training

- **Lesson 16-1** Education & Training Today ... 479
- **Lesson 16-2** Education & Training Jobs ... 486
- **Lesson 16-3** Building a Career in Education & Training ... 495
- **Lesson 16-4** Education and Training for Education & Training Opportunities ... 498
- **Lesson 16-5** Working Conditions in the Education & Training Industry ... 506
- **Lesson 16-6** Trends in Education & Training ... 509

Chapter 17: Law, Public Safety, Corrections, & Security

- **Lesson 17-1** Law, Public Safety, Corrections, & Security Today ... 514
- **Lesson 17-2** Law, Public Safety, Corrections, & Security Jobs ... 521
- **Lesson 17-3** Building a Career in Law, Public Safety, Corrections, & Security ... 529
- **Lesson 17-4** Education and Training for the Law, Public Safety, Corrections, & Security Opportunities ... 532
- **Lesson 17-5** Working in the Law, Public Safety, Corrections, & Security Industry ... 540
- **Lesson 17-6** Trends in Law, Public Safety, Corrections, & Security ... 545

Chapter 1

Exploring Your Future

Chapter Topics

1-1 Introducing Your Future
1-2 Building a Career
1-3 Education and Training
1-4 Trends

Essential Questions

By the end of the chapter, you will be able to answer the following questions:

- **1-1** How can you explore career options?
- **1-2** How can you match your skills and interests with the right job?
- **1-3** What training and education is needed for your career journey?
- **1-4** What are major trends in career journeys?

1-1 Introducing Your Future

This textbook is about you. You may have access to the accompanying eBook and online materials, which are also about you. Many students have not deeply thought about their future career. Most students know of about a dozen possibilities out of the thousands of options. When you find an opportunity that fits your needs and allows them to contribute to others in a valuable way, they feel good about their career. This textbook will introduce you to possible future careers and guide you through the journey you will take after graduating high school.

1-1 Essential Question

As you read this section, keep this question in mind:

How can you explore career options?

Preparation

In 1969, *Apollo 11* carried three people to the moon. Two landed on the dusty, rocky surface and walked for the first time on a place different than the earth. Futurists optimistically projected that by the year 2000, humans would be living in orbit around the earth and the moon, and in bases on the moon. Other bold predictions included development of fusion, a limitless, clean, renewable energy source, and underwater cities. Which of these are realities today?

Instead of the advances mentioned above, we have found a way to communicate and connect globally—the Internet. We have video telephone calls. Medicine has advanced in many ways, such as finding treatments for diseases like AIDS and COVID-19 and understanding genetics down to the tiniest detail.

Industries with jobs that once were held exclusively by individuals with bachelor's degrees and beyond have opened to a broader workforce and offer many opportunities with medium- and high-paying salaries. These include occupations such as mechanical technician, paralegal, and nursing assistant. Occupations requiring hands-on attention to build and fix things, such as shipbuilding, automotive repair, and heavy machine operation, have continued to thrive. However, when considering their future, students often overlook these important

2   Chapter 1 • Exploring Your Future

occupations. Most new jobs include the use of technologies that make work safer and more efficient.

Why is all this important to know? You are learning about and preparing for a world that does not yet exist! By the time you graduate high school, new industries and jobs will be created, while many old occupations will need fewer workers or disappear. It is simply not possible to accurately predict what the jobs of the 2030s, 2040s, and 2050s will be. What can you do about that?

Most occupations evolve. If you can find a field in which you are interested and prepare for success, you will find success as that field evolves. An important part of that preparation involves professional skills, sometimes referred to as soft skills or employability skills. Examples include communication, problem-solving, time management, and good personal and professional habits. Your professional skills comprise the most significant set of skills that predict and support your future success!

This program is designed to introduce you to the occupations of today. It will tell you about the variety of jobs in many fields and how to build careers in these fields. It will also provide opportunities to practice the skills that will help you succeed.

Exploring Your Career

Finding a job that interests you is the first step in managing your career. To be successful, however, you will need to explore many job and career possibilities. What if your goals change? What if a shift in the labor market or the economy occurs? You may need, or want, to change jobs or even careers.

When considering a career, it is important to know all you can about it. Which jobs project the greatest growth? Which offer opportunities for advancement? Which jobs align most closely with your own abilities and interests?

Keep these questions in mind as you explore each chapter in this book. Every chapter is designed to help you answer these questions. Do the answers make you more or less likely to want to work in a particular industry? If you feel an industry may be right for you, make note of that, and find out more about it. Share your thinking with your teacher and others and try to learn more about the realities of the industries and occupations that are of interest to you.

Also, sample some of the real-world scenarios included in each chapter. These practice questions provide a starting point from which you can get a glimpse at the work that is done in that industry. The questions focus on reading for information, decoding charts and graphs, and completing basic math in real-world scenarios. Do not worry if your reading and math skills are not perfect for each question or exercise. You have plenty of time left to learn more about reading and math!

Evaluating Career Choices

Choosing a career is challenging. Now is a good time to start thinking about what kind of career path you would like to follow. A well-chosen career can bring satisfaction and success in life.

Self-knowledge is the key to making wise career choices. The more you learn about your interests and strengths, the better quality of choices you will make. Also, while weaknesses are often areas for which you need more help, they can become strengths if you work on them. Friends, teachers, and family members may offer helpful suggestions for potential careers. However, you are ultimately in charge of making your own career decisions.

You may feel that your personality, the way you think and behave, is well suited to an industry or occupation. You should allow your interests to influence your career decisions. What activities do you most enjoy? In some cases, your aptitude, or ability in a certain area, will shape your career goals. Ask yourself what skills come naturally to you. Also, you should consider the growth you will experience between now and high school graduation.

Values are another factor to consider when selecting a career. Values are the principles and beliefs that you live by. You might value courage, independence, or creativity. Your values will shape all areas of your life. For example, if you value being a responsible family member, you might seek a job that allows for flextime and provides good vacation benefits.

Don't worry if you change your mind about your career path. This happens to many people. It often takes time to find the right path. You can always change your career path regardless of where you are in your chosen profession.

1-1 Essential Question Reflection

So, let us revisit our essential question:

How can you explore career options?

1-2 Building a Career

There may be several steps in your career journey before you reach your ultimate career goal. For example, science technicians usually start as trainees. In this entry-level position, your tasks might include monitoring experiments and maintaining lab equipment. With more experience, you might conduct research. In time you might become a supervisor. You would then oversee training technicians. Finally, if you continued your education, you might become a biologist or a chemist.

1-2 Essential Question

As you read this section, keep this question in mind:

How can you match your skills and interests with the right job?

Jobs

Finding a job is seldom easy, but finding a job in a new career field can be especially hard.

Changing Jobs

Many people jump from one career right into another. They may feel that their job does not match their skills or interests. They may believe the job does not offer enough room to advance. A new career can offer new opportunities.

If you find a job that you would like to pursue, spend time investigating the qualifications required. You might speak to someone who works in the industry. Learn everything you can to ensure the career cluster is right for you.

Look for ways to gain experience that will help you in your search. If the new career involves working with people, volunteer for tasks in which you will interact with people.

You should spend time networking or reaching out to people who can help in your job search. This may include family, friends, or colleagues from current or former jobs. Try to meet new people to expand your network. One good way to do this is to use online networking sites.

1-2 Essential Question Reflection

So, let us revisit our essential question:

How can you match your skills and interests with the right job?

Based on what you learned in this section, please answer this question in detail.

1-3 Education and Training

Each industry differs in how much training and education are needed to get started. As you build your career, more education and training may benefit you. You may acquire more skills, abilities, and knowledge. You also may attain more professional skills. College and a college degree are admirable and important goals but not always needed as starting points for many well-paying careers. Sometimes you may earn a degree while starting your career and earning money. Many employers even have tuition reimbursement programs and other ways to help you learn while you earn. The result is that you eventually have the education you need without the potentially crippling debt that a college education can entail.

1-3 Essential Question

As you read this section, keep this question in mind:

What training and education is needed for your career journey?

Preemployment Training

Preemployment training for jobs may involve completing one or more of the following:

- An apprenticeship or internship
- A certification or degree program at a technical or career school
- A degree program at a college or university

Apprenticeships

An apprenticeship is a way to gain real-life work experience. In an apprenticeship, an inexperienced worker learns by working alongside an expert. The apprenticeship may last up to five years. During this period, the apprentice receives very little pay. However, workers who have completed these programs are often well respected and well paid. For more information about apprenticeship opportunities, the U.S. Department of Labor's Office of Apprenticeship is an excellent source.

Internships

An internship is an opportunity to gain supervised practical experience in a field. Internships are usually shorter than apprenticeships. They may offer the opportunity to learn about various departments or jobs in an organization. An intern often receives little or no pay. However, completing an internship can improve your chances of getting a job.

Formal Training and Education Options

Formal training and education for your future career may include one of the following options:

- Technical or career school
- Associate degree
- Bachelor's degree
- Graduate degree
- On-the-job training
- Technical and soft skills

It is important to note that obtaining a high school diploma or equivalent is vital to being able to pursue the postsecondary (i.e., after high school) educational opportunities listed above. To address the needs of busy professionals, many schools now offer online programs.

Before choosing a postsecondary educational program, make sure that the program will prepare you for the job you want. Consider the length of the program and its rate of job placement. Find out whether the program is nationally accredited or state licensed. Consider the school's reputation in the field and the expertise of its faculty.

Technical and Career Schools

If you're interested in a position that requires some training, a technical school is a promising option. A technical school offers skills-oriented programs. For example, it may offer programs in electrical or mechanical engineering that could help you become a technician in one of those fields. In addition to certification programs, technical schools sometimes offer associate degree programs.

Career schools specialize in training for a certain career or group of related careers. They may specialize in business, computer technology, or environmental health. Career schools that meet state requirements receive special licenses to operate.

Associate Degree

An associate degree is an academic program of study taken at the undergraduate level at a junior or community college. Students who are interested in obtaining an associate degree must obtain a high school diploma or equivalent and complete an application.

It typically takes two years of full-time study to complete an associate degree. Cost for obtaining an associate degree is often much lower than a bachelor's or master's degree. Attending community college and earning an associate degree can be an affordable way to dip your toes into higher education before transferring to a four-year program.

Bachelor's Degree

A bachelor's degree is an undergraduate degree in which you study a subject of your choice at a university. Obtaining a bachelor's degree enhances your access to job opportunities, exposes you to new ideas and opinions, and boosts your earning potential. Bachelor's degrees typically take most students between four and five years of full-time study. To obtain a bachelor's degree, students must usually earn 120 credits. Most universities offer a wide variety of programs of study, including computer science, business, nursing, and English.

Graduate Degree

Postgraduate education occurs after earning a bachelor's degree. Most people who seek postgraduate education enroll in a master's or doctoral degree program at a university's graduate school. Having a master's or doctoral degree gives a job candidate an edge over candidates without advanced degrees.

On-the-Job Training

On-the-job training is on-site instruction in how to perform a particular job. It has two main advantages over other forms of training.

First, you are usually paid while you train. However, even if the job is not paid, you will be gaining knowledge and skill without paying tuition.

Second, the training is tailored to the job. When you complete the training, you'll feel comfortable in your position.

Even jobs requiring advanced education often have on-the-job training. Many companies provide continued training for even their most experienced workers.

Many paid apprenticeships qualify as on-the-job training, especially if they are sponsored by the company employing the apprentice.

1-3 Essential Question Reflection

So, let us revisit our essential question:

What training and education is needed for your career journey?

Based on what you learned in this section, answer this question in detail.

1-4 Trends

Industries, occupations, and jobs are constantly changing. Knowing about the trends and forces that produce these changes can help you make better decisions about your future path and preparation. Throughout the book, you will read about trends that affect the industry discussed in each chapter.

1-4 Essential Question

As you read this section, keep this question in mind:

What are major trends in career journeys?

Remote Work

Technology improvements have made working from home or other remote workplaces easier, effective, and efficient. Working remotely has several advantages for both workers and employers; however, it is not always possible.

Technology

What do you think of when you hear the word *technology*? Chances are, if you are like most people, something related to computers and the Internet is at the top of your list. However, there are other examples of technology. Improvements in sensors have made warehouses and factories much safer. Improvements in robotics have made it possible for people to reduce how often they put themselves in risky situations. As technology continues to evolve, it will change how and where we work.

Gig and Contract Work

The ability to work at any time from almost anywhere has helped millions of workers take on work in a way that was rare until 5 to 10 years ago. Working on a contract-by-contract basis, or "gig" work, is when someone does a certain job for a customer and is paid based on completing the task. The work may take a week, a few months, or several years. Some construction and artistic work has almost always been contracted. But today, everything from blog copywriting to audio creation is "gig" work.

1-4 Essential Question Reflection

So, let us revisit our essential question:

What are major trends in career journeys?

Based on what you learned in this section, answer this question in detail.

Chapter 2
Science, Technology, Engineering & Mathematics (STEM)

❓ Essential Questions

By the end of the chapter, you will be able to answer the following questions:

- **2-1** What types of opportunities are available in STEM?
- **2-2** Which opportunities may be right for you?
- **2-3** How can I match my skills & interests with the right job?
- **2-4** What training & education is needed for a job in STEM?
- **2-5** What are typical work environments in STEM?
- **2-6** What factors affect trends in STEM?

Chapter Topics

2-1 STEM Today

2-2 STEM Jobs

2-3 Building a Career in STEM

2-4 Education and Training for STEM Opportunities

2-5 Working Conditions in the STEM Industry

2-6 Trends in STEM

2-1 STEM Today

Throughout history, people have thought about the world around them. People have invented tools and designed structures to improve their lives. Technology and engineering apply science and math in practical ways to make these tools and structures. As a result, a person born today can expect to live past the age of 80!

Career opportunities in Science, Technology, Engineering, and Mathematics are valuable because they improve the quality of life for people. These fields together are often referred to as "STEM."

2-1 Essential Question

As you read this section, keep this question in mind:

What types of opportunities are available in STEM?

Science

Science is the systematic study of the world. Scientists use the scientific method. They observe an aspect of the world and form a hypothesis, or an educated guess, that explains why something is the way it is. They then perform research experiments to test the hypothesis. They report the results to other scientists, who conduct their own tests. Only when many scientists have confirmed the findings does the hypothesis become a theory (a widely accepted explanation for why something happens). Science occupations are divided into three subcategories.

Table 2.1: Branches of Science

Category	Description	Examples of Occupations
Life Science	Focus on living things	Medical Researchers Geneticists Biologists Ecologists Environmental Scientists
Physical Science	Focus on nonliving things	Chemists Physicists Astronomers Geologists Meteorologists
Social Science	Focus on human behavior	Economists Psychologists

Life Science

Life sciences focus on the study of living things. This branch includes medical research, genetics, and biology. It also includes environmental science and ecology, the study of how organisms react with their physical environment.

Physical Science

Physical sciences deal mainly with studying nonliving things through chemistry, physics, astronomy, geology, and atmospheric science. Chemistry involves the makeup, structure, and behavior of substances. Physics deals with how objects interact with one another and with their surroundings. Astronomy examines the planets,stars, and other objects in space. Geology studies volcanoes, earthquakes, and the materials that make up Earth. Atmospheric science surveys the gases that surround Earth and includes the study of weather and climate.

Social Science

In the social sciences, the scientific method is used to study human behavior. This branch includes economists and psychologists. Economists study how humans produce and distribute goods and how they use wealth. Psychologists analyze the mental and emotional processes of humans.

Technology

Technology is the use of special tools or techniques to solve problems. Technology is closely related to science and engineering. For example, a scientist comes up with a theory about how hydrogen can be used to create energy. Then an engineer designs something that uses hydrogen to power motor vehicles. That invention, known as a hydrogen fuel cell, is an example of technology. Someone skilled in operating the tools of technology is called a technician. A laboratory technician uses equipment in a laboratory. Technicians often assist scientists and engineers with the more practical tasks involved their work.

Engineering

Engineering applies science and mathematics to the practical problems of designing and building new things. For example, aerospace engineers design aircraft. Robotics engineers design robots.

Mathematics

Mathematics examines the relationships between numbers. Theoretical mathematics studies the logic of mathematics; the fields of algebra and geometry, for example, are a part of theoretical mathematics. Applied mathematics uses mathematics to solve real-world problems.

Career Journeys in STEM

There are two major paths along which your journey in STEM might be shaped. People commonly move into and out of different paths. Each path contains a group of careers requiring similar skills as well as similar certifications or education. The paths are:

- Science and Math
- Engineering and Technology

Science and Math

This career path includes natural scientists, social scientists, and mathematicians. It also includes the researchers and lab technicians who collaborate with scientists.

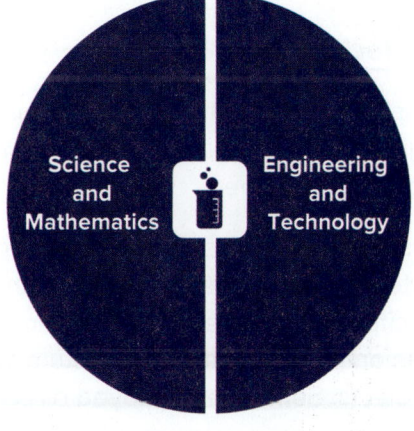

Most natural scientists work in research and development. They usually specialize in a particular area. Botanists, for example, focus on plant life. Zoologists focus on animals. Organic chemists study carbon-based compounds, which are the building blocks of life. Inorganic chemists focus on metals, salts, acids, and bases.

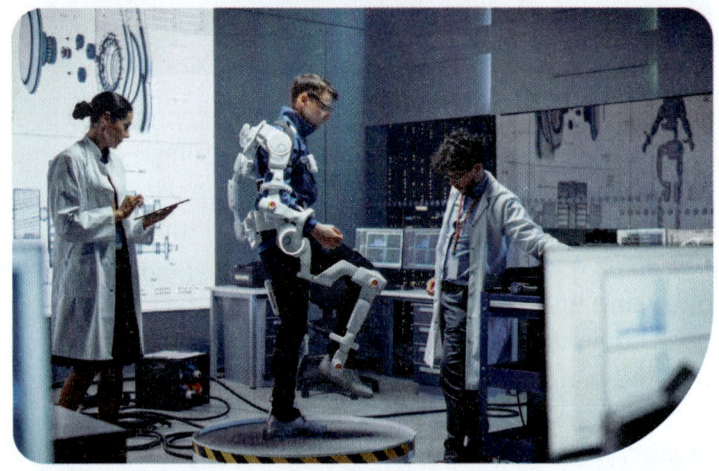

Some natural scientists work for colleges and universities. Others work for local, state, or federal government. For example, epidemiologists, who study diseases, may work for government health agencies. Meteorologists, who study and predict the weather, may work for the National Weather Service. Many life scientists and physical scientists work for private companies. An inorganic chemist, for instance, might help develop new fabrics for clothing manufacturers. Medical scientists often do research and development for drug companies.

Social scientists may work for colleges and universities, or they may work for private industries, the government, or nonprofit organizations. A political scientist, for instance, may work for a political research organization. A psychologist with special training may work with patients at hospitals or students in public schools.

Applied mathematicians often work for government agencies or businesses. A statistician, for example, might work for the US Department of Labor, gathering and interpreting data about jobs and job outlooks. Data scientists work for private companies or the government and develop useful insights from large amounts of data. In contrast, theoretical mathematicians usually work in universities.

Most scientists and mathematicians who do research at colleges and universities also teach. Some of them teach in places other than schools. An astronomer, for example, may explain the skies to visitors at a planetarium.

Scientists who work at colleges and universities often rely on grant money to support their research. That grant money may come from government programs or from private companies or organizations. A company seeking to produce fuel from crops, for example, may give grant money to a college biology department so scientists can conduct the needed research.

Engineering and Technology

This career path includes engineers and the technicians who assist them. There are many kinds of engineers. The three most common are civil engineers, mechanical engineers, and industrial engineers.

Civil engineers design and oversee the construction of roads, bridges, tunnels, dams, airports, water and sewage systems, and other public structures. Many specialize in a specific area, such as water resources or urban streets. Civil engineers are often employed by the architectural and engineering firms hired for government projects. Some are employed directly by government.

Mechanical engineers design tools, engines, and machinery. They are often employed by companies trying to develop new or better products. Mechanical engineers may design anything from a bicycle to a life-support system needed in a hospital. Sometimes they work on power-producing machines such as electric generators and gas turbines. At other times, they work on machines such as refrigerators, elevators, and small power tools. Many mechanical engineers specialize in one type of design. For example, one mechanical engineer may specialize in designing car engines. Another may specialize in building robots.

Other types of engineers are less common, partly because their work is more specialized. A computer hardware engineer designs computers and related equipment. A petroleum engineer develops methods of extracting oil from the earth. A marine engineer designs and supervises the building of boats and ships.

Industrial engineers come up with ways to help people, machines, materials, and other resources work together to create a product or service.

Engineers are often assisted by engineering technicians. An industrial engineering technician, for instance, may work with an industrial engineer to formulate a more productive way for a company to distribute its goods.

STEM Future Outlook

The outlook for jobs in the STEM industry is better than average. It is especially good in the Science and Mathematics career path. The Bureau of Labor Statistics expects jobs in STEM to increase by about 33 percent from 2020 to 2030. That compares to only 8 percent growth in all job types. Competition for these jobs is expected to be strong. Since the jobs in this path will grow and pay well, many people will want these jobs. This means that candidates with the most experience or education—or both—are likely to land the best jobs.

Table 2.2: Employment in STEM Occupations, 2020 and Projected 2030

Occupation Category	Employment Change, 2020–30	Percent Employment Change, 2020–30	Median Annual Wage, 2021
Total, all occupations	11,879,900	7.7	$45,760
STEM occupations	1,074,500	10.5	$95,420
Non-STEM occupations	10,805,400	7.5	$40,120

Source: *U.S. Bureau of Labor Statistics*

In the Engineering and Technology career path, the job outlook is about average overall. However, prospects vary greatly, depending on the specific engineering area.

The best growth is expected to be in the life science and related engineering specialties, such as biomedical engineering. The nation's aging population will create a demand for new drugs and medical treatments. That, in turn, will result in the demand for more medical research. The need to feed the world's rising population will increase job growth in areas such as agricultural and food sciences. The social sciences are expected to see higher-than-average job growth. Many of these jobs will be with nonprofit organizations that develop public policy.

Table 2.3: Job Forecast for a Sample of Occupations over the Next 10 Years

Occupation	Expected Growth Rate
Geographic Information Systems Technicians	5%–10%
Environmental Scientists and Specialists	5%–10%
Industrial Ecologists	5%–10%
Biological Technicians	5%–10%
Chemists	5%–10%
Surveyors	1%–5%
Blockchain Engineers	5%–10%
Computer and Information Scientists, Researchers	15% or more
Mechanical Engineers	5%–10%
Data Scientists	15% or more
Architectural Drafters	Little or no growth

Source: *O*NET Occupational Network Database*

2-1 Essential Question Reflection

So, let us revisit our essential question:

What types of opportunities are available in STEM?

Based on what you learned in this section, which path of STEM is the most interesting to you? Explain your answer.

Practice 2-1

Skills Practice

When reading workplace graphics and gauges, such as a diagram for a spacecraft, STEM workers must know what information to look for. The key information may be in one or more graphics. Workers must be able to sift through unimportant or distracting information to find what is needed. **Practice this skill!**

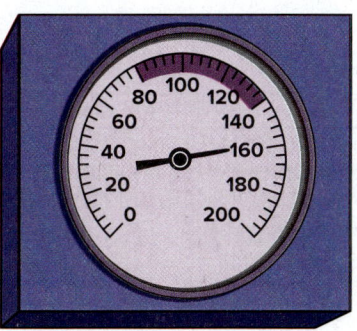

The above gauge measures pressure in pounds per square inch. Use the gauge to answer the two questions that follow.

1. As a water treatment plant operator, one of your jobs is to regularly check the pressure gauges on the 500-gallon water vessels. What is the current pressure for this water vessel?

   A. 145 pounds per square inch

   B. 150 pounds for square inch

   C. 160 pounds per square inch

   D. 165 pounds per square inch

   E. 170 pounds per square inch

2. The shaded area indicates the ideal pressure range required for this water vessel to operate safely and properly. The pressure is currently too high. You want to lower the pressure. As the pressure lowers, at which point will you be back in a safe operating zone?

   A. 140 pounds per square inch

   B. 155 pounds per square inch

   C. 160 pounds per square inch

   D. 185 pounds per square inch

   E. 190 pounds per square inch

The chart below shows how different groups process information to get dollars from the U. S. government for a local project. Use the chart to answer the two questions that follow.

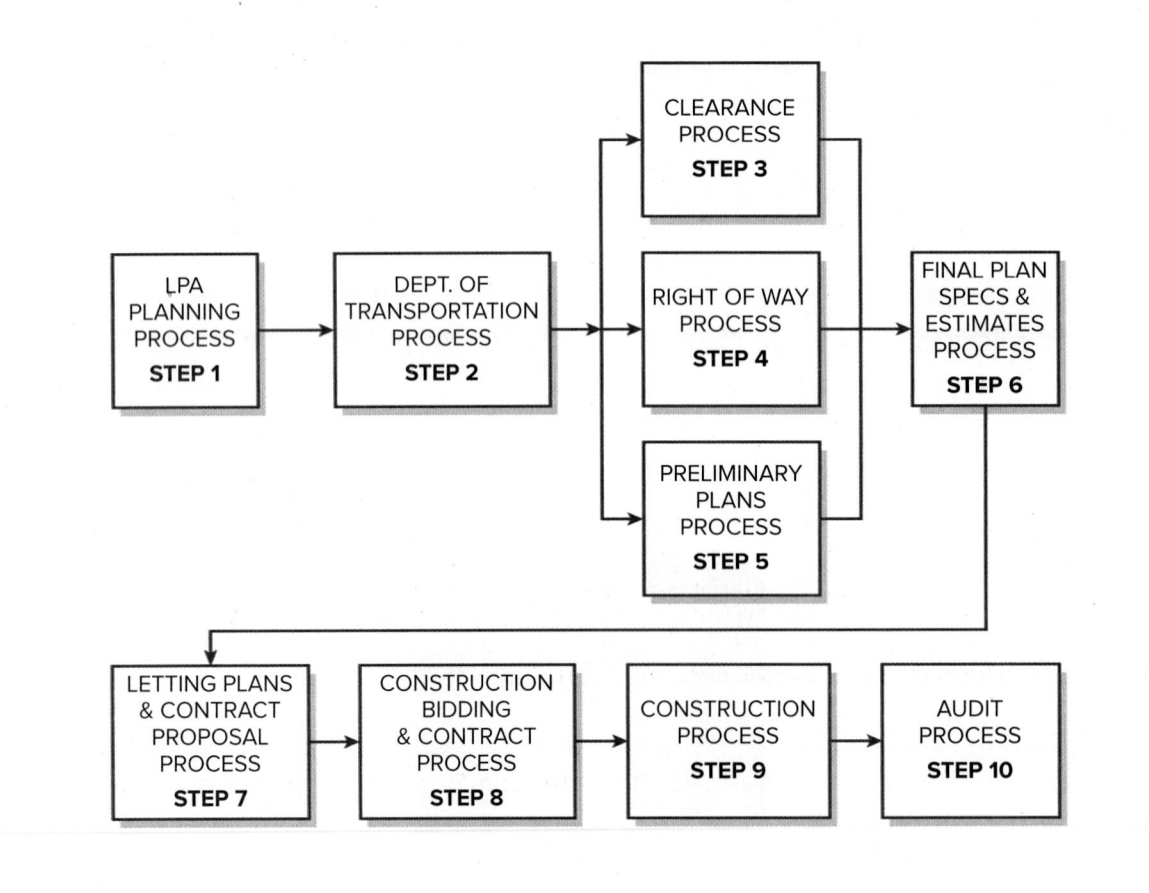

3. You are an entry-level transportation engineer working for your state Department of Transportation. You must refer to Local Public Agency (LPA) policy guidelines for any project using federal funds. According to your flow chart, which steps in the upcoming federal aid project occur simultaneously?

A. Steps 1, 2, and 3

B. Steps 3, 4, and 5

C. Steps 2, 4, and 6

D. Steps 6, 7, and 8

E. Steps 8, 9, and 10

4. You typically help coordinate the bidding process. At which point will you become involved?

A. Step 3

B. Step 5

C. Step 6

D. Step 8

E. Step 9

To access more problems that will help you grow professional skills and are real-world examples in STEM, go online.

18 Chapter 2 • Science, Technology, Engineering & Mathematics

2-2 STEM Jobs

Many kinds of jobs are available in the STEM industry. Some workers conduct research to cure diseases, develop a new food product, or identify criminals. Others design a water treatment center or find ways to dispose of toxic material. Jobs are available in private companies, at colleges, in the government and military, and with nonprofit organizations. They are also available with local, state, and federal governments. Some workers in this field start their own business. Here are some industry jobs and the skills they require.

2-2 Essential Question

As you read this section, keep this question in mind:

Which opportunities may be right for you?

Occupation With the Most People Employed:

Maintenance and Repair Workers

- Maintain and fix objects that range in size from the width of a human hair to the largest buildings in the world
- Exciting opportunities in the future from repairing drones and robots to maintaining machines that are networked through small computer chips in them

Fast Facts:

Employment: 1.44 million in 2020, expected to grow to 1.56 million in 2030
Annual Openings: 152,000 – the size of a large city!
Median Annual Wage: $43,000
Education Needed: High school diploma
Other: Some on-the-job training

Fastest-Growing Occupations:

Wind Turbine Service Technicians

- Inspect, adjust, or repair large wind turbines (windmills)
- Diagnose and fix any problem that could cause the turbine to shut down unexpectedly

Fast Facts:
   Employment: 6,900 in 2020, expected to grow to 11,700 in 2030
   Did You Know: 1 out of 8 are self-employed
   Education Needed: High school diploma and on-the-job training

Engineers in Advanced Systems

- Research, design, develop, and test parts and systems that apply to wind and solar energy, nanosystems, robotics, photonics, and mechatronics
- Engineers are on the cutting edge of products that are the result of applying science. They are responsible for making and testing the machines of today and of the future.

Fast Facts:
   Employment: 1.72 million in 2020, expected to grow to 1.85 million in 2030
   Median Annual Wage: $99,040
   Education Needed: Master's degree

Occupation Where Most Work for Themselves:

Solar Cell Installers

- Assemble, install, or maintain solar energy systems on roofs or other structures in compliance with site assessment and schematics
- Measure, cut, assemble, and bolt structural framing and solar modules

Fast Facts:

Employment: 11,800 in 2020, expected to grow to 17,900 million in 2030
Percent Change in Employment: 52%
Median Annual Wage: $47,670
Education Needed: High school diploma
Did You Know: Solar energy is a form of energy that reduces carbon emissions.

Highest-Wage Occupation:

Physicists

- Conduct research into physical universe, develop theories from of observation and experiments, and devise ways to apply physical laws and theories
- Famous physicists include Albert Einstein and Isaac Newton.

Fast Facts:

Employment: 17,400 in 2020, expected to grow to 18,900 million in 2030
Percent Change in Employment: 8.8%
Median Annual Wage: $152,430
Education Needed: Doctoral degree
Did You Know: Physicists publish papers in journals and are critical to innovative advances, such as the James Webb telescope and electric vehicle development.

Great Job! – Associate Degree Needed:

Aerospace Engineering Technicians

- Operate, install, adjust, and maintain systems, consoles, simulators, and other data acquisition, test, and measurement instruments and equipment, which are used to launch, track, position, and evaluate air and space vehicles
- Technicians work alongside scientists and engineers and make their visions and concepts to reality.

Fast Facts:

Employment: 11,900 in 2020, expected to grow to 12,900 million in 2030

Median Annual Wage: $73,580

Education Needed: Associate degree

Did You Know: This is a "high-flying" occupation where the work you do eventually becomes part of making a vehicle fly.

Great Job! – High School Diploma Needed:

Nuclear Power Reactor Operators

- Operate or control nuclear reactors
- Move control rods, start and stop equipment, monitor and adjust controls, and record data in logs
- Implement emergency procedures when needed
- Respond to abnormalities, determine cause, and recommend corrective action

Fast Facts:

Employment: 5,300 in 2020

Median Annual Wage: $104,260

Education Needed: High school diploma, or equivalent

Did You Know: As technology becomes better and the need for energy generated from non–fossil fuels, nuclear power reactor operators will be needed worldwide.

2-2 Essential Question Reflection

So, let us revisit our essential question:

Which opportunities may be right for you?

Based on what you learned in this section, what 2 or 3 opportunities are the most interesting? Explain your answer.

Case Study: Environmental Science & Protection Technicians

Also called: Environmental Technicians, Laboratory Technicians, Public Health Sanitarians, Sanitarians

What do they do?

- Perform laboratory and field tests to monitor the environment and investigate sources of pollution, including those that affect health, under the direction of an environmental scientist, engineer, or other specialist
- Collect samples of gases, soil, water, and other materials for testing

What would you do?

- Discuss test results and analyses with customers
- Record test data and prepare reports, summaries, or charts that interpret test results
- Develop or implement programs for monitoring of environmental pollution or radiation

What do you need to know?

Arts and Humanities
English language

Math and Science
Biology
Arithmetic, algebra, geometry, calculus, or statistics

Safety and Government
Law and government
Public safety and security

Business
Customer service

What skills do you need?

Communication
Listen to others, do not interrupt, and ask good questions
Read work-related information

Problem Solving
Notice a problem and figure out the best way to solve it

People and Technology Systems
    Think about the pros and cons of different options and pick the best one
    Figure out how a system should work and how changes in the future affect it

What abilities must you be good at?

Verbal
    Listen to and understand what people say
    Read and understand what is written

Ideas and Logic
    Notice when problems happen
    Use rules to solve problems

Math
    Add, subtract, multiply, or divide
    Choose the right type of math to solve a problem

Visual Understanding
    Quickly compare groups of letters, numbers, pictures, or other things

Who does well in this occupation?

    People who like activities that include ideas, thinking, and figuring things out

People who do well at these jobs need:
    Integrity
    Dependability
    Attention to detail
    Analytical thinking
    Initiative
    Adaptability/flexibility

What educational level is needed?

- Bachelor's degree or associate degree

Practice 2-2

Skills Practice

STEM workers must sometimes analyze graphics to identify trends. They might search data for evidence that conditions have changed over time. Geodetic surveyors, for example, need to study data from satellite images to measure changes in the earth's surface. Being able to identify common trends from several pieces of data can be helpful in a variety of jobs in this industry. **Practice this skill!**

1. As an assistant in the science department at your college, you track e-mails that are received each month. Based on this graph, what trend can you identify?

   A. The number of e-mails increased every month.

   B. The number of e-mails received decreased every month.

   C. The number of e-mails stayed consistent throughout the year.

   D. The number of e-mails stayed relatively consistent but decreased in the last two months.

   E. The number of e-mails stayed relatively consistent but increased in the last 2 months.

2. Based on this graph, which of the following general statements can you make?

   A. There is a large increase in e-mails in the summer months.

   B. There is a large increase in e-mails at the beginning of the year.

   C. There is a large increase in e-mails every other month.

   D. There is a large increase in e-mails at the end of the year.

   E. There is a large increase in e-mails in July.

2-2 • STEM Jobs   25

Skills Practice

When workers look at a graphic such as a diagram or a bar graph, they need to analyze and make sense of the information. It may be necessary to summarize the information or outline only the most important facts. For example, health and safety engineers may need to summarize graphics showing statistics on the hazards they find in a particular location. Being able to summarize allows workers to make sense of varying information. **Practice this skill!**

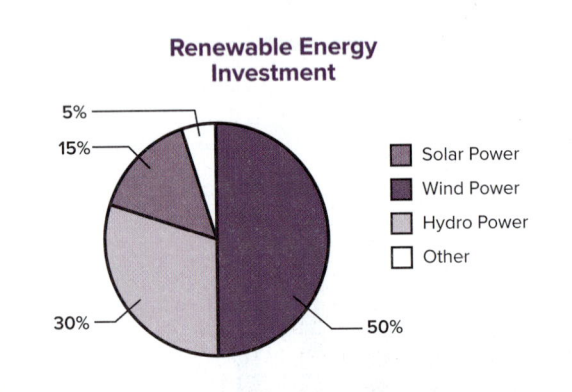

3. As an agricultural engineer, you have researched and created a graph showing the percentage of dollars invested in different forms of energy. How would you summarize the investment in energy sources from your chart?

   A. From greatest to least, companies have invested the most in wind, hydro, other, and solar power, in that order.

   B. From greatest to least, companies have invested the most in hydro, other, solar, and wind power, in that order.

   C. From greatest to least, companies have invested the most in wind, hydro, solar, and other power, in that order.

   D. From greatest to least, companies have invested the most in other, solar, wind, and hydro power, in that order.

   E. From greatest to least, companies have invested in solar, wind, hydro, and other power, in that order.

4. Your team is considering designs for a machine that can work using any type of energy. The team is trying to get money to fund building the machine. You and your team think that the greater the investment amount, the better the chances that a type of energy will be best.

   Based on the graph showing the percentage of investments in renewable energy sources, what is your recommendation to gain the most financial support?

   A. You recommend solar power for the new machine.

   B. You recommend hydro power for the new machine.

   C. You recommend hydro and solar power for the new machine.

   D. You recommend wind and hydro power for the new machine.

   E. You recommend solar and other types of power for the new machine.

To access more problems that will help you grow professional skills and are real-world examples in STEM, go online.

26   Chapter 2 • Science, Technology, Engineering & Mathematics

2-3 Building a Career in STEM

Building a career in STEM can take many years. For example, a science technician usually starts as a trainee. Your tasks might include monitoring experiments and maintaining lab equipment. With more experience, you might conduct research. In time you might become a supervisor. You would then oversee training technicians. Finally, if you continued your education, you might become a biologist or a chemist.

Do not worry if you change your mind about your career path. This happens to many people. It often takes time to find the right path. You can always change your career path regardless of where you are in your chosen profession.

2-3 Essential Question

As you read this section, keep this question in mind:

How can I match my skills & interests with the right job?

Are You More Interested in Working With Data, People, or Things?

When planning your career path, consider what balance of data, people, and things you want in a career. Many online resources can help you determine opportunities that match your skills and interests.

Careers That Involve Working With Data

Examples include drawing up industrial blueprints, solving complex equations, analyzing population statistics, and writing a lab procedures manual. Meteorologists are another example of people who work with data.

Almost all jobs in STEM involve working with data. Engineers, for example, often run tests and then analyze the data when designing a new product or improving an old one. Actuaries assess risks by studying data. Meteorologists examine data to make predictions about the weather. Science technicians often perform calculations and record data from experiments.

Scientists of all kinds must carefully record, collect, and analyze data when performing experiments or making observations. They also work with data in the form of scientific principles and formulas. Mathematicians work almost exclusively with data in the form of numbers, formulas, and principles.

Careers That Involve Working With People

Examples of working with people in the STEM industry includes coordinating work teams, sharing theories with colleagues, teaching students, and working with a construction crew on a civil engineering project. All these activities require strong communications skills.

If you are a manager or part of a team of workers, you will spend much time working with other people. If you are employed at a university, you will interact with students, teaching assistants, and colleagues. As a scientist or mathematician, you are likely to consult with people in your field. You may benefit from attending conferences where you can share your findings.

Careers That Involve Working With Things

In STEM working with things might involve experimenting with chemicals or constructing engineering prototypes. It may mean working with tiny microchips or enormous telescopes.

Many careers in STEM involve extensive work with things. Botanists, for example, spend much of their day working with plants, plant samples, and laboratory equipment. Electrical engineers may use circuits, machines, or power-generating equipment. Hazardous materials technicians use air samplers, water samplers, and special equipment for removing physical waste.

> **2-3 Essential Question Reflection**
>
> **So, let us revisit our essential question:**
>
> *How can I match my skills & interests with the right job?*
>
> Based on what you learned in this section, please answer this question in detail.

2-4 Education and Training for STEM Opportunities

The STEM industry perhaps has mostly training-intensive jobs. Most jobs require a college degree.

2-4 Essential Question

As you read this section, keep this question in mind:

What training & education is needed for a job in STEM?

Training and Education for STEM

To get a job as a technician, you may need to complete a training program or earn a certificate. However, most higher-level jobs require a college degree.

Jobs Requiring Specific Training or Certification

Almost all jobs in STEM deal with complex problems. Virtually all of them require at least a high school diploma and some training, or education in a specific job skill or professional area, after high school. Additionally, most careers in this industry require a license or certification. These licenses are often required by government agencies and are obtained by passing an exam.

Many environmental services technician jobs only require special training after high school. To become a hazardous waste removal technician, you need a high school diploma and 40 hours of formal training on the job or at an EPA-approved school. The training requires completing a program in chemistry, environmental technology, and safe waste handling.

To become a nuclear power plant operator, you need a high school diploma plus experience in a nuclear power plant. You may also need to obtain a special license, depending on the state or area in which you wish to work. Preference is often given to graduates of the U.S. Navy's Nuclear Field Program. This intensive 18-month training program is open to high school graduates with a proven talent in math and science.

Radon measurement technicians are certified by the National Environmental Health Association (NEHA) or the National Radon Safety Board (NRSB). For certification, you must complete an approved 8- or 16-hour training course. You also must pass an exam.

Some jobs as lab assistants require a high school diploma along with special training and certification. Technical or vocational schools often offer this training. Lab assistants who wish to rise to the position of lab technician can continue their education and obtain an associate degree.

Jobs Requiring an Associate Degree

Not all jobs in the STEM industry require advanced degrees. Technicians and research assistants in several science and engineering fields may need only an associate degree. An associate degree is a degree awarded after two years of successful study.

Engineering technicians, for example, generally require only an associate degree. Many obtain their degree at community colleges or technical schools. Some receive their training in the armed forces. The U.S. Army, for example, offers training in technical engineering and pharmacy technology. Drafters, who make the detailed drawings used in building and manufacturing, may also receive training in the armed forces or at technical schools.

Jobs Requiring a Bachelor's, Master's, or Doctoral Degree

Most jobs in STEM require an advanced education. If you want to become a scientist, a mathematician, or an engineer, you will need at least a bachelor's degree in your field. Most scientists and mathematicians obtain a master's and often a doctoral degree. These advanced degrees lead to far more job opportunities and higher pay. For example, a master's or doctoral degree in physics could prepare you for work in the government space program or with an airplane manufacturer. Scientists and mathematicians who wish to conduct advanced research and publish their findings must obtain a doctoral degree.

Chapter 2 • Science, Technology, Engineering & Mathematics

Engineers whose work affects life, health, or property and engineers who work for the government must obtain a state license. To be licensed as a professional engineer, you generally need a bachelor's degree and four years of job experience. You must also pass a state exam. Engineers who work with nuclear materials must obtain a special license from the U.S. Nuclear Regulatory Commission (NRC).

Table 2.4: Education Required for STEM Jobs

Level of Education	Job Title
High school diploma & other training	Hazardous Material Remover Workers Nuclear Power Plant Operators Water Treatment Plant Operators Lead Sampling Technicians
Associate degree	Automotive Engineering Technicians Electrical Engineering Technicians Genetic Engineering Research Assistants Lab Assistants
Bachelor's, master's, or doctoral degree	Biochemical Engineers Electrical Engineers Wind Energy Engineers Archaeologists Chemists Environmental Scientists

STEM Skill Standards

Skills standards in the STEM industry vary considerably. Funding provided by the U.S. Department of Education has let several groups develop specific standards and programs for entry-level employees. For instance, beginning- to middle-level bioscience technical specialists must now meet specific requirements consisting of 34 integrated skills standards. For each standard, candidates are asked to demonstrate how they would handle a particular problem.

Standards have also been established for entry-level chemical lab technicians. These standards assess a candidate's mastery of math and statistics, computer skills, communication skills, workplace skills, and general laboratory skills. One general laboratory skill requires competency in handling lab equipment.

In some cases, mastery of specific skills leads to certification or licensing. This shows that the person has achieved a high level of competence in a field. Scientists are generally not licensed, but many engineers and technicians are. Employers and clients often value licenses, and many companies require that senior engineers be licensed.

License regulations for engineers vary from state to state. Most require that a candidate has a four-year engineering degree from a program approved by the state board and four years of qualifying engineering experience. Candidates must also pass exams on engineering fundamentals, principles, and practices.

Professional Skills

Communications Skills   In the STEM industry, communication skills are necessary when giving instructions and explaining procedures. They are essential for scientists and mathematicians who teach students. They are also important for communicating with coworkers.

Listening Skills   Listening skills are key to following instructions safely and precisely. They are very important in discussing ideas and information with colleagues. Good listening skills also help in understanding other ideas and viewpoints. They are essential to teachers when they interact with students.

Problem-Solving Skills   Problem solving is key to many jobs in STEM. For example, an environmental engineer might try to design the best way to clean up a toxic spill. An industrial chemist might aim to figure out why a new formula for furniture polish leaves spots on the furniture. Problem solving requires creativity, logical thinking, and persistence.

Technology Skills   The impact of technology on this industry is enormous. Many scientists and engineers work with new technologies such as fiber optics, lasers, and robots. They must be able to keep up with cutting-edge advances. Workers in this field must be able to use sophisticated lab equipment.

Decision-Making Skills   STEM jobs often involve making important decisions. Civil engineers, for example, must decide on the safest, most practical ways to make improvements to infrastructure. Environmental engineers may need to decide on the best way to clean up a polluted site. Being able to gather and analyze information quickly and to think clearly under pressure are very important skills for virtually all workers in this industry.

Organizing and Planning Skills
Engineering a product or conducting an experiment involves many steps. Organization and planning are crucial to the success of any project. Engineers and scientists often work on complex research projects that require long-term, far-sighted planning. The ability to organize teams, schedules, and processes is essential.

Teamwork Skills Scientists and engineers rarely work entirely on their own. They are required to work with various teams, departments, managers, colleagues, and sometimes customers to complete a job. Teamwork requires leadership skills, communication skills, and respect for the thoughts and feelings of others.

Social Skills Social interaction makes for a more enjoyable and productive work environment. It is also very important when working with students and colleagues at colleges and universities. Private consultants need effective social skills to help them obtain and work with clients. Social scientists need strong social skills when conducting studies in which they need to interview human subjects.

Adaptability Skills Change is a fact of life in the STEM industry. Job descriptions, work environments, and technologies are constantly changing. Workers must view change positively and be flexible.

2-4 Essential Question Reflection

So, let us revisit our essential question:

What training & education is needed for a job in STEM?

Based on what you learned in this section, please answer this question in detail.

Practice 2-4

Skills Practice

When reading documents, workers in the STEM industry need to be able to identify the main idea. The main idea tells what the document is about. They must also find details supporting the main idea. For example, as a biologist studying a particular animal, you may need to find the main ideas and details in research papers. Details provide more information that helps explain the main idea. **Practice this skill!**

As a conservation biology field assistant, you help protect sea turtle hatching areas. Your manager has given you information to distribute to residents and business owners around the beach. The following is the flyer they have given you:

LEARN TO SET UP LIGHTS FOR SEA TURTLES!

March 22, 3–5 p.m.

Turtle Beach Annex Building

Come participate in a special lighting workshop where you can learn how to set up safe lights for our sea turtle mothers and hatchlings in kind ways! We'll show you how artificial light affects sea turtles, which lights are the most turtle-friendly, and how to get ready for hatching season.

Please RSVP to Donna Smith by March 8.

You can also contact Donna for more information at dsmith@turtlebeachconservation.org or via phone at 555-3232 ext. 15.

Brought to you by the Turtle Beach Conservation Organization.

1. What is the main idea of this flyer?

   A. Artificial lights hurt sea turtles.

   B. People can attend a workshop to learn how to install lighting that is safe for turtles.

   C. Residents must leave the beach during hatching season.

   D. Mother turtles will not lay eggs if artificial light is around the beach.

   E. Business owners should learn to be more turtle friendly.

2. One of the business owners you speak to has more questions about the workshop. What does the email suggest they should do to get more information?

   A. Visit the Turtle Beach Annex Building.

   B. Talk to other business owners in the area.

   C. Find someone to talk to on Turtle Beach.

   D. Call or e-mail Donna Smith.

   E. Write a letter to the Turtle Beach Conservation Organization.

To access more problems that will help you grow professional skills and are real-world examples in STEM, go online.

2-5 Working Conditions in the STEM Industry

When choosing a career path, knowing what it is like to work in the industry is important. Understanding the work environment, hazards, and benefits of a job can help you make informed decisions.

2-5 Essential Question

As you read this section, keep this question in mind:

What are typical work environments in STEM?

Work Environment

Work environment refers to factors that affect workers' health and satisfaction on the job. These include the physical surroundings and the working hours. They also include the physical activities required to perform the job.

Physical Environment

People in STEM work in a variety of settings. Researchers, professors, and managers usually work in laboratories, classrooms, or offices. These worksites are generally clean, modern, well lit, and well equipped. Nevertheless, lab work can be hazardous, especially if it involves work with chemicals, biological agents, heat, or dangerous machinery.

These volcanologists are ready for a fast exit as this volcano erupts. Volcanology is hazardous but exciting!

Sometimes scientists and engineers need to work outdoors. Volcanologists study volcanoes and work in some of the most extreme conditions possible. Some environmental scientists or engineers gather information by taking water samples or monitoring animal populations. Some aerospace engineers go to test ranges or airstrips to observe tests of vehicle designs or electronic equipment. In these cases, engineers may have to work outdoors regardless of the weather conditions.

Some scientists and engineers must travel or live abroad to work. For example, mining engineers often work in parts of the world that are rich in certain minerals. Archaeologists must gather physical evidence in the regions of the world that they specialize in. Sometimes the climate and living conditions in foreign lands present an increased risk of health problems or environmental dangers. The political climate may also present hazards. When working overseas, it is generally a good idea to keep in touch with the U.S. State Department and organizations such as American Citizens Abroad (ACA).

Work Hours

The work hours for careers in STEM vary greatly. Some experiments must be constantly monitored. Some workplaces must remain secure around the clock. For these reasons, many labs and other facilities rely on shift work. Shift work divides the day into blocks of time. Some workers start their shifts early in the morning. Others start late at night. In addition, many workers do not have weekends or holidays off. Science technicians, engineers, and power plant operators might all work shifts.

Most scientists, mathematicians, and engineers work 40 hours a week during standard working hours. However, they may need to work overtime to meet deadlines. Often, they face long evening and weekend hours when a project nears its deadline. For example, a deadline might require a satellite component to be finished by a certain date so that other specialists can plan how their components will fit together.

Because professionals, like scientists and engineers, are paid a salary, they are often not paid for overtime work. A salary is a fixed wage, usually set for a year. Workers who earn an hourly pay wage generally do earn overtime pay.

Some scientists, mathematicians, engineers, and technicians may work flextime. Flextime is a type of schedule that allows employees to choose the hours and days they work, if they work a standard total number of hours per week. For example, a worker who must put in 40 hours a week may choose to work ten hours on four days a week instead of eight hours on five days.

College professors have fixed schedules for teaching classes and for office hours when students meet with them. The time they spend doing their own research or examining student work is usually flexible. Nevertheless, professors may put in long hours to get their work done.

Essential Physical Activities

Workers in STEM are usually not required to be in excellent physical condition. However, those who work outdoors do need to be in good shape so they can tolerate various climates and rugged conditions. Many scientists work in laboratories or offices. They might be required to spend long periods of time on their feet. Those who work with microscopes and small tools, wiring, and other small items need good hand-eye coordination. Good vision is also a must for scientists who study minute objects or read thermometers, gauges, and meters.

Science and Mathematics

Life Scientists and Technicians

- Those who work in labs often stand for long periods of time.
- Some scientists make field trips that can involve strenuous activity.
- Those working with dangerous organisms or toxic substances must follow strict safety procedures.

Physical Scientists and Technicians

- Chemists may work outdoors gathering samples. They must follow safety procedures when working with potentially harmful chemicals.
- Physicists may need to travel and use special equipment for research.
- Hydrologists and geologists often work outdoors.
- Oceanographers may spend long periods at sea on research ships.

Social Scientists

- Archaeologists, anthropologists, sociologists, linguists, and geographers often work in the field gathering data or artifacts.
- Historians may spend long hours doing research in libraries.
- Psychologists sometimes work in clinics or hospitals.

Mathematicians

- Mathematicians may spend long hours working at computers or pouring over spreadsheets; this work can cause eyestrain.
- Statisticians may need to do field work gathering data.

Engineering and Technology

Engineers and Engineering Technicians

- Most work in offices, labs, or industrial plants.
- Those who work in labs or industrial plants are often on their feet for long periods.
- Some may be exposed to hazardous equipment, chemicals, or materials.
- Mining, geological, and petroleum engineers may work overseas.

Environmental Services Technicians

- Most work outdoors in all weather conditions, and they are exposed to noise, toxic substances, and unpleasant odors.
- Many do repetitive, physically demanding work.
- Waste and wastewater treatment plant operators must stoop, reach, and climb. They may work in hazardous conditions.
- Hazardous materials removers may do strenuous physical labor. They wear safety gear and follow safety rules to avoid toxic substances.
- Nuclear plant operators must comply with strict safety rules to avoid endangering themselves and others.

Source: *O*NET*

Some jobs in the STEM industry can be physically demanding. Hazardous materials technicians, for example, may need to shovel, lift heavy objects, crawl into tight spaces, or work on scaffolding.

Hazards and Environmental Dangers

Eye injuries are a major concern in laboratories. Goggles are required to prevent damage from sharp objects or exposure to chemicals and extreme light. Showers and eye baths must be available to workers at risk for eye damage. Scientists, mathematicians, and engineers who often read gauges, dials, or detailed written material may suffer from eyestrain.

Scientists, engineers, and technicians may be exposed to chemicals or other substances that are dangerous to touch or breathe. For example, some lab workers risk skin injuries from acids or strong alkaline solutions. Safety shoes, gloves, and respirators must be available to all workers exposed to dangerous substances. Some workers, such as hazardous materials removers, may need to wear protective gear whenever they are on the job.

Because accidents happen on the job, safety must be a priority. Workers must follow all safety procedures. They must be especially careful with sharp tools, lab animals, explosions, broken lab glass, electricity, and hazardous or radioactive materials.

In addition to on-the-job-injuries, workers may face more chronic health problems. Over time, they may suffer from musculoskeletal disorders (MSDs). A musculoskeletal disorder is a chronic problem with the muscles, nerves, tendons, joins, cartilage, or spinal discs. One kind of MSD is a repetitive stress injury (RSI), an ailment that can develop when the same motions are performed repeatedly. Scientists, mathematicians, and engineers who spend many hours using a computer may suffer from repetitive stress injuries (RSIs) because they repeat the same motions hundreds of times a day.

The federal government helps protect workers by creating workplace safety standards and laws to help prevent accidents and job-related illnesses. The Occupational Safety and Health Administration (OSHA) is the government agency that sets most job safety standards and inspects job sites. Many states also run their own OSHA programs.

2-5 Essential Question Reflection

So, let us revisit our essential question:

What are typical work environments in STEM?

Based on what you learned in this section, please answer this question in detail.

2-6 Trends in STEM

Few industries change as rapidly as the STEM industry. New technology means new directions for research and new ways of conducting research. Changes in society create new demands on what scientists study and engineers design.

> **2-6 Essential Question**
>
> As you read this section, keep this question in mind:
>
> What factors affect trends in STEM?

Technology in the STEM Industry

New technology and a commitment to use "green" products and processes are changing the STEM industry. Researchers today use the technology of the Internet and computer databases—rather than paper—to gather and store information. Many scientists are employed to find ways of improving the environment through renewable energy and sustainable design.

Artificial Intelligence and Sensor Technology

Artificial intelligence (AI) is the technology that develops computer programs to do human tasks. It has been applied extensively in aerospace engineering. NASA uses AI software to guide satellites and spacecraft. Computers react to changes in their surroundings and perform functions without aid from ground controllers.

A sensor can detect and record objects and movement. With sensor technology, machinery is "aware" of its surroundings. Some electric wheelchairs, for example, have been equipped with ultrasonic sensors that enable the wheelchair to avoid bumping into objects. The U.S. Defense Advanced Research Projects Agency (DARPA) is encouraging the development of biosensors that detect dangerous microorganisms, small living things that could be used in a terrorist attack.

Robotics, another AI application, is the technology of designing, building, and operating robots. A robot is made up of a small computer "brain," mechanical devices that enable movement, and sensors that allow the robot to respond to its surroundings. Today's robots are becoming much more adaptable. Carnegie Mellon University has successfully tested the navigation/sensor system of a robot helicopter. Such a craft may one day be able to evacuate soldiers or others in dangerous situations without putting pilots at risk.

Neuromorphic engineering copies structures in the human brain and nervous system to design computers and robots capable of sensing. This technology could eventually create computer systems that will recognize objects by sight.

Natural language processing (NLP) attempts to build computers that understand human language. Using NLP, computers may be able to translate or summarize texts or understand exactly what users are looking for when they conduct web searches.

Nanotechnology and Biotechnology

Nanotechnology is the ability to control matter at the level of individual atoms and molecules (the smallest pieces of matter) to build tiny devices. Physics, chemistry, and engineering all contribute to the field of nanotechnology. Nanotechnology can create computers the size of a single molecule. This technology has hundreds of applications. For example, a tiny layer of particles placed in household paint could be programmed to make the paint resistant to fires. A pill-sized camera swallowed by a patient can check for diseases. The use of nanotechnology in health and medicine is called nanomedicine.

Nanotechnology has produced the atomic force microscope (AFM). This tool helps scientists see tiny things in great detail. Biologists can use it to observe how cells interact.

DNA is the molecule that is the "blueprint" for a living organism. This tiny material is made up of genes that determine what an organism looks like and how it is different from other organisms. In 2003, the Human Genome Project completed its effort to identify and map all 25,000 genes in human DNA. The effort helped create the biotechnology industry, which uses DNA to improve, create, or modify living things. Biotechnology has led to the discovery of important drugs like human insulin and growth hormone. It is the basis of genetic engineering, which modifies foods and other organisms. Genetic engineering can develop crops that are resistant to insects.

Sustainability in STEM

Sustainability is a major trend in STEM today. It refers to economic activity that does not harm the environment. Examples of sustainable technology include renewable energy, green chemistry, and sustainable design.

Renewable Energy

Renewable energy is generated from natural sources that do not run out. It causes less pollution than energy from petroleum-based fuels like oil and gasoline. Many scientists and engineers are working to find the best forms of renewable energy and the best ways to use them. Solar energy systems engineers design and maintain systems that get energy from sunlight. Engineers in nanotechnology are working on less costly solar panels to help generate solar energy. Wind energy engineers design wind farms where wind is collected and used for energy. Wind resource analysts are helping them decide where to locate these wind farms.

Geoscientists work with engineers on two other types of renewable energy: geothermal energy and hydropower. Geothermal energy uses the heat inside the earth as an energy source. Hydropower is energy produced by moving water. Dams on rivers have long been a source of hydropower. Now efforts are being made to use the energy of the ocean waves.

Renewable energy also comes from biofuels, which are fuels produced from easy-to-grow plants, such as corn, and the waste materials of plants, like leftover cooking oil. Biofuels work well in motor vehicles, such as buses, boats, and trucks. The most widely used biofuels today are ethanol and biodiesel. Biological scientists continue to identify the best plants or plant products to use. Engineers continue to design new ways to use them.

Green Chemistry

One growing trend in the field of chemistry is green chemistry. The goal of green chemistry is to avoid products and processes that harm the environment. To achieve this goal, scientists work to design products that are less hazardous to people and the environment. They design products that take less energy or fewer materials to produce. Scientists look for ways to reuse or recycle chemicals or to treat existing chemicals to make them less hazardous. Finally, they work to ensure that chemicals are disposed of without doing harm to the environment.

Sustainable Design

Sustainable design focuses on the design and use of processes and products that lower the risk of harm to human health and the environment. It stresses the use of "green" chemistry, chemical products that are not harmful. It encourages the use of building materials from renewable sources. The American Society of Civil Engineers (ASCE) has set sustainable design as a goal for its members.

> ### 2-6 Essential Question Reflection
>
> **So, let us revisit our essential question:**
>
> *What factors affect trends in STEM?*
>
> Based on what you learned in this section, please answer this question in detail.

Chapter 3: Manufacturing

❓ Essential Questions

By the end of the chapter, you will be able to answer the following questions:

- **3-1** What types of opportunities are available in Manufacturing?
- **3-2** Which opportunities may be right for you?
- **3-3** How can I match my skills & interests with the right job?
- **3-4** What training & education is needed for a job in Manufacturing?
- **3-5** What are typical work environments in Manufacturing?
- **3-6** What factors affect trends in Manufacturing?

Chapter Topics

3-1 Manufacturing Today

3-2 Manufacturing Jobs

3-3 Building a Career in Manufacturing

3-4 Education and Training for Manufacturing Opportunities

3-5 Working Conditions in the Manufacturing Industry

3-6 Trends in Manufacturing

Copyright © McGraw Hill Shutterstock

3-1 Manufacturing Today

Look around you. How much of what you see has been made by combining materials in creative, effective ways? The chair on which you sit, the walls around you, your phone, and even much of what you eat and drink have all been made. Manufacturing is the process of making products by hand or by machine. The term "production" sometimes means the same thing as "manufacturing." For example, apparel manufacturers produce the clothes you wear, and breakfast cereal is created at food processing plants. Manufactured products can be as simple as paper clips or as complicated as robots and computers. Manufacturers create their products by hand or by using highly specialized machinery that they purchase from other manufacturers.

The United States is the world's largest manufacturing economy. It produces products worth $1.6 trillion each year. The Manufacturing industry includes 18.6 million jobs. This is about one in every six jobs in the private sector, or private and non-government companies.

3-1 Essential Question

As you read this section, keep this question in mind:

What types of opportunities are available in Manufacturing?

Career Journeys in Manufacturing

There are six major paths along which your journey in Manufacturing might be shaped. Each field contains a group of careers requiring similar skills as well as similar certifications or education. These paths are:

- Production
- Manufacturing Production Process Development
- Maintenance, Installation, and Repair
- Quality Assurance
- Logistics and Inventory Control
- Health, Safety, and Environmental Assurance

Companies in the Manufacturing industry fall into three broad categories:

- **Producers** make and sell a product directly to the public or retail merchants.
- **Suppliers** are manufacturing businesses that make parts or components. They then sell these parts to other manufacturers.
- **Distributors** sell the products of suppliers.

Production

Workers in the Production path include people who work on the shop floor of manufacturing plants. These workers may use machines to make electronic parts. They may construct or assemble housing. They may weld metal, or they may print books.

Machinists use tools like lathes and grinders to produce precision metal parts. Foundry workers melt and mix metals and pour them into molds. Sheet metal workers shape and weld flat sheets of metal into large products, such as heating ducts and drainpipes. Tool and die makers create metal parts used to form all kinds of products, from wood furniture to ceramic bowls.

This path is not limited to making products. Hydroelectric plant technicians make sure their plants are running smoothly. Other workers operate chemical and nuclear plants. Millwrights install, move, and take apart heavy machinery. Boilermakers assemble, maintain, and repair boilers and other vessels that hold liquids and gases.

Workers in this path must be good at working with their hands. They often must be physically strong. They should have good problem-solving skills and be able to work well on their own. Many workers in this field take part in apprenticeships or train at community colleges.

Manufacturing Production Process Development

Employees in this career path supervise product design and the design of the manufacturing process itself. They make sure that products meet or exceed customer expectations. They also monitor the materials used to manufacture products.

A variety of engineering jobs are included in this path. These include design engineers, electronics engineers, and industrial engineers. Engineers design new products, using computers to analyze and test their designs.

There are a variety of other jobs in this path. Process improvement technicians work to find the most efficient processes for creating a product. Production managers coordinate all the people and equipment involved in the production process. Precision inspectors, testers, and graders make sure the products meet required quality standards.

Workers in this path must have good problem-solving skills and mathematical abilities. They must exercise good judgment and have a detailed knowledge of the production process. Many jobs in this field require a bachelor's degree.

Maintenance, Installation, and Repair

This career path is wide-ranging. It includes all jobs involved with installing, maintaining, and repairing a broad range of devices. These devices can be small, such as cellular phones, computers, and home security systems. Or they can be large, such as nuclear power generators and satellites. This field is vital to every area of the Manufacturing industry.

Jobs in installation and maintenance require highly developed technical skills. These skills may be learned through apprenticeships, technical schools, community colleges, and on-the-job training. Workers in this career path need to understand electrical wiring and components. They must also be able to diagnose and repair complex systems.

Quality Assurance

Employees in the Quality Assurance path make sure that standards are met and procedures are followed. They are responsible for fulfilling the performance requirements that customers expect from various products and services. Some employees in this path monitor and maintain the quality of parts, while others inspect raw materials to see that they meet specifications. Still other employees measure and test products and parts to make sure they meet customer satisfaction.

3-1 • Manufacturing Today

Jobs in this career path include food science technicians, medical and health services managers, aerospace engineers, and managers of computer and information systems. Employees may have titles such as inspector, tester, sorter, sampler, and weigher.

Good communication skills are required in this path. A quality control systems manager, for instance, meets with the marketing and sales departments of a company to define client expectations. He or she supervises the tracking of test results and product defects. A manager in this field oversees supervisors, inspectors, and laboratory workers engaged in testing activities.

Logistics and Inventory Control

Employees in this path move products and materials around. Jobs in this field include storage and distribution managers, shipping and receiving clerks, cargo and freight agents, and transportation managers. Employees move raw materials to the production line, unload trucks with raw materials, and communicate with traffic managers. Organizational skills are very important in this path.

Logistics analysts, for example, work with data that tells whether a product is available, how well the production process is working, and how the product is being transported to the next location. They meet and communicate with management teams to make sure the materials required for production are available and not too expensive. People involved in logistics make sure deliveries are made on time and all orders are fulfilled. They keep track of inventory, the amount of the product available to be shipped. They also manage systems that make sure the price of a product considers the cost of producing and shipping it.

Health, Safety, and Environmental Assurance

Employees in this career path ensure the safe use of workplace equipment. They design and install safety procedures for new production processes. They carry out health and safety investigations. Many jobs in this path focus on preventing health problems. People in this path train other workers in health, safety, and environmental issues.

For example, environmental science and protection technicians often perform laboratory and field tests to monitor the impact of manufacturing firms on the environment. They investigate sources of pollution and other things that may endanger a person's health. Skills needed for this job include knowledge of biology, chemistry, computers, and public safety and security.

Manufacturing Future Outlook

Industry outlook refers to the projected job growth or decline in a particular industry. According to the Bureau of Labor Statistics, growth will be slow in the Manufacturing industry in the years up to 2030. The greatest growth will be in the areas of high-tech equipment and pharmaceuticals. Other areas will see declines.

Table 3.1: Job Forecast for a Sample of Manufacturing Occupations

Occupation	Expected Growth Rate
Welders, Cutters, Solderers, and Brazers	5%–10%
Purchasing Agents	−1% or lower
First-Line Supervisors	1%–5%
Machinists	5%–10%
Machine Tool Operators (CNC automated)	5%–10%
Industrial Production Managers	5%–10%
Power Plant Operators	−1% or lower
Telecommunications Equipment Installers	−1% or lower
Security and Fire Alarm Installers	15% or higher!
Medical Equipment Repairers	5%–10%
Inspectors, Testers, and Sorters	−1% or lower
Quality Control Systems Managers	5%–10%
Logistics Analysts	15% or higher!
Cargo and Freight Agents	5%–10%
Environmental Engineers	1%–5%
Health and Safety Engineers	5%–10%

3-1 Essential Question Reflection

So, let us revisit our essential question:

What types of opportunities are available in Manufacturing?

Based on what you learned in this section, which field of Manufacturing is the most interesting to you? Explain your answer.

Practice 3-1

Skills Practice

The details in workplace documents are not always clearly stated. For example, a help wanted ad for a machine repairer might ask for related experience. People applying need to identify what would qualify as related experience and determine whether they have that experience. It may sometimes be necessary to infer, or make a logical guess, when a detail is suggested rather than stated. **Practice this skill!**

WAREHOUSE AND OPERATIONS SPECIALIST

Description

Responsibilities include keeping accurate records on warehouse inventory, truck loading and unloading (manually and using a forklift), and primary shipping/receiving. Forklift driving certificate may be required.

Primary Responsibilities
- Operate equipment and/or a forklift safely and efficiently
- Track, receive, and store incoming items efficiently using established procedures and automated devices including barcode scanners
- Maintain accurate, complete records of incoming, outgoing, and stored product including partial cases of returned product

Desired Experience
- Experience in high-speed warehouse or shipping environment
- Forklift driving experience or certificate
- Experience in tracking and managing inventory
- Computer experience including using spreadsheets, proprietary applications, and hand-held devices such as barcode scanners

---

Use the above job posting for a Warehouse and Operations Specialist to answer the questions that follow.

1. As a warehouse and operations specialist, you are interested in applying for this job. Which one of the following jobs listed on your resume should you highlight because it relates directly to the type of experience the employer is looking for?

    A. restaurant busser; cleaned tables and refilled beverages

    B. theme park operator; operated a roller coaster

    C. cafeteria cashier; rang up customers' orders

    D. stock clerk; used a barcode scanner to check inventory levels

    E. fry cook; managed the fryer

2. You also have additional skills and achievements listed on your resume. According to the job description's list of desired experience, which of the following should you highlight?

    A. your forklift driving certificate

    B. your experience as a telemarketer

    C. your experience as a clothing store sales clerk

    D. your certificate to teach cooking classes

    E. your Employee of the Month award at a fast-food restaurant

To access more problems that will help you grow professional skills and are real-world examples in Manufacturing, go online.

3-2 Manufacturing Jobs

The field of Manufacturing contains jobs that represent a variety of skills and abilities. You might find yourself working at an auto plant assembling cars, or you might work in a lab creating robots. Here are some common industry jobs and the skills they require.

3-2 Essential Question

As you read this section, keep this question in mind:

Which opportunities may be right for you?

Occupation With the Most People Employed:

Supervisors

- Directly supervise and coordinate the activities of production and operating workers
- Keep records of employees' attendance and hours worked
- Inspect materials, products, or equipment to detect defects or malfunctions

Fast Facts:
Employment: 616,000 in 2020, expected to grow slightly to 640,000 in 2030
Annual Openings: 63,000
Median Annual Wage: $61,790
Education Needed: High school diploma

Great Job! – Associate Degree Needed:

Drafters

- Prepare detailed working diagrams of objects requiring assembly
- Sometimes called CAD Designer (Computer Aided Design Designer), CAD Operator (Computer Aided Design Operator), Design Drafter, Drafter

Fast Facts:
Employment: Approximately 100,000
Median Annual Wage: $61,000
Education Needed: Associate degree
Did You Know: This is a "high flying" occupation, where the work you do eventually becomes part of making a vehicle fly.

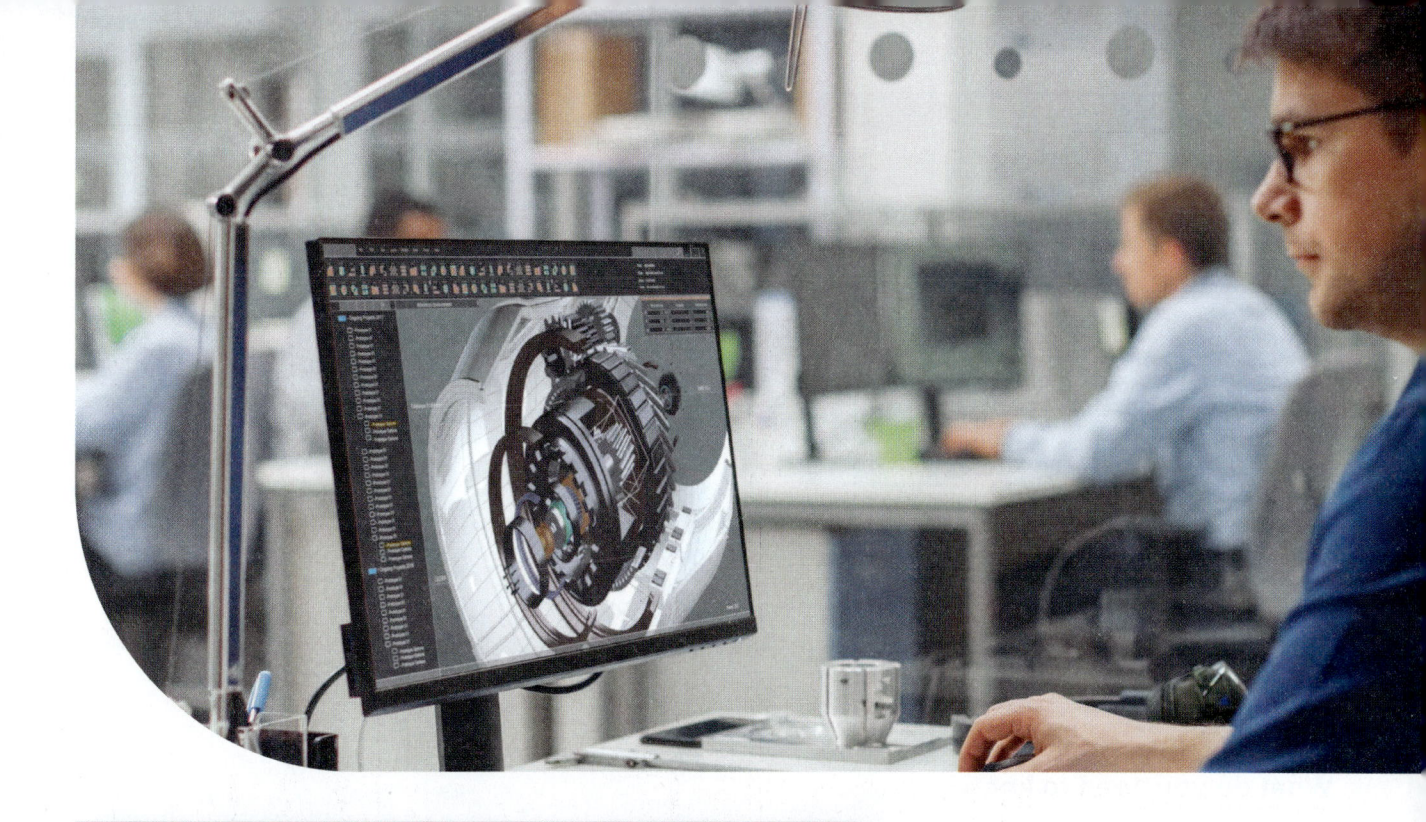

Great Job! – High School Diploma Needed:

Mapping Technicians

- Perform mapping duties, usually under supervision
- Obtain data used for construction, mapmaking, boundary location, mining, or other purposes
- May calculate mapmaking information and create maps from source data

Fast Facts:

Employment: 54,800

Median Annual Wage: $46,910

Education Needed: High school diploma, or equivalent

Did You Know: In this field you contribute to everything from weather maps to map apps used by drivers!

3-2 Essential Question Reflection

So, let us revisit our essential question:

Which opportunities may be right for you?

Based on what you learned in this section, please answer this question in detail.

Case Study: Computer Numerically Controlled (CNC) Programmers

What do they do?

- Develop programs to control machining or processing of materials by automatic machine tools, equipment, or systems
- Set up, operate, or maintain equipment

What would you do?

- Write programs in the language of a machine's controller and store programs on media, such as punch tapes, magnetic tapes, or disks
- Determine the sequence of machine operations and select the proper cutting tools needed to machine workpieces into the desired shapes
- Revise programs or tapes to eliminate errors and retest programs to check that problems have been solved

What do you need to know?

Engineering and Technology
Computers and electronics
Mechanical

Math and Science
Arithmetic, algebra, geometry, calculus, or statistics

Manufactured or Agricultural Goods
Manufacture and distribution of products

Arts and Humanities
English language

What skills do you need?

Basic Skills
Keep track of how well people and/or groups are doing in order to make improvements

Figure out how to use new ideas or things

Problem Solving
Notice a problem and figure out the best way to solve it

People and Technology Systems
Figure out how a system should work and how changes in the future will affect it

Think about the pros and cons of different options and pick the best one

What abilities must you be good at?

Math
Choose the right type of math to solve a problem

Add, subtract, multiply, or divide

Ideas and Logic
Order or arrange things

Notice when problems happen

Visual Understanding
Quickly compare groups of letters, numbers, pictures, or other things

See hidden patterns

Verbal
Listen and understand what people say

Who does well in this occupation?

People interested in this work like activities that include data, detail, and regular routines

People who do well at these jobs need:
- Attention to detail
- Independence
- Analytical thinking
- Dependability
- Integrity
- Achievement/effort

What educational level is needed?

- High school diploma, or equivalent
- Certificate, can be obtained during or after high school

Practice 3-2

Skills Practice

Manufacturing workers must sometimes analyze graphics to identify trends. They might search for data that has increased or decreased over time. An industrial safety and health engineer might analyze tables of accident statistics in a factory over several years. Being able to identify common trends from several pieces of data can help with a variety of jobs in this industry. **Practice this skill!**

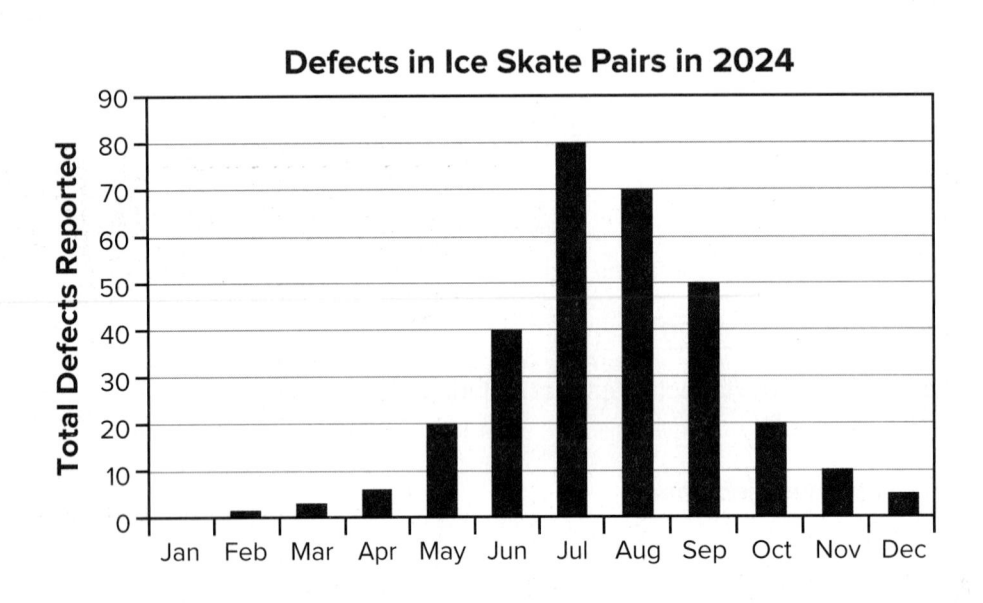

Defects in Ice Skate Pairs in 2024

Month	Total Defects Reported
Jan	0
Feb	1
Mar	3
Apr	6
May	20
Jun	40
Jul	80
Aug	70
Sep	50
Oct	20
Nov	10
Dec	5

Use the chart above to answer the questions that follow.

56   Chapter 3 • Manufacturing

1. As a shift manager in a production plant that makes ice skates, you have received the defect report for your shift's production over the past year. In what month were the defects at their highest point?

    A. January

    B. March

    C. April

    D. June

    E. July

2. By how much did the defect rate change between May and June?

    A. It doubled.

    B. It was reduced by half.

    C. It stayed the same.

    D. It fell slightly.

    E. There were no defects in June.

To access more problems that will help you grow professional skills and are real-world examples in Manufacturing, go online.

3-3 Building a Career in Manufacturing

Once you have found a field that interests you, look ahead and consider your overall career path and where you should start. For example, many robotics engineers begin their career as an apprentice. After a few years, their responsibility might increase to include designing and managing projects. Robotics engineers with significant experience generally become more involved with clients and upper-level executives. Some senior-level engineers might even start their own companies.

> **3-3 Essential Question**
>
> As you read this section, keep this question in mind:
>
> *How can I match my skills & interests with the right job?*

Are You More Interested in Working With Data, People, or Things?

Environmental engineers, for example, work mainly with data. Labor relations managers work primarily with people. Welders work mostly with things. When planning your career path, consider what balance of data, people, and things you want in a career.

Careers That Involve Working With Data

Examples of working with data include preparing financial statements and drawing up budgets, making measurements and calculations, and scheduling the steps needed to manufacture a product.

Many Manufacturing jobs focus on data. Machinists and tool and die makers review blueprints before calculating where and how to cut into something. Engineers may be called upon to design new products or improve existing ones. This requires conducting research, running tests, and collecting and analyzing data. Engineers may also perform calculations and make projections based on collected data.

Some managers in Manufacturing also need to work with data. A production manager, for instance, may need to study spreadsheets that display rates of production to determine whether a particular procedure is efficient and cost-effective.

Careers That Involve Working With People

Examples of working with people include training employees, mediating conflicts among coworkers, negotiating prices with suppliers, and advising customers. All these activities involve strong communication skills.

Many Manufacturing jobs enable you to spend a great deal of time working with others. Production managers or supervisors must effectively supervise and lead teams of workers. Assemblers rely heavily on teamwork, which requires the ability to follow directions and communicate ideas to other members.

Careers That Involve Working With Things

Examples of working with things include setting up and operating machinery, driving a forklift, and welding metal. For instance, someone who works with machinery might start, stop, and observe the operations and actions of equipment. A tender (a worker who attends to machines) may need to adjust materials or controls of a machine. He or she may change guides, adjust timers and temperature gauges, turn valves to allow the flow of materials, and flip switches in response to lights.

This carpenter is using a plane. Carpenters spend much of their time working with tools and machines.

Setting up requires preparing machines or equipment for operation by planning the order of the steps. Employees with this focus adjust the positions of parts or materials, set controls, and verify the accuracy of machine capabilities. These employees evaluate the properties of materials. They use tools, equipment, and work aids such as precision gauges and measuring instruments. This job requires experience and good independent judgment.

Most careers in Manufacturing involve working primarily with things. For example, welders, assemblers, and machinists spend a majority of their day working with tools, machines, and other equipment.

Working with things, though, may occur in a wide variety of settings. For instance, boiler tenders are responsible for handling and monitoring large equipment. Boiler tenders work in a variety of Manufacturing industries. Some, for example, are employed at plants that produce lumber, paper, chemicals, iron, or steel. Others work at public facilities, such as schools or government buildings.

3-3 Essential Question Reflection

So, let us revisit our essential question:

How can I match my skills & interests with the right job?

Based on what you learned in this section, please answer this question in detail.

3-4 Education and Training for Manufacturing Opportunities

Jobs in the Manufacturing industry require varying levels of education. Many jobs in the industry require little or no formal training. For others, it is necessary to have specific education and experience.

> **3-4 Essential Question**
>
> As you read this section, keep this question in mind:
>
> *What training & education is needed for a job in Manufacturing?*

Training and Education in Manufacturing

The level of training necessary to succeed in the Manufacturing industry varies by career. Jobs can be categorized into three groups—jobs requiring little or no training, jobs requiring some training, and jobs requiring advanced training.

Jobs Requiring Little or No Training

Positions such as precision assembler, machine tool operator, and hand packer usually require little previous training. The training for jobs such as these, and similar on-the-floor production jobs, is usually provided by your employer when you are hired.

However, getting a high school education or the equivalent is important. Many employers look for workers who earned solid grades in high school. Failing to complete high school may hurt your chances of advancing in your field.

Jobs Requiring Some Training or Certification

Many jobs in Manufacturing require some specialized training. If you are interested in working as a welder, electrician, machinist, or mechanical drafter, you will need to pursue specialized degrees or certifications.

You can complete apprenticeships to prepare for many of the more skilled trades in Manufacturing. Technical colleges offer programs in such fields as electronics servicing, mechanical drafting, and electronic engineering technology. Some programs will provide you with an associate degree upon completion.

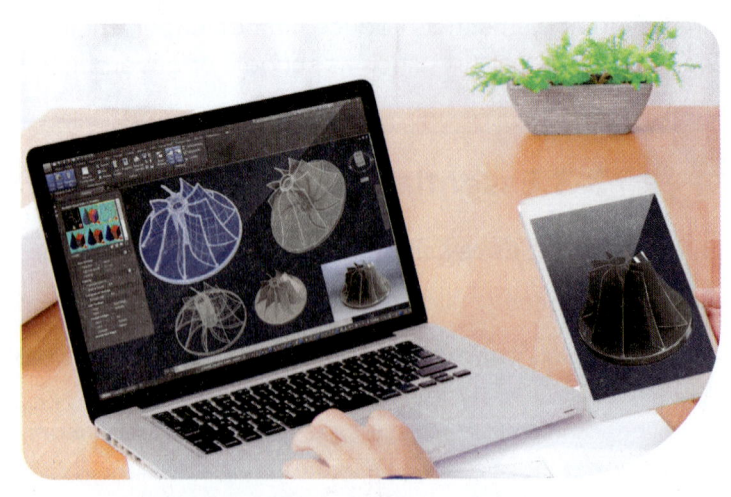

Drafting, as well as many other Manufacturing roles, may require a specialized credential.

Trade organizations, or organizations representing a specific industry or type of job, often offer certification programs. These programs provide training for a specific occupation. Specialized certification exists in a wide variety of Manufacturing careers, including occupations in plastics and welding. These programs might require a minimum number of hours on the job and a minimum score on a standardized test.

Earning an associate degree or a nationally recognized certification can help you prosper in your field. For more information about such programs, contact trade organizations or community colleges and technical schools in your area.

Jobs Requiring Advanced Training

Jobs in Manufacturing that require extensive training usually involve business management, science, or engineering. Such jobs generally require at least a bachelor's degree. Some may require study at the master's or doctoral level.

Manufacturing professionals who work in scientific or engineering positions often need extensive schooling. The Manufacturing industry has a wide variety of scientific and engineering jobs.

For example, the aerospace industry employs many physicists. Most physicists have doctoral degrees in physics. Other Manufacturing fields, such as drug manufacturers, employ chemists with degrees in chemistry.

Table 3.2: Training Required for Manufacturing Jobs

Level of Training	Job Title
Little or No Training	Boiler Tenders Cooling and Freezing Equipment Operators Machine Tool Operators Shipping Clerks
Some Training	Boilermakers Computer Technicians Machinists Patternmakers Quality Control Technicians Tool and Die Makers
Advanced Training	Computer Engineers Industrial Engineers Mechanical Engineers Robotics Engineers Technicians

The Manufacturing industry also employs many engineers, particularly in the automotive and aerospace industries. To become an engineer, you must have at least a bachelor's degree in engineering. Common types of engineers in Manufacturing include mechanical, chemical, electrical, and civil engineers. Many engineers eventually pursue advanced degrees (master's or doctoral degrees) in their fields. Some companies hire technicians who have high school diplomas and some college training, usually less than two years. Many of these companies then pay for the employee to finish college and earn their degree.

Manufacturing Skill Standards

The Manufacturing Skill Standards Council (MSSC) represents individuals and organizations from the Manufacturing industry. These include labor unions, companies, educators, and public interest groups. Members of the council have worked together to create a set of core knowledge and skills. The standards stress the importance of specific job skills. They also emphasize general workplace skills. The standards call for knowledge in 17 academic areas, such as math, science, computer technology, and writing. The standards also define three main technical areas: safety procedures, the manufacturing process, and business policies and procedures.

The MSSC has developed skill standards for jobs in the six Manufacturing career paths. These are Production; Manufacturing Production Process Development; Maintenance, Installation, and Repair; Quality Assurance; Logistics and Inventory Control; and Health, Safety, and Environmental Assurance. These standards outline how work should be performed. The standards also define the level of knowledge and skill required for specific careers.

Professional Skills

Communication Skills   In Manufacturing, workers need good communication skills when offering instruction to the people they manage or when bringing problems to management's attention. Good communication is also needed to develop good, productive relationships with coworkers.

Listening Skills   Listening is the foundation of learning. Active listening skills are vital to effective communication. Listening skills are essential for following instructions safely and precisely. In the Manufacturing industry, this is necessary to ensure a safe working environment. Good listening skills also help colleagues understand each other's ideas and points of view.

Problem-Solving Skills   Employers value workers who can spot problems and take action to find solutions. Solving problems requires creativity and self-reliance. A production supervisor, for example, may need to solve complex problems occurring on the production line or between departments. Maintenance, Installation, and Repair workers confront a broad range of problems almost every day. They must identify problems and then evaluate potential solutions. The same is true for employees in the Logistics and Quality Assurance career paths.

Technology Skills   Technology has an ever-increasing impact on production processes. Many plants now use computer automation instead of human workers to produce items more quickly and efficiently. Line workers, such as assemblers, may be required to run computer programs and operate high-tech machinery.

Decision-Making Skills Time is of the essence in Manufacturing. The ability to gather and analyze information rapidly, and to think clearly under pressure, is key to this industry. A boiler tender, for example, might be faced with an equipment breakdown or problem during a night shift that will require him or her to make effective decisions quickly. Employees in the Health, Safety, and Environmental Assurance path must make important decisions daily to ensure a safe work environment.

Organizing and Planning Skills Because manufacturing involves so many steps, organization is crucial. Planning requires the ability to set goals and to visualize the sequence of steps leading up to those goals. Robotics engineers, for example, might be called on to develop new products on a deadline. They would then have to make a plan and organize different departments, teams, and processes to make sure the deadline is met.

Teamwork Skills Teamwork is key in Manufacturing. For example, a successful manufacturing firm brings hundreds, perhaps even thousands, of products to market. To do so, producers must work with maintenance and repair employees, logisticians, quality assurance workers, and health and safety inspectors. Good communication is one of the most important foundations of teamwork.

Social Skills In a production factory, workers might interact with individuals from various levels of the company, from apprentices to managers. They should keep an open mind and use the opportunity to learn from others. Some studies have shown that between 80 to 85 percent of a person's success in the workplace is due to the person's social skills. These skills build an excellent foundation for advancement opportunities.

Adaptability Skills In Manufacturing, job descriptions, work environments, and production processes are constantly changing because of technological innovation. Workers should keep an open mind and be ready to acquire new skills. Remember that for every firm in the Manufacturing industry, the image of being on the cutting edge is highly desirable.

3-4 Essential Question Reflection

So, let us revisit our essential question:

What training & education is needed for a job in Manufacturing?

Based on what you learned in this section, please answer this question in detail.

Practice 3-4

Skills Practice

Some jobs in the Manufacturing industry require workers to calculate costs and discounts. A plumber, for example, needs to be able to calculate a mark-up that will bring in a profit while being acceptable to the client. **Practice this skill!**

1. As a manager at a paper recycling facility, you buy recycled cardboard boxes. Your supplier offers 1,000 boxes (minimum purchase) at $0.50 a box plus a 7% sales tax. How much do you end up paying for the recycled cardboard boxes?

   A. $515
   B. $520
   C. $525
   D. $530
   E. $535

2. You are a quality assurance assistant working in a semiconductor manufacturing plant. The supervisor just announced the introduction of a new line, using an innovative method of manufacturing semiconductors. To learn more about the new technology about to be introduced, you order a book from an online vendor. The book costs $30. Shipping is 3% of your purchase, but sales tax is free. How much do you end up paying for the book?

   A. $29.25
   B. $29.50
   C. $30.25
   D. $30.90
   E. $32.75

To access more problems that will help you grown professional skills and are real-world examples in Manufacturing, go online.

3-5 Working Conditions in the Manufacturing Industry

Understanding the work environment, hazards, and benefits of Manufacturing jobs can help you make informed decisions about your future career path.

3-5 Essential Question

As you read this section, keep this question in mind:

What are typical work environments in Manufacturing?

Work Environment

There are many factors that can impact work environments in the Manufacturing industry, including workers' satisfaction, health, and the physical activities they are asked to perform on a daily basis. It is important to consider these factors before accepting an opportunity in the Manufacturing industry.

Physical Environment

Some jobs require workers to spend long days on their feet in noisy factories. Other jobs require them to handle chemicals and toxic substances. Most factory buildings are clean and have good lighting and ventilation. Some factories even have outdoor facilities.

In the aerospace, apparel, pharmaceutical, electronics, automotive, textile, and computer industries, employees usually enjoy a reasonably pleasant work environment. In every industry, however, production workers confront greater environmental stresses than administrators and engineers do. Workers in the iron and steel industries, for example, are often exposed to intense heat and noise. In glassmaking, which requires the use of high temperatures and heavy machinery, there is the risk of cuts and burns.

Production

- Workers are sometimes exposed to high noise levels, and heavy lifting may be required in some jobs.
- Part-time work is unusual.
- In chemical plants, split, weekend, and night shifts are common, but pay is usually higher for non-traditional hours.
- Many food industry production jobs involve repetitive, physically demanding work.

Manufacturing Production Process Development

- In the computer industry, research and development (R&D) personnel may work long hours of overtime.
- Many food manufacturing plants have redesigned equipment and increased the use of job rotation.
- In textiles, travel is an important part of the job for many managers and designers.

Maintenance, Installation, and Repair

- In steel mills, computer-controlled machinery helps to move iron and steel through the production processes, reducing the need for heavy labor.

Quality Assurance

- In pharmaceuticals, the danger of contamination means that there is rigorous attention needed in keeping plants and equipment clean.
- In food manufacturing, managers and employees must comply with numerous government standards and regulations.

Logistics & Inventory Control

- In motor vehicle manufacturing, overtime is especially common during periods of peak demand.

Health, Safety, & Environmental Assurance

- Environmental engineers and health and safety engineers spend much of their time in offices working on plans and safety reports.
- Engineers may travel on-site to inspect facilities and machinery. In some cases, they may spend time near hazardous materials and situations to find ways to reduce the hazard's impact and improve safety.

Source: *U.S. Department of Labor*

Work Hours

The work hours of jobs in Manufacturing vary greatly. Because the equipment in many manufacturing plants requires 24-hour supervision, shift work is vital in this industry. Shift work divides the day into blocks of time, generally eight hours. Shift work allows Manufacturing companies to operate around the clock. It also allows workers to select hours to meet their needs. Shift work is common for assemblers, boiler tenders, quality control inspectors, and production supervisors.

Flextime is a trend affecting all industries, including Manufacturing. Flextime allows workers to choose the hours and days they work. However, employees must maintain a standard total number of hours per week. Workers may adjust their hours to suit their personal needs. One employee may choose to work ten hours only four days a week, for example. Another employee may work six and one-half hours six days a week. Flextime is especially important for workers who have young children or other family commitments.

Machinists, tool and die makers, and precision assemblers typically work eight-hour shifts. Although they do most of their work during standard working hours, they may need to work overtime to meet production demands. Most welding technicians work 40 hours per week, although opportunities for overtime are usually available. Boiler tenders also generally work 40 hours per week. However, because boilers operate around the clock, most boiler tenders are required to work some nights, weekends, and holidays.

Many workers in Manufacturing must deal with tight deadlines. A deadline might require that a specific number of cars be produced for a certain launch date, for example. This deadline would affect production supervisors, assemblers, and line workers. Manufacturing engineers and robotics engineers often face tight deadlines when developing new and innovative products.

Essential Physical Activities

Production workers in Manufacturing must be in good physical shape to withstand the demands of their jobs. Heavy lifting and the operation of powerful equipment is required for most production jobs. It is vital that workers be trained to handle heavy equipment properly. Although some production jobs are not strenuous, most workers are required to stand, walk, stoop, bend, or climb ladders regularly during the day.

Good vision is a must for production workers who must test products by color. Good eyesight is also necessary for the accurate reading of thermometers, gauges, charts, and meters.

Manufacturing workers should be skilled with their hands. Many assembly-line workers handle small pieces and parts and detailed machinery. Machinists and precision assemblers must have good hand-eye coordination to work with the machinery and components.

Hazards and Environmental Dangers

Because accidents can happen on any job, safety must be a priority. The federal government protects individual workers on the job through agencies such as the Occupational Safety and Health Administration (OSHA). These agencies create safety standards and laws that help prevent accidents. They also ensure that accident victims are helped. OSHA certification credentials require sitting through a 10-hour or 30-hour course and are usually needed for a person to be present on a jobsite. These credentials may be earned while you are in high school and may be taken remotely.

Injuries and Illnesses

Many Manufacturing jobs involve operating heavy equipment and machinery that can be dangerous if improperly used. Proper training and common sense are therefore necessary for tasks involving machinery. Workers must follow all safety procedures. They should take advantage of breaks in line work to rest tired muscles. They should also vary their tasks when possible. They should notify managers if they feel pain or stiffness.

Another job hazard is eye injuries. Goggles are necessary during exposure to chemicals, extremely bright lights, and sharp pieces. Workers who focus on very detailed machinery, such as tool and die makers, may suffer from eyestrain.

Developments in ergonomics are helping to create a healthier work environment. Ergonomics is the study of creating and adjusting work equipment and practices to make workplaces safer and more comfortable. Ergonomically correct production lines, for example, are set at a comfortable height. Workers can maintain a healthy and appropriate stance and posture. Ergonomic workstations can be adjusted to accommodate workers of different heights.

3-5 Essential Question Reflection

So, let us revisit our essential question:

What are typical work environments in Manufacturing?

Based on what you learned in this section, please answer this question in detail.

3-6 Trends in Manufacturing

Manufacturing is constantly evolving. People's needs for products change. Advances in technology continue to improve Manufacturing.

3-6 Essential Question

As you read this section, keep this question in mind:

What factors affect trends in Manufacturing?

Technology in Manufacturing

Technology continues to make Manufacturing more efficient and safe. Improvements have occurred so often that today's manufacturing machines and processes are referred to as "advanced manufacturing," "clean manufacturing," or "manufacturing 4.0." Companies that once dealt with suppliers in person or by telephone now use e-mail and websites to make purchases. Manufacturers also use the Internet to participate in online auctions. These auctions allow companies to bid on parts, products, or services over the Internet.

Hi-tech manufacturing uses strict safety and cleanliness practices to produce many different things. Here you can see a silicon "wafer" used in the computer chip industry as it reflects a glowing rainbow of color.

Computer Numerical Control (CNC) and Manufacturing

An example of the rapid changes in Manufacturing is the use of programmable machine tools. Imagine using simple programming to tell a machine what to make. This is referred to as "computer numerical control" or "CNC" manufacturing. Machines may be programmed to cut three-dimensional (3D) shapes out of wood, metal, stone, plastic, and many other materials.

3D Printing

Imagine making a house anywhere, anytime. 3D printing has made this a reality. 3D printing uses portable machines to cut all the objects needed to make a home into the right shapes. All people need to do is put the objects together in the right way.

This technology exists for mobile and at-home manufacturing of a vast number of products. As this technology improves and becomes more mobile, only the available materials will limit the possibilities. The photo in this section shows the representation of a fingerless glove on the computer. That "recipe," a specific program that tells where to cut a block of material, is sent to the printer, which looks like a small kiln or microwave oven. A block of the needed material, in this case a plastic, is placed in the printer. The printer then cuts and shapes the material like a sculptor, and the glove is produced.

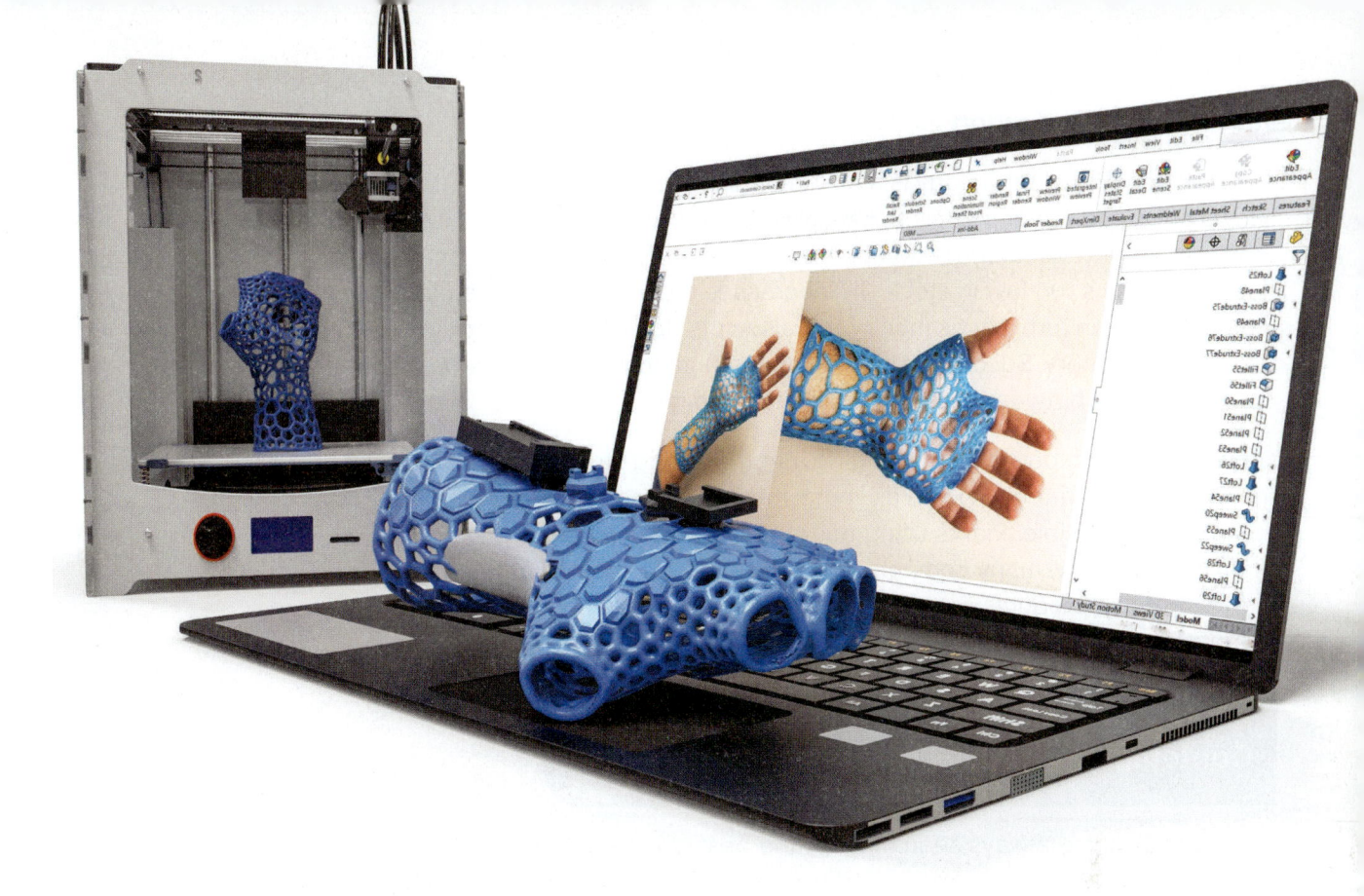

Automation

Robotics is the technology used in designing, constructing, and operating robots. It is perhaps the most useful development in computer-aided manufacturing. Creating and programming robots to perform production tasks is an example of automation. Automation is the operation and control of machinery by electronic devices. Robots can be programmed to do a wide range of jobs, such as spotwelding parts of an automobile frame.

The automotive industry is one of the biggest users of robots. However, other areas of Manufacturing are introducing robots into production processes as well. These include the aerospace, electronics, food processing, and pharmaceutical industries. For example, robotic devices have been used by NASA to collect and analyze soil samples on distant planets. The International Federation of Robotics predicts that worldwide sales of industrial robots may near the 500,000 mark in 2024, more than five times as many as in 2013. Some critics argue that robots are taking jobs away from people. However, robots are essential in performing jobs that are too dangerous for people to do.

3-6 • Trends in Manufacturing

Just-in-Time Production

Another benefit of technology is a just-in-time (JIT) inventory system. This system allows parts and raw materials to be delivered to production plants just before they are needed. A computer keeps track of supplies. Orders are placed when necessary items run low in stock. JIT decreases the inventory that a plant must maintain. This, in turn, saves money. JIT also cuts down on overstock, or having too much inventory. Successful just-in-time manufacturing depends on frequent communication between manufacturer and supplier.

Computer technology is also changing manufacturing strategies. The traditional manufacturing strategy, known as "push manufacturing," is to produce as much inventory as possible. Plants using this strategy often create an oversupply of products. Today, many companies are switching to "pull manufacturing." In this strategy, products are created in response to consumer demand. "Pull manufacturing" offers better responsiveness to special orders.

Contemporary Issues in Manufacturing

Manufacturers are always searching for the best way to get the job done. New methods are constantly being tested to produce goods that use environmentally safe processes. In addition, manufacturers want to reduce waste. They are also discovering that outsourcing, or sending jobs to other companies, often overseas, helps to improve production in a variety of ways.

Green Manufacturing

Green manufacturing emphasizes conserving resources and minimizing pollution and waste. The Manufacturing industry generates more waste than any other industry. A growing number of environmental laws, as well as increasing consumer demand for environmentally sound products and processes, are creating new challenges for many companies.

The goal of green manufacturing is to create no waste at all. In some cases, remanufacturing can accomplish this. *Remanufacturing* is the process of taking apart, cleaning, repairing, and putting back together products for reuse. Instead of going to landfills or having their parts melted down for raw materials, products like vending machines and photocopiers are rebuilt and resold.

Outsourcing in Manufacturing

Outsourcing is the process of turning over control of certain tasks or duties to other companies. The contracting company specifies the desired result but does not specify how the result should be achieved. For example, an automobile factory might outsource the production of axles. The factory does not specify which machines, part numbers, or brands the outsource company should use. Instead, the contractor depends on the outsourced company to complete the job in the most cost-effective and efficient manner. Many large electronics manufacturers practice outsourcing. Companies must do a great deal of research before choosing the right outsource firm.

Companies that outsource must maintain a close relationship with the outsource company. The two firms must work toward a common goal. Outsourcing relationships work best when the partner companies share similar values, goals, and expectations.

3-6 Essential Question Reflection

So, let us revisit our essential question:

What factors affect trends in Manufacturing?

Based on what you learned in this section, please answer this question in detail.

Chapter 4
Information Technology (IT)

Essential Questions

By the end of the chapter, you will be able to answer the following questions:

- **4-1** What types of opportunities are available in IT?
- **4-2** Which opportunities may be right for you?
- **4-3** How can I match my skills & interests with the right job?
- **4-4** What training & education is needed for a job in IT?
- **4-5** What are typical work environments in IT?
- **4-6** What factors affect trends in IT?

Chapter Topics

4-1 IT Today

4-2 IT Jobs

4-3 Building a Career in IT

4-4 Education and Training for IT Opportunities

4-5 Working Conditions in the IT Industry

4-6 Trends in IT

4-1 IT Today

Since its invention in the middle of the 20th century, the computer has dramatically changed the way people perform their jobs. Computing technology has made information sharing easier. It has spawned advancements like the Internet, cloud computing, and "wearable" watches. In addition, millions of jobs have been created in the field of Information Technology (IT). IT is the practical knowledge used to design, develop, set up, operate, and support computer systems.

How does IT affect you? Cars and appliances use IT in the form of interconnected computing chips. Payments are taken electronically, and digital currencies like Bitcoin are increasingly used. When was the last time you saw a "cash register" that was not electronically connected to a computer? IT has enabled the creation of many new medical tests.

Businesses cannot function without Information Technology. In one way or another, most companies rely on computers to keep their business going. Workers in the IT industry keep those computers are working.

4-1 Essential Question

As you read this section, keep this question in mind:

What types of opportunities are available in IT?

Career Journeys in Information Technology

There are four major paths along which your journey in IT might be shaped. People commonly move into and out of different paths. Each path contains a group of careers requiring similar skills as well as similar certifications or education. This industry is divided into four main career paths:

- Network Systems
- Information Support and Services
- Web and Digital Communications
- Programming and Software Development

The Information Technology industry is a relatively young part of the economy, but it offers many job opportunities. The close connection between the paths mean that skills may be transferable from one path to another.

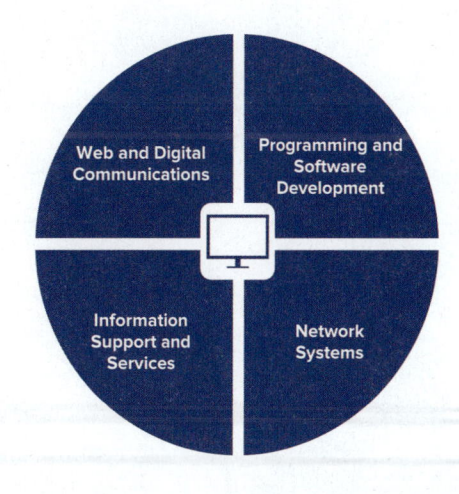

IT Products and Services

Workers in the Information Technology industry deal in four main product and service areas: computer hardware, computer software, web and digital programming, and IT services.

- **Computer hardware** refers to physical pieces of computer equipment. Mainframe computers—large, powerful computers that do complex calculations and tasks—are hardware. Personal computers, tablets, smartphones, and accessories such as keyboards and printers are also examples of hardware.
- **Software** includes all the programs and information that make hardware work. These include application software, such as word processors and photo editors.
- **Web and digital programming** are used to design websites. This programming allows for the creation of pages with text, images, video, and links.
- **IT services** are used by people and companies use to improve and maintain their technology. These services include installing software and maintaining websites.

Network Systems

A network is a system that links several computers together so that multiple users have access to the same files, applications software, and other features. Most networks are used in offices where people can share printers and files.

A network that links computers within a single office is known as a local area network (LAN). This kind of network can include as few as two and as many as several hundred computers. Other kinds of networks link people over larger areas, even throughout the world. The Internet is the world's largest network. It is a network of networks. Each day many billions of people around the world log on to this network, which gives them access to billions of sites.

Many companies maintain their own private, secure, internal networks called intranets. Intranets work like a private collection of linked documents. Only specified internal personnel are allowed access to information or resources on an intranet.

More businesses are developing external networks for customers, partners, and suppliers. These extranets allow designated users to use a portion of an organization's internal network. There is an increased need for workers who can find ways to ensure the privacy and security of such networks.

Many people work in the Network Systems career path. They support the operation of networks, resolve communication problems, or develop new ways for businesses to deliver important information to employees (both on-site workers and remote workers) customers, and suppliers. Ensuring the safe transfer of information across networks is the work of cybersecurity experts. These networking professionals are responsible for securing personal information, like credit card numbers, and preventing destructive attacks to networks.

Network managers must have strong technical skills and be excellent problem solvers. They deal with wiring, so network administrators must understand how to work safely with electricity. Some network managers have degrees in math or computer science.

Information Support and Services

Workers in Information Support and Services path provide a wide range of services. Database managers are responsible for managing the huge quantities of detailed information stored in computer systems. Technical writers prepare the manuals that explain how to use hardware and software. Computer support specialists help people who have questions about their computers.

Information Support and Services professionals need both technical and communication skills. Systems analysts, computer support specialists, and technical writers, for example, need to be able to understand technical problems and communicate solutions to non-experts.

Information Support and Services jobs are found across a wide range of fields. These jobs exist in companies that write customized software programs. Other jobs can be found in companies that sell computers and related hardware and software. Still others are available in businesses that teach people how to use IT.

Some companies in the IT industry provide support and services instead of producing hardware or software. They may help businesses determine their IT needs. Others design systems to meet those needs. Still others test and install systems, integrate hardware and software, and then operate the systems.

Some Information Support and Services providers have college degrees in computer science or related fields. Others may have degrees in unrelated fields, but they also have excellent IT skills.

Web and Digital Communications

Web and Digital Communications is the newest path in IT, and it is growing quickly. This path includes web-related jobs (jobs that involve work on Internet sites) and jobs in digital media. Any content that can be sent over the Internet—whether the content is text, graphics, audio, or video—is digital media. When the web was new, there were websites but not much else. The impressive capacity of the Internet now makes many more types of communication, such as video conferencing, possible. This field continues to expand.

Some of the people who work in this career path are the multimedia artists and animators who create graphics and animation for websites. Others deal with streaming media, the video or audio that plays from a website. Some specialize in virtual reality or in search engine optimization (the strategy for writing web pages so they appear at the top of Internet searches). There are jobs for social networking specialists, blog developers, and electronic commerce specialists.

Many industries are investing in digital or computer-enhanced media. This field is evolving rapidly, so many workers learn on the job. However, there are degree programs and courses available to those interested in learning how to create and manage digital media.

Programming and Software Development

People in the Programming and Software Development career path design, develop, and produce computer software, the coded instructions that direct the computer to carry out specific tasks. Structuring how the software will work in a system is called software design and development. Translating the design into coded statements that computer hardware can interpret is called coding or programming.

As new technologies emerge, new or updated software is needed. Demand for computer software engineers, in both applications and systems software, is expected to be very strong. Computer software engineers modify existing software and design new programs. They may work with clients to identify problems or needs. They may also design new software based on industry needs.

Computer programmers must be able to use various computer programming languages like Python. They must be logical thinkers who pay close attention to detail and work well under pressure. Most programmers have bachelor's degrees. Some receive their training at technical schools. Many programmers hold degrees in computer science, math, or information systems.

IT Future Outlook

The industry outlook for IT is excellent. In fact, this industry is one of the fastest-growing areas of the U.S. economy. "Cloud" computing refers to a virtual way to access programs through the Internet rather than through one's own computer. Mobile and wireless access to the Internet through cell phones, smartphones, and computer tablets is creating a need for new or adapted products. Strong growth is expected for jobs in this field. Most online businesses need people who can solve the latest security challenges.

Demand for many jobs in IT is expected to grow faster than average. These jobs include computer support specialists, computer security specialists, database administrators, network and computer systems administrators, telecommunications specialists, and computer systems analysts.

Table 4.1: Forecast for Occupations over the Next 10 Years

Occupation	Expected Growth Rate
Software Developers	15% or higher!
Software Quality Assurance Analysts and Testers	15% or higher!
Computer User Support Specialists	5%–10%
Computer Systems Analysts	5%–10%
Computer and Information Systems Managers	10%–15%
Digital Forensic Analysts	5%–10%
Network and Computer Systems Administrators	5%–10%
Information Security Analysts	15% or higher!
Computer Network Specialists	5%–10%
Database Administrators	5%–10%
Software Developers	15% or higher!

Source: *O*NET Online*

4-1 Essential Question Reflection

So, let us revisit our essential question:

What types of opportunities are available in IT?

Based on what you learned in this section, please answer this question in detail.

Practice 4-1

Skills Practice

It may be necessary to follow multi step instructions in a variety of situations, such as when setting up a new computer network. Workers must read carefully to know when to take each step, and they must be able to apply the same instructions in a variety of situations. **Practice this skill!**

PROCEDURE FOR INSTALLING A NEW GRAPHICS CARD

1. Gather the tools you'll need: new graphics card, screwdriver, and antistatic wrist strap.
2. Uninstall the current graphics card drivers on the PC.
3. Turn off the PC, and unplug it from the wall.
4. Put on antistatic wrist strap to prevent damage to computer components.
5. Open the computer casing, and locate the graphics card slot.
6. Remove the small screw that holds the graphics card in place, and then remove the card.
7. Install the new card in the slot. Press firmly to make sure it is all the way in place.
8. Secure the card with a screw.
9. Close the computer casing, and power up the PC.
10. Install the driver for the new graphics card.

Use the Procedure for Installing a New Graphics Card above to answer the questions that follow.

1. As a computer support specialist, you occasionally upgrade computer components such as graphics cards. According to the procedure shown, what must you do before opening the computer casing and handling components?

   A. install a new graphics card
   B. install a new graphics driver
   C. put on an antistatic wrist strap
   D. locate the graphics card slot
   E. secure the card with a screw

2. According to the procedure shown, when should you install the new graphics card driver?

   A. after you turn off the PC
   B. before you remove the old graphics driver
   C. before you remove the old graphics card
   D. before you have installed the new graphics card
   E. after you have installed the new graphics card

To access more problems that will help you grow professional skills and are real-world examples in IT, go online.

4-2 IT Jobs

There are many kinds of jobs in the Information Technology industry. You can find jobs at all skill levels and in a variety of working environments. You can work at some jobs with a minimum of experience, while others require significant education and training. Here are some common IT jobs and the skills they require.

> **4-2 Essential Question**
>
> As you read this section, keep this question in mind:
>
> *Which opportunities may be right for you?*

Occupation With the Most People Employed:

Software Developers

- Research, design, and develop computer and network software or specialized utility programs
- Analyze user needs and develop software solutions
- Update software or enhance existing software capabilities

Fast Facts

Employment: Approximately 1,847,900 in 2020, expected to grow to 2,257,400 in 2030

Annual Openings: 18,920

Median Annual Wage: $120,730

Education Needed: Associate or bachelor's degree

Fastest-Growing Occupation:

Software Quality Assurance Analysts and Testers

- Develop software programs and tests to identify problems and their causes
- Test system modifications to prepare for implementation
- Create and maintain databases of known defects

Fast Facts
   Employment: Approximately 1,847,900
   Annual Openings: 18,920
   Median Annual Wage: $98,220
   Education Needed: Associate or bachelor's degree

Highest Wage Occupation:

Computer and Information Research Scientists

- Conduct research into fundamental computer and information science as theorists, designers, or inventors
- Develop solutions to problems in the field of computer hardware and software

Fast Facts
   Employment: Approximately 33,000
   Annual Openings: 3,200
   Median Annual Wage: $131,490
   Education Needed: Master's degree

Great Job! – High School Diploma Needed:

Computer Support Specialists

- Answer user inquiries regarding computer software or hardware operation to resolve problems
- Oversee the daily performance of computer systems
- Set up equipment for employee use, performing or ensuring proper installation of cables, operating systems, or appropriate software

Fast Facts

Employment: Approximately 654,800

Annual Openings: 5,800

Median Annual Wage: $49,770

Did You Know: Computer support specialists oversee the daily performance of computer systems which means they make sure others can do their jobs!

Great Job! – Associate Degree Needed:

Computer Network Support Specialists

- Back up network data
- Configure security settings or access permissions for groups or individuals
- Analyze and report computer network security breaches or attempted breaches

Fast Facts

Employment: 189,800

Annual Openings: 1,550

Median Annual Wage: $62,760

Education Needed: Associate degree

Other: Computer network support specialists keep networks operating with minimal interruption. They keep us online!

4-2 Essential Question Reflection

So, let us revisit our essential question:

Which opportunities may be right for you?

Based on what you learned in this section, what 2 or 3 opportunities are the most interesting? Explain your answer.

Case Study: Information Security Analyst

Also called: Information Security Officer

What do they do?

- Plan, implement, upgrade, or monitor security measures for the protection of computer networks and information
- Assess system vulnerabilities for security risks and propose and implement risk mitigation strategies

What would you do?

- Develop plans to safeguard computer files against accidental or unauthorized modification, destruction, or disclosure and to meet emergency data processing needs
- Monitor current reports of computer viruses to determine when to update virus protection systems
- Encrypt data transmissions and erect firewalls to conceal confidential information as it is being transmitted and to keep out tainted digital transfers

What do you need to know?

Engineering and Technology
  Computers and electronics
  Product and service development

Arts and Humanities
  English language

Business
  Management
  Customer service

Communications
  Telecommunications

What skills do you need?

Basic Skills
  Read work-related information
  Think about the pros and cons of different ways to solve a problem

Problem Solving
  Notice a problem, and figure out the best way to solve it

People and Technology Systems
  Figure out how a system should work and how changes in the future will affect it
  Think about the pros and cons of different options, and pick the best one

What abilities must you be good at?

Verbal
  Listen and understand what people say
  Read and understand what is written

Ideas and Logic
    Make general rules, or come up with answers from lots of detailed information
    Notice when problems happen

Visual Understanding
    See hidden patterns
    Quickly compare groups of letters, numbers, pictures, or other things

Who does well in this occupation?

People interested in this work like activities that include data, detail, and regular routines.

They do well at jobs that need:
    Attention to detail
    Dependability
    Integrity
    Analytical thinking
    Cooperation
    Adaptability/flexibility

What educational level is needed?

- High school diploma, or equivalent
- Certification

Practice 4-2

Skills Practice

When workers look at a graphic such as a diagram or a bar graph, they need to analyze and make sense of the information. It may be necessary to summarize the information. For example, a help desk technician might need to summarize the cause of a problem for a user. Being able to summarize allows workers to make sense of varying information. **Practice this skill!**

Network Space Allocation

Drive #	Department	Space Available
1-2000-16P	Production	200 Gb
1-2001-17M	Marketing	50 Gb
1-2002-18D	Development	25 Gb
1-2003-19C	Corporate	150 Gb
1-2004-20G	Graphics	15 Gb

Department	Avg Usage Rate
Corporate	1 Gb / day
Development	25 Gb / day
Graphics	150 Gb / day
Marketing	5 Gb / day
Production	100 Gb / day

Use the Network Space Allocation table above to answer the questions that follow. Note, 1 gigabyte (Gb) is a unit of space for storage of information.

1. As a network administrator, you manage hard drive space and usage. Your manager asks you which drive is priority. What should you tell her?

   A. Drive 1-2001-17M is priority because it has a small amount of space and low usage.

   B. Drive 1-2004-20G is priority because it has the least free space and the highest usage.

   C. Drive 1-2003-19C is priority because it has a large amount of free space and the lowest usage.

   D. Drive 1-2002-18D is priority because it has space available for one day of usage.

   E. Drive 1-2000-16P is priority because it has the most free space and moderate usage.

2. Your manager asks you to summarize the Production team's network details. What can you tell him?

   A. Production uses an average of 1 Gb per day and has 15 Gb of space available on its drive.

   B. Production uses an average of 15 Gb per day and has 150 Gb of space available on its drive.

   C. Production uses an average of 25 Gb per day and has 150 Gb of space available on its drive.

   D. Production uses an average of 100 Gb per day and has 200 Gb of space available on its drive.

   E. Production uses an average of 5 Gb per day and has 50 Gb of space available on its drive.

To access more problems that will help you grow professional skills and are real-world examples in IT, go online.

4-3 Building a Career in IT

In most businesses, IT professionals who are just beginning their careers perform simple technical tasks. They take on more responsibilities and increasingly complex problems as their careers progress. A junior IT professional may provide IT services to a small office or group, while a more senior-level person may support several departments or groups and may oversee other IT workers. As IT professionals advance in their careers, they increase their technical knowledge and their knowledge of their employer's business.

For example, a software designer may start out as a computer programmer. After a few years, they could move into a job that involves managing projects. Eventually, the programmer could advance to software design. Don't worry if you change your mind about your career path. This happens to many people. It often takes time to find the right path. You can always change your career path regardless of where you are in your chosen profession.

4-3 Essential Question

As you read this section, keep this question in mind:

How can I match my skills & interests with the right job?

Are You More Interested in Working With Data, People, or Things?

Most jobs focus mainly on a combination of people, places, and things. Database administrators, for example, work mainly with data. Computer support specialists work closely with people. Software designers work mostly with things. When planning your career path, consider what balance of data, people, and things you want in a career.

Careers That Involve Working With Data

Examples of careers in IT that involve working with data include programming and testing software, setting up a database, and designing a website.

Most people in IT work with data. Database administrators manage huge databases in which millions of pieces of information are stored. Systems analysts bring together data from many sources and use the data to devise solutions. IT managers work with spreadsheets, which they use to analyze sales, market share, costs, and profits.

Careers That Involve Working With People

In IT, workers may consult with clients, have team meetings, and help people with their computer problems. All of these activities require strong communication skills.

Most people in IT work closely with the colleagues and clients. Computer support specialists, for example, spend much of their time answering questions posed by computer users. Network administrators regularly meet with network users to solve problems and understand user needs. IT instructors teach people how to use information technology, usually by giving courses or training sessions. Salespeople spend their time meeting with prospective buyers, trying to convince these people to buy their company's products. Managers direct entire staffs.

Careers That Involve Working With Things

The IT industry has many jobs that involve designing, creating, and repairing things, such as computer hardware and peripherals (such as printers and scanners). Examples of working with things include setting up and operating computers and taking apart computers for repair.

People in IT who work with things may assemble computer components, set up computer hardware, or manage data backup systems. They operate, maintain, and repair computers.

4-3 Essential Question Reflection

So, let us revisit our essential question:

How can I match my skills & interests with the right job?

Based on what you learned in this section, please answer this question in detail.

4-4 Education and Training for IT Opportunities

Jobs in the Information Technology industry require varying levels of education. Some jobs in this industry require little or no formal training. For many others, it is necessary to have specific education and experience.

4-4 Essential Question

As you read this section, keep this question in mind:

What training & education is needed for a job in IT?

Training and Education for Information Technology

The level of training necessary to get a first job and then succeed in the IT industry varies by job and by field. However, almost all jobs in this industry require some training and education. If your interests lie in IT, you should start planning now to get the relevant training and education you will need. The more research you do before entering the workforce, the greater your chances of achieving your goals.

Jobs Requiring Little or No Training

Almost all IT jobs require some education or training. In computer hardware manufacturing, most employers require that their employees have at least a high school education. Employers look for workers with relevant course-work and good communication and people skills.

Jobs Requiring Some Training

There are many options for training in IT jobs. You can get the training you need through a certification program, through a two- or four-year college program, or on the job.

A certification program can teach you what you need to know to do a job. Becoming certified shows employers that you have mastered a set of skills and are able to perform a specific job.

Certification exists in many IT fields. For example, you can become a certified network administrator, a certified database manager, or a certified systems engineer. Many companies that focus on technology offer several different certifications in database management, for instance, so it is possible to have multiple certifications in one field. When certification is offered by a company, that certification shows your expertise in the company's products.

The Institute for Certification of Computing Professionals (ICCP) is an umbrella organization for testing in IT field. It seeks to establish professional standards in the industry. ICCP offers several dozen tests in fields ranging from web development to system security to programming languages.

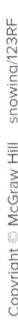

Certification programs require concentrated work, and the programs can be expensive. For this reason, you need to think carefully about which IT field attracts you most. Look for free or low-cost courses on the Internet to avoid spending time and money on certification before you really know which area you want to specialize in. Community colleges offer relatively inexpensive IT courses that can help you gain expertise in a variety of areas.

In addition to becoming certified, many people obtain college degrees in IT. Community colleges and some universities offer two-year Associate degrees. Some of these programs offer most or all of their courses online.

Obtaining an Associate degree or a nationally recognized certification can help you get started in your career field.

Jobs Requiring Advanced Training

Many people holding IT jobs have a bachelor's degree in computer science or engineering. Software designers and architects, senior programmers, test engineers, and systems architects often have a master's degree. Computer scientists usually have a PhD.

If you're interested in any of these fields but you do not yet have a bachelor's degree, it's a good idea to consider a college program. When choosing a program, consider its reputation, cost, location, and rate of job placement. If you plan to work and go to school at the same time, be sure the program has an option for part-time study.

Table 4.2: Training Required for Information Technology Jobs

Level of Training	Job Title
Little or No Training	Computer Operators Data Entry Keyers
Some Training	Computer Support Specialists Software Quality Assurance Analysts and Testers Network Systems and Data Communications Analysts Web Administrators Web Developers
Considerable Training	Computer and Information Systems Managers Computer Programmers Computer Security Specialists Computer Systems Analysts Computer Systems Engineers/Architects Computer Software Engineers Network and Computer Systems Administrators Network Designers Software Designers

Professional Skills

Communication Skills To be effective, IT workers must be able to communicate well, especially when interacting with nonexperts. Those who manage others or lead teams, like IT project managers, must also have good communication skills. Anyone trying to establish productive relationships with coworkers and clients will find the task easier if they can communicate clearly with others.

Listening Skills Listening skills are very important for IT professionals. This is especially true for computer support specialists and computer systems analysts. They often work on problems others bring to their attention. Failure to listen carefully could mean working on the wrong problem or providing software or hardware that doesn't meet the client's needs. Good listening skills help employees understand coworkers' ideas and points of view.

Problem-Solving Skills IT workers are asked to solve problems regularly. Computer support specialists, for example, do nothing but solve problems brought to them by computer users. Systems analysts, software designers, and many other IT professionals and technicians also solve problems. Solving problems requires confidence, creativity, and self-reliance.

Technology Skills Since the basis of the industry is technology, every worker must have excellent technology skills. This is true even at the entry level. Different skill levels are required depending on the position. Instructors or support staff who teach or assist users need a thorough grounding in the software being used and the way the system works. Computer hardware engineers need to know the internal workings of the hardware in use so they can identify and repair problems.

Decision-Making Skills
IT professionals must make decisions regularly. A systems analyst, for example, has to decide how best to collect information. A programmer must decide how to fix bugs in a new program. The ability to gather and analyze information rapidly and the ability to think clearly under pressure are critical in IT careers.

Organizing and Planning Skills People in IT often work on large projects that involve many people and tight deadlines. Organizing and planning are vital skills for managing teams of workers. Planning requires the ability to set goals and to visualize the sequence of steps leading to those goals.

Teamwork Skills Teamwork is key in Information Technology. IT professionals work with many different people to get a job done. A team that is healthy has members that listen and communicate well with each other. They share their ideas and draw out the ideas of others. Ideally each person on the team will see to it that all team members contribute and that no one dominates, or takes over, the group.

Social Skills Almost all jobs involve interacting with coworkers. Listening and being patient and cooperative helps colleagues get along with one another. Remaining polite and positive encourages team members be more productive.

Adaptability Skills Job descriptions, work environments, and workflow are constantly changing due to business developments and technological advances in IT. Workers must keep an open mind and be ready to acquire new skills and new certifications. The more employees can adapt to change, the more valuable they will be.

4-4 Essential Question Reflection

So, let us revisit our essential question:

What training & education is needed for a job in IT?

Based on what you learned in this section, please answer this question in detail.

4-5 Working Conditions in the IT Industry

Because careers in IT vary greatly, it is important to know what it is like to work in this industry. Before accepting any job, you should ask questions to understand the work environment, hazards, and benefits in order to make an informed decision.

> **4-5 Essential Question**
>
> **As you read this section, keep this question in mind:**
>
> *What are typical work environments in IT?*

Work Environment

Work environment, or factors that affect workers' health and satisfaction on the job, should an important factor you consider when thinking about possible career paths in IT. This includes the physical surroundings, the working hours, and the physical activities required to perform a job in IT.

It is important to note that few IT jobs are physically demanding, as most involve working in offices or seated at a computer. Many are tiring, though, because they require strenuous mental activity and long hours.

Physical Environment

Most IT workers worked in offices until 2020. Many workers began to work remotely because of the COVID-19 pandemic. Some continue to work remotely, and that change may be permanent. Network and computer systems administrators and computer support specialists may spend part of their time installing, maintaining, or repairing equipment at a work site. Some computer and information scientists work in laboratories.

Work Hours

Many people in IT work regular hours. However, they tend to work slightly longer hours than average. Some people work flextime. Flextime allows workers to choose the hours and days they work, if they keep to a standard total number of hours per week. Workers may adjust their hours to suit their needs. One employee may choose to work 10 hours a day, four days a week. Another may work six and a half hours a day, six days a week.

Flextime is helpful for workers with young children or other family commitments. Many young people, who often prefer to start work late in the morning and stay late in the evening, also like flextime. Not all companies offer flextime, and flextime isn't practical for all positions. For many employees, however, flextime is an important job benefit. Part-time work is uncommon in this industry.

Many workers in IT must meet tight deadlines. A company may announce that a new software product will be released by a certain date. Everyone working on the product may have to work long hours to make sure the deadline is met.

Since most people working in this field are professionals who receive annual salaries rather than hourly wages, IT workers are usually not paid for the extra time they work. To reward workers for their efforts, some companies provide cash bonuses. Others allow employees to take paid days off. These days off are known as "comp time." They are compensation for the extra time worked.

Essential Physical Activities

Most people in IT do not perform strenuous physical activities as part of their jobs. Computer programmers, electronic commerce specialists, and web designers typically do not need to have physical strength or physical skills to perform their jobs.

Some jobs in IT do require physical skills, however. Network and computer systems administrators need to be good with tools. They also need to be able to climb ladders, lift heavy equipment, and spend much of the day on their feet. They may do a lot of walking as part of their job. Faulty equipment or wires can be difficult to track down.

Network and computer systems administrators also spend time checking wiring in hard-to-reach places. In facilities with raised floors, workers must pull up heavy floor tiles to lay wiring. Running wire may require pulling up and replacing heavy flooring.

Injuries and Illnesses

Most workers in IT face a much lower-than-average risk of being hurt or becoming ill on the job. IT workers are, however, exposed to certain health risks. Musculoskeletal disorders are a particular concern. The U.S. Department of Labor defines a musculoskeletal disorder (MSD) as an injury or a disorder of the muscles, nerves, tendons, joints, cartilage, and spinal discs. MSDs do not include disorders caused by an accident on the job, such as a slip, trip, fall, or by a motor vehicle accident. Musculoskeletal disorders are the result of muscle overuse, bad posture, and repeated motions.

Repetitive stress injuries (RSIs), a type of musculoskeletal disorder, can develop when the same motions are performed over and over. Spending many hours working at a keyboard, for example, can damage the tendons of the wrist. Over time, injuries from these repetitive actions can cause severe pain and disability.

Employees who bend their heads to view their computer monitors are also at risk. According to OSHA, bending the head forward is a "hidden lifting task." This is because the head weighs about 15 pounds. Working with a bent head for long periods of time can obstruct blood flow. Muscle and eye fatigue and soreness can result.

Table 4.3: Preventing Occupational Injuries in the Information Technology Workplace

Hazard	Cause	Preventative Action
MSD (musculoskeletal disorder)	Repetitive head tilting, bending of wrist while using fingers, long periods in seated position with head looking down and to the side	• Rest at least five minutes every hour, and take at least one 15-minute break every two hours. • Sit at a workstation in which you can easily change your position. • Whenever possible, mix computer- and noncomputer-related tasks, to relieve tension on muscles and tendons. • Make sure the keyboard and mouse are directly in front of you so you do not need to reach for them.
RSIs (repetitive stress injuries)	Rapid, frequent, and sustained use of tendons of the hand when using a keyboard	• Rest at least five minutes every hour, and take at least one 15-minute break every two hours. • Stretch and move fingers during breaks. • Whenever possible, mix computer- and noncomputer-related tasks, to relieve tension on muscles and tendons. • Periodically switch the hand with which you use your mouse to relieve tension on muscles and tendons.
Fatigue, headache, and back problems	Working with head bent forward to view monitors located at desk height	• Rearrange the workstation so you can view the screen without tilting your head more than 15 degrees.
Neck, shoulder, and upper-back strain	Computer monitor that is too high, too low, or placed to the side of the user	• Keep monitor directly in front of you. • Make sure top line of screen is no higher than your eyes.
Decreased circulation to the hands and feet	Chair that is too large, too small, or the wrong shape	• Use chairs that support comfortable posture and allow change of position. • Make sure that the seat fits you and is padded, with a rounded edge.
Headache and eyestrain	Glare from computer monitor caused by an upward tilt so that overhead lighting is reflected on screen or viewing monitors that are too close or too far away	• Rearrange lighting so that it is not directly overhead. • Use nonglare computer screens. • Rest your eyes by focusing on objects at least 20 feet away. Blink periodically. • Position your monitor at arm's length from your face.

Ergonomics

Ergonomics is the study of creating and adjusting equipment and work procedures to make workplaces safer and more comfortable. One of the main goals of ergonomics is to reduce the number of MSDs. Ergonomically designed workstations can help prevent injuries. OSHA provides specific recommendations on desk height, legroom, and keyboard and monitor placement.

4-5 Essential Question Reflection

So, let us revisit our essential question:

What are typical work environments in IT?

Based on what you learned in this section, please answer this question in detail.

4-6 Trends in Information Technology

Technology has changed work processes and working conditions for jobs in every industry. Thanks to the rapid development of high-speed Internet, people around the world can communicate more rapidly and effectively.

It is hard to imagine how people operated without today's technology. Yet it hasn't been long since people made the switch from ordering supplies over the phone to ordering them over the Internet or from storing data in paper files to storing data electronically.

The people who made these advances possible work in the IT industry. The changes that occur in IT affect businesses and workers throughout the economy.

Because technology continues to advance quickly and companies and individuals rely on it more heavily, demand in this industry will continue to grow.

4-6 Essential Question

As you read this section, keep this question in mind:

What factors affect trends in IT?

Technology in the Industry

People in IT are always searching for new technologies and new ways of doing business. IT companies compete to develop better, more powerful software and to make computers and other hardware that do more, weigh less, take up less space, and work faster than previous equipment. They also compete to perfect new technologies, such as cloud computing, wireless networks, and mobile platforms and to solve problems such as faulty computer security.

Improvements in Hardware and Software

New technologies have resulted in faster streaming speeds over the Internet. There are still areas of the planet that cannot access broadband speeds on the Internet using computers or mobile devices. Over the next 5 to 10 years, connectivity will become available through a variety of means, including satellites beaming high-speed Internet to remote parts of the world. This will allow the half of Earth's population that cannot access the Internet now to enjoy the same level of access as most people in North America.

Artificial Intelligence and Machine Learning

Computers have developed since the late 1990s when IBM's Deep Blue beat the world chess champion, Garry Kasparov. Technology has developed to where computers have great speed and programming capabilities. Every day we move closer to writing programs that allow for learning and independent action by computers. Computers are doing everything from creating authentic artworks to seeking cures for diseases. These capabilities will become more useful over time and create opportunities for people who understand these technologies and business.

The Metaverse

Science fiction of the 1990s speculated that a shared, connected experience was to come. *Ready Player One,* a novel that was made into a popular movie, gave people a whimsical sense of what a "metaverse" experience is like.

Companies and organizations are rapidly developing environments that are now accessible, viable versions of a metaverse. Metaverses will create new ways to teach and learn, conduct business, and make friends from all over the world. While this is still an emergent technology, metaverses may be as important in the future as the Internet is today.

Cloud Computing

More companies and individuals are turning to cloud computing, software accessed on the web rather than on the computer. Such software has several advantages. For example, it doesn't require space on your computer to store programs; therefore, you don't need to purchase new equipment as often. Also, you don't have to worry about updating software. Storing documents over the Internet means people in different locations can easily work on them. Cloud computing is expected to grow as companies and individuals look to use more applications online.

Electronic Commerce

Electronic commerce, or e-commerce, is still expanding, though at a slower rate than it once did. Many thousands of businesses, large and small, already maintain e-commerce websites. This number will continue to grow. To remain competitive, sites must evolve as new technologies become available.

From a business point of view, e-commerce has many advantages. Selling products over the Internet does not require maintaining retail outlets or paying salespeople to staff stores.

With Internet use growing around the globe, U.S. companies are trying to expand into worldwide markets. E-commerce allows businesses, including small businesses, to market their products all over the world.

One of the challenges in e-business is ensuring credit card security. To prevent credit card numbers from being stolen, most e-commerce sites use encryption. Encryption is the use of a "key" to code messages. The longer the key, the harder the message is to decrypt or decode.

Blockchain

Blockchain is a technology where records of transactions are kept on various, random computers world-wide, but are accessible when needed for recordkeeping or proof of ownership. The most well-known use of blockchain is cryptocurrency, money that uses blockchain to track these transactions. Many other applications of blockchain are being developed including real estate records and electronic artwork.

Blockchain will be used more as time passes and may include how your grades are kept, how diplomas, degrees, and credentials are awarded and accessed, and proof of driver's licenses and insurance. These are uses that are widely varied, and the jobs that will use blockchain and that will be created to further develop this technology will be significant.

Internet of Things

The Internet has allowed people to be connected in ways that were previously inconceivable. It has also made it possible for objects with computer chips that are programmed to communicate. The future of appliances and repair depends on the "Internet of Things," also known as the "IoT". Most appliances are computerized and record data of use patterns and operating conditions and communicate this data through the Internet. This allows you to use your cell phone to watch your pet at home on a camera that remotely follows your directions.

4-6 Essential Question Reflection

So, let us revisit our essential question:

What factors affect trends in IT?

Based on what you learned in this section, please answer this question in detail.

Chapter 5 — Arts & Media

❓ Essential Questions

By the end of the chapter, you will be able to answer the following questions:

- **5-1** What types of opportunities are available in Arts & Media?
- **5-2** Which opportunities may be right for you?
- **5-3** How can I match my skills & interests with the right job?
- **5-4** What training & education is needed for a job in Arts & Media?
- **5-5** What are typical work environments in Arts & Media?
- **5-6** What factors affect trends in Arts & Media?

Chapter Topics

5-1 Arts & Media Today

5-2 Arts & Media Communications Jobs

5-3 Building a Career in Arts & Media

5-4 Education and Training for Arts & Media Opportunities

5-5 Working Conditions in the Arts & Media Industry

5-6 Trends in Arts & Media

5-1 Arts & Media Today

Careers in the Arts & Media industry are related in one important way: they all involve communication. Writing a drama may seem very different from installing and repairing cell towers. However, both jobs help people communicate with one another. Every job in this industry works in some way to help people share information, ideas, and feelings.

Imagine the world without the Arts & Media industry. There would be no Internet, movies, radio, cellphones, online social media, game sharing, paintings, or photographs. Printed and digital books, newspapers, or magazines would not exist. Just imagining such a world shows the extraordinary importance of the arts and communication. Communication skills are foundational for all careers. More opportunities are available for "gig" workers who want the freedom of being self-employed than in most other fields. It is no wonder that one-third of the fastest-growing occupations are found in the arts!

5-1 Essential Question

As you read this section, keep this question in mind:

What types of opportunities are available in Arts & Media?

Career Journeys in Arts & Media

People in Arts & Media commonly move into and out of different paths due to similar certifications or education requirements. Six of the most common paths are:

- Journalism and Broadcasting
- Performing Arts
- Visual Arts
- Audio and Video Technology and Film
- Telecommunications
- Printing Technology

Journalism and Broadcasting

The Journalism and Broadcasting career path is one of the most popular in this industry. It includes jobs in book publishing, as well as work at online news and information websites. Jobs in this path include station managers, radio and broadcast announcers, broadcast technicians, publishers, editors, and reporters.

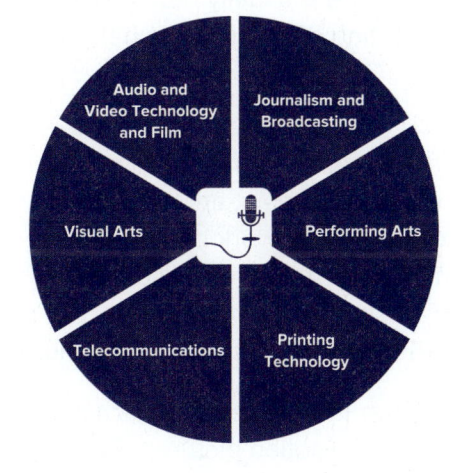

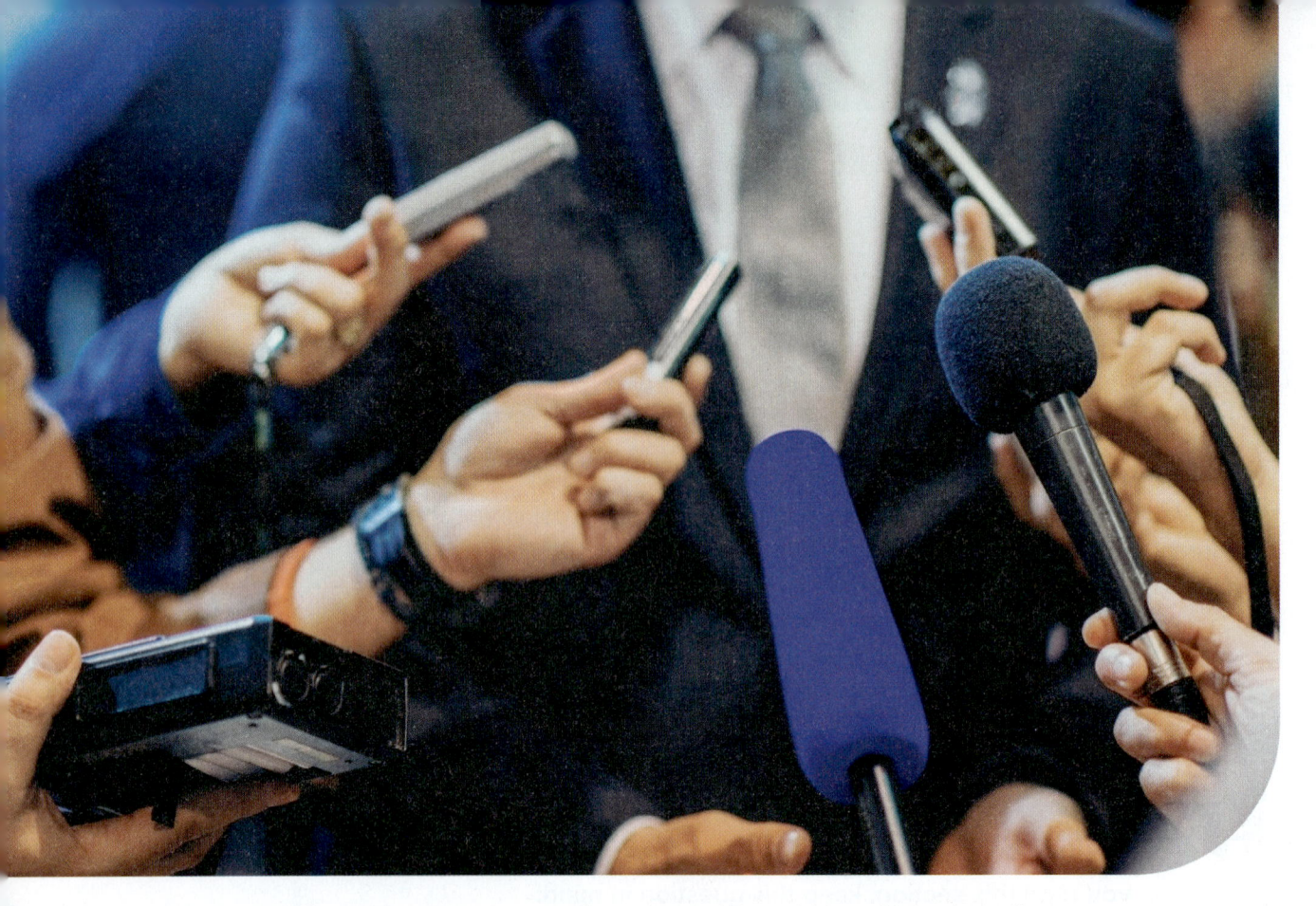

Nearly three-quarters of broadcasting workers are employed by radio and media stations that have 50 or more employees. Although jobs are found all over the United States, larger stations are in big cities.

Jobs are extremely competitive. More people try to create content like news, podcasts, and opinion-based blogs and videos than can make a living at these jobs. Those who pursue such jobs must be driven to succeed. They need to work well under pressure. Broadcast and control-room technicians need strong technological skills. Good communications skills are essential for almost all jobs in this path. A college degree is usually required. A bachelor's or master's degree in journalism or broadcasting often provides helpful preparation.

Performing Arts

The Performing Arts career path involves performing for an audience. Actors, singers, dancers, digital designers, and musicians work in this path. There are many people in this career path who work behind-the-scenes to make performances possible. For example, directors, production managers, film editors, composers, playwrights, visual artists, and makeup artists. The path also covers those who teach performing arts, like drama coaches and music teachers.

Many jobs in live theater last only as long as a particular play runs. Often the jobs are seasonal. Jobs in motion pictures, TV, and videos are mostly centered in Los Angeles and New York City. However, there are small production studios throughout the United States.

More than 40 percent of people who work as musicians, singers, composers, and music directors work part-time. About half of all performing artists are self-employed, and nearly one-third of them work for organizations. For example, an organist is sometimes employed by a church. Performing artists give private lessons or perform at restaurants, on cruises, or at weddings and other events.

Actors, singers, and other performers must have talent, confidence, and good stage presence. They must be persistent because jobs are scarce and competition is fierce. Behind the scenes, workers must be creative, energetic, and organized. Training is necessary for most jobs in the performing arts. A degree in film, in addition to practical experience, is helpful for jobs in motion pictures or theater. Good networking skills are essential in the performing arts. Workers are often hired based on word-of-mouth recommendations.

Audio and Video Technology and Film

Audio and video technology and film are used to display information so that it can be heard or seen. This area includes the technology used to produce film equipment, videos, special effects, animation, DVDs, CDs, MP3s, and streaming services. This career path includes the engineers and technicians who design, install, and repair audio and video equipment. It also includes those who manufacture and sell the equipment. Some people in this path work for manufacturers and dealers. Others operate the equipment for schools, conferences, convention centers, the government, the military, or other organizations. Above-average technological skills are a must for success in this field. Workers must be able to learn new software quickly.

Visual Arts

The Visual Arts path includes careers that create the forms of art we look at. The art may be created with simple tools such as a paintbrush or pottery wheel, or with more advanced technology such as a camera or a computer design program. The Visual Arts path includes fine artists, such as painters and sculptors, who create original work for its artistic value. This path also includes commercial artists, fashion designers, and interior designers who create art for more practical purposes.

Many visual artists work for advertising agencies, design firms, or publishing companies. About 60 percent of visual artists are self-employed. Self-employed commercial artists work on a freelance basis; that is, various companies hire them for specific jobs. Fine artists usually sell their paintings at galleries or try to get special commissions. For example, a business or a community may commission an outdoor sculpture and pay the self-employed artist for their work.

This path is highly competitive. To succeed, artists need talent, skill, and persistence. Training at an art school can help to develop skill. It is also a good way to network, or develop connections, with others in the field. Graphic design credentials may be earned without a diploma or degree. Many high-value credentials are related to Adobe® products like Photoshop. Working at an art gallery or as an assistant to an established artist is another good way to learn more about the field and to network with other artists.

Telecommunications

Those working in Telecommunications provide telephone, Internet, cable, and other services. They design, manufacture, and repair equipment such as cellphones and land-based telephones. Some people in this path work for equipment manufacturers. Others work for service providers, including cable and phone companies.

Most jobs in this path require training in electronics and computer technology. Workers who are in frequent contact with clients and customers need good communication skills and a professional attitude.

Printing Technology

Printing technology is used to print newspapers, books, and magazines. It is also used to print brochures, wedding announcements, menus, and other materials. Workers in this path include those who operate printing equipment. Jobs involving desktop publishing or website design are also part of this path.

108 Chapter 5 • Arts & Media

Workers in this path usually work with sophisticated technology that is constantly changing due to new innovations. An associate degree from a two-year college or a bachelor's degree from a four-year college is helpful.

Arts & Media Future Outlook

The job outlook in the Arts & Media industry is mixed. Many traditional jobs are shrinking because of new technologies. Others are growing for the same reason. For instance, demand for cable technicians will drop as equipment improves and repairs can be made virtually instead of in person. However, technicians who hook up cable subscribers to high-speed Internet lines or set up wireless networks will see more job opportunities.

Table 5.1: Occupations in Arts & Media with Most Job Openings

Occupation	Number of Job Openings
Graphic Designers	80,000 +
Musicians and Singers	50,000 +
Telecommunications Line Installers and Repairers	40,000 +
Telecommunications Equipment Installers	30,000 +
Producers and Directors	30,000 +

Jobs for printing press operators will decline as many printing functions become automated. Jobs in print media will also decline as more people turn to the Internet for news and other information. However, electronic publishing will provide many job opportunities.

As always, there will be huge competition for highly creative jobs, such as directors, broadcasters, and visual artists. Many jobs in theater, film, and music will remain part-time or short-term. The use of freelance or contract workers for projects will continue in publishing and in the visual arts.

5-1 Essential Question Reflection

So, let us revisit our essential question:

What types of opportunities are available in Arts & Media?

Based on what you learned in this section, which field of Arts & Media is the most interesting to you? Explain your answer.

Practice 5-1

Skills Practice

When reading documents, workers in the Arts & Media industry need to be able to identify the main idea. For instance, broadcast news analysts need to find the main idea in news reports. They must also find details supporting the main idea. The main idea tells what the document is about. Details provide more information that helps explain the main idea. **Practice this skill!**

E-MAIL

To: Mary Elis

From: K. Burker, Supervisor

I have decided we need to change the look of the brochure you are working on. I want the brochure to look more fun and more appealing to children. I like the colors you have chosen, but they are too sophisticated for the audience. I would like to see the color scheme with brighter, primary colors. I think we need the font to be somewhat larger with more contrast between the font color and the background. Some of the kids we are trying to reach with this brochure are young and just beginning to read. Having more contrast will help them follow the content. Finally, I would like to see photos with more interesting treatments—silhouettes, tilted images, that king of thing. You might even think about separating an image into different components and scattering them around the brochure. I have a meeting first thing in the morning, but please start working on some options. Thank you!

1. You work as a desktop publishing specialist, and your boss has given you specific instructions to be carried out at work the next day. What is the main idea of her e-mail to you?

   A. Your boss changes her mind a lot with designs.
   B. Your boss wants a new color scheme.
   C. The look of the brochure needs to be changed.
   D. Photos in the brochure should be larger.
   E. The new design should be more fun.

2. Which detail best explains why your boss has asked you to perform this work?

   A. She wants to see some new options soon.
   B. She is worried about the meeting she has first thing in the morning.
   C. Colors should be less sophisticated and brighter.
   D. She wants to make the design more appealing to children.
   E. She would like to see photos have more interesting treatments.

To access more problems that will help you grow professional skills and are real-world examples in Arts & Media, go online.

5-2 Arts & Media Jobs

You can find a variety of exciting jobs in the Arts & Media industry at all skill levels, from entry level to managerial. Video editors and content creators help create cutting-edge information and entertainment. Graphic designers make print and online publications more appealing to readers. The following job profiles will introduce you to some of the professions in this industry.

5-2 Essential Question

As you read this section, keep this question in mind:

Which opportunities may be right for you?

Occupation With the Most People Employed:

Graphic Designers

- Determine size and arrangement of illustrative material and copy and select style and size of type
- Confer with clients to discuss and determine layout design
- Create designs, concepts, and sample layouts based on knowledge of layout principles and esthetic design concepts

Fast Facts:

Employment: 264,400 currently employed

Annual Openings: About 630

Median Annual Wage: $50,710

Education Needed: Varies; high school diploma, associate degree, bachelor's degree, plus high-value industry-recognized credentials

Fastest-Growing Occupations:

Amusement and Recreation Attendants

- Sell tickets and collect fees from customers
- Stay informed of shutdown and emergency evacuation procedures

Fast Facts:

Employment: 81,500 currently employed in 2020, expected to increase by 50,400 in 2030, 62% faster than average

Annual Openings: 8,400

Median Annual Wage: $24,500

Education Needed: High school diploma

Exercise Trainers and Group Fitness Instructors

- Observe participants and inform them of corrective measures necessary for skill improvement
- Evaluate individuals' abilities, needs, and physical conditions and develop suitable training programs to meet any special requirements
- Plan routines, select appropriate music, and choose different movements for each set of muscles, depending on participants' capabilities and limitations

Fast Facts:
Employment: 309,800 currently employed
Annual Openings: 6,910
Median Annual Wage: $19.57 hourly, $40,700 annual
Education Needed: High school diploma, or certificate

Occupations Where Most Work for Themselves:

Actors

- Collaborate with other actors as part of an ensemble
- Portray and interpret roles using speech, gestures, and body movements to entertain, inform, or instruct radio, film, television, or live audiences

Fast Facts:
Employment: 51,600 currently employed
Annual Openings: 820
Median Annual Wage: $23.48 hourly

Education Needed: High school diploma

Other: You will work closely with directors, other actors, and playwrights to find the interpretation most suited to the role.

Athletes and Sports Competitors

- Assess performance following athletic competitions, identify strengths and weaknesses, and adjust to improve future performance
- Maintain equipment used in a particular sport
- Attend scheduled practice or training sessions

Fast Facts:

Employment: 16,700 currently employed

Annual Openings: 3,400

Median Annual Wage: $77,300, but varies drastically based on contract

Education Needed: High school diploma

Other: As of 2022, the world's highest-paid athlete is Argentine soccer star Lionel Messi, who earns around 130 million dollars annually!

Great Job! - High School Diploma Needed:

Ushers, Lobby Attendants, and Ticket Takers

- Greet patrons attending entertainment events
- Sell or collect admission tickets, passes, or facility memberships from patrons at entertainment events
- Clean facilities

114 Chapter 5 • Arts & Media

Fast Facts:

Employment: 81,500 currently employed

Annual Openings: 5,040

Median Annual Wage: $24,440

Other: People interested in this work like activities that include helping people, teaching, and talking.

5-2 Essential Question Reflection

So, let us revisit our essential question:

Which opportunities may be right for you?

Based on what you learned in this section, please answer this question in detail.

Case Study: Sound Engineering Technicians

Also called: Recording Engineer

What do they do?

- Assemble and operate equipment to record, synchronize, mix, edit, or reproduce sound, including music, voices, or sound effects for theater, video, film, television, podcasts, sporting events, and other productions

What would you do?

- Record speech, music, and other sounds onto media using appropriate equipment
- Confer with producers, performers, and others to determine and achieve the desired sound for a production, such as a musical recording or a film
- Separate instruments, vocals, and other sounds, and combine sounds during the mixing or postproduction stage

What do you need to know?

Engineering and Technology
  Computers and electronics
  Product and service development

Communications
  Multimedia
  Telecommunications

Business
  Customer service
  Management

Arts and Humanities
  English language

116   Chapter 5 • Arts & Media

What skills do you need?

Basic Skills
Listen to others, not interrupt, and ask good questions
Talk to others

Problem Solving
Notice a problem and figure out the best way to solve it

People and Technology Systems
Think about the pros and cons of different options and pick the best one
Figure out how a system works and how changes in the future will affect it

What abilities must you be good at?

Verbal
Communicate by speaking
Listen and understand what people say

Ideas and Logic
Order or arrange things
Create new and original ideas

Attention
Pay attention to something without being distracted

Hearing and Speech
Tell the difference between sounds

Who does well in this occupation?

People interested in this work like activities that include practical, hands-on problems and solutions.

What educational level is needed?

- High school diploma, or equivalent
- One to two years of on-the-job training through an apprenticeship program

Practice 5-2

Skills Practice

Workers in the Arts & Media industry must sometimes analyze graphics to identify trends. Being able to identify common trends from several pieces of data can be helpful in a variety of jobs in this industry. A business reporter, for example, must review key statistics of a corporation to analyze its performance over time. **Practice this skill!**

Finances for Start-Up Graphic Design Business

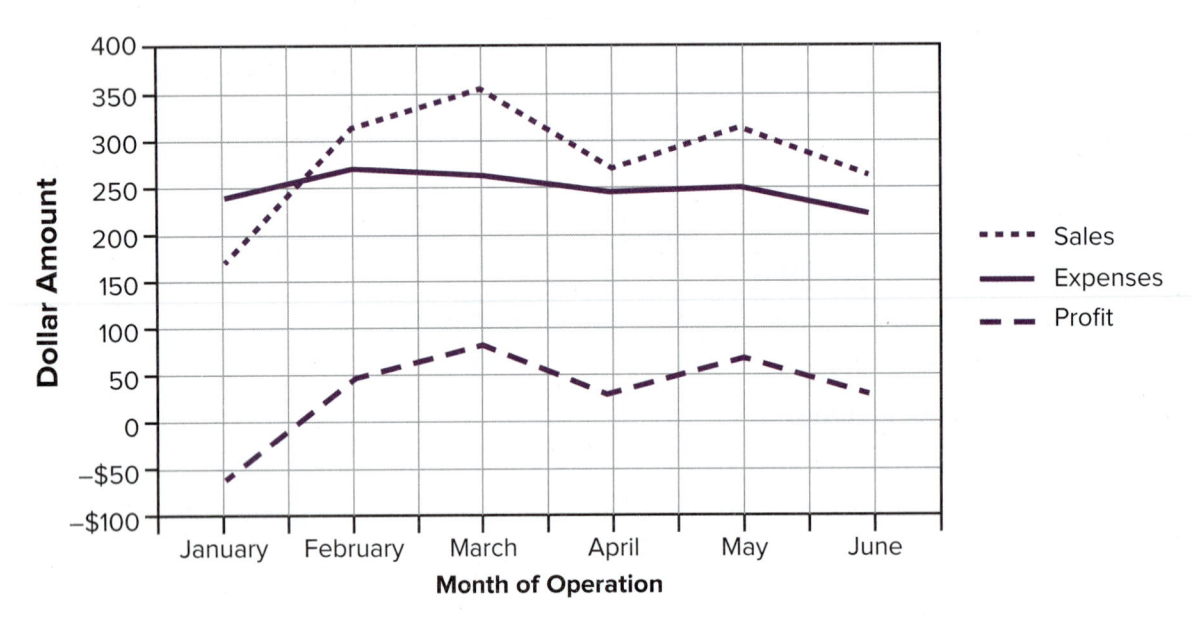

Monthly Financial Data

	January	February	March	April	May	June
Sales	$170	$315	$356	$270	$318	$263
Expenses	$237	$270	$276	$245	$249	$239
Profit	–$67	$45	$80	$25	$69	$24

1. You have started your own graphic design firm and have been charting your financial activity. From the chart, what trend can you identify?

   A. Profits have been in a steady decline since the beginning of the year.
   B. When expenses increase, sales go down.
   C. Profits go up as sales go down.
   D. Profits, expenses, and sales all increase at the same rate.
   E. When expenses are stable, profits parallel sales.

2. Assuming that July was your third most profitable month, what dollar range would your profits be in?

   A. $24–$25
   B. $26–$45
   C. $46–$68
   D. $69–$80
   E. $81–$130

To access more problems that will help grow professional skills and are real-world examples in Arts & Media, go online.

5-3 Building a Career in Arts & Media

If this industry is interesting to you, be aware of the special challenges in the Arts & Media industry. One challenge is intense competition for many jobs in the industry. More people want to be artists, filmmakers, performers, and journalists than there are opportunities available. Another challenge is that some job opportunities are shrinking. Jobs at print newspapers are on the decline, for example. While online journalism offers more opportunities, some online ventures go out of business quickly, and many pay little or no money. Recent government funding cuts may mean fewer jobs in the fine and performing arts.

Given these challenges, the best way to move forward in your career path in this industry is to be flexible and persistent. You may have to start at an entry-level position to gain experience before finally landing a job.

5-3 Essential Question

As you read this section, keep this question in mind:

How can I match my skills & interests with the right job?

Are You More Interested in Working With Data, People, or Things?

Do you like to work with data, people, or things more? Editors, for example, work mainly with data. Musical coaches work primarily with people. Technicians work mostly with things. When planning your career path, consider what balance of data, people, and things you want in a career.

Careers That Involve Working With Data

Examples of working with data include researching and writing a news article or preparing a cost analysis of a movie production.

Many jobs in the Arts & Media industry involve working with data in the form of words. Editors spend time reading manuscripts and editing documents on a computer. Screenwriters and playwrights create scripts, and actors read them. Journalists, like all other writers, use words as the basic tools of their trade.

Some jobs in the industry involve working with data in the form of numbers. A telecommunications manager, for example, may need to study spreadsheets that display production costs to determine whether a particular project is efficient or cost-effective. Sound engineers may need to make calculations, run tests, and analyze test results.

Careers That Involve Working With People

Jobs that focus on working with people are based on human relationships. Examples include organizing a photo shoot, conducting an orchestra, or selling cable or satellite services. All these activities require strong communication skills.

Many people in this industry spend a great deal of time working with others. Journalists interview and observe people when researching articles. Film directors work with performers, producers, and a large technical staff. Art gallery directors spend much of their day working with clients, artists, and gallery staff. Actors and musicians interact not only with their colleagues but also with the audience.

Careers That Involve Working With Things

In this industry, working with things often means using tools or equipment to create, perform, or communicate in some way. Fashion designers work with things when they use pen and ink or a computer to design clothes or when they use fabric and sewing machines to create samples. Musicians work with things when they perform on musical instruments. Radio broadcasters work with things when they use electronic equipment to communicate.

Many technical careers in the industry involve working mainly with things. Telecommunications technicians, printing press operators, and commercial photographers, for example, spend a large portion of their day working with tools, machines, and equipment. Other careers in the industry that involve working with things include makeup artists and film editors who work with film and the machines and computer programs that cut film footage.

5-3 Essential Question Reflection

So, let us revisit our essential question:

How can I match my skills & interests with the right job?

Based on what you learned in this section, please answer this question in detail.

5-4 Education and Training for Arts & Media Opportunities

Jobs in the Arts & Media industry require varying levels of education and training. Some jobs require technical skills, such as knowledge of electronics or computer-aided design (CAD). Others require special talents, such as the ability to draw or sing. Some require advanced training that can take years to complete.

5-4 Essential Question

As you read this section, keep this question in mind:

What training & education is needed for a job in Arts & Media?

Training and Education for the Industry

The level of training necessary to succeed in the Arts & Media industry varies by career. Jobs can be categorized into three groups—those requiring little or no training, those requiring some training, and those requiring advanced training.

Jobs Requiring Little or No Training

Some telecommunications jobs need no advanced training. Line workers and cable splicers, who build and service telephone wires, may receive their training on the job after they are hired. They might start out as helpers, trimming trees or working on the ground. They would then be gradually trained to do more complex tasks.

Perhaps the job that interests you requires little or no training. It is still important to keep in mind that getting a high school education, or the equivalent, is necessary for almost every job. Many employers look for workers who earned solid grades in high school. Even if you do get a job without having a high school diploma, not having one may jeopardize your chance of advancement.

Jobs Requiring Some Training

Many jobs in this industry require some training. One way to get that training is by attending school. Technical schools and community colleges offer programs that can prepare you for jobs that demand special training – these schools can cost a lot less than attending a four-year university. For example, many technical schools or community colleges have programs for jobs in broadcasting or filmmaking, such as camera operation or film editing.

An associate degree is awarded after two years of successful study at a community college. It usually involves general study as well as concentration in a particular subject.

A certificate is awarded after completing study in a particular area. Getting a certificate usually takes less time than getting an associate's degree. Some certificate programs offer home study online. For example, you can study at home to become a telecommunications technician and then apply for certification.

Training may be obtained through trade organizations, or groups that represent a specific career or industry. Such groups often offer certification programs that provide thorough training for a certain job. The program may require a minimum number of hours on the job and a minimum score on a test. Those who meet the requirements are then certified as trained professionals. For example, the International Association for Radio, Telecommunications, and Electromagnetics (iNARTE) offers training in telecommunications at various levels and provides certification after the trainee has passed a test. The Society of Broadcast Engineers (SBE) offers certificates to broadcast engineers at different levels of experience.

Earning an associate degree or certification can help you obtain a job or advance in your field. For more information about such programs, contact community colleges, technical schools, and national trade organizations in your area.

Jobs Requiring Advanced Training

Many jobs in Arts & Media require more extensive training or formal education. They often require a bachelor's degree, which is usually obtained after four years of undergraduate study at a college or university. Some jobs even require a master's or doctoral degree.

Almost everyone entering journalism today has at least a bachelor's degree. They usually major in English, journalism, or communications. Some attend a special school of journalism, and they may obtain a graduate degree in the field. Telecommunications engineers usually have a bachelor's degree in a technical area. It may be in electrical or electronic engineering, computer science, or telecommunications technology. Workers who combine such a degree with a master's degree in business have the best chance to advance to a management position.

Many arts professionals have advanced degrees. Curators at art museums typically have a graduate degree in art history or museum studies or both. Artists can enter special degree programs in painting, sculpture, or new media. Programs exist for special areas of music, dance, theater, and other performing arts.

Table 5.2: Training Required for Arts & Media Jobs

Level of Training	Job Title
Little or No Training	Amusement and Recreation Attendants Ushers Lobby Attendants Ticket Takers Actors
Some Training	Camera Operators; Television, Video, and Film Broadcast Technicians
Considerable Training	Graphic Designers Special Effects Artists and Animators

Job and Workplace Skills

When considering job candidates, employers look for both job-specific skills and general workplace skills. Job-specific skills are those skills necessary to do a particular job. For example, using computer-aided design (CAD) or operating a printing press is a job-specific skill. General workplace skills can be used in a variety of jobs. Developing these skills will make you more marketable in any job situation.

Arts & Media Skill Standards

Skill standards have been established in many areas of the Arts & Media industry. State education departments often set skill standards for teaching particular subjects. Professional organizations also set standards for turning out quality workers. For instance, the National Association of Schools of Music accredits schools or programs that meet its standard for teaching music.

In some cases, workers must pass a test to show skill proficiency. To be an interpreter for the U.S. Department of State, for example, it is necessary to pass the Interpreting Skill Test as well as meet other requirements.

In some cases, mastery of specific skills leads to licensing or certification. The license or certificate shows that the person has reached a recognized level of proficiency in a field. Several states require that interior designers obtain licenses, for example. The National Council for Interior Design Qualification (NCIDQ) administers the licensing exam. The Society of Broadcast Engineers (SBE) offers certification for broadcast technicians. The Academy of Certified Archivists offers certification to archivists, workers who research and catalog museum collections. The Jewelers of America offers certificates at various skill levels for those who work with jewelry.

Professional Skills

Communications Skills   Communication skills are key to an industry that is all about communication. News broadcasters, journalists, actors, and screenwriters are all in the business of communicating with audiences. Those who direct or manage others must communicate clearly about tasks and performances. Communication with coworkers is vital in working together on a broadcast, concert, museum exhibit, or any other group effort.

Listening Skills   Film casts need good listening skills to understand directors' requests. Repair workers need good listening skills to understand customers' complaints. Interior designers and other commercial artists need good listening skills to create what clients want.

Problem-Solving Skills Problem solving is essential to many technical jobs, where workers must often solve problems with equipment. It is also important in creative jobs, where artists may be asked to rework their material to solve a particular problem. Screenwriters, for example, must sometimes rewrite scenes at the last minute. Graphic designers must find new ways to present information visually.

Technology Skills Most jobs and companies in the industry use technology. Newspapers use sophisticated computer networks to control their presses. Multimedia artists and graphic designers need to be familiar with computer-aided design (CAD). Broadcast technicians and music composers use highly sophisticated computer programs and equipment to do their jobs. Film editors use digital equipment to cut and rearrange scenes in movies.

Decision-Making Skills Being able to gather and analyze information quickly and think clearly under pressure are requirements for many jobs in Arts & Media. News editors need to decide which stories to run. Senior cable TV engineers need to decide which projects to bid on. Movie producers decide which film projects to take on.

Organizing and Planning Skills Planning is essential to many jobs in management or directing. Senior telecommunications engineers, for example, may be called on to develop a new product by a certain deadline. They then need to organize departments and processes to ensure the deadline is met. Art directors must often do the same for a new ad campaign.

Teamwork Skills Teamwork is vital to completing many projects in the arts, audio/video technology, or communications industry. For example, teamwork is essential to opening an art exhibit, putting on a ballet, or broadcasting the news.

Social Skills Jobs that require frequent interaction with others, such as reporters, photographers, makeup artists, or telecommunications line installers, must have strong social skills. Social interaction with coworkers also makes for a better work atmosphere.

Adaptability Skills Job tasks and work sites are constantly changing. Customer preferences, artistic trends, and advances in technology all contribute to these changes. Workers must be flexible and ready to acquire new skills.

5-4 Essential Question Reflection

So, let us revisit our essential question:

What training & education is needed for a job in Arts & Media?

Based on what you learned in this section, please answer this question in detail.

Practice 5-4

Skills Practice

When reading workplace graphics, such as a diagram of a camera, workers in the Arts & Media industry must know what to look for. The information may be in one or more graphics. They must be able to sift through irrelevant or distracting information to find what is needed. **Practice this skill!**

Floor Plan

- 18", 20", 52"
- Door to Patio
- Oven
- Sink
- Bay Window
- 120"
- Table
- Refrigerator
- Door to Living Room
- 10", 30", 10", 24", 70"
- 144"

5-4 • Education and Training for Arts & Media Opportunities

1. As an interior designer, you are making a drawing of a kitchen you are designing, recording accurate measurements as you take them. How wide is the door to the living room?

   A. 30 inches
   B. 52 inches
   C. 30 inches
   D. 120 inches
   E. 144 inches

2. What is located on the same wall as the door to the patio?

   A. bay window
   B. sink
   C. table
   D. refrigerator
   E. oven

To access more problems that will help you grow professional skills and are real-world examples in Arts & Media, go online.

5-5 Working Conditions in the Arts & Media Industry

Understanding the work environment, hazards, and benefits of a job in Arts & Media can help you make informed decisions.

> **5-5 Essential Question**
>
> As you read this section, keep this question in mind:
>
> *What are typical work environments in Arts & Media?*

Work Environment

Work environment refers to factors that affect workers' health and satisfaction on the job. These include physical surroundings and working hours. They also include the physical activities required to perform the job.

Physical Environment

People in this industry work in a variety of settings. They may work at newspaper offices, publishing houses, or print shops. They may work at movie studios or TV or radio stations. Some work at ad agencies or high-tech companies. Others work in museums or other public spaces. Working conditions are different in each setting. For example, some employees spend the day sitting at a desk. Others spend little or no time in the office. Here we will study the physical environment of a few select occupations in this industry.

Table 5.3: Physical Environment in the Arts & Media Industry

Occupations	Physical Environment
Actors	Spend much of their workday on set, but may venture out to a location to film
Museum Curators	Spend much of their workday at the museum, but also work in their office or a research lab
Journalists	Spend much of their workday interviewing people and collecting information, and then return to the newsroom to write
Cable Technicians	Spend much of their workday outdoors or in customers' homes

Work Hours

Many industry employees work irregular hours. Broadcast journalists and technicians often begin their workdays before sunrise or end them past midnight. Musicians, dancers, and stage actors often perform at night and on weekends.

Directors, film editors, and others in film production may work 12 or more hours a day, especially when they have a deadline to meet. Journalists at daily papers often work more than 40 hours a week. They get to work earlier than most workers and stay late to write or edit stories until press time.

In contrast, most people in telecommunications work regular hours. Repair technicians may have to work overtime during a crisis, however, such as when a storm knocks out equipment. Commercial artists generally work 40 hours a week, but they sometimes work overtime to meet deadlines.

Some printing presses run 24 hours a day. That means that employees must work in shifts. Shift work divides the day into blocks of time, usually eight hours. Some workers start their shifts early in the morning. Others finish late at night. Still others work night shifts.

Essential Physical Activities

Some jobs in the industry can be physically demanding. Telephone and cable technicians often climb up poles or ladders. Set decorators and lighting designers work on scaffolds with heavy equipment. On-stage performers stand and exert themselves for long periods of time. Those who give nightly performances may find the work exhausting. Operating a printing press can be tiring and tedious.

Hazards and Environmental Dangers

Accidents occur in every industry. In the Arts & Media industry there are many hazards and dangers. Camera operators and broadcast technicians can be injured while lifting and setting up heavy equipment. Telecommunications workers may suffer a fall while making repairs. Outdoor workers may suffer problems from extreme heat or cold. Dancers may injure themselves while on stage. Because so many accidents can happen on the job, safety must be a priority. The Occupational Safety and Health Administration (OSHA) sets job safety standards and inspects job sites. Many states also run their own OSHA programs.

5-5 Essential Question Reflection

So, let us revisit our essential question:

What are typical work environments in Arts & Media?

Based on what you learned in this section, please answer this question in detail.

5-6 Trends in Arts & Media

Many factors have influenced the arts, audio/video technology, and communications industry. New technology means changes in the workplace and in the products consumers want. Over the next decade, technological and other workplace trends will continue to change the industry.

5-6 Essential Question

As you read this section, keep this question in mind:

What factors affect trends in Arts & Media?

Technology in the Industry

Technology changes have greatly affected the Arts & Media industry. Online news sites can post the news as it happens. Satellites allow live broadcasts from all over the globe. Animators and graphic artists use computers as tools in their craft. Websites promote films, plays, and concerts, and they sell tickets to performances. Musicians and authors not only sell their products directly, but they can also chat with fans. New technology will continue to result in industry changes.

VPNs, Smartphones, and Other Telecommunications Advances

Telecommunications is a constantly changing field. Most companies and private users now have broadband Internet services. These services are available in homes and on mobile devices, which makes access available from most places most of the time. Improved service makes it easy to hold video conferences, virtual meetings that bring people together through audio and video connections. Now a museum curator can confer with overseas colleagues and show them the art objects being discussed. Video connections also help in distance learning, which saw an increase during the COVID-19 pandemic. Many students used telecommunication tools, such as video conferencing, to complete their schooling.

Virtual private networks (VPNs) offer a way for companies to hold video conferences and to exchange files securely over the Internet. Members of a film crew working on location might use a VPN to communicate with the home studio.

Wireless service, which gives laptop computers and cellphones Internet access, is now being added to buses and trains. Both advances are helpful to people who travel or work on location. For example, a photographer can access records and then e-mail photos to clients. Journalists can do Internet research, write articles, and e-mail the articles as they travel.

Access to the Internet has increased drastically over the past 10 years and completely transformed this industry. For example, more access to the Internet means more use of social media. People who work in this industry, including artists, authors, actors, and musicians, are increasingly using social media, such as TikTok and Instagram, to promote their work.

Contemporary Issues in Arts & Media

Modern technology and other developments are impacting the workplace in the Arts & Media industry in a variety of ways. Workers in this industry must keep pace with changing technology. The decrease in printed products is a very significant development in the industry. Telecommuting has changed the way offices operate.

Decrease in Printed Products

As more people turn to the Internet for their news and to e-books for their reading, the result is a decline in printed text. In recent years, many print-based newspapers have gone out of business or have laid off staff. In turn, many printers and booksellers have gone out of business. Publishers have had to change their businesses to cater to the e-book market and pursue other digital innovations.

A positive result of the decrease in printed products is that fewer natural resources are being used. A decrease in printed books, magazines, and newspapers means less energy use and less waste. The need for paper, ink, and packaging has decreased. These changes benefit the environment.

The conversion from print to electronic format also affects writers. Authors can self-publish e-books more easily than printed books because they do not have to pay for printing. They can promote their books on a website. As a result, some authors have become less dependent on publishing companies. Similarly, journalists and other writers can produce blogs and news sites on their own, rather than relying on established companies. As traditional journalism jobs have decreased, independent bloggers have become more common. Most bloggers rely on online advertising to pay their salaries.

Remote Work

New technology has also caused a growth in remote work. Remote work is working from home, generally on a computer, instead of going to the workplace. Most remote workers submit their work by e-mail. Many self-employed writers and visual artists work remotely.

The Economy and the Arts & Media Industry

Today we live in a global economy linked by the Internet. Many movies are global productions, filmed at various locations, both in the United States and overseas. The film industry can sell its products overseas much more easily than it could in the past. In fact, some Hollywood films make more money abroad than in the United States.

Outsourcing and Downsizing

Some companies set up divisions in other countries so certain activities can be done at overseas branches of the company. Other companies outsource jobs; that is, they contract work out to foreign companies. Many technical support jobs in telecommunications are now performed overseas.

New technology has allowed many companies to downsize or cut their workforce. For example, some jobs in printing firms that used to require hands-on employees can now be done by computers. Downsizing also occurs when companies consolidate, or join together, as a new, larger company. Staff members who do the same job as others are often let go. The recent consolidation of publishing companies, for example, has resulted in many job losses.

> ### 5-6 Essential Question Reflection
>
> **So, let us revisit our essential question:**
>
> *What factors affect trends in Arts & Media?*
>
> Based on what you learned in this section, please answer this question in detail.

Chapter 6: Architecture & Construction

❓ Essential Questions

By the end of the chapter, you will be able to answer the following questions:

- **6-1** What types of opportunities are available in Architecture & Construction?
- **6-2** Which opportunities may be right for you?
- **6-3** How can I match my skills & interests with the right job?
- **6-4** What training & education is needed for a job in Architecture & Construction?
- **6-5** What are typical work environments in Architecture & Construction?
- **6-6** What factors affect trends in Architecture & Construction?

Chapter Topics

6-1 Architecture & Construction Today

6-2 Architecture & Construction Jobs

6-3 Building a Career in Architecture & Construction

6-4 Education and Training for Architecture & Construction Opportunities

6-5 Working Conditions in the Architecture & Construction Industry

6-6 Trends in Architecture & Construction

6-1 Architecture & Construction Today

Take a look out the window. Do you see houses and apartments? Are there stores and offices? Can you see a bridge or a highway? Every single one of these structures is there due to the hard work and resilience of workers in the Architecture & Construction industry.

The structures these workers design, build, and maintain fulfill a wide variety of human needs. Houses and apartment buildings provide shelter. Offices and factories serve as places to provide services and make products. Roads and highways help move goods and people. In capital buildings and courts, officials make and enforce laws.

Beyond fulfilling basic needs, the Architecture & Construction industry also gives us beauty and artistry. Think of a soaring, gleaming skyscraper or a stately bridge. Good design, high-quality materials, and solid construction result in structures that are useful, attractive, and safe.

6-1 Essential Question

As you read this section, keep this question in mind:

What types of opportunities are available in Architecture & Construction?

Career Journeys in Architecture & Construction

There are three major paths along which your journey in Architecture & Construction might be shaped. People commonly move into and out of different paths. The paths are:

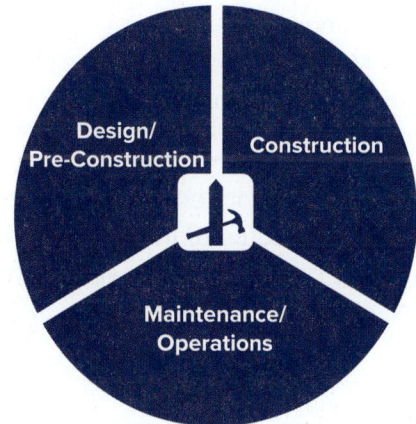

- Design/Pre-Construction
- Construction
- Maintenance/Operations

The Architecture & Construction industry truly shapes the way we live. Architecture involves the design, or planning, phase. All structures, from garages to skyscrapers, require the efforts of designers, builders, and operations staff. Construction workers turn plans into reality when they build structures. Maintenance and operations workers make needed repairs so buildings stay in good condition.

Design/Pre-Construction

The Design/Pre-Construction path includes architects, surveyors, civil engineers, environmental designers, urban planners, and many more workers related to planning the building of structures.

Architects design buildings such as houses, offices, and stores. They create structures that meet the planned uses and are pleasing to the eye. They must consider the safety of the structure and the best materials to use. Civil engineers plan public structures such as highways, airports, and sewer systems. They choose materials based on how long the structure is supposed to last and how much use it will receive. They make sure that the structure will be safe and that it will not harm the environment. Landscape architects design outdoor spaces, such as backyards and city parks. They think about how their designs will look and how easy it will be to maintain plants in the climate where they will be placed. All these designers and planners must keep their client's budget in mind as they create their designs.

Designers begin by finding out their client's needs and wishes. They make sketches that show their ideas for a structure. Then the client reviews these drawings. The designer moves forward only if the client approves this work. The design process may involve many meetings and several revisions. As the final step, the designer draws up detailed plans and specifications for building the structure.

Other workers assist throughout the process. Surveyors measure the size and shape of the land where the structure will be built. Drafters create some of the detailed drawings that are needed. Modelers build smaller versions of the structure so clients can better visualize how the structure will look.

Some workers help plan how the structure will be built. Mechanical engineers help architects design heating and cooling systems in the building. Cost estimators determine how much a project will cost to build.

Designers must be able to think in terms of spatial relationships, or how the space is used, and visualize the outcome of their plans and designs. They need excellent communication skills and problem-solving skills. They pay attention to detail and are able to work well with others on a team.

138 Chapter 6 • Architecture & Construction

Construction

Jobs in the Construction path can be grouped into three areas:

- **Building construction** involves building houses, offices, stores, and factories. Projects can be as small as building an addition to a home and as large as building a skyscraper. Large projects can be very costly and may take more than a year to complete.
- **Civil engineering construction** involves projects paid for and organized by the government for the public good. Projects include dams, highways, tunnels, hospitals, and schools. These projects are often very complex. They can take months or years to build.
- **Specialty trade construction** involves all other types of construction workers, including those who are skilled in a particular area, such as heating and cooling systems or electrical systems.

Typically, construction projects are managed by general building contractors who work for contracting firms. Their firm is hired for a project, and they take the responsibility of carrying out the project according to the plan. To do the work, they may hire subcontractors, such as independent carpenters and electricians. General contractors may do some of the building work as well. Most contracting firms specialize in either building construction or civil engineering.

Workers in the Construction path need good communication, math, and problem-solving skills. Problem-solving skills are especially important when dealing with large-scale projects. Since these projects often cost many millions of dollars, it is important to prevent problems and solve them as soon as they arise.

Some jobs in building construction require little or no pre-employment training. For instance, workers who install drywall or work as manual laborers are usually trained on the job. Other jobs require several years of experience and sometimes even a license to work in the field. Electricians and plumbers, for example, may train for three to four years under experienced workers. Additionally, they must be licensed by the state in which they work.

Workers entering this field can learn basic construction techniques and procedures while working in home construction. These projects are mostly smaller in scale than commercial structures like hotels and hospitals. Once workers gain experience, they may begin working in commercial or public works construction, which deals with larger, more complex projects.

Maintenance/Operations

The Maintenance/Operations path includes jobs related to maintaining, repairing, and upgrading structures.

Plumbers and electricians are important careers in this path. Plumbers install, connect, and repair pipes, valves, and faucets. Electricians install, test, and maintain the electrical systems in buildings. They work on everything from light switches to the power systems needed for elevators.

Another important career in this path involves taking care of systems that provide heating, ventilation, and air conditioning, also known as HVAC. HVAC mechanics maintain these systems. When the systems have problems, these mechanics identify the source of the trouble and fix it.

Like workers in the Construction path, workers in the Maintenance/Operations path should have good math and problem-solving skills. Communication skills are also important because workers need to be able to explain problems and solutions to people who do not have the same technical knowledge they do. Workers should be able to work independently, follow directions, and read technical diagrams such as blueprints.

Most workers in this path attend technical schools or train on the job with experienced workers. Employers prefer candidates with high school diplomas and some technical training. Jobs in this path rarely require college degrees.

Architecture & Construction Future Outlook

The outlook for the Architecture & Construction industry is better than average.

Table 6.1: Job Forecast for a Sample of Architecture & Construction Opportunities

Occupation	Expected Growth Rate
Wind Turbine Service Operators	15% or higher!
Civil Engineers	5–10%
Architects	1–5%
Operating Engineers	5–10%
Construction Laborers	1–5%
Heating and Air-Conditioning Mechanics	5–10%
First-Line Supervisors	1–5%
Geothermal Technicians	5–10%
Carpenters	1–5%
Construction Managers	5–10%
Surveyors	1–5%
Refrigeration Mechanics and Installers	5–10%
Painters	1–5%
Landscaping Workers	5–10%
Solar Energy Installation Managers	15% or higher!
Electricians	5–10%
Plumbers	1–5%
Cost Estimators	−2%

Source: *O*Net*

Growth in this industry is affected by two factors. First is the demand for building new structures or for remodeling of standing structures. These demands are affected by the state of the economy. Construction booms when the economy is growing. In an economic slowdown, on the other hand, demand for new buildings drops. That means less work for construction workers, although specialty trade contractors can still find work in these times. Those workers often carry out

6-1 • Architecture & Construction Today

remodeling projects, which are more common than new construction in hard economic times.

Second is the increase of public construction. This area is expected to grow in the future. Population growth leads to rising demand for roads, bridges, and similar projects. These construction projects mean increased demand for design and pre-construction workers such as civil engineers.

Demand for jobs within the industry is expected to vary widely in the future. Jobs requiring special skills—such as supervisors, construction workers, plumbers, and civil engineers—will see faster-than-average growth. Other jobs, such as structural steel workers, iron workers, painters, and roofers, are expected to see slower growth and may even decline.

The likelihood of getting a job varies from career to career. Generally, workers seeking lower-level positions have the most difficulty finding a job. They face more competition and have fewer skills to attract employers. Experienced and highly skilled workers will find it somewhat easier to get work.

6-1 Essential Question Reflection

So, let us revisit our essential question:

What types of opportunities are available in Architecture & Construction?

Based on what you learned in this section, which field of Architecture & Construction is the most interesting to you? Explain in detail.

Practice 6-1

Skills Practice

It may be necessary to follow multi-step instructions in a variety of situations, such as when installing insulation to weatherize a building. Workers must read carefully to know when to take each step, and they must be able to apply the same instructions in a variety of situations. **Practice this skill!**

PROCEDURES TO INSTALL INSULATION FOR A QUALITY THERMAL ENVELOPE

The following steps should be followed in the installation of insulation to ensure efficiency and comfort:

1. Work with the architect and framer to minimize spaces that are difficult to insulate.
2. Use materials that meet California quality standards.
3. Select the R-values that meet or exceed design specifications.
4. Install insulation to completely fill all cavities, without gaps and with minimal compression.
5. Account for special characteristics of the materials used, such as settling, flammability, or water permeability.
6. Inspect the job to ensure a quality installation.

1. You are working for an insulation installation crew on a new home in California and are reviewing the procedures. When should you check to see whether the materials you are using meet California quality standards?

   A. before meeting with the architect
   B. after installing the insulation
   C. after checking for gaps in the insulation
   D. before selecting the R-values
   E. during your final inspection of the job

2. When placing insulation for a quality thermal envelope, which step must you perform immediately before you inspect the work?

   A. Install R-values that meet California quality standards.
   B. Use properly labeled insulation.
   C. Minimize spaces that are difficult to insulate.
   D. Account for special characteristics of the material.
   E. Install the insulation without gaps.

To access more problems that will help you grow professional skills and are real-world examples in Architecture & Construction, go online.

6-2 Architecture & Construction Jobs

Are you interested in helping to build a home from the ground up? Do you want to use 3-D modeling software to design buildings? Do you want to be outdoors planting trees and tending gardens? You can find jobs at all skill levels, from entry-level to managerial, in the Architecture & Construction industry. The following job profiles will introduce you to some professions in this industry.

6-2 Essential Question

As you read this section, keep this question in mind:

Which opportunities may be right for you?

Fastest-Growing Occupation:

Construction Workers

- Build structures, such as roadways, bridges, and office buildings
- Follow construction plans and instructions from supervisors or more experienced workers
- Clean and prepare construction sites by removing debris and possible hazards

Fast Facts:

Employment: 1,572,200 currently employed

Annual Openings: 14,320

Median Annual Wage: $18.04 hourly $37,520 annually

Education Needed: On-the-job training

Occupations With the Most People Employed:

Construction Equipment Operators

- Clean and maintain equipment, making basic repairs as necessary
- Coordinate machine actions with crew members using hand or audio signals

Fast Facts:
 Employment: 466,900 currently employed
 Annual Openings: 4,540
 Median Annual Wage: $23.22 hourly, $48,290 annually
 Education Needed: High school diploma, or equivalent, and certification

Sheet Metal Workers

- Repair or install sheet metal product
- Fasten seams or joints by welding, bolting, riveting, or soldering
- Measure and mark dimensions and reference lines on metal sheets

Fast Facts:
 Employment: 129,100 currently employed
 Median Annual Wage: $25.69 hourly, $53,440 annually
 Education Needed: High school diploma, or equivalent, and some on-the-job training

Great Job! – Associate Degree Needed:

Environmental Engineering Technologists and Technicians

- Implement plans that environmental engineers develop
- Collect and analyze samples, such as of ground water, for monitoring pollution or treatment
- Set up, test, operate, and modify equipment used to prevent or clean up environmental pollution

Fast Facts:
 Employment: 15,500 currently employed
 Annual Openings: 600
 Median Annual Wage: $23.27 hourly, $48,390 annually
 Education Needed: Associate degree

Great Job! – High School Diploma Needed:

Surveying and Mapping Technicians

- Visit sites to record survey measurements and other descriptive data
- Select needed information from databases to create maps

Fast Facts:
Employment: 59,800 currently employed
Annual Openings: 220
Median Annual Wage: $22.55 hourly, $46,910 annually

6-2 Essential Question Reflection

So, let us revisit our essential question:

Which opportunities may be right for you?

Based on what you learned in this section, please answer this question in detail.

Case Study: Solar Photovoltaic Installers

What do they do?

- Assemble, install, or maintain solar photovoltaic (PV) systems on roofs or other structures in compliance with site assessment and schematics
- Measure, cut, assemble, and bolt structural framing and solar modules
- Perform minor electrical work such as current checks

What would you do?

- Install photovoltaic (PV) systems in accordance with codes and standards, using drawings, schematics, and instructions
- Assemble solar modules, panels, or support structures as specified
- Apply weather sealing to array, building, or support mechanisms

What do you need to know?

Engineering and Technology
Mechanical
Building and construction

Arts and Humanities
English language

Business
Customer service

Manufactured or Agricultural Goods
Manufacture and distribution of products

What skills do you need?

Basic Skills
Listen to others, do not interrupt, and ask good questions
Think about the pros and cons of different ways to solve a problem

Problem Solving
Notice a problem and figure out the best way to solve it

What abilities must you be good at?

Hand and Finger Use
Put together small parts with your fingers
Hold or move items with your hands

148 Chapter 6 • Architecture & Construction

Ideas and Logic
    Notice when problems happen
    Order or arrange things

Who does well in this occupation?

People interested in this work like activities that include practical, hands-on problems and solutions.

People who do well at this job need:
    Cooperation
    Dependability
    Attention to detail
    Integrity
    Initiative
    Self-Control

What educational level is needed?

- High school diploma, or equivalent
- Associate degree

Practice 6-2

Skills Practice

Architecture & Construction workers must sometimes analyze graphics to identify trends. They might search for data that has increased or decreased over time. An urban planner, for example, might use a graph of population trends to plan new community housing. Being able to identify common trends from several pieces of data can be helpful in a variety of jobs in this industry. **Practice this skill!**

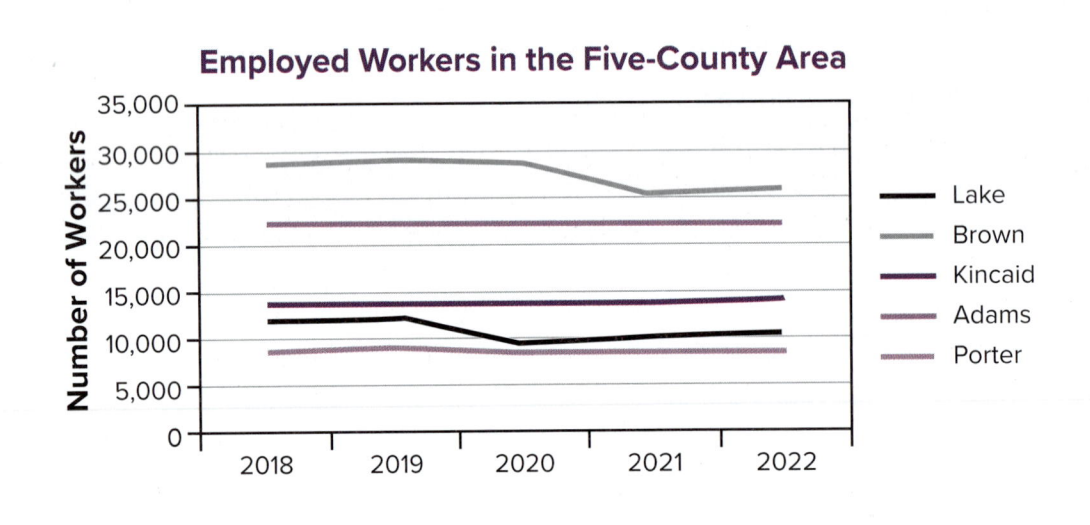

Employed Workers in the Five-County Area

1. You are a general trade union steward in a five-county area that has a mixture of agriculture and some light industry. You keep close track of the effects of economic trends in employment. In January 2020 a manufacturing plant that was a major employer closed down. In which county was the manufacturing plant most likely located?

   A. Adams
   B. Brown
   C. Kincaid
   D. Lake
   E. Porter

2. Which county experienced an overall rise in employment numbers over the five-year period covered by the graph?

   A. Adams
   B. Brown
   C. Kincaid
   D. Lake
   E. Porter

To access more problems that will help you grow professional skills and are real-world examples in Architecture & Construction, go online.

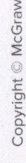

150 Chapter 6 • Architecture & Construction

6-3 Building a Career in Architecture & Construction

An architect usually begins by serving as an intern at an architectural firm. An intern-architect works under a licensed architect for three years to learn more about the profession. In that time, intern-architects research building codes and materials, write specifications, prepare construction drawings, and perhaps design parts of projects. After three years, they are eligible to take their state's licensing exam. Passing that exam makes them a registered architect.

? 6-3 Essential Question

As you read this section, keep this question in mind:

How can I match my skills & interests with the right job?

Are You More Interested in Working With Data, People, or Things?

Most careers offer opportunities to work with a combination of data, people, and things. Cost estimators, for example, work mainly with data. Architects often work with people. Plumbers work mostly with things. When planning your career path, consider what balance of data, people, and things you want in a career.

Careers That Involve Working With Data

Working with data means working with words, numbers, concepts, and ideas. Examples of working with data include drawing up budgets for a project, analyzing building codes, and scheduling the steps required to construct a large office building.

Some Architecture & Construction jobs that focus on data include: cost estimators, specification writers, civil engineers, and mechanical drafters. Cost estimators need to look at the materials and labor needed for a building project so they can determine the cost. They analyze costs of an ongoing project to make sure it does not run over budget. A civil engineer may work on redesigning a highway to make traffic flow more smoothly. Carrying out this project requires conducting research, running tests, and collecting and analyzing data.

Careers That Involve Working With People

Human relationships are an important part of most jobs in Architecture & Construction. Examples of tasks that involve working with people include training construction laborers, mediating conflicts among coworkers, negotiating prices with suppliers, and working with clients on the designs of buildings. All of these activities require strong communication skills.

Many Architecture & Construction jobs require working with others. Construction projects rely heavily on teamwork. Construction managers and supervisors have to supervise and lead teams of workers. They must have the ability to ensure that team members work well together. At the same time, all members of the work crew need be able to communicate clearly to each other.

Careers That Involve Working With Things

In Architecture & Construction, working with things involves designing, creating, using, and repairing machines, tools, and structures. Examples of working with things include painting, pouring concrete, carving stone, installing flooring, repairing pipes and faucets, and making architectural models.

Many careers in Architecture & Construction involve working primarily with things. Carpenters, electricians, and drywall installers spend most of their days working with tools, machines, and building materials. Construction equipment operators run large machines like cranes and shovels.

> **6-3 Essential Question Reflection**
>
> **So, let us revisit our essential question:**
>
> *How can I match my skills & interests with the right job?*
>
> Based on what you learned in this section, please answer this question in detail.

6-4 Education and Training for Architecture & Construction Opportunities

Architecture & Construction jobs require varying levels of education and training. Many jobs in this industry require little or no formal training. For others, it is necessary to have specific education and experience.

6-4 Essential Question

As you read this section, keep this question in mind:

What training & education is needed for a job in Architecture & Construction?

Training and Education in This Industry

The level of training necessary to succeed in the Architecture & Construction industry varies by career. Jobs can be categorized into three groups—those requiring little or no training, those requiring some training, and those requiring advanced training.

Jobs Requiring Little or No Training or Education

Entry-level jobs in Architecture & Construction require little or no formal training. This is often the case with hands-on jobs such as construction laborers and drywall and ceiling-tile installers. The training for those occupations often takes place on the job.

However, getting a high school education or the equivalent is very important. Many employers look for workers who earned solid grades in high school. Failing to complete high school may hurt your chances for advancement. Here are some examples of jobs in the Architecture & Construction industry that may require little training or education.

Table 6.2: Jobs Requiring Little Training or Education

Little Training or Education	
Drywall Installers, Ceiling Tile Installers, and Tapers	Flooring Installers
Painters	Construction Laborers
Roofers	Tile and Stone Setters

Jobs Requiring Some Training or Education

Many jobs in Architecture & Construction require specialized training and education past a high school diploma for many skilled trades. You can get the necessary training in an apprenticeship program. In addition, technical colleges offer programs in many fields.

Trade organizations, or organizations representing a specific industry or type of job, often offer certification programs, which provide training for an occupation. For instance, the National Glass Association (NGA) offers three levels of certification for glaziers, workers who install or repair glass. Certification might require a certain amount of work experience and a minimum score on a standardized test. Here are some examples of jobs in the Architecture & Construction industry that may require some training or education.

Table 6.3: Jobs Requiring Some Training or Education

Some Training or Education Required	
Architectural and Civil Drafters	Aerospace Engineering and Operations Technologists
Mechanical Drafters	Electrical and Electronic Engineering Technologists
HVAC Technicians	Environmental Engineering Technologists

Jobs Requiring Advanced Training or Education

Some jobs in Architecture & Construction require extensive preparation. Typically, these are jobs that involve design, business management, or engineering. Some jobs require at least a bachelor's degree, while others may require study at the master's or doctoral level. Most workers who have these more advanced jobs must have several years' work experience in the field and a license allowing them to practice.

For example, architects must have a college degree from an architecture program. In addition, they must complete an internship and take a test to earn their license. Some states even require continuing education to maintain a license. Here are some examples of jobs in the Architecture & Construction industry that may require advanced training or education.

Table 6.4: Jobs Requiring Advanced Training or Education

Advanced Training or Education	
Surveyors	Agricultural Engineers
Bioengineers and Biomedical Engineers	Aerospace Engineers
Marine Engineers and Naval Architects	Environmental Engineers
Mining and Geological Engineers	Electrical Engineers

Job and Workplace Skills

Job-specific skills are the skills necessary to do a particular job. They may include installing wiring or building a model to scale. General workplace skills are skills that can be used in a variety of jobs.

Architecture & Construction Skill Standards

Skill standards for many construction careers have been developed by the LIUNA Training and Education Fund. This fund is set up by the Laborers' International Union of North America (LIUNA). The standards include basic academic skills, such as math and reading; employability skills, such as knowledge of safe behaviors; and specific job skills. LIUNA runs more than 50 training programs at centers across the country, and many construction workers become members of this program.

In addition to LIUNA, there are the National CAD drafting standards (NCS). These standards specify how to plot and draft data in computer-aided design (CAD) software. Because of these standards, workers from different companies can understand each other's work more easily.

Often mastery of a specific set of skills leads to certification or licensing. Crane operators can be certified by the National Commission for the Certification of Crane Operators. Concrete flatwork finishers and technicians can receive certification from the American Concrete Institute International. Earning certification can help you advance in your career.

Workers in some other skilled trades, such as electricians and plumbers, are also required to earn licenses. Architects and civil engineers need to obtain licenses as well. This step ensures that all workers have a strong base of knowledge about the trade and relevant building codes.

Professional Skills

Professional skills differ from academic or job-specific skills.

Communication Skills   Being able to communicate effectively is important in the Architecture & Construction industry, where many levels of employees are dependent on one another to make a project work. Communication skills are needed when giving instructions. They are just as necessary when bringing problems to the attention of a supervisor. Those who work with clients, such as architects, must be able to explain plans clearly.

Listening Skills   Listening skills are vital to all workers. Construction workers must pay careful attention to safety instructions. To execute projects correctly, architects and contractors must be able to listen closely to their clients.

Problem-Solving Skills   Employers value workers who can spot problems and take steps to solve them. Problems, such as increases in material costs and unexpected structural issues, often occur during construction projects. A construction manager may be called on to troubleshoot technical problems or to resolve tensions and conflicts that arise between workers.

Technology Skills   Workers with solid technology skills often earn more and have greater success than workers without these skills. Many construction professionals need to be able to use specialized scientific software, such as industrial control software, in order to do their jobs. Architects and drafters need to be skilled at using CAD software.

Decision-Making Skills   The ability to gather and analyze information rapidly and to think clearly under pressure are important skills in this field. A contractor must make decisions that impact the safety of buildings and of work crews. A plumber needs to be able to quickly analyze the cause of a major leak and act decisively to repair it.

Organizing and Planning Skills Because planning and building structures involve so many steps, organization is crucial. Planning requires being able to set goals and to sequence all the steps needed to achieve these goals. A civil engineer might be asked to design a new highway and to oversee its construction by a certain date. Civil engineers must organize a large quantity of materials and many workers. They also need to develop a complex schedule to make sure that all the work is done on time.

Teamwork Skills Teamwork is very important in the Architecture & Construction industry. On a single project, an architect or contractor might need to work with clients, drafters, government zoning officials, inspectors, construction workers, and skilled craft workers. Being an effective collaborator and a good team member is key to success in this industry.

Social Skills Workers often interact with people at different levels, from apprentices to general building contractors. These people have various levels of knowledge, experience, and authority. Learning to adapt to these differences and have positive conversations with people of different backgrounds can make the interactions go more smoothly.

Adaptability Skills The Architecture & Construction industry is a dynamic field. Job descriptions, work environments, and architecture and construction methods are constantly changing. New technology, economic changes, and changing customer tastes require workers to adapt to new materials, techniques, or styles. Workers in this industry must be ready to acquire new skills. Being able to change increases a worker's chance of employment.

6-4 Essential Question Reflection

So, let us revisit our essential question:

What training & education is needed for a job in Architecture & Construction?

Based on what you learned in this section, please answer this question in detail.

Practice 6-4

Skills Practice

When reading workplace graphics, such as a diagram for a heating and air conditioning system, Architecture & Construction workers must know what information to look for. The key information may be in one or more graphics. Workers must be able to sift through unimportant or distracting information to find what is needed. **Practice this skill!**

Job Site Rules
1. No smoking permitted at any time.
2. Job site speed limit is 15 miles per hour.
3. Protective safety equipment must be worn at all times.

Type of Personal Protective Safety Equipment	Equipment Attributes Required
Hard hats	Must meet ANSI standards
Safety glasses	Must have rigid side shields
Safety footwear	Must have steel toes and a heel
Gloves	Must be rubber
Fire-resistant clothing	Outermost layer must be fire-resistant

1. As a construction laborer, you are responsible for ordering and organizing safety equipment around a hospital building site. The superintendent has asked you to order safety glasses. According to the chart, what special attribute do the safety glasses need to have?

   A. unbreakable lenses
   B. rigid side shields
   C. flexible side shields
   D. multiple layers
   E. ANSI approval

2. Your construction company is required to post speed limits around the site in accordance with the contractor's safety program. As a laborer, you are to post the signs. What speed limit should be on the signs?

   A. 15 miles per hour
   B. 15 kilometers per hour
   C. 25 miles per hour
   D. 25 kilometers per hour
   E. 30 kilometers per hour

Skills Practice

Some calculations used by Architecture & Construction workers may require using conversions and formulas. A stonemason who uses imported materials may need to convert currencies to calculate costs, for example. Other calculations require working with mixed units, such as when a plumber needs to measure pipes using meters and centimeters. **Practice this skill!**

3. As the leader of a painting crew who is preparing a bid for the job, you need to calculate the time it will take to finish painting the new bank branch. There are 6 rooms in all, and each room will take 90 minutes to paint. How much time should be allotted for painting the entire facility?

   A. 6 hours
   B. 7 hours, 30 minutes
   C. 8 hours, 30 minutes
   D. 9 hours
   E. 10 hours, 30 minutes

4. You are a drywall taper and have been asked to pick up three quart-sized containers of joint compound. You happen to have the exact amount due in cash. You give the store clerk (1) ten-dollar bill, (1) five-dollar bill, (3) one-dollar bills, (5) quarters, (3) nickels, and (7) pennies. How much did you pay for all three containers?

   A. $18.92
   B. $19.47
   C. $19.52
   D. $19.82
   E. $20.47

To access more problems that will help you grow professional skills and are real-world examples in Architecture & Construction, go online.

6-5 Working Conditions in the Architecture & Construction Industry

Understanding the work environment, hazards, and benefits of a job can help you make informed decisions.

6-5 Essential Question

As you read this section, keep this question in mind:

What are typical work environments in Architecture & Construction?

Work Environment

Working in the Architecture & Construction industry requires physical stamina. Some jobs require long days on your feet at noisy, cluttered construction sites. Others require you to run heavy machinery or to work around hazardous materials, such as asbestos. Workers must use their common sense to stay safe on the work site.

Physical Environment

In the Architecture & Construction industry, the physical work environment varies by job and by company. Some jobs require working outdoors, even in bad weather, and other jobs are done indoors. Sometimes outdoor work may take place in extreme weather conditions.

In this industry, most of the outdoor jobs are done at construction sites, which are often dirty and noisy. Construction workers, especially those who work on roadway projects or on skyscrapers, may face increased risk to their health or even death at work.

Work Hours

The work hours for careers in Architecture & Construction vary greatly. Because construction crews often need to work through the night, shift work is common in this industry. Shift work divides the day into blocks of time, generally into eight-hour blocks. By using shift work, a construction company can keep working at a job site around the clock. This can benefit workers as well. They can select hours to suit their schedules. Shift work is common in heavy construction because projects such as highways must be worked on during off-peak hours.

Most workers in Architecture & Construction work 40-hour weeks. Many workers in the industry must meet tight deadlines to finish projects on time. As a result, they may need to work overtime to keep a project on schedule. The need for overtime can increase as the deadline for a project nears. In addition to overtime, working on weekends and holidays is not uncommon. Workers who work overtime are heavily compensated for doing so.

Essential Physical Activities

Many workers in Architecture & Construction must be in good physical condition. Several jobs in the industry have heavy physical demands. Most workers must stand, walk, stoop, bend, and climb regularly during the day. Heavy lifting is common. Workers often handle heavy equipment.

Some workers are required to be skilled with their hands. Some workers lay bricks or tiles in complicated patterns. Other workers use their hands to service equipment.

Good vision is a must for electricians. They install and repair electrical systems that use different colored wires. They read gauges, charts, and meters. Other workers in the industry need good eyesight as well. Plumbers sometimes work in poorly lit areas. Building inspectors must be able to spot small but important flaws in a building's construction.

Hazards and Environmental Dangers

Because so many accidents can happen on the job, safety is a high priority. The federal government protects workers by creating workplace safety standards and laws to help prevent accidents and ensure that accident victims are offered assistance. According to the Bureau of Labor Statistics (BLS), more than 1,061 workers in the Architecture & Construction industry died in 2019. This was the second highest number for any industry. Leading causes of death were falls and transportation accidents. Because of the dangers involved in construction, the government works hard to protect workers in this industry.

The Occupational Safety and Health Administration (OSHA) is the branch of the U.S. Department of Labor that sets standards for workplace safety. OSHA has many rules for the construction industry. Several states have passed laws that require construction workers to complete and pass an OSHA-certified safety course. They cover such issues as working with power tools, building and using scaffolds, and working with materials such as asbestos and concrete. OSHA representatives inspect work sites to make sure that the standards are being met.

One common safety practice is to require workers to wear hard hats when working at a construction site. OSHA requires workers on any job site who might be struck on the head by falling materials to wear some kind of protective hat. Construction workers must follow this rule.

Injuries and Illnesses

Workers in this industry may experience occupational injuries and illnesses. An occupational injury is any injury that occurs at work. Injuries may include cuts, fractures, and sprains. These injuries can be caused by falls, equipment not working properly, or contact with harmful materials.

An occupational illness is a short- or long-term health problem caused by being exposed to harmful substances at a workplace. A worker might develop rashes or skin disease, respiratory problems, side effects of exposure to extreme heat or cold, or poisoning from toxic materials. Illnesses can be caused by common materials such as paint, drywall, carpeting, plastics, and insulation. All these materials can give off gases that are dangerous to breathe. Even dust in the air can harm the lungs.

To help reduce workplace injuries and illnesses, adequate safety training and safety precautions are essential. Even workers in management positions are required to have training in on-site safety. Workers should take breaks to rest overworked muscles, vary their work when possible, and notify their managers when they feel pain or stiffness. Showers and eye baths must be available to workers who are at risk of exposure to dangerous materials. Workers who may be exposed to chemicals must have safety shoes, gloves, and respirators.

6-5 • Working Conditions in the Architecture & Construction Industry

Ergonomics

Ergonomics is the study of how to design work equipment and work procedures with safety in mind. Tools, such as hammers, drills, and saws, are now being made using ergonomic principles. These designs cause less stress on the wrist. Seating in heavy equipment, such as bulldozers and front-end loaders, is now equipped with support for the lower back that eases back strain.

A major goal of ergonomics is to reduce the rate of repetitive stress injuries (RSIs). Repetitive stress injuries can develop when a person performs the same motion many times. Plumbers, roofers, and sheet metal workers may suffer from RSIs because they use the same tools and motions every day. To prevent RSIs, the federal government and state governments have passed laws that mandate safe workplace design.

6-5 Essential Question Reflection

So, let us revisit our essential question:

What are typical work environments in Architecture & Construction?

Based on what you learned in this section, please answer this question in detail.

6-6 Trends in Architecture & Construction

Humans have been designing and building structures for thousands of years. Yet, the Architecture & Construction industry is constantly changing. New technology gives workers updated materials and tools to work with. Demands, based on changes in the population, affect the work that people in the industry perform. The economy also has a tremendous impact on this industry.

6-6 Essential Question

As you read this section, keep this question in mind:

What factors affect trends in Architecture & Construction?

Technology in the Industry

Technology has had a huge impact on the Architecture & Construction industry. Changes have affected how buildings are designed, how supplies are purchased, how projects are managed, and the way workers do their jobs. Technological innovations have impacted both paths of this industry.

Design and Pre-Construction

For some time now, computers have been vital tools for the Design and Pre-Construction career path. Cost estimators use programs to budget a project. Architects and drafters frequently use computer-aided design (CAD) programs. This software makes it easier to change a design after showing draft ideas to a client. Once designs are final, the CAD system produces exact plans faster than could be done in the past. In addition, plans have fewer errors because CAD systems identify structural problems.

Construction

Technology has changed the Construction path as well. Over the past several years, lasers have become widely used. A laser is an extremely intense beam of light that can be used to perform many different construction tasks, including leveling and drawing perfectly straight lines. Laser devices are also used to measure distance. This has allowed quicker completion of construction projects.

In addition, lasers are being used to remove contaminated materials from metals. Heavy-construction contractors, for example, use special laser systems to remove lead paint from bridges. These laser systems are safer than strong chemicals, which can harm the environment.

Computers have had an impact on construction as well as design. Online project management software allows members of a planning team to check the progress of a project using a website. The website allows users to store and retrieve documents and to communicate with one another. In some companies, that communication takes place using Internet conferencing.

Firms may use web-based cameras to manage projects. Contractors install these cameras at job sites. Project managers can then use the Internet to see building progress and check in on their workers.

Demographic Trends in the Architecture & Construction Industry

The demographics of the United States are changing. Demographics refer to the statistics that describe a population. They include personal characteristics such as age, gender, and ethnic background. One of today's most significant demographic changes is the aging of the American population.

Aging Population

According to the U.S. Census Bureau, the number of people 65 years old and older will continue to rise Older Americans will be an increasing share of the whole population. This increase in older people will lead to an increase in demand for housing targeted at senior citizens. That building surge will provide jobs for the Architecture & Construction industry.

Sustainability and Adaptive Reuse in the Architecture & Construction Industry

Another major change in the industry is the growing demand for green building, or sustainable design. Green building is designing, building, and operating structures so that they do the least harm to the environment. The goal is to plan a building so it uses less energy and other natural resources. Businesses and homeowners are also turning to green building in the hope that these designs will cut operating costs.

Green building ideas include using skylights and large windows to reduce the need for artificial light and installing low-flow showerheads to conserve water. Builders use materials made of recycled content. A key part of green building is designing energy-efficient heating and cooling systems. In addition, green roofs have seen a recent rise in popularity. Green roofs help to offset carbon dioxide and in turn purify air, which also lowers operating costs.

Another trend in the industry is called adaptive reuse. It involves adapting older buildings for new uses while retaining the historic features of these buildings. In Philadelphia, a turn-of-the-century bank was remodeled to be a luxury hotel.

Adaptive reuse has several benefits. Older buildings often have high-quality materials, excellent craftsmanship, or special features that make them valuable architecturally. Older buildings are also valuable as a physical record of the past. Adaptive reuse has social benefits too. Many of these old buildings sit unused in decaying downtown areas. Putting old buildings to new use helps renew urban centers.

The Economy and the Architecture & Construction Industry

Like all industries, the Architecture & Construction industry is affected by the health of the economy. When the economy is strong, more people purchase new houses. Businesses hire more workers. This increases their need for offices, warehouses, and other kinds of space. Those trends create jobs in the Architecture & Construction industry. When the economy slows, individuals and businesses are less eager to invest in new space. Work for members of the industry is harder to find.

Changes in demand for construction work are constant in the Architecture & Construction industry. Workers in this industry are used to the cycles of high demand, followed by slow periods. In the coming decades, two trends driven by economics are expected to shape the industry. They are the need to rebuild the nation's infrastructure and the increasing use of contract workers.

Rebuilding Infrastructure

A nation's infrastructure is its network of roads and bridges, sewer and water lines, and power and communications systems. A growing population will create a need to expand this infrastructure. This trend will create jobs for civil engineers, highway construction workers, and skilled workers from plumbers to electricians. Demand will be particularly high in the south and west, where population growth is most rapid.

One area of infrastructure improvement that is expected to grow in the future is alternative energy. Companies are investing in wind power, solar power, and other alternative power sources in the hope of cutting energy costs and preserving natural resources.

Contract Workers

Many companies in the Architecture & Construction industry are making a strong effort to keep costs down. One approach is to rely more on contract workers than on employees. Companies must pay benefits to employees and must continue paying wages, even in down times. By contracting with independent workers when extra workers are needed, companies avoid these costs. Contract workers have more independence than employees. They can pick and choose which company to work for—as long as there is plenty of work. Contract workers have little job security, however. Workers who do high-quality work and are efficient and reliable will be in the greatest demand.

6-6 Essential Question Reflection

So, let us revisit our essential question:

What factors affect trends in Architecture & Construction?

Based on what you learned in this section, please answer this question in detail.

Chapter 7

Agriculture, Food, & Natural Resources

Chapter Topics

7-1 Agriculture, Food, & Natural Resources Today

7-2 Agriculture, Food, & Natural Resources Jobs

7-3 Building a Career in Agriculture, Food, & Natural Resources

7-4 Education and Training for Agriculture, Food, & Natural Resources Opportunities

7-5 Working Conditions in the Agriculture, Food, & Natural Resources Industry

7-6 Trends in Agriculture, Food, & Natural Resources

Essential Questions

By the end of the chapter, you will be able to answer the following questions:

- **7-1** What types of opportunities are available in Agriculture, Food, & Natural Resources?
- **7-2** Which opportunities may be right for you?
- **7-3** How can I match my skills & interests with the right job?
- **7-4** What training & education is needed for a job in Agriculture, Food, & Natural Resources?
- **7-5** What are typical work environments in Agriculture, Food, & Natural Resources?
- **7-6** What factors affect trends in Agriculture, Food, & Natural Resources?

7-1 Agriculture, Food, & Natural Resources Today

In the past, more Americans worked in agriculture than in any other field. But by 2021, the United States had one-third the number of farmers it had in 1900. Today, many family-owned farms have been combined into large farms owned by corporations. As a result, farms are generally larger than in the past. Still, agriculture plays a large part of every American's life because it produces the food we eat.

How can we produce enough food and energy to satisfy our needs while protecting the environment? Workers in this industry are trying to find answers to this question.

7-1 Essential Question

As you read this section, keep this question in mind:

What types of opportunities are available in Agriculture, Food, & Natural Resources?

Career Journeys in Agriculture, Food, & Natural Resources

There are seven major paths along which your journey in Agriculture, Food, & Natural Resources might be shaped. People commonly move into and out of different paths. Each path contains a group of careers requiring similar skills as well as similar certifications or education. This industry is divided into seven main career paths:

- Plant Systems
- Animal Systems
- Agribusiness Systems
- Food Products and Processing Systems
- Natural Resources Systems
- Environmental Services Systems
- Power, Structural, and Technical Systems

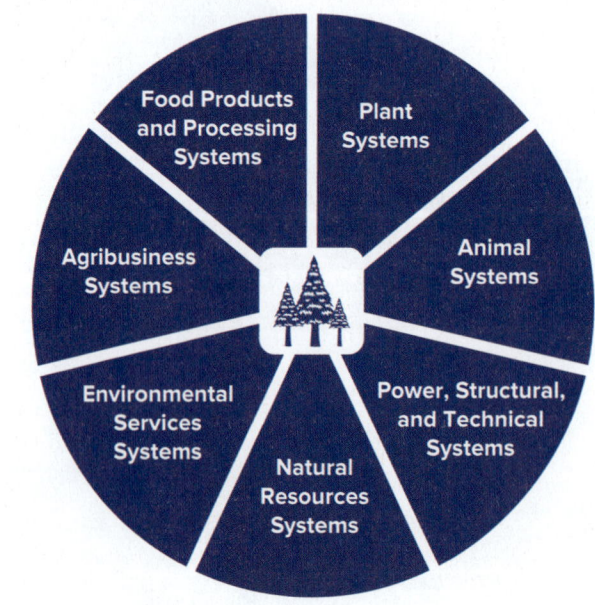

Plant Systems

Workers in this path grow plants to sell or to study. Most of these jobs do not require specific education or training, but some scientific careers may require advanced degrees.

Farmers use planting methods that will yield, or result in, the best harvests. Farmers need to understand crops and growing conditions and have business skills to succeed.

Agricultural scientists help keep the food supply safe. They also look for ways to improve yield, control pests and weeds, and conserve water and soil.

Animal Systems

Workers in Animal Systems look for better ways to raise animals to produce meat, poultry, eggs, and dairy products. Scientists study animals, while others breed, raise, or care for them. Most jobs in this path require a college degree.

Veterinarians provide health care for pets and for farm animals. Some veterinarians work in research and in human and animal disease prevention. Veterinarian technologists and technicians help them do their work.

Many farmworkers care for the animals on a farm or a ranch, including animals raised for the products they produce.

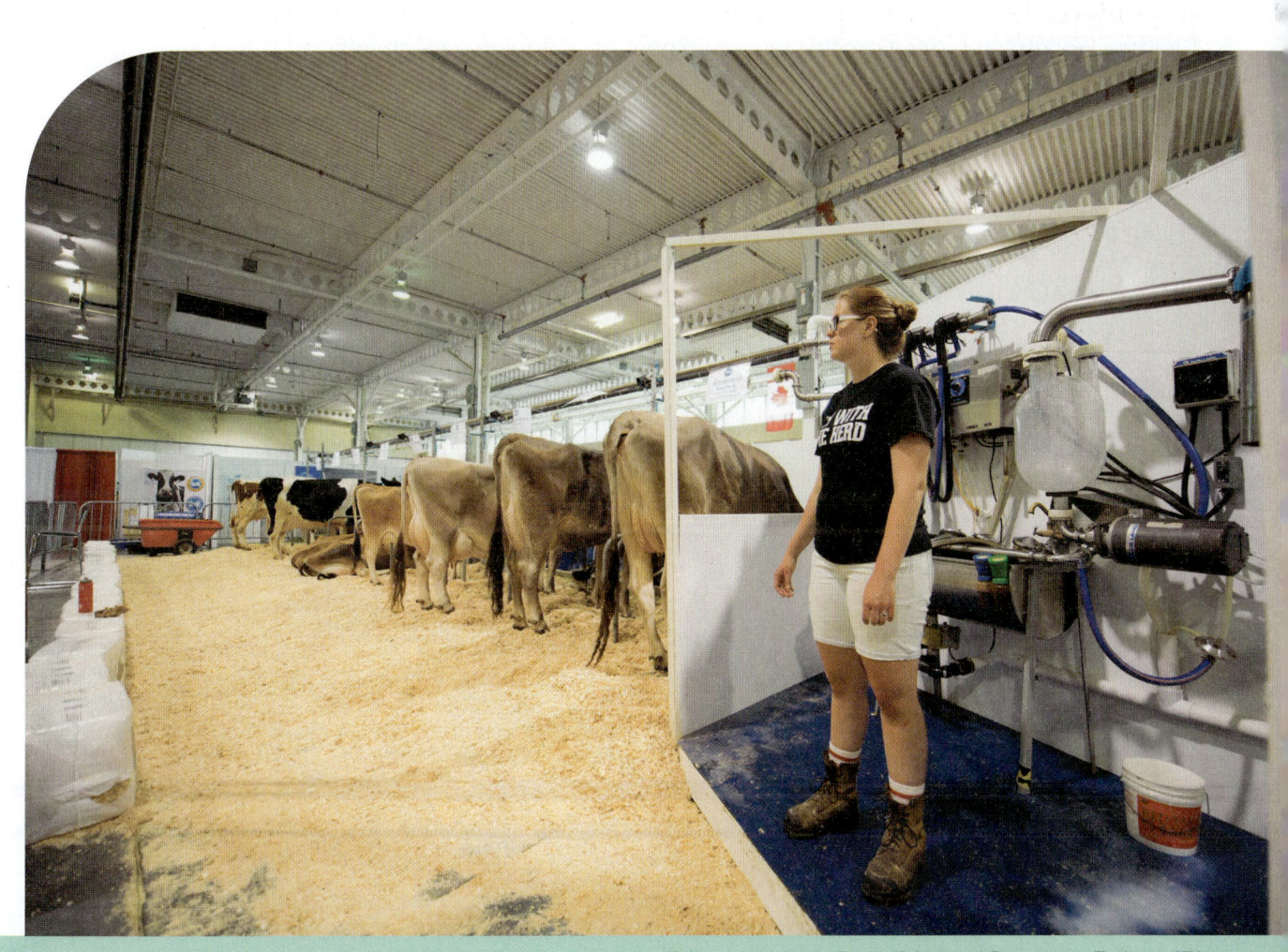

Animal breeders choose which animals on a farm or ranch will have offspring. They aim to produce animals with certain characteristics, such as high egg or wool production.

Agribusiness Systems

Workers in Agribusiness Systems coordinate a range of activities related to producing agricultural products. Using the latest technology, they operate in the marketplace for everything from food to fiber to natural resources. They work to make these markets efficient and profitable.

Workers in this path include farm managers, who run farms for the owners, and farmworkers. Jobs are available on many types of farms, including vegetable farms, dairy farms, cattle ranches, poultry farms, fish farms, and cash grain farms. Cash grain farms are farms on which crops are grown specifically for sale. Examples of cash grain crops are corn, soybeans, and wheat. Some agribusiness jobs, such as farm laborers, require little or no training. Jobs such as farm manager require several years of experience and even a degree.

Food Products and Processing Systems

Workers in the Food Products and Processing Systems path develop food products package and process food, and study its contents. Workers involved in preparing or packaging food may only need a high school diploma. Others, such as food scientists, require advanced training.

Cannery workers and dairy processing equipment operators use machines to process meats, vegetables, fruits, and dairy products into packaged form. Industrial machinery mechanics keep all the equipment in a food processing plant running.

Some workers in this path are responsible for food safety. Agricultural inspectors enforce government health regulations. To do so, they examine food processing plants and check animals for disease.

Natural Resources Systems

Workers in this path focus on natural resources. Some make use of these resources to create products for human consumption. Others look for ways to conserve and maintain these resources. The skills required for most careers in this path are learned on the job.

Foresters manage forested lands. They oversee the use of forests for commercial and recreational needs. They also protect forests from environmental damage. Forest technicians collect data on the size, content, and condition of forests. Forest workers maintain roads and campsites and carry out the work of reforesting and protecting forested land. Loggers harvest trees and process them for use in products from chairs to toothpicks.

A wide range of jobs are involved in building and operating gas and oil wells and mines. Geologists analyze geological maps (maps of what makes up the earth), seismic (earth vibrations) data, and other information. Some geologists head operations exploring for oil or coal.

In the oil and gas industry, petroleum engineers plan and manage drilling operations that extract oil or gas from the earth. At the extraction site, rotary drillers operate the machines that control drill speed and pressure. Derrick operators work on platforms high up on the rigs, helping to run pipe in and out of well holes.

Mining machine operators extract and move metal, coal, or rock at a mine. This equipment includes cutting machines, drilling machines, loading machines, and shuttle cars. Mine safety inspectors check work areas for dangerous gases, loose roofs, inadequate ventilation, or other hazards.

Environmental Service Systems

Workers in the Environmental Service Systems path handle waste treatment and recycling. Some monitor and prevent pollution or handle hazardous materials. Others make sure that workplaces are safe. Many of the jobs in this path, such as pest control workers, require no previous training, while others, such as environmental engineers, require college degrees.

Water and liquid waste treatment plant and system operators work in waste water treatment plants. They take samples of waste water and give them to technicians for testing. Refuse and recyclable material collectors collect trash and recycled materials. They also deliver the refuse to landfills and recycling centers.

Occupational health and safety specialists try to make workplaces as free as possible from hazards. They create systems meant to limit workplace injuries and illnesses. They often visit workplaces to see what conditions are like.

Power, Structural, and Technical Systems

Workers in the Power, Structural, and Technical Systems path work with power systems, controls, electronics, and computer systems. These workers include machine operators, who run equipment, and electronics systems technicians, who maintain it. Power systems are typically controlled by computers. As a result, this path includes computer service technical support technicians, who help computer users when they encounter problems. Other occupations include parts salespeople and equipment and parts managers. When machinery breaks down, service technicians contact the parts workers to obtain needed replacement parts. Many of the skills in this path can be learned through on-the-job training, but a few jobs require advanced training.

Agriculture, Food, & Natural Resources Future Outlook

According to the Bureau of Labor Statistics (BLS), three agriculture paths including Plant Systems, Animal Systems, and Agribusiness are not expected to see much change in the number of workers in the coming years. The same is true of the Food Products and Processing Systems paths. The outlook in the other paths differs greatly from job to job, however.

Table 7.1: Job Forecast for a Sample of Agriculture, Food, & Natural Resources Opportunities

Occupation	Expected Growth Rate
Farmworkers and Laborers	0%_5%
Nursey Workers	5%–10%
Crop and Livestock Managers	Little to no change
Farmers and Ranchers	5%–10%
First-Line Supervisors	5%–10%
Farmworkers	0% or lower
Nonfarm Animal Caretakers	15% or higher
Veterinary Technicians	10%–15%
Veterinarians	15% or higher
Meat, Poultry, and Fish Cutters	1%–5%
Food Batch Makers	5%–10%
Precision Agriculture Technicians	5%–10%
Natural Sciences Managers	5%–10%
Environmental Compliance Inspectors	5%–10%
Refuse and Recyclable Material Collectors	10%–15%
Recycling and Reclamation Workers	5%–10%
Environmental Science and Protection Technicians	10%–15%
Agricultural Equipment Operators	10%–15%

Source: *O*Net*

7-1 Essential Question Reflection

So, let us revisit our essential question:

What types of opportunities are available in Agriculture, Food, & Natural Resources?

Based on what you learned in this section, please answer this question in detail.

Practice 7-1

Skills Practice

When studying graphics such as the readings on gauges, Agriculture, and Food, & Natural Resources workers must know what information to look for. The key information may be in one or more documents. Workers must be able to sift through irrelevant or distracting information to find what is needed. **Practice this skill!**

Crop Planning Calendar

Crops	Dates to Plant (Central Iowa)	Inches Between Plants	Inches Between Rows
Lima Beans	May 20 – June 20	3 to 4	18 to 24
Tomato	May 20 – June 10	12 to 26	36 to 40
Broccoli	April 1 – May 20	9 to 12	20
Brussels Sprouts	April 15 – May 25	18 to 24	20
Spinach	April 10 – May 10 July 1 – August 1 (fall)	3 to 6	9 to 18
Carrots	April 15 – May 30	1 to 2	14 to 24
Cauliflower	May 15 – May 30	18 to 24	24 to 30
Sweet Corn	May 1 – June 15	9 to 12	18 to 36

1. You are a farmworker at a collective farm in Iowa and are planning your vegetable garden for the fall. When should you plant brussels sprouts?

   A. between April 25 and May 15
   B. between May 1 and June 25
   C. between June 15 and July 5
   D. between April 15 and May 25
   E. between July 1 and August 15

2. You have decided to plant lima beans. How many inches should you allow between rows?

   A. 3 to 4 inches
   B. 18 to 24 inches
   C. 12 to 26 inches
   D. 36 to 40 inches
   E. 12 to 18 inches

176 Chapter 7 • Agriculture, Food, & Natural Resources

Gamen Nursery and Greenhouse
1111 Main Street, Cable, IL 22222 (555) 222-0000

Order Date: *5/12/20xx*	Delivery Date: *5/14/20xx*	Taken By: *Juan Align*	Order #:

Delivery Information:

Name: *Anna Jones*
Address: *22 E. Front St.*
Cable, IL 22222

Telephone:
(555) 222-9876

Item Type:	Quantity:	Detailed Description:
☐ Plants ☒ Trees ☐ Seeds ☐ Chemicals ☐ Hardware ☐ Other	*12*	*6-foot flowering crabapple trees*

Special Instructions: *Call 30 minutes before arriving. Deliver from alley in back.*

Purchaser:
Name: *Wanda Jones*
Mobile: *(555) 112-9988*
Address: *901 Elm St.*
Cable, IL 22222

Payment Method:
Amount: *$360.00*
☒ VistaCard   ☐ Bankocard
☐ First Ameribanc   ☐ Cash/Check
Cardholder Name: *Wanda Jones*
Card Number: *1122-0099-7725*

Delivery Request Form

Date: *5/14/20xx*
Deliver To:
Name: *Anna Jones*
Address: *22 E. Front St.*
Cable, IL 22222
Phone Number: *(555) 222-9876*

From:
Name: *Wanda Jones*
Address: *901 Elm St.*
Cable, IL 22222
Phone Number: *(555-)112-9988*

Special Instructions:
Deliever by noon on 5/14. Reference Order Number: 99006.
Call 30 minutes before arriving. Deliver from alley in back.

Bill To: *Prepaid*
Account Number: *XJ1234*
Amount: *$27.00*

---

3. As a plant handler in a commercial nursery, you often help fulfill orders from customers. Based on the forms, what type of item has been ordered, and who placed the order?

   A. trees; Juan Align
   B. trees; Wanda Jones
   C. plants; Wanda Jones
   D. other; Juan Align
   E. plants; Anna Jones

4. Based on the forms, who took the order, and where should the order be delivered?

   A. Anna; 1111 Main St.
   B. Juan; 901 Elm St.
   C. Juan; 22 E. Front St.
   D. Wanda; 901 Elm St.
   E. Anna; 901 E. Front St.

To access more problems that will help you grow professional skills and are real-world examples in Agriculture, Food, & Natural Resources, go online.

7-2 Agriculture, Food, & Natural Resources Jobs

You can find jobs at all skill levels, from entry-level to managerial, in the Agriculture, Food, & Natural Resources industry. Would you like to protect the environment through a career in forestry? Perhaps you are interested in making the food supply safer and more nutritious as a food scientist. Here are some common industry jobs and the skills they require.

> **7-2 Essential Question**
>
> As you read this section, keep this question in mind:
>
> Which opportunities may be right for you?

Occupation With the Most People Employed:

Agricultural Workers

- Direct and monitor the work of casual and seasonal help during planting and harvesting
- Participate in the inspection, grading, sorting, storage, and post-harvest treatment of crops
- Harvest, transplant, pot, or label plants

Fast Facts:

Also Called: Farm Laborer, Farmer, Field Irrigation Worker, Gardener, Greenhouse Worker, Grower, Harvester, Nursery Worker, Orchard Worker, Picker

Employment: 526,300 employees

Median Annual Wage: $14.25 hourly, $29,60 annually

Education Needed: No high school diploma or GED required

Fastest-Growing Occupation:

Agricultural Equipment Operators

- Load and unload crops or containers of materials manually or using conveyors, hand trucks, forklifts, or transfer augers
- Mix specified materials or chemicals and dump solutions, powders, or seeds into planter or sprayer machinery
- Manipulate controls to set, activate, and adjust mechanisms on machinery

Fast Facts:

Employment: 65,000 employees

Annual Openings: 1,170

Median Annual Wage: $17.48 hourly, $36,360 annually

Education Needed: No high school diploma or GED required

Highest Wage Occupation:

Food Scientists and Technologists

- Inspect food processing areas to ensure compliance with government regulations and standards for sanitation, safety, quality, and waste management
- Check raw ingredients for maturity or stability for processing and finished products for safety, quality, and nutritional value
- Develop new or improved ways of preserving, processing, packaging, storing, and delivering foods, using knowledge of chemistry, microbiology, and other sciences
- Test new products for flavor, texture, color, nutritional content, and adherence to government and industry standards

Fast Facts:

Employment: 15,000 employees
Annual Openings: 1,700
Median Annual wage: $37.66 hourly, $78,340 annually
Education Needed: Doctoral degree
Other: People interested in this work like activities that include ideas, thinking, and figuring things out.

Occupation Where Most Work for Themselves:

Fishing and Hunting Workers

- Patrol trap lines or nets to inspect settings, remove catch, and reset or relocate traps
- Obtain permission from landowners to hunt or trap on their land
- Travel on foot, by vehicle, or by equipment such as boats, snowmobiles, helicopters, snowshoes, or skis to reach hunting areas
- Steer vessels and operate navigational instruments
- Skin quarry, using knives, and stretch pelts on frames to be cured

Fast Facts:

Employment: 32,300 employees
Annual Openings: 530
Median Annual Wage: $14.36 hourly, $29,860 annually
Education Needed: May require a high school diploma

7-2 Essential Question Reflection

So, let us revisit our essential question:

Which opportunities may be right for you?

Based on what you learned in this section, what 2 or 3 opportunities are the most interesting? Explain your answer.

Case Study: Veterinary Technologists & Technicians

Also called: Certified/Licensed Veterinary Technician, Veterinary Technician (Vet Tech)

What do they do?

- Perform medical tests in a laboratory environment for use in the treatment and diagnosis of diseases in animals
- Prepare vaccines and serums for prevention of diseases
- Prepare tissue samples, take blood samples, and execute laboratory tests, such as urinalysis and blood counts
- Clean and sterilize instruments and materials and maintain equipment and machines
- Assist a veterinarian during surgery

What would you do?

- Administer anesthesia to animals, under the direction of a veterinarian, and monitor animals' responses to anesthetics so that dosages can be adjusted
- Care for and monitor the condition of animals recovering from surgery
- Maintain controlled drug inventory and related log books

What do you need to know?

Health
Medicine and dentistry

Business
Customer service

Arts and Humanities
English language

Math and Science
Biology

What skills do you need?

Basic Skills
Listen to others, do not interrupt, and ask effective questions
Think about the pros and cons of different ways to solve a problem

Problem Solving
Notice a problem and figure out the best way to solve it

What abilities must you be good at?

Verbal
Communicate by speaking

Listen to and understand what people say

Ideas and Logic
Make general rules or come up with answers based on lots of detailed information

Use rules to solve problems

Hand and Finger Use
Hold or move items with your hands

Keep your arm or hand steady

Attention
Pay attention to something without being distracted

Who does well in this occupation?

People interested in this work like activities that include practical, hands-on problems and solutions.

They do well at jobs that need:
Attention to detail

Stress tolerance

Dependability

Integrity

Adaptability/flexibility

Cooperation

What educational level is needed?

- Associate degree and sometimes a certification

Practice 7-2

Skills Practice

Agriculture, Food, & Natural Resources workers must sometimes analyze graphics to identify trends. They might search for data that has increased or decreased over time. A farmer or farm manager may need to interpret historical price trends to determine what crops to plant. Being able to identify common trends from several pieces of data can help with a variety of jobs in this industry. **Practice this skill!**

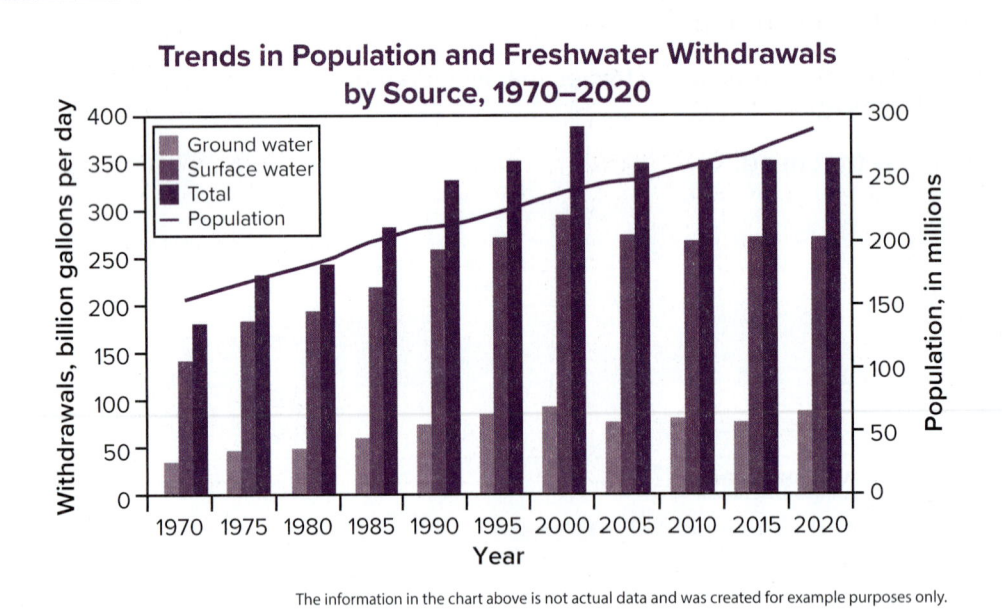

Trends in Population and Freshwater Withdrawals by Source, 1970–2020

Legend: Ground water, Surface water, Total, Population

The information in the chart above is not actual data and was created for example purposes only.

1. You are a conservation analyst for a nonprofit conservation agency and are studying how water is used (withdrawn from available water supplies) in the United States. What trend do you see in total water withdrawals?

    A. They increased steadily between 1970 and 2020.

    B. They increased steadily between 1970 and 2000.

    C. They decreased steadily between 1970 and 1980.

    D. They remained about the same from 1990 to 1995.

    E. They decreased from 1990 to 1995.

2. During which time period did the United States see a decrease in total water withdrawals?

    A. between 1970 and 1975

    B. between 1975 and 1980

    C. between 1980 and 1985

    D. between 2000 and 2005

    E. between 2015 and 2020

184 Chapter 7 • Agriculture, Food, & Natural Resources

Skills Practice

When reviewing workplace graphics, it may be necessary to compare trends in one or more graphics. A forest and conservation technician, for example, may need to review graphics to compare the growth, varieties of vegetation, and conditions of different forests. Workers must know how different graphics relate to each other and be able to compare information and trends within them. **Practice this skill!**

May						
Sunday	Monday	Tuesday	Wednesday	Thursday	Friday	Saturday
	1	2	3 Saplings arrive after noon	4	5	6
7	8	9 Prune trees- English Walled garden	10 Put up protective barriers for seedings – east circle garden	11	12	13

Worker Name	Availability
Jacob	Monday, Friday and Weekends
Suzanne	Weekends only
Rene	Tuesday – Thursday
Milo	Weekends only
Donna	Tuesday – Friday
Hector	Monday – Tuesday

3. As a senior botanist at a state park, you supervise several workers who assist in maintaining the park's plants. This week you will need two workers to set up protective barriers for more than 100 seedlings that you have started. Which workers are available on the day that you have scheduled the task?

   A. Jacob and Suzanne
   B. Suzanne and Rene
   C. Rene and Jacob
   D. Donna and Rene
   E. Donna and Hector

4. Next week, you have a shipment of 300 tree saplings arriving. The saplings will take three people (plus you) two consecutive days to plant. You want the same people to work both days. On which days will the trees be planted, and who will you hire to plant them?

   A. May 4, 5; Rene, Donna, Hector
   B. May 5, 6; Jacob, Suzanne, Donna
   C. May 6, 7; Jacob, Suzanne, Milo
   D. May 7, 8; Jacob, Suzanne, Hector
   E. May 8, 9; Jacob, Rene, Hector

To access more problems that will help you grow professional skills and are real-world examples in Agriculture, Food, & Natural Resources, go online.

7-3 Building a Career in Agriculture, Food, & Natural Resources

If a career in Agriculture, Food, & Natural Resources interests you, consider what you will need to do to achieve it. Many attractive options require advanced degrees for which you want to be prepared. There may be several steps that will help you reach your ultimate goal. Entry-level positions often lead to greater opportunity, so don't overlook starting positions.

Purchasing agents, for example, usually begin in an entry-level job working under an experienced purchasing agent. In that position, they learn about the goods that their firm purchases and about the industry. After a few years of training, they may be ready to move to a more independent position. Some firms require them to obtain continuing education credits and certification.

7-3 Essential Question

As you read this section, keep this question in mind:

How can I match my skills & interests with the right job?

Are You More Interested in Working With Data, People, or Things?

Agricultural educators work primarily with people. Miners work mostly with things. When planning your career path, consider what balance of data, people, and things you want in a career.

Careers That Involve Working With Data

Working with words, ideas, concepts, and numbers are ways you can work with data. Other examples of working with data include taking and analyzing readings from a global positioning system (GPS) receiver, planning when and where to plant crops, or scheduling the steps required to perform veterinary surgery.

Agriculture, food, and natural resources workers whose jobs focus on data include farm managers, soil and plant scientists, researchers, and mining engineers. A soil and plant scientist, for example, may be hired to analyze the soil in a particular area to see whether it is suitable for planting a particular crop. This type of job requires conducting research, running tests, and collecting and analyzing data.

Careers That Involve Working With People and Animals

Some jobs in Agriculture, Food, & Natural Resources focus on relationships. This can include relationships with both people and animals. Examples of working with people and animals include explaining to a cat's owner how to administer medicine, breeding racehorses, and explaining the natural features of an area to park visitors. Working with people requires strong communication skills. Working with animals requires empathy—the ability to understand another living thing's feelings—and the ability to recognize nonverbal signs.

Many Agriculture, Food, & Natural Resources jobs enable you to spend a great deal of time working with others. Managers and crew leaders must effectively supervise and lead teams of workers. Operating farms, mines, fishing vessels, and timber companies requires teamwork. All team members must be able to follow directions and communicate ideas to other members.

Careers That Involve Working With Things

Working with things in Agriculture, Food, & Natural Resources, involves designing, creating, using, and repairing machines, tools, and structures. Examples of working with things include setting up and operating logging machinery, inspecting crops, and processing fish.

Many careers in Agriculture, Food, & Natural Resources involve working primarily with things. Food processing workers, miners, oil and gas production workers, and loggers spend a majority of their day working with tools, machines, and other equipment, as well as natural resources. Farm equipment operators are responsible for handling and monitoring large equipment.

7-3 Essential Question Reflection

So, let us revisit our essential question:

How can I match my skills & interests with the right job?

Based on what you learned in this section, please answer this question in detail.

7-4 Education and Training for Agriculture, Food, & Natural Resources Opportunities

For some jobs in Agriculture, Food, & Natural Resources, it is necessary to have education and experience to perform what is needed. Other jobs require little or no formal training. It is important to pay attention to the requirements for the jobs you are interested in.

7-4 Essential Question

As you read this section, keep this question in mind:

What training & education is needed for a job in Agriculture, Food, & Natural Resources?

Training and Education for Agriculture, Food, & Natural Resources

Each career has a different level of training needed to succeed in Agriculture, Food, & Natural Resources. These jobs can be grouped into three areas, based on the level of training required – little or no training, some training, and advanced training.

Jobs Requiring Little or No Training

Many entry-level jobs in Agriculture, Food, & Natural Resources require little or no formal training. For example, farmworkers, fishers, and meatpacking workers are trained after they are hired.

Jobs Requiring Some Training

Many jobs in Agriculture, Food, & Natural Resources require specialized training. If you're interested in working as a veterinary technician, mining technician, or farm labor contractor, you'll need to pursue specialized degrees or certification.

Additional education also gives you a chance to learn more about this industry. Technical colleges offer associate degree programs in such fields as agricultural science, agricultural economics, and mining.

Other programs may combine study with worksite training. Trade associations, or organizations representing a specific industry or type of job, often offer certification programs. These programs provide thorough training for a specific occupation. When trainees complete the programs, they are certified as trained professionals. Obtaining certification might require a minimum number of hours on the job and a minimum score on a standardized test.

Special certification exists in many Agriculture, Food, & Natural Resources careers. For example, the Retail Bakers of America offers certification programs for bakers. This credential shows that a baker has the knowledge required to work in a bakery. Some workers, such as captains of large fishing vessels, must pass approved courses. Other occupations require licenses. Specific requirements for licenses vary, but they all require knowledge of the trade and of relevant laws and regulations.

Obtaining an associate degree or certification can help you get a job and prosper in your career. For more information about such programs, contact trade and professional associations related to the field you are interested in. You may also be able to obtain information from community and technical colleges in your area.

Jobs Requiring Advanced Training

Jobs in Agriculture, Food, & Natural Resources that require advanced training usually involve management, engineering, science, or complex farm operations. Some of these jobs require at least a bachelor's degree. For other jobs, workers must earn a master's or doctoral degree. Most of these jobs also require several years of work experience in the field. For some jobs, the workers must obtain a license.

Veterinarians, for example, must have a bachelor's degree as well as a Doctor of Veterinary Medicine (DVM) degree. They earn that degree at a college of veterinary medicine. All 50 states and the District of Columbia also require these professionals to obtain a license in order to practice. States do not recognize licenses issued by other states. As a result, a veterinarian who wishes to practice in two states must obtain a license from both.

A bachelor's degree in forestry is required for a career as a conservation scientist and forester. Most foresters who teach or conduct research have a doctoral degree. Many land-grant universities have schools or colleges of agriculture that give degrees in this field. Seven states require a license to practice forestry. To obtain the license, foresters must complete a minimum amount of training and pass an examination.

Table 7.3: Training Required for Agriculture, Food, & Natural Resources Jobs

Level of Training	Job Title
Little or No Training	Agricultural Equipment Operators Butchers and Meat Cutters Farmworkers Food Batchmakers Logging Equipment Operators Nonfarm Animal Caretakers Nursery Workers Veterinary Assistants
Some Training or Preparation	Agricultural Inspectors Animal Breeders Farmers and Ranchers Forest and Conservation Technicians Gas Plant Operators Precision Agricultural Technicians Recycling Coordinators Veterinary Technicians
Considerable Training or Preparation	Animal Scientists Environmental Engineers Fish and Game Wardens Food Scientists and Technologists Foresters Veterinarians

Agriculture, Food, & Natural Resources Skill Standards

Job-specific skill standards have been developed for many careers in Agriculture, Food, & Natural Resources. Workers who show they have mastered specific skills can often gain certification or licensing. The American Society of Farm Managers and Rural Appraisers offers accreditation for four jobs, including farm managers and agricultural consultants. The Society of American Foresters has a Certified Forester program.

Loggers can be certified through programs such as New York's Trained Logger Certification (TLC) or Maine's Master Logger Certification (MLC). To earn certification, a candidate may need to pass a written exam. Some programs call for candidates to pass a practical exam showing they can do the work required.

Professional Skills

Academic or job-specific skills are different than professional skills. Professional skills can be learned inside and outside the classroom and are transferable from job to job. They can also be transferred from career to career. As such, developing these skills in one job will make you more marketable in other jobs.

Communication Skills Good communication skills lead to productive relationships among coworkers. In this industry, managers need good communication skills so they can give instructions, and other workers need to be able to explain problems. Those who work as educators, such as recycling coordinators or extension specialists, must be able to explain ideas clearly.

Listening Skills Listening skills are vital to workers. For instance, loggers and food batchmakers must pay careful attention to safety instructions. To make wise decisions, purchasing agents must listen carefully to what suppliers say about the products they sell.

Problem-Solving Skills Employers value workers who can spot problems and take steps to solve them. Mining engineers might be called on to solve problems in digging the mine. Supervisors often have to settle differences that arise between workers. Food engineers may have to solve difficult scientific problems.

Technology Skills Workers with solid technology skills often earn more and have greater success than workers without them. Even traditionally "low-tech" industries like farming now make use of advanced technology. Cattle farmers, for example, might use a GPS receiver to keep track of their herds. A greenhouse manager may need to select, install, and operate equipment to track levels of humidity and temperature.

Decision-Making Skills The ability to gather and analyze information rapidly will serve you well in your career. Many workers need to think clearly under pressure. Veterinarians are sometimes faced with life-or-death situations that require quick decisions. Miners and loggers face many hazards on the job. They must think on their feet during accidents and emergencies.

Organizing and Planning Skills Planning calls for the ability to set goals and to see the sequence of steps needed to achieve those goals. Vegetable farmers have to make plans for their fields well in advance of planting time. They must order seeds and other supplies so they will be available when needed. Later in the season, these farmers contract with the laborers they will need at harvest time.

Teamwork Skills Teamwork is key to all jobs in Agriculture, Food, & Natural Resources. All levels of workers are required to work together to get a job done. Commercial divers depend on a ship's crew for their survival underwater. Oil and gas drilling teams must work together to drill a well properly.

Social Skills Social interaction makes for a more enjoyable and productive work atmosphere. It also presents the opportunity to learn. Social skills are important for all workers in this industry—from veterinary intern to processing plant manager.

Adaptability Skills Job descriptions, work environments, and methods are constantly changing. New technology, economic changes, and changing customer tastes can require workers to be able to adapt to new materials, techniques, or styles. Be ready to acquire new skills. Use change as a chance to increase your employability.

7-4 Essential Question Reflection

So, let us revisit our essential question:

What training & education is needed for a job in Agriculture, Food, & Natural Resources?

Based on what you learned in this section, please answer this question in detail.

Practice 7-4

Skills Practice

When reading documents, such as procedures for sorting materials at a recycling plant, workers in the Agriculture, Food, & Natural Resources industry need to be able to identify the main idea. They must also find details supporting the main idea. The main idea tells what the document is about. Details provide more information that helps explain the main idea. **Practice this skill!**

PLANT SAFETY STANDARDS

According to statistics from the Occupational Safety and Health Administration (OSHA), 15 percent of all accidental deaths in meat processing plants are the result of slips, trips, and falls. These accidents are due to slippery floor surfaces, workers wearing inappropriate footwear, or recklessness when moving about the processing plants.

All Food Safety and Inspection Services (FSIS) workplaces are subject to OSHA's requirements for walking and working surfaces, which include the following:

- Wear skid-resistant shoes; replace all shoes with worn tread.
- Do not run in FSIS processing plants.
- Use handrails when available, especially when ascending or descending stairs.
- Use extra caution when walking on slippery surfaces; shuffling is recommended.

1. You have just been hired to work in a meatpacking plant. Before you begin working at the plant, you must fully understand the safety guidelines. What are major causes of accidents in meatpacking plants?

   A. forklift and heavy equipment mishaps
   B. hands and feet trapped in machinery
   C. slips, trips, and falls
   D. electrocution incidents
   E. explosions and fires

2. Based on the information in the guidelines, what clothing is appropriate for your workplace?

   A. warm, loose-fitting clothing
   B. warm, tight-fitting clothing
   C. layered clothing
   D. skid-resistant shoes
   E. leather-soled shoes

Skills Practice

Many jobs in the Agriculture, Food, & Natural Resources industry require workers to calculate costs and discounts. For example, an animal health products distributor might need to calculate charges and discounts for clients. **Practice this skill!**

3. As a grain farmer, you use your tractor constantly. Today is Saturday, and your tractor has broken down. You call a farm equipment agency to have them send out a mechanic. Normally, the agency charges $70/hour for the mechanic's time. Because it is Saturday, however, the agency charges a 50% markup for the mechanic's time. It takes 5 hours to repair your tractor. How much do you pay the agency for the mechanic's work?

   A. $425
   B. $497.50
   C. $500
   D. $512.50
   E. $525

4. You are an apple orchard manager, and you sell your apples at a local produce market. The Fuji apples cost $30 per bushel. Honeycrisp apples are a premium item and are much more expensive. A half-bushel of Honeycrisp apples sells for 15% more than a full bushel of Fujis. Your customer buys 2 bushels of Fuji apples and 1 full bushel of Honeycrisp apples. How much do you charge your customer, in all?

   A. $125
   B. $126
   C. $127
   D. $128
   E. $129

To access more problems that will help you grow professional skills and are real-world examples in Agriculture, Food, & Natural Resources, go online.

7-5 Working Conditions in the Agriculture, Food, & Natural Resources Industry

Understanding the work environment, hazards, and benefits of a job will help you make an informed decision.

> **7-5 Essential Question**
>
> **As you read this section, keep this question in mind:**
>
> *What are typical work environments in Agriculture, Food, & Natural Resources?*

Work Environment

The factors that make up and affect a worker's health and satisfaction on the job are known as the work environment. The physical surroundings, physical activities required to perform the job, and the working hours are factors that make up a job's work environment.

Physical Environment

The physical work environment in Agriculture, Food, & Natural Resources varies greatly by job and by setting. Some workers enjoy a beautiful outdoor environment in a forest or on a tree farm. Others—such as fishers—must work outdoors in extreme heat or cold and other bad weather. Still others work indoors with animals in a laboratory or a clinic. Some miners work underground in dark, damp, and often hot tunnels. Many in the food processing industry work in hot, noisy factories. Managers usually work in offices, though they often visit the field to check progress.

New equipment, safety precautions, and other advances have cut down on dangerous and unpleasant conditions in the industry. Conditions on farms, in mines, and at other work sites have improved over time. Nevertheless, there are still dangers that many workers in this industry face every day.

Table 7.4: Working Conditions in Agriculture, Food, & Natural Resources

Career Path	Working Conditions
Plant Systems	• Farmers, supervisors of work crews, equipment operators, and farm laborers often work every day during planting and harvesting seasons. • Work may be seasonal; many people in the industry must find other kinds of work during slow seasons.
Animal Systems	• Veterinarians work in clinics and also in the field. They may be called on at any hour to handle emergencies. • Workers on dairy farms must tend to animals every day. • Many workers in this path spend much of their time outdoors in all kinds of weather.
Agribusiness Systems	• Financial managers carry a heavy responsibility, and they may work as many as 60 hours a week. • Purchasing agents and buyers work in offices. They often work overtime.
Food Products and Processing Systems	• Food processing plants are often noisy, and workers may have little contact with other workers. • Workers in retail stores may have contact with customers. • Many workers in food manufacturing plants spend much of their work hours standing.
Natural Resources Systems	• Loggers face many dangers, including falling trees and branches, powerful saws, poisonous plants, and wild animals. • Fishers who work on large ocean-going vessels may be at sea for long periods of time. They usually have to share small, tight living spaces with other crew members.
Environmental Service Systems	• Occupational health and safety specialists work in offices, but they may travel to inspect worksites. • Frequent travel may be required of recycling coordinators, who teach local groups about recycling.
Power, Structural, and Technical Systems	• Equipment maintenance technicians may work in cramped spaces and in extreme hot or cold.

Source: *U.S. Department of Labor*

Work Hours

Work hours for careers in Agriculture, Food, & Natural Resources vary greatly. Because some businesses operate around the clock, shift work is important in this industry. Shift work divides the day into blocks of time, generally into eight-hour blocks. Shift work allows workers to select hours to meet their needs. Shift work is common in kennels, veterinary practices, food processing plants, large farms, and fishing vessels. Some landscaping and groundskeeping companies may require workers to work morning and evening shifts.

A relatively new trend in many workplaces is flextime. With flextime, workers choose the hours and the days they work, if they meet a required total number of hours for the week. A worker may work ten hours on four days a week or six-and-a-half hours on six days. Workers can adjust their hours to suit personal needs. Flextime is especially convenient for workers with young children or other family commitments. In this industry, veterinary technicians, agricultural scientists, and food processing workers might be offered flextime.

The number of hours worked per week varies in this industry. Most employees in food processing work about 40 hours a week. Many workers in mining or oil and gas extraction may have 12-hour days and often work as many as 50 hours a week. After working several very long days, they may have a couple of days off. With some jobs, longer workdays or workweeks are seasonal. Farmers and farmworkers, for instance, put in extra hours at planting and harvesting times. They may even work seven days a week during these times.

Essential Physical Activities

Many jobs in this industry require that workers be in good physical condition. Heavy lifting is a part of most Agriculture jobs. It is also vital that workers be trained to handle heavy equipment properly. Many jobs are strenuous at times, and most workers are required to stand, walk, stoop, or bend regularly during the day.

Agriculture, Food, & Natural Resources workers should be skilled with their hands as well. Farmworkers must be able to pick crops quickly, as some are paid by the amount they harvest. Some workers in food processing must be able to cut and slice quickly and accurately. Veterinarians must be good with their hands because they perform surgery.

Good vision is a must for many workers in the Agriculture, Food, & Natural Resources industry as well. Fishing vessel captains, for example, must be able to see potential dangers in the water at night and in foggy conditions. Good eyesight is also essential for workers who operate heavy equipment and for those who read thermometers, gauges, charts, and meters.

Hazards and Environmental Dangers

Mining, fishing, logging, and farming can be dangerous. These tasks involve working underground, at sea, with toxic agricultural chemicals, or with heavy equipment or blades. All these jobs require thorough training and good common sense. Because of these risks, both workers and managers are required to have safety training.

Federal laws and rules set workplace safety standards aimed at preventing accidents. Other laws ensure that accident victims receive help. OSHA sets job standards and inspects job sites. OSHA inspectors visit and review companies to ensure that working processes and conditions are safe. More than two dozen states also run job safety programs.

To prevent injury, workers must follow all safety procedures. It is recommended that workers take breaks to rest overworked muscles and vary their tasks when possible. Workers should notify their managers if they feel pain or stiffness.

Workers also need to be aware of the presence of chemicals that are dangerous to touch or breathe. Safety shoes, gloves, and respirators must be made available to all workers who are exposed to dangerous substances.

Airborne debris, chemicals, and tools or materials with sharp edges are things workers may be exposed to, and therefore goggles are needed. Showers and eye baths should be available to workers who are at risk for eye damage.

As time moves on and technology continues to change the field, adjustments and updates to work equipment and processes continue to make workplaces safer and more comfortable. The study of creating and adjusting work equipment and processes for increased safety and comfortability is ergonomics. A main goal of ergonomics is to reduce the occurrence of musculoskeletal disorders (MSDs).

These disorders include any injury to muscles, nerves, tendons, joints, cartilage, and spinal discs. MSDs do not include those disorders caused by an accident, such as a fall or a motor vehicle accident. A common MSD is carpal tunnel syndrome, a swelling of tendons in the wrist, which can result from frequent repetition of a task using the hands. Fish processors, loggers, and crop workers can suffer from carpal tunnel syndrome because they repeat the same motions hundreds of times in a day. The federal government and state governments have set rules for workplace design to help prevent the occurrence of MSDs.

7-5 Essential Question Reflection

So, let us revisit our essential question:

What are typical work environments in Agriculture, Food, & Natural Resources?

Based on what you learned in this section, please answer this question in detail.

7-6 Trends in Agriculture, Food, & Natural Resources

Humans have been growing and processing food and working with natural resources for thousands of years. Yet the Agriculture, Food, & Natural Resources industry is constantly changing. For example more consumers are demanding organic foods, and new equipment requires more highly trained workers.

> **7-6 Essential Question**
>
> **As you read this section, keep this question in mind:**
>
> *What factors affect trends in Agriculture, Food, & Natural Resources?*

Technology in the Industry

Loggers once cut down trees with hand tools. Miners once hauled coal out of mines manually. Fishing vessel captains once navigated with only a compass. Today, farmers work with computers. Geologists use sound imaging to look for possible sources of oil and gas inside the earth.

Technology in Plant Systems, Animal Systems, and Agribusiness Systems

Computers are becoming more and more important to many fields in agriculture, food, and natural resources. Analyzing crop yields (the amount of crops harvested), navigating ships, and even milking cows can all be done with computers. Computers are so widely used that farmers need several kinds of monitors. A new communications standard called the ISOBUS has been adopted by the International Standards Organization. With this standard, various monitors can share information with one another.

Another major change in the industry is precision farming. This practice means adapting farming to the different varieties of soil in different sections of a farm. Precision farming allows farmers to boost production. One method of precision farming involves using sensors on farm equipment that can test soil and adjust the amount of fertilizer applied.

Remote sensing also helps farmers. In remote sensing, sensors on airplanes or satellites gather information about Earth's surface and atmosphere. The data enables farmers to gather precise information about their land and crops. For example, farmers can use it to analyze soil types or to measure the surface temperature of their crops.

Some farmers are using GPS technology. GPS receivers allow users to precisely locate themselves or something else. Crop farmers use GPS to guide equipment over their fields. Livestock farmers use it to track their herds. A fishing captain can use GPS signals to chart the ship's course and navigate more accurately.

Biotechnology is another growing trend in food production. This term refers to a number of scientific techniques. Genetic engineering is used to create or improve living things. Genetic engineering changes the characteristics of living things by altering their genetic makeup. Foods changed in this way are known as genetically modified (GM) foods. Genetic engineering is being used to make food plants resistant to insects, herbicides (weed killers), disease, drought, and cold. Some foods, such as rice, have been genetically engineered to contain additional vitamins and minerals. GM foods are controversial because many people remain concerned that the foods have not been tested enough.

Technology in Food Products and Processing Systems

An area of research in food processing involves nanotechnology. Nanotechnology uses extremely tiny bits of matter to make machines that do useful work but are microscopic in size. Researchers are using this approach to make sensors that can tell when food is spoiling.

Another area of research is trying to find new, safer additives. Many processed foods have chemicals added to them. These chemicals are used to give the food a certain color or a longer shelf life. Some additives have been found to be unhealthy. Researchers are working to find replacements.

Technology in Natural Resources Systems

Seismic prospecting has brought a huge change in the oil and gas industry by decreasing the risk in locating underground oil and gas reserves. This process measures how long it takes sound waves to move to the earth's surface from underground formations. The data is analyzed by a computer, which creates a model of the underground formations. This model shows where the oil and gas are most likely located and pinpoints the best areas to drill. Large oil and gas companies use seismic prospecting to test unexplored areas.

Mining equipment now includes computer controls that help complete tasks more precisely. Lasers are used to make cutting more accurate.

Contemporary Issues in the Agriculture, Food, & Natural Resources Industry

Every year more resources are needed to feed, clothe, and shelter the world's growing population. As cities expand and open land is used for housing, less land is available for farming and forestry. Intensive agriculture, which requires large amounts of money, labor, and chemicals, meets the need by producing more and more food each year. However, chemical fertilizers and pesticides may harm the environment. To address these concerns, workers in Agriculture, Food, & Natural Resources are developing new ways to increase production while protecting the environment.

Sustainability in the Agriculture, Food, & Natural Resources Industry

As citizens become more concerned about the environment, sustainable resource use has become an important goal. Sustainability refers to economic activity that does not harm the environment. Sustainable farming aims to improve agriculture while balancing profitability, the conservation of resources, and people's quality of life. Methods include planting a greater variety of crops and reusing crop leftovers and manure for fertilizers. Another sustainability activity is using crop remains as a source of energy. Plant material used in this way is called biomass.

Organic farming is one type of sustainable farming. The goal is to make soil, plants, animals, and people as healthy and productive as possible. This approach requires the use of all-natural products in crop and livestock production. Animals must be fed organic feed, and they may not be treated with hormones, which are often used to promote muscle growth. Foods certified as organic must meet strict United States Department of Agriculture (USDA) standards. Organic farming requires more worker hours than traditional farming. As a result, organic food often costs more than traditional foods. However, many customers are willing to pay this higher price.

Biodiversity

Biodiversity, or biological diversity, refers to the variety of living things. According to the California Academy of Sciences Biodiversity Resource Center in San Francisco, more than 10,000 species go extinct each year. Destruction of natural habitats by humans is the main cause.

Tropical rainforests are one focus of concern. Though they account for only about 7 percent of the earth's surface, these forests contain about 50 to 80 percent of all species. Yet millions of acres of rainforest are cut down each year. Scientists estimate that a quarter of the world's diverse species could be extinct within two or three decades. Increasingly, scientists in the Natural Resources Systems path are working with environmental groups and government agencies to preserve the earth's life-forms.

Mine Reclamation

Mine reclamation is the process of restoring land damaged by mining so that it can be safely used again. The U.S. Department of the Interior's Office of Surface Mining Reclamation and Enforcement (OSM) is responsible for this restoration. OSM verifies that mining companies are following safety procedures. It also makes sure that the land is restored once companies are finished mining an area. The OSM protects the public from the hazards of abandoned mines, such as underground fires, landslides, and the seeping of acid into the water supply.

Reclaimed mines can be used for many purposes. Some are planted with native plants and turned back into wilderness areas. Many unused mines are being preserved as habitat for bats. Bats are useful to agriculture because they help with pest control by consuming large numbers of insects.

The Economy and the Agriculture, Food, & Natural Resources Industry

The Agriculture, Food, & Natural Resources industry is, in some ways, less affected by conditions in the economy than other industries. People need to eat, and they need natural resources that provide energy.

The United States is a major exporter of agricultural products to other countries. The most exported goods are food grains, oil seeds, and wheat. The United States exports products all over the world. Japan is the main market for corn and wheat, China for soybeans, and Russia for poultry meat.

As a result of globalization (the worldwide link between people), workers in Agriculture, Food, & Natural Resources may work on projects with people in other countries. Opportunities for overseas travel and relocation exist for upper-level employees in the industry. Many groups working to save natural areas, for example, have projects all around the world. Many mining and oil and gas extraction companies have divisions in other countries.

7-6 Essential Question Reflection

So, let us revisit our essential question:

What factors affect trends in Agriculture, Food, & Natural Resources?

Based on what you learned in this section, please answer this question in detail.

Chapter 8

Government & Public Administration

Chapter Topics

8-1 Government & Public Administration Today

8-2 Government & Public Administration Jobs

8-3 Building a Career in Government & Public Administration

8-4 Education and Training for Government & Public Administration Opportunities

8-5 Working Conditions in the Government & Public Administration Industry

8-6 Trends in Government & Public Administration

Essential Questions

By the end of the chapter, you will be able to answer the following questions:

- **8-1** What types of opportunities are available in Government & Public Administration?
- **8-2** Which opportunities may be right for you?
- **8-3** How can I match my skills & interests with the right job?
- **8-4** What training & education is needed for a job in Government & Public Administration?
- **8-5** What are typical work environments in Government & Public Administration?
- **8-6** What factors affect trends in Government & Public Administration?

8-1 Government & Public Administration Today

Government is the institution that maintains social order, provides public services, and enforces laws. Public Administration is the management of the administrative structures of government.

Workers in this industry keep our highways, courts, and schools running smoothly. Public service employees teach our children. They deliver mail. They give assistance to people with disabilities and people who are retired. They work to make heat, electricity, and water available in homes and workplaces. They keep people safe.

8-1 Essential Question

As you read this section, keep this question in mind:

What types of opportunities are available in Government & Public Administration?

Career Journeys in Government & Public Administration

There are seven major paths along which your journey in Government & Public Administration might be shaped. People commonly move into and out of different paths. Each path contains a group of careers requiring similar skills as well as similar certifications or education. This industry is divided into seven main career paths:

- Governance
- National Security
- Foreign Service
- Planning
- Revenue and Taxation
- Regulation
- Public Management and Administration

Governance

Workers in the Governance career path include governors, mayors, and their staffs. They also include legislators, legislative aides, and legislative policy researchers. Legislators include U.S. senators and representatives; state senators and representatives; and county, city, and town lawmakers.

Legislators propose new laws and make changes to existing laws. To prepare legislative proposals, known as bills, officials must do research. They study reports and consider input from citizens, interest groups, and lobbyists. Legislators also vote on proposed budgets and tax increases. They help choose people to fill appointed positions in the government. The U.S. Senate, for example, must confirm the president's choices to head the cabinet departments.

Legislative aides and policy researchers work with government executives. They help executives and legislators organize and conduct research.

National Security

The National Security path is made up of the U.S. Department of Defense, which includes all branches of the armed forces. The three largest branches of the U.S. military are the Army, the Navy, and the Air Force. The other three branches of the military are the Coast Guard, Space Force, and the Marine Corps.

All the branches of the armed forces have both officers and enlisted personnel. Officers, who usually have college degrees, are the leaders and managers of the armed forces. Enlisted personnel carry out a huge range of necessary duties. Enlisted personnel often have specific job titles, such as health care specialist. Military personnel repair vehicles and equipment, provide medical and social services, keep records, fight fires, and cook and serve food.

The Department of Defense (DOD) works with intelligence agencies to safeguard national security. The gathering of intelligence is a crucial part of national security. Intelligence is knowledge of another nation's activities, plans, or technologies. The U.S. Intelligence Community is a large group of agencies and organizations. Its members include the Central Intelligence Agency (CIA), the National Security Agency (NSA), and the Federal Bureau of Investigation (FBI).

The Intelligence Community warns military leaders of possible immediate crises and informs them of long-term dangers. It works to counter terrorist threats and drug trafficking. It keeps watch for foreign bribery, espionage (spying), and other illegal activities. Intelligence workers include military intelligence officers and specialists, intelligence and counterintelligence agents, and intelligence analysts.

Foreign Service

The Foreign Service is a group of professionals who represent the United States in foreign countries. The U.S. Department of State oversees this group. The Foreign Service helps carry out U.S. foreign policy in the countries that the United States has diplomatic relations with. It safeguards U.S. citizens and their interests in other countries. The Foreign Service employs people for diplomatic missions and people who work in embassies and consulates around the world. An ambassador is a diplomatic agent appointed to represent the government. A consul is an official who represents U.S. economic interests in a foreign country.

The Foreign Service path is divided into two main job groups:

Foreign Service officers are the chief U.S. diplomatic and consular personnel. The U.S. Senate must confirm appointments to the Foreign Service Officer Corps.

Foreign Service specialists provide important technical, support, or administrative services. They may be engineers, scientists, communications specialists, security officers, clerical staff, or information management technicians.

Planning

The Planning career path refers to drawing up guidelines for how land in a particular area should be used. The purpose of planning is to make sure that states, counties, cities, and neighborhoods are developed in a well-planned manner. To be successful, planners must balance business interests, quality of life, environmental protection, and recreational use of space.

Part of the planning process involves collecting information about people living in an area. Census clerks and census enumerators are responsible for collecting and analyzing population data for a particular state, county, or city. The chief of vital statistics keeps records of the births, deaths, marriages, and divorces. Accurate analysis of data helps planners create communities that serve the needs of local populations. Business leaders and governments officials must work together to plan the economic development in an area.

Revenue and Taxation

Federal, state, and local governments get most of their income from taxes. The money collected pays for government programs and services. Federal taxes include personal income tax and corporate income tax. State and local governments receive money from individual income tax and corporate income tax, too. They also collect sales tax, property tax, and fees such as building permits.

The Internal Revenue Service (IRS) is a branch of the U.S Department of the Treasury. It is the tax collection agency for the federal government. It is responsible for collecting and reviewing the tax returns of taxpayers. Individual states also have revenue departments responsible for collecting state taxes.

Government accountants and auditors maintain government accounting records. They audit private businesses and individuals who owe taxes. At the federal, state, and local levels, accountants make sure that tax payments are received and spent according to the law. Tax examiners, collectors, and revenue agents are responsible for reviewing tax returns and collecting overdue taxes.

Regulation

Regulation is the process of enforcing the laws and government rules. Regulation is intended to ensure that businesses meet certain standards. For example, it ensures that businesses pay their workers at least a minimum wage and that they sell safe products. It enforces rules related to toxic waste. Careers in the Regulation path include health and safety regulators, environmental regulators, communications regulators, and utilities regulators.

Regulatory agencies need technicians and scientists to perform tests. Environmental and pollution control technicians, for example, perform tests to monitor pollutants in the air, water, and soil. Environmental health technicians work to ensure that food, water, air, and soil meet government standards.

Public Management & Administration

Employees in the Public Management & Administration path seek to apply principles of management similar to those used in private companies to public organizations. A city manager is similar to the chief executive officer (CEO) in a business. Members of a city council can be compared to members of a board of directors.

Public administration workers include employees of the city, the county, the chamber of commerce, and the court system. Workers who manage public programs, like librarians, postal service workers, social workers, and human resources personnel, are also a part of the Public Management & Administration career path.

Government & Public Administration Future Outlook

According to the Bureau of Labor Statistics (BLS), the employment outlook for Government & Public Administration is fair. Employment in state and local governments is expected to increase by 8 percent between 2021 and 2031 because some public services jobs will transfer from the federal government to the state and local levels. This is slightly lower than the 11 percent average growth expected across all industries. Employment in the federal government, not including the postal service, is expected to increase by 10 percent. This increase is due in part to projected retirements. Scientists and engineering workers will be in demand.

Table 8.1: Job Forecast for a Sample of Government & Public Administration Opportunities

Occupation	Expected Growth Rate
Legislators	1%–5%
Enlisted Personnel	1%–5%
Commissioned Officers	1%–5%
Warrant Officers	1%–5%
Interviewers	1%–5%
Compliance Officers	1%–5%
Urban and Regional Planners	10%–15%
Economists	1%–5%
Appraisers and Assessors	1%–5%
Tax Examiners and Collectors	1%–5%
Detectives and Criminal Investigators	1%–5%
Meter Readers	10%–15%
Financial Examiners	1%–5%
Transportation Security Screeners	0%–5%
Postal Service Mail Carriers	5%–10%

Source: *O*Net*

Government employment is often influenced by the priorities of each new elected politician. Changes in public policy, for example, may result in increased spending and employment in some programs and decreases in others.

8-1 Essential Question Reflection

So, let us revisit our essential question:

What types of opportunities are available in Government & Public Administration?

Based on what you learned in this section, please answer this question in detail.

Practice 8-1

Skills Practice

It may be necessary to follow multi step instructions in a variety of situations, such as when conducting cargo inspections. Workers in the Government & Public Administration industry must read carefully to know when to take each step, and be able to apply the same instructions in a variety of situations. **Practice this skill!**

TRAVELING WITH KIDS

We specially train our security officers, and they understand your concern for your children. They will approach your children gently and treat them with respect. If you child becomes uncomfortable or upset, security officers will consult you about the best way to relieve your child's concern.

- All carry-on baggage, including children's bags and items, must go through the X-ray machine. Examples include diaper bags, blankets, and toys.
- All child-related equipment that will fit through the X-ray machine must go through the X-ray machine. Examples include: strollers, umbrella-strollers, baby carriers, car and booster seats, and backpacks.
- When you arrive at the checkpoint, collapse or fold your child-related equipment. Secure items that are in the pockets, baskets, or attached to the equipment, and place them on the X-ray belt for inspection. Plastic bins are provided to deposit such items.
- If any of your child-related equipment does not fit through the X-ray machine, security officers will visually and physically inspect it.

1. As an airport security officer, you provide information to families traveling with children. Based on the instructions, when should a parent fold a stroller?

   A. after going through security
   B. when arriving at the security checkpoint
   C. after placing the stroller in the X-ray machine
   D. upon request by the screener
   E. before arriving at the airport

2. When will screeners visually inspect equipment?

   A. if it will not fit through the X-ray machine
   B. if an alarm sounds
   C. before it is placed in the X-ray machine
   D. after it is placed in the X-ray machine
   E. when the parent requests an inspection

To access more problems that will help you grow professional skills and are real-world examples in Government & Public Administration, go online.

8-2 Government & Public Administration Jobs

The government is concerned with our economic, social, and cultural life. As a result, this industry contains many kinds of jobs. You could work overseas as a Foreign Service officer. You could help shape your city by serving on a zoning board. Perhaps maybe a career in the armed forces might be right for you.

> **8-2 Essential Question**
>
> As you read this section, keep this question in mind:
>
> *Which opportunities may be right for you?*

Occupation With the Most People Employed:

Compliance Officers

- Warn violators of infractions or penalties
- Evaluate applications, records, or documents to gather information about eligibility or liability issues

Fast Facts:
Employment: 334,340 employees
Median Annual Wage: $33.20 hourly, $69,050 annually
Education Needed: High school diploma, or equivalent

Fastest-Growing Occupation:

Paralegals and Legal Assistants

- Investigate and gather the facts of a case
- Write or summarize reports to help lawyers prepare for trials

Fast Facts:
Employment: 352,800 employees
Annual Openings: 4,990
Median Annual Wage: $27.03 per hour, $56,230 annually
Education Needed: Associate degree
Did You Know: Unlike lawyers who must complete seven years of formal

education and pass the bar exam to practice, you can become a paralegal through an associate degree program in about two years.

Highest-Wage Occupations:

Information Security Analysts

- Monitor their organization's networks for security breaches and investigate when breaches occur
- Check for vulnerabilities in computer and network systems

Fast Facts:

Employment: 163,000

Annual Openings: 5,650

Median Annual Wage: $49.33 per hour, $102,600 annually

Education Needed: Bachelor's degree

Other: Some workers enter the occupation with a high school diploma and relevant industry training and certifications.

Lawyers

- Interpret laws, rulings, and regulations for individuals and businesses
- Present facts in writing and verbally to their clients or others, and argue on behalf of their clients

Fast Facts:

Employment: 833,100

Annual Openings: 8,020

Median annual wage: $61.54 per hour, $127,990 annually

Education Needed: Juris Doctor degree (J.D.) followed by the acquisition of a lawyer's license by passing the bar exam.

Other: Earning potential in this occupation is extremely varied. The lowest 10 percent earned less than $61,400, and the highest 10 percent earned more than $208,000.

8-2 • Government & Public Administration Jobs

Occupation Where Most Work for Themselves:

Management Analysts/Consultants

- Gather and organize information on problems or procedures
- Analyze data gathered and develop solutions or alternative methods of proceeding

Fast Facts:

Employment: 87,100 employees
Annual Openings: 994
Median Annual Wage: $44.71 per hour, $93,000 annually
Education Needed: Bachelor's degree or master's degree

Great Job! – Associate Degree Needed:

Climate Change Analysts

- Provide analytical support for policy briefs related to renewable energy, energy efficiency, or climate change
- Prepare study reports, memoranda, briefs, testimonies, or other written materials to inform government or environmental groups on environmental issues, such as climate change

Fast Facts:
- **Employment:** 87,100 employees
- **Annual Openings:** 940
- **Median Annual Wage:** $36.79 per hour, $76,530 annually
- **Education Needed:** Associate degree

Great Job! – High School Diploma Needed:

Title Examiners, Abstractors, and Searchers

- Search real estate records, examine titles, or summarize pertinent legal documents for a variety of purposes
- May compile lists of mortgages, contracts, and other instruments pertaining to titles

Fast Facts:
- **Employment:** 61,200 employees
- **Annual Openings:** 120
- **Median Annual Wage:** $47,310
- **Education Needed:** High school diploma, or equivalent

Police and Detectives

- Protect lives and property
- Write detailed reports and fill out forms
- Prepare cases for legal proceedings and testify in court

Fast Facts:
- **Employment:** 808,200 employees
- **Annual Openings:** 120
- **Median Annual Wage:** $31.74 per hour, $66,020 annually
- **Education Needed:** High school diploma, or equivalent
- **Other:** Most police and detectives must graduate from their agency's training academy before completing on-the-job training.

8-2 Essential Question Reflection

So, let us revisit our essential question:

Which opportunities may be right for you?

Based on what you learned in this section, what 2 or 3 opportunities are the most interesting? Explain your answer.

Case Study: Social and Human Service Assistants

Also called: Advocates

What do they do?

- Assess clients' cognitive abilities and physical and emotional needs to determine appropriate interventions
- Develop and implement behavioral management and care plans for clients
- Keep records or prepare reports for owner or management concerning visits with clients

What would you do?

- Work with clients and other professionals, such as social workers, to develop treatment plans
- Help clients complete paperwork to apply for assistance programs
- Check in with clients to ensure that services are provided appropriately

What do you need to know?

Business
  Customer service
  Administrative services

Math and Science
  Psychology
  Sociology and anthropology

Health
  Therapy and counseling

Arts and Humanities
  English language

What skills do you need?

Basic Skills
  Listen to others, do not interrupt, and ask good questions
  Talk to others

Social
    Understand people's reactions

    Look for ways to help people

Problem Solving
    Notice a problem and figure out the best way to solve it

What abilities must you be good at?

Verbal
    Communicate by speaking

    Communicate by writing

Ideas and Logic
    Notice when problems happen

    Use rules to solve problems

Who does well in this occupation?

People interested in this work like activities that include data, detail, and regular routines.

What educational level is needed?

- Varies; some companies may require a bachelor's degree while other may only require a high school diploma.

Practice 8-2

Skills Practice

Government & Public Administration workers must sometimes analyze graphics to identify trends. They might search for data that have increased or decreased over time. An urban planner, for example, might use a graph of population trends to plan a new housing community. Being able to identify common trends from several pieces of data can be helpful in a variety of jobs in this industry. **Practice this skill!**

Electricity Generated by Fuel, 1990–2035

Information beyond 2021 is a projected forecast

1. As an engineer for the Department of Energy, you are using the graph to prepare a report about projected energy production. Which fuel type is expected to generate the same amount of electricity in 2035 as it did in 2010?

   A. coal
   B. renewables
   C. natural gas
   D. nuclear
   E. petroleum

2. Which statement about fuel usage in 2010 is true?

   A. Coal generated more energy than any other fuel source.
   B. Renewable fuel generated less energy than any other fuel source.
   C. Natural gas generated more energy than any other fuel source.
   D. Nuclear fuel generated less energy than any other fuel source.
   E. Petroleum generated more energy than any other fuel source.

To access more problems that will help you grow professional skills and are real-world examples in Government & Public Administration, go online.

8-3 Building a Career in Government & Public Administration

Urban and regional planners usually begin work at an agency of a city or state government. Recent graduates usually work on small projects with experienced planners. As they gain experience, they take on more responsibility.

Within a few years, a planner may be handling large jobs such as the design of a shopping center. Urban and regional planners can later move on to direct entire projects. Planners may also move to a larger agency. They may work for a city with more challenging programs, or they may work in a related occupation, such as community or economic development.

> **? 8-3 Essential Question**
>
> **As you read this section, keep this question in mind:**
>
> *How can I match my skills & interests with the right job?*

Are You More Interested in Working With Data, People, or Things?

Many careers in Government and Public Administration offer opportunities to work with data, people, and things. However, most jobs focus mainly on one of these. Policy analysts, for example, work mainly with data. Instructors do a great deal of work with people. Technicians work mostly with things.

Careers That Involve Working With Data

Examples of working with data include analyzing public policy, calculating social security benefits, writing speeches for political candidates, and drawing up zoning plans.

Many jobs in Government & Public Administration involve working with data. A mayor, for example, must oversee the city budget and study policy options. A field commander in the army must read intelligence reports and compose battle tactics. An urban planner must gather data on all aspects of a project and then perform calculations and make projections based on the data. Internal Revenue Service workers examine tax returns and accounting records. They must stay informed about all new tax laws.

Careers That Involve Working With People

Many jobs in this industry focus on human relationships. Examples of working with people include discussing political issues with voters and meeting with lawmakers.

Environmental compliance officers might interview company representatives during an inspection. Equal opportunity representatives may need to talk to employers and employees to solve hiring problems. Members of the Foreign Service might meet with representatives of other countries. All of these activities require strong communication skills.

Many Government & Public Administration jobs enable you to spend a great deal of time working with others. For example, workers at social service offices, in the armed forces, and in regulatory agencies work with coworkers, members of the public, and nongovernmental employees. Many government workers, particularly legislators and city council members, work with others in committees dealing with specific issues. Officers in the armed forces must supervise and lead enlisted personnel and inspire their trust.

Careers That Involve Working With Things

Working with things includes creating, using, and repairing machines, tools, engines, and instruments. Although most jobs in Government & Public Administration involve working with data and people, some jobs have a large "things" component. Jobs in the armed forces, for examples, often involve operating tanks and other military equipment. Postal service mail sorters must handle letters, packages, and postal equipment.

8-3 Essential Question Reflection

So, let us revisit our essential question:

How can I match my skills & interests with the right job?

Based on what you learned in this section, please answer this question in detail.

8-4 Education and Training for Government & Public Administration Opportunities

Jobs in the Government & Public Administration industry require varying levels of education. If you are interested in entry-level work, you might need little or no formal training to perform the job. However, if you're interested in a specialized or management-level position, you will need specific education and experience.

8-4 Essential Question

As you read this section, keep this question in mind:

What training & education is needed for a job in Government & Public Administration?

Training and Education in This Industry

The level of training necessary to succeed in the Government & Public Administration industry varies by career. Jobs can be categorized into three groups—those requiring little or no training, those requiring some training, and those requiring advanced training.

Jobs Requiring Little or No Training

Some jobs in Government & Public Administration do not require extensive pre-employment training. Joining the military requires only a high school diploma.

Many clerical and administrative jobs, such as office or program assistants, require little or no training after high school. The training for these jobs is often given by experienced employees or through on-the-job training programs.

In the federal government, mail and file clerks and equipment operators can find employment with only a high school diploma. Field representatives and census takers for the U.S. Census Bureau do not need a college degree.

Government jobs such as laborers, sanitation workers, and custodians require little training, but some jobs require passing a standardized exam. Candidates are also evaluated on reliability and dependability.

Jobs Requiring Some Training

Many jobs in Government & Public Administration require some specialized training. Examples include careers in accounting, auditing, zoning, and electoral politics. These positions usually require an associate or bachelor's degree.

Other programs combine study with on-site training. These are designed to meet the requirements for specific types of certifications. Trade organizations representing specific industries may have certification programs for specific jobs. Certification programs often require a minimum number of hours on the job and a minimum score on a standardized test.

Several professional certifications can help you find employment in Government & Public Administration. The National Environmental Health Association, for example, awards the Certified Environmental Health Technician designation to those who pass an examination and meet postsecondary requirements in environmental health.

Workers in government finance can become accredited financial examiners by completing a bachelor's degree in accounting, completing two years of work experience, and passing a test administered by the Society of Financial Examiners. The Institute of Internal Auditors certifies internal auditors.

Jobs Requiring Advanced Training

Some jobs in Government & Public Administration require extensive training. These include upper-level administration positions and jobs that require a high level of technical expertise. For example, jobs in policy analysis, environmental regulation, urban planning, and international relations require advanced training.

To be an urban planner, for example, you will need a bachelor's degree or a master's degree in urban planning or civil engineering. To be a city manager or agency director, you will need a master's degree in Public Administration. Foreign Service officers need at least a bachelor's degree, although a master's degree in history, international relations, languages, or cultural studies is extremely helpful.

Often, advanced positions in Government & Public Administration require experience as well as formal education. Many high-level government agency positions are filled by promoting individuals with experience. An assistant city manager, for example, may become a city manager through a series of promotions. Inspectors often become supervisors or heads of departments by advancing up the civil service ranks.

Others work for private companies before entering a government career. Many legislators, for example, work first as lawyers or community activists. Tax inspectors and IRS investigators may have begun their careers as accountants. Inspectors in environmental compliance may have gained expertise by working in a business, for a nonprofit organization, or on a farm.

Table 8.2: Training Required for Government & Public Administration Jobs

Level of Training	Job Title
Little or No Training	Interviewers Postal Service Mail Carriers Court Clerks
Some Training	Legislators Postmasters Tax Examiners Assessors
Considerable Training	Climate Change Analysts Urban and Regional Planners Coroners Financial Examiners Equal Opportunity Representatives

Government & Public Administration Skill Standards

In government, skill standards vary by agency and by job. In choosing candidates for the job of taxpayer resolution representative, for example, the IRS looks for candidates who can provide excellent customer service. These people must have effective communications skills and understand accounting. Elected officials, by contrast, do not need to meet skill standards at all. The public decides whether they are qualified to serve. They must meet only basic age and citizenship requirements.

Professional Skills

Communication Skills Communication skills are important for legislators, who must be able to clearly express the purpose of bills they are proposing and convince others to vote for these bills.

Listening Skills Listening skills are necessary for following instructions safely, which is critical for military personnel during combat.

Problem-Solving Skills Employers value workers who can spot problems and take action to find solutions. An FBI special agent, for example, must find evidence that will help solve crimes.

Technology Skills Most records are now stored electronically, so it is increasingly important that workers have good computer skills. For example, IRS workers must be able to process online tax forms. Workers must be able to adapt to new technology.

Decision-Making Skills   Making decisions is a part of every job. For example, while armed services personnel are guided by their commanding officers, they must have a good deal of independence while on duty. It is imperative that they have good decision-making skills.

Organizing and Planning Skills   An urban planner must develop a schedule and a workflow that ensures the project will be completed on time.

Teamwork Skills   Teamwork is key to nearly every job in government. City managers count on a team of department heads such as tax collectors, police commissioners, and fire department chiefs to work together.

Social Skills   As a legislator, you must be able to interact with your constituent as well as staff and fellow legislators. Social interaction is key to success in the Foreign Service.

Adaptability Skills   Job descriptions, work environments, and procedures are constantly changing along with technological advancements, political shifts, population growth, and changing government priorities. The ability to adapt to change is an important skill in every job.

8-4 Essential Question Reflection

So, let us revisit our essential question:

What training & education is needed for a job in Government & Public Administration?

Based on what you learned in this section, please answer this question in detail.

Practice 8-4

Skills Practice

When reading documents, such as an article about advances in intelligence-gathering methods, workers in the Government and Public Administration industry need to be able to identify the main idea. They must also find details supporting the main idea. The main idea tells what the document is about. Details provide more information that helps explain the main idea. **Practice this skill!**

DNA PROFILING

One of the most important advances in criminal investigation is DNA profiling. DNA, the acronym for deoxyribonucleic acid, is a molecule found in all living things, and contains the genetic material that makes each organism unique. The DNA found in blood, hair, or other bodily tissue or fluid on the victim can provide criminologists the genetic makeup of the persons at the scene of a crime. DNA profiling serves three purposes. First, it can either link a suspect to a crime or eliminate the suspect from suspicion. DNA profiling can match genetic material from a crime scene to a DNA database in order connect crimes or identify a suspect. It also can clear convicted criminals of crimes years after their convictions if DNA profiling was not available at the time of the trial. DNA profiling would be very useful, for example, in cases where a murderer's blood was found at the scene of a crime after a deadly struggle or in an assault case where samples of the attacker's bodily tissue could be collected from the victim.

1. As an FBI agent, you must be familiar with the latest advances in detection and identification. What is the main idea in this text about DNA profiling?

   A. Everyone has a unique genetic profile.
   B. DNA is present in all forms of life.
   C. DNA profiling is useful in criminal investigations.
   D. Bodily substances contain DNA.
   E. DNA databases contain crime scene samples.

2. Which detail mentioned would be useful in the DNA profiling process?

   A. molecules
   B. hair
   C. crime scene
   D. wrongful convictions
   E. positive matches

Skills Practice

Many jobs in the Government & Public Administration industry require workers to calculate costs and discounts. A worker at a city's Department of Public Works, for example, may need to decide which road salt supplier to use based on the amount of road salt needed and the discount offered. **Practice this skill!**

3. You are the fleet supervisor for a municipal utility company. Your fleet uses diesel fuel, which has been becoming more expensive. Last year, it cost $0.44 a mile to operate one of your vans. This year, the cost of diesel fuel has increased by 25 percent, and you need to figure out how much fuel money you should request from your manager. How much does it cost to fuel a van per mile now?

   A. $0.29
   B. $0.33
   C. $0.55
   D. $0.66
   E. $0.89

4. As the information technology specialist in a state office, you are responsible for purchasing new computers. The computer you wish to purchase costs $679, but you receive an 11 percent discount for being a government employee. How much does one computer cost you?

   A. $74.69
   B. $575.99
   C. $583.25
   D. $604.31
   E. $753.69

To access more problems that will help you grow professional skills and are real-world examples in Government & Public Administration, go online.

8-5 Working Conditions in the Government & Public Administration Industry

When choosing a career path, understanding the work environment, hazards, and benefits of a job can help you make informed decisions.

> **8-5 Essential Question**
>
> **As you read this section, keep this question in mind:**
>
> *What are typical work environments in Government & Public Administration?*

Physical Environment

The physical work environment in Government & Public Administration varies by path, location, and job. Soldiers in combat zones may work in tanks, on naval ships, or with aircraft. Members of the armed services in noncombat jobs often work in conditions similar to workers in the civilian world.

Government administrators, commissioners, city managers, auditors, and treasurers usually work in modern offices. However, office work can be stressful when it involves dealing with issues and problems on a regular basis.

Highway maintenance workers, meter readers, and sanitation managers spend most of their workdays outdoors. Their jobs can be physically strenuous. Legislators divide their time between their home office and their office in the state or national capital. They also spend time on the campaign trail.

Work Hours

The work hours for jobs in this industry are varied. Most administrators, regulators, planners, and office personnel work 40-hour weeks. Foreign Service officers usually work standard hours, but they often attend evening and weekend events. CIA agents may work long hours on missions abroad.

Legislators work long hours reading reports or meeting with staff and advisors. Election officials usually work 40-hour work weeks, but they may work more hours at election time. Other elected officials, such as mayors, spend evening and weekend hours attending political and ceremonial functions such as community meetings, charity banquets, and fundraising dinners.

Some government services require around-the-clock work. In these areas, shift work is common. It allows services to be performed at all times. It may also allow workers to select hours to meet their needs. Shift work is common for armed services personnel, corrections officers, and utility workers.

Many Government & Public Administration employees work overtime. For example, customs offices are open around the clock, so most customs agents are required to work some nights, weekends, and holidays. While most political aides work eight-hour days, five days each week, campaigns or other important projects may involve working extra hours.

Workers in Government & Public Administration often must meet tight deadlines. Postal service workers, for example, face a deluge of mail each December. IRS employees receive millions of tax returns just after April 15th. At times of war, members of the armed forces are called for intensive training and preparation.

Essential Physical Activities

Many workers in Government & Public Administration must be in good physical condition. Mail handlers are required to perform heavy lifting. Maintenance workers may need to handle heavy equipment. All members of the armed forces are expected to remain in good physical condition during their career. This includes professional officers such as physicians and accountants.

Good vision is necessary for inspectors. Air Force pilots must have good vision to navigate by sight and read instrument panels, gauges, and charts.

Injuries and Illnesses

Some government employees, such as members of the armed forces or police officers, regularly encounter hazardous conditions. In this industry, there is a higher rate of on-the-job injuries and illnesses than office workers, such as legislators. However, work-related injuries and illnesses can happen even in an office setting.

> **8-5 Essential Question Reflection**
>
> **So, let us revisit our essential question:**
>
> *What are typical work environments in Government & Public Administration?*
>
> Based on what you learned in this section, please answer this question in detail.

8-6 Trends in Government & Public Administration

Using technologies and protecting the environment are two important trends in the Government & Public Administration industry. The government has taken the lead in protecting the environment by limiting pollution and encouraging the development of renewable forms of energy.

> **? 8-6 Essential Question**
>
> **As you read this section, keep this question in mind:**
>
> *What factors affect trends in Government & Public Administration?*

Campaigning and Voting

Politicians use the Internet to interact with citizens and to encourage people to vote. Online polls allow voters to voice their opinions on campaign issues. Candidates can send messages to millions of people. They can stream videos of speeches, meetings, and rallies on the Internet.

Military Technology

Every year, the Department of Defense spends billions of dollars on research and development of military technology, such as vehicles and weapons. Today, military research focuses on small adaptable weapons guided by computer systems. More effective nonlethal weapons keep soldiers and civilians safe during military operations. Service members have also benefited from the increased safety of equipment.

The intelligence community invests billions of dollars in technology that improves intelligence. Intelligence can be gathered through the interpretation of words and images. This information can be used to suit the needs of the military.

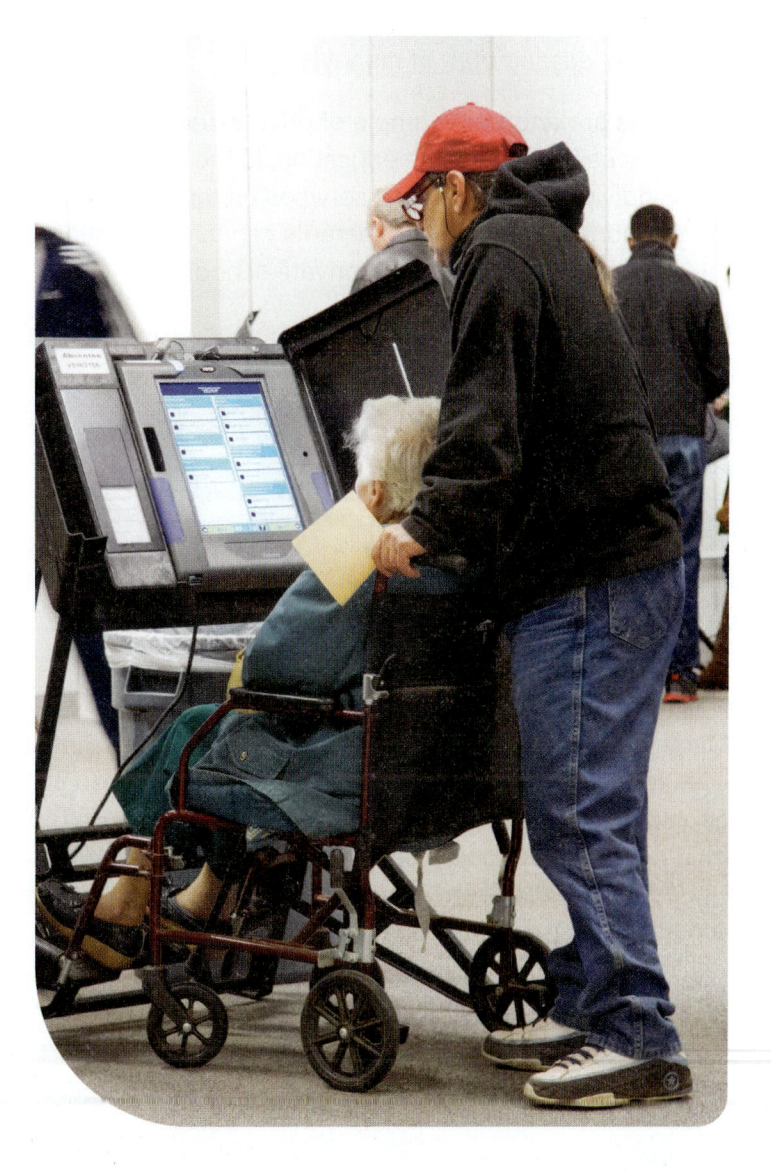

8-6 • Trends in Government & Public Administration   235

Trends in the Industry

Various factors can cause changes in the Government & Public Administration industry. Changes in public opinion and changes in other parts of the world affect U.S. practices and policies.

Privatization

Government agencies are turning to privatization, which is the transfer of public services into private hands. This can make operations more cost efficient. Several states have hired private businesses to manage prisons. Many governments contract out the operation of wastewater plants to private companies. Outsourcing these tasks frees the government from the responsibility of hiring, training, and managing workers.

Private-sector competition is one result of privatization. When government organizations bid against nongovernmental organizations for government contracts, efficiency may be increased. If two companies want to manage the same project, each must submit a bid. Contracts are awarded to the company that can do the best job for the least amount of money.

Vouchers are another example of private-sector competition. The government pays for some services, such as education, in the form of vouchers. These vouchers allow individuals to purchase services on the open market rather than from the government. In some states, parents can use education vouchers to help pay for their children's education at a private school.

Many privatization proposals have been controversial. This debate will continue.

Sustainability and the Industry

Environmental and sustainability issues have become high-priority challenges for the Government & Public Administration industry. High among these concerns are pollution and energy issues.

Environmental Regulation

Many lawmakers believe the government should protect the environment by limiting pollution. In 2021, President Biden introduced an economic plan that set a goal to make 50 percent of all vehicles sold in the United States run on electricity by 2030. New standards have been set for vehicle emissions, and recently, the United States has seen an increase in the sale of electric vehicles (EVs) that run solely on electricity instead of gasoline. In addition, proposals have been made that will limit the pollution caused by businesses.

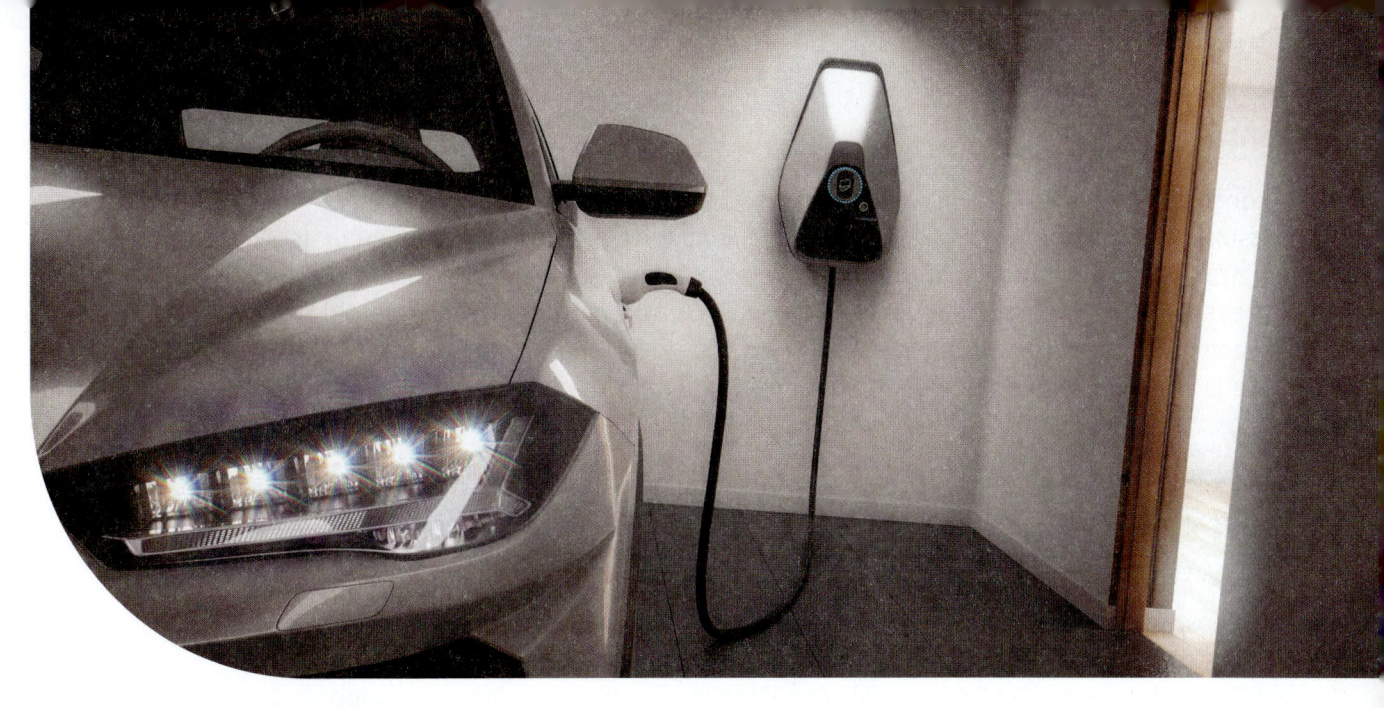

Green Energy Initiatives

Government leaders have sought to protect the environment in other ways. New programs aimed at reducing the amount of energy people consume have been introduced. For example, people who made their homes more energy efficient by adding insulation and replacing windows were given a tax credit. Billions of dollars have been invested in developing clean and renewable forms of energy, which include solar and wind-powered energy, hydroelectric power, and biofuels.

The Economy and the Industry

The Government & Public Administration industry are affected by changes in the economy. Unlike private businesses, however, government agencies are not driven by the need to make a profit. In recent years, the federal government and many state and local governments have spent more money than they have taken in. This is known as a budget deficit.

The deficits grow worse during recessions. Governments collect less money in taxes because people earn lower incomes at times when there is less economic activity. In addition, governments may be spending more to provide unemployment benefits and other services to people in need.

Growing deficits add pressure on legislators to reduce government spending. Government workers may be laid off or asked to take furloughs (unpaid leave). Benefits, such as pensions and health care, may be reduced. Cuts are often made first to programs that are least popular with voters. Some workers, such as military personnel, may feel fewer effects.

Workplace Trends in the Industry

The Government & Public Administration industry is affected by the changes taking place in the U.S. economy. The popularity of consultants and temporary workers are some of today's major trends.

Consultants

A consultant provides specialized services for one or more clients. Some consultants are employed by one client for a long-term project. Other consultants work for several clients at once. A consultant is typically a highly specialized professional. Consultants may be called in when a new project starts, or an old project is reevaluated. A labor relations specialist, for example, may be called in if there is conflict between union employees and management.

Consultants are hired by a variety of state and local government agencies. They perform tasks such as policy research, opinion polling, and strategic planning. They may analyze health, environmental, educational, and economic issues.

Political consultants advise candidates running for public office. They may serve as the overall campaign strategy planner. They may specialize in a particular area, such as the creation and placement of advertising. Large numbers of people run for political office each year, so political consulting is a rapidly growing profession.

Temporary Workers

Some government offices and agencies need workers only during certain times of the year. Temporary workers often receive assignments through temporary employment agencies. If an agency has an important deadline to meet or if key workers are on vacation, a temporary worker might be called to fill a position. Temporary workers have little job security and few benefits. Campaign volunteers and aides are examples of temporary workers in Government & Public Administration. During tax season, the IRS hires temporary workers as telephone operators to field taxpayers' questions.

8-6 Essential Question Reflection

So, let us revisit our essential question:

What factors affect trends in Government & Public Administration?

Based on what you learned in this section, please answer this question in detail.

Chapter 9
Business Management & Administration

Chapter Topics

9-1 Business Management & Administration Today

9-2 Business Management & Administration Jobs

9-3 Building a Career in Business Management & Administration

9-4 Education and Training for Business Management & Administration Opportunities

9-5 Working Conditions in the Business Management & Administration Industry

9-6 Trends in Business Management & Administration

Essential Questions

By the end of the chapter, you will be able to answer the following questions:

- **9-1** What types of opportunities are available in Business Management & Administration?
- **9-2** Which opportunities may be right for you?
- **9-3** How can I match my skills & interests with the right job?
- **9-4** What training & education is needed for a job in Business Management & Administration?
- **9-5** What are typical work environments in Business Management & Administration?
- **9-6** What factors affect trends in Business Management & Administration?

9-1 Business Management & Administration Today

Business is all around us. We use business services when we buy clothing, eat out, or use a credit card. What is business? Business is activity that provides goods and services.

All businesses rely on management and administration. Managers and administrators set the goals and policies of an organization. They decide how the organization should be run and how many people to hire. They also make sure the organization has enough money.

Workers in this industry are responsible for a wide variety of business functions. They provide administrative services, handle mail, and manage the storage of documents. They plan conferences, manage the payroll, and train new employees. Millions of people work in business management and administration.

9-1 Essential Question

As you read this section, keep this question in mind:

What types of opportunities are available in Business Management & Administration?

Career Journeys in Business Management & Administration

There are five major paths along which your journey in Business Management & Administration might be shaped. People commonly move into and out of different paths. Each path contains a group of careers requiring similar skills as well as similar certifications or education. This career is divided into five main career paths:

- General Management
- Business Information Management
- Human Resources Management
- Operations Management
- Administrative Support

240   Chapter 9 • Business Management & Administration

General Management

The General Management path includes careers in a variety of fields. All industries have management and executive positions. Managers are responsible for making decisions that help guide a business toward its goals. Most managers have advanced training, including a bachelor's degree or higher.

Managers perform many important tasks including planning, organizing, staffing, directing, and controlling their department or business. For example, restaurant managers select and price menu items. They arrange for the delivery of fresh food and beverages. They hire, train, and fire staff. They supervise the kitchen and dining room. They may also oversee the bookkeeping. Bookkeeping involves recording daily sales, managing payroll, and tracking inventory. Juggling all these tasks requires self-discipline and leadership skills.

Most large organizations have three levels of managers.

- First-line managers directly supervise the workers who perform specific duties. For example, in a manufacturing plant, the first-line manager may supervise machinists working on the floor. There may be several first-line managers who are supervised by a mid-level manager.

- Mid-level managers are responsible for setting the goals and objectives for a department or a business unit. They decide dress code policies and the number of hours employees can work. They also determine the responsibilities of the first-line managers. In some companies, mid-level managers are called directors. In banks, they are often called assistant vice president. Many companies have several levels of mid-level managers. For example, department stores that are part of national chains may have regional managers who oversee the operation of several stores. Those managers generally answer to top-level management.

- Top-level managers include the chief executive officer (CEO). It also includes the president and vice presidents of the company. Top-level managers set overall goals and policies for their organizations. They direct the activities of mid-level managers. Ultimately, they are accountable for the success or failure of their companies.

Business Information Management

The Business Information Management career path includes employees who manage the finances of a company. This includes tracking sales and expenses. It may include planning budgets, invoicing, and making sure staff is paid. These employees ensure that financial records are accurate. During tax season, they prepare tax statements. This path includes occupations such as bookkeeper, auditor, accountant, and accounting clerk.

Bookkeeping is the process of recording the finances of a business, and bookkeepers are usually part of the accounting department. Bookkeepers and accounting clerks may use both computers and paper files to keep financial records.

Accountants and auditors are employees who have expertise in financial operations. They may work for a private or public company, or even the government. They are typically responsible for budgeting, tax preparation, and internal auditing. Internal auditors are responsible for verifying the accuracy of a company's financial records and checking for mismanagement of funds or fraud.

Human Resources Management

Human Resources Management is the management of people. HR managers work on a day-to-day basis with the employees in their company. They recruit, or try to attract, qualified new employees, and they interview job candidates. They advise management on hiring decisions and arrange for employee training. They often work to improve employee health and productivity. Some HR workers are responsible for writing the company's newsletter. They answer questions related to pay and benefits. Workers in this path generally have a college degree, and some more have additional certifications.

Companies compete for the best employees. Executives rely on human resources professionals to help the company with the recruitment, hiring, and training of these talented professionals.

Operations Management

Operations Management is concerned with the production, sales, and distribution of goods and services. Occupations in this path include sales managers and customer service supervisors. This path also includes careers that involve marketing and public relations. For most careers, a bachelor's degree in an area such as accounting, finance, or business is preferred.

Many positions in this path involve interacting with customers. Sales representatives work to get new customers. They also sell new products to existing customers. Sales managers train and supervise sales representatives. Sales managers and sales representatives work together to attain sales goals.

Customer service representatives resolve problems that customers encounter. They keep records of their interactions with customers. At times, customer service representatives may refund the money a customer paid or take other action to resolve customer issues.

Administrative Support

Administrative Support personnel are responsible for various administrative and clerical duties, and they work in a variety of fields. They are the employees who answer phones, file papers, type reports, and schedule meetings. Administrative assistants with more experience may write reports, do research, and prepare spreadsheets. Some jobs in this path require college degrees, while many others do not.

The duties of administrative support workers vary depending on the company or department. Some administrative support personnel have expertise in a certain field. Legal secretaries, for example, must understand the legal profession. Their work includes the preparation of complaints, motions, and other legal documents.

Business Management & Administration Future Outlook

The Bureau of Labor Statistics (BLS) projects that most job openings in the Business Management & Administration industry will be in occupations assigned to the administrative support path—including customer service representatives, the occupation expected to have the largest number of job openings in the career.

The skills developed in this career field are found in every industry, and as a result, job growth is tied to growth of these industries. For example, careers in medical and health services management are expected to grow about 16 percent. This is due to growth and change in the health-care industry. Students who are uncertain about their career path are able to confidently begin their training in this career field since all careers use similar skill sets found in Business Management & Administration.

Table 9.1: Forecast for Occupations over the Next 10 Years in Business Management & Administration

Occupation	Expected Growth Rate
First-Line Supervisors of Personal Service Workers	15% or higher
Project Management Specialists and Business Operations Specialists	5%–10%
Marketing Managers	10%–15%
Agents and Business Managers of Artists, Performers, and Athletes	10%–15%
Claims Adjusters, Examiners, and Investigators	Little or no growth
Accountants and Auditors	5%–10%
Medical Secretaries	10%–15%
Training and Development Specialists	5%–10%
Couriers and Messengers	Little or no growth

Source: *O*Net*

9-1 Essential Question Reflection

As you read this section, keep this question in mind:

What types of jobs are available in Business Management & Administration?

Based on what you learned in this section, please answer this question in detail.

Practice 9-1

Skills Practice

It may be necessary to follow multi-step instructions in a variety of situations, such as when closing a store at the end of the day and preparing the nightly bank deposit. Workers must read carefully to know when to take each step and be able to apply the same instructions in a variety of situations.
Practice this skill!

SCHEDULING INTERVIEWS

1. Applicants who have met initial screening requirements will be invited to call our department to schedule a phone interview.
2. When you receive a call, ask for the applicant's full name and telephone number. We use this information to identify applicant records in our database.
3. From the candidate's record, determine the appropriate hiring manager. Schedule a 30-minute phone interview within a week, and pass this information on to the hiring manager for follow up.
4. Read the information for the appropriate job description to the applicant. Remember not to promise the applicant a job or coach them on what to say.
5. Thank the caller and let the applicant know that the hiring manager will follow up soon to schedule the interview.
6. Refer unsolicited callers to our website to fill out the online application. If callers are checking the status of an application, kindly remind them that they will be notified via e-mail of any next steps.

1. You are a recruitment specialist for a publishing company. Based on this procedure, when should you schedule a phone interview?

   A. after you have determined the appropriate hiring manager

   B. before the applicant has met the initial screening requirements

   C. whenever you receive an unsolicited call from a candidate

   D. as soon as the applicant responds to your e-mail

   E. once you have checked that the applicant meets the screening requirements

2. You receive a call from an unqualified applicant. What should you do?

   A. Let them know that the hiring manager will be calling soon.

   B. Tell them how to prepare for the 30-minute phone interview.

   C. Remind them that they will receive an e-mail explaining any next steps.

   D. Verify that you have their correct name and telephone number.

   E. Read them the information for the appropriate job description.

To access more problems that will help you grow professional skills and are real-world examples in Business Management & Administration, go online.

9-2: Business Management & Administration Jobs

There are variety of jobs to pick from in the Business Management & Administration industry. You can find jobs at all skill levels, from entry level to managerial. Are you interested in working with a company's finances? Would you like to use your people skills in a human resources department? The following job profiles will introduce you to some professions in this industry.

9-2 Essential Question

As you read this section, keep this question in mind:

Which opportunities may be right for you?

Occupation With the Most People Employed:

Project Management Specialists

- Monitor project progress, budget, and timeline
- Assign duties or responsibilities to other project personnel

Fast Facts:

Employment: 1,777,300 employees

Annual Openings: 14,190

Median Annual Wage: $45.43 hourly, $94,500 annually

Education Needed: Bachelor's degree

Did You Know: People who have strong organizational skills excel in this occupation.

Fastest-Growing Occupations:

Agents and Business Managers of Artists, Performers, and Athletes

- Keep informed of industry trends and deals
- Collect fees, commissions, or other payments, according to contract terms
- Send samples of clients' work and other promotional material to potential employers to obtain auditions, sponsorships, or endorsement deals

Fast Facts:
Employment: 18,700 employees
Annual Openings: 3,400
Median Annual Wage: $37.70 hourly, $78,410 annually
Education Needed: High school diploma/GED or bachelor's degree

Medical Secretaries

- Schedule and confirm patient diagnostic appointments, surgeries, or medical consultations
- Complete insurance or other claim forms

Fast Facts:

Employment: 611,200 employees

Annual Openings: 7,520

Median Annual Wage: $18.01 hourly, $37,450 annually

Education Needed: High school diploma or associate degree

Other: If you are interested in working in health care, but not ready to make a commitment, this is a great place to gain knowledge and exposure!

First-Line Supervisors of Personal Service Workers

- Assign work schedules to ensure quality and timely delivery of service
- Observe and evaluate workers' performance to ensure quality service and compliance with specifications
- Train workers in proper operational procedures and functions and explain company policies

Fast Facts:

Employment: 200,400 employees

Annual Openings: 2,860

Median Annual Wage: $37.70 hourly, $78,410 annually

Education Needed: High school diploma, or equivalent

Occupations With Some Travel:

Training and Development Specialist

- Obtain, organize, or develop training procedure manuals, guides, or course materials, such as handouts or visual materials
- Evaluate modes of training delivery, such as in-person or virtual, to optimize training effectiveness, training costs, or environmental impacts

Fast Facts:

Employment: 354,800 employees
Annual Openings: 2,890
Median Annual Wage: $29.60 hourly, $61,570 annually
Education Needed: Bachelor's degree

Great Job! - High School Diploma Needed:

Claims Adjusters, Examiners, and Investigators

- Examine claims forms and other records to determine insurance coverage
- Analyze information gathered from investigation and report findings and recommendations

Fast Facts:

Employment: 333,800 employees
Annual Openings: 2,400
Median Annual Wage: $31.29 hourly, $65,080 annually
Did You Know: Certifications offer steps toward your career journey and unlock many jobs that sometimes feel out of reach.

9-2 Essential Question Reflection

So, let us revisit our essential question:

Which opportunities may be right for you?

Based on what you learned in this section, what 2 or 3 opportunities are the most interesting? Explain your answer.

Case Study: Tax Preparers

Also called: Enrolled Agent, Tax Advisor, Tax Consultant

What do they do?

- Prepare tax returns for individuals or small businesses

What would you do?

- Use all appropriate adjustments, deductions, and credits to keep clients' taxes to a minimum
- Compute taxes owed or overpaid, using adding machines or personal computers, and complete entries on forms, following tax form instructions and tax tables
- Interview clients to obtain additional information on taxable income and deductible expenses and allowances

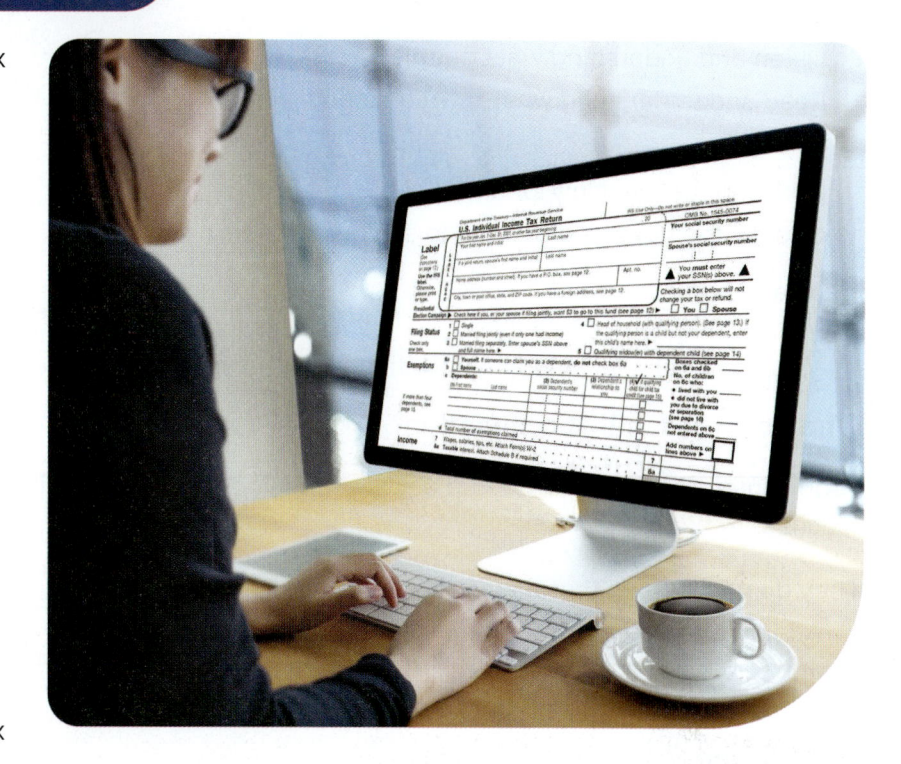

What do you need to know?

Business
Customer service
Accounting and economics

Arts and Humanities
English language

Engineering and Technology
Computers and electronics

Safety and Government
Law and government

What skills do you need?

Basic Skills
Read work-related information
Listen to others, do not interrupt, and ask good questions

Problem Solving
Notice a problem and figure out the best way to solve it

What abilities must you be good at?

Verbal
- Listen and understand what people say
- Read and understand what is written

Math
- Add, subtract, multiply, or divide
- Choose the right type of math to solve a problem

Ideas and Logic
- Use rules to solve problems
- Make general rules or come up with answers from lots of detailed information

Who does well in this occupation?

People interested in this work like activities that include data, detail, and regular routines.

They do well at jobs that need:
- Attention to detail
- Integrity
- Dependability
- Self-control
- Cooperation
- Stress tolerance

What educational level is needed?

- High school diploma/GED

Practice 9-2

Skills Practice

When reviewing workplace graphics, it may be necessary to compare information in one or more graphics. A public relations manager may need to review graphs showing trends in advertising and consumer buying habits. Workers must know how different graphics relate to each other and be able to compare information and trends within them. **Practice this skill!**

Weekly Schedule March 30–April 5

Sunday	Monday	Tuesday	Wednesday	Thursday	Friday	Saturday
30 David	31 Nancy	1 Donna	2	3	4	5

Employee Name	Availability
David	Mondays, Fridays and Weekends
Suzanne	Weekends only
Nancy	Tuesdays – Thursdays
Juan	Weekends only
Donna	Tuesdays – Fridays
Hector	Mondays only

1. As the manager of a print shop, you are responsible for completing the weekly employee schedule. Based on the information provided, which employees are available to work on April 2?

   A. Nancy and Hector
   B. Nancy and Donna
   C. Donna and Hector
   D. Hector and Juan
   E. Juan and David

2. How many employees are available to work on weekends?

   A. 1
   B. 2
   C. 3
   D. 4
   E. 5

To access more problems that will help you grow professional skills and are real-world examples in Business Management & Administration, go online.

9-3: Building a Career in Business Management & Administration

The Business Management & Administration industry has a positive outlook and there are many exciting careers to choose from. At the beginning of your career, you may have to spend time as a clerk, coordinator, or other entry-level position. A human resources clerk who works for a large company can be promoted to a position as trainer. In smaller companies, the human resources coordinator may be responsible for training. A trainer is often responsible for reviewing company policies with new employees and answering the questions that new employees have.

A trainer can be promoted to recruiter, who represents the company to potential new employees. Recruiters often travel to college campuses or employment fairs to fill positions within the company. After gaining work experience in the field, an individual may be promoted to human resources manager.

9-3 Essential Question

As you read this section, keep this question in mind:

How can I match my skills & interests with the right job?

Are You More Interested in Working With Data, People, or Things?

Occupations such as project managers and executives require people to work with a combination of data, people, and things, but a few careers don't. Accountants, for example, work mainly with data. Human resources managers work primarily with people. Clerks work mostly with things. When mapping out your career path, consider what balance of data, people, and things best suits your skills.

Careers That Involve Working With Data

Preparing financial statements, drawing up budgets, analyzing sales figures, preparing payroll, transcribing spoken information, and preparing written documents are all examples of working with data in this industry.

Some jobs in the Business Management & Administration industry require expertise at analyzing data. Many of these careers are found in the business information management path. They include auditor, payroll manager, database manager, and systems analyst. Administrative assistants, medical transcriptionists, and researchers all use words and numbers in their work, too.

Most managers in business and administration need to work with data. A database manager, for instance, collects data throughout the company. The manager oversees the inputting of this data and then analyzes spreadsheets that display the data.

Careers That Involve Working With People

Some Business Management & Administration jobs focus on human relationships. These careers often include recruiting, interviewing, and training employees. They may involve mediating, or helping settle, conflicts between coworkers. Many management positions involve analyzing business processes with clients and advising customers. All these activities require strong communication skills. They also require an understanding of the complex network of human relationships in a business or a community.

Many Business Management & Administration jobs enable you to spend a great deal of time working with others. Office managers or supervisors must effectively supervise and lead teams of workers. Human resources workers need the ability to interview candidates for a job, hire new employees, and train new workers.

Careers That Involve Working With Things

Working with things in this industry involves using office machines and equipment to accomplish tasks. Transcribing information from a recording to a typewritten document and entering information into a database are examples of working with things in this industry. Financial managers and accountants need to work with a computer system that stores information for an entire company.

Most careers in Business Management & Administration involve working primarily with data and people and only occasionally working with things. Virtually every position depends heavily on computer use. For example, bookkeepers, clerks, administrative assistants, and accountants all work with numbers and words in nearly every task. Human resources workers, public relations specialists, and training and development specialists all work closely with people, training them and helping to resolve their problems.

Even in jobs that deal mainly with people or data, however, you'll need skill at working with things. Administrative assistants need to be able to use computers. General managers must be able to use the equipment their employees rely on, such as cash registers.

9-3 Essential Question Reflection

So, let us revisit our essential question:

How can I match my skills & interests with the right job?

Based on what you learned in this section, please answer this question in detail.

9-4 Education and Training for Business Management & Administration Opportunities

Jobs in the Business Management & Administration industry require varying levels of education and training.

9-4 Essential Question

As you read this section, keep this question in mind:

What training & education is needed for a job in Business Management & Administration?

Training and Education for the Industry

The level of training necessary to be successful in the Business Management & Administration industry varies by career. Jobs can be categorized into three groups—those requiring little or no training, those requiring some training, and those requiring advanced training.

Jobs Requiring Little or No Training

A wide variety of entry-level Business Management & Administration jobs do not require extensive education or training. Businesses need many support people to perform administrative and clerical duties. As a result, some positions are available to high school graduates with little or no training. You could be a receptionist, a mail clerk, or a file clerk. Most companies provide on-the-job training for these new employees.

Jobs Requiring Some Training

Many jobs in Business Management & Administration require some specialized training. Examples include legal secretaries, auditing clerks, and database managers. For these positions, you'll need a degree or certification.

Technical colleges offer programs in areas such as accounting, administrative support, and medical support. Programs are also offered in human resources and financial administration. Some programs award an associate degree. Other programs combine study with onsite training to meet the requirements for certification. Trade organizations, or organizations representing a specific industry or type of job, often have certification programs that provide training for an occupation. Certification tells employers that you can do a certain job.

Certification programs usually require a minimum number of hours on the job and a minimum score on a standardized test. Certification programs cover a wide variety of business and administration careers. For example, a legal secretary can earn certification as an Accredited Legal Secretary (ALS) by the Certifying Board of the National Association of Legal Secretaries. The American Institute of Professional Bookkeepers awards the Certified Bookkeeper designation to those who have at least two years of bookkeeping experience, pass a four-part test, and adhere to a code of ethics.

Earning an associate degree or a certification can help you advance in your field. For more information about such programs, contact trade organizations or community colleges and technical schools in your area.

Jobs Requiring Advanced Training

Some jobs in Business Management & Administration require extensive training. These usually involve business and financial management. Such jobs generally require at least a bachelor's degree, and some require study at the master's degree level.

If you want to be an accountant, auditor, manager, information systems manager, or labor relations specialist, you will need at least a bachelor's degree in your field. Managers may have undergraduate degrees in business and administration or in their specialized field. If you want to become a high-level manager, you should consider pursuing a master's degree. One common option is a Master of Business Administration (MBA). Keep in mind that a degree is not out of any student's reach. The demand for knowledge-based workers is high, and employers are building methods to afford the cost of education to interested employees. Your career is a journey; don't let the distance overwhelm you before you begin.

As you consider college programs, keep in mind your long-term goals. Investigate schools that have programs in business management, human resources, or the specific field you want to pursue. When choosing a program, consider its reputation, cost, location, and rate of job placement.

Table 9.3: Training Required for Business Management & Administration Jobs

Level of Training	Job Title
Little or No Training	Couriers and Messengers Data Entry Keyers Mail Clerks Payroll and Timekeeping Clerks Receptionists and Information Clerks
Some Training	Advertising Sales Agents Bookkeeping, Accounting, and Auditing Clerks Court Reporters Administrative Assistants General and Operations Managers
Considerable Training	Accountants and Auditors Human Resources Managers Management Analysts Operations Research Analysts Public Relations Managers Training and Development Specialists Treasurers and Controllers

Business Management & Administration Skill Standards

Skills required in business management include business planning, employee management, and financial management. Managers may oversee operations or production. Workers in business management also need job-specific skills related to their duties. Administrative support personnel in a lawyer's office need skill in preparing legal documents. Administrative supervisors must have skill in supervising other workers.

Workers in business finance need the ability to organize and plan, maintain records, and use software applications. They must also have knowledge of accounting and banking operations, including the loan process. In addition, workers in business finance also need job-specific skills related to their duties. Workers in accounting departments, for example, require skill in accounting and tax preparation. Workers who oversee employee pension plans need to understand investment strategies.

Professional Skills

Communication Skills   In this industry, workers need to give instructions to the people they manage and discuss problems with those who oversee their work. They may need to speak with customers and suppliers over the phone or in person. Strong relationships with coworkers are founded on good communication.

Listening Skills   Managers meet their customer's and employee's needs by listening to their concerns. Listening skills are necessary for following instructions safely and precisely, which is the foundation of a safe working environment. Good listening also helps workers understand other points of view. For example, listening to employees helps a training and development specialist create training programs that make employees more productive at their jobs.

Problem-Solving Skills   All employees in Business Management & Administration must solve problems that arise in the course of their work. For example, a human resources manager will likely be called on to solve problems between coworkers. Solving problems requires creativity, inventiveness, and critical thinking skills.

Technology Skills   Nearly all workers are expected to be skilled at using computers and other office technology. Most businesses invest significant resources in their computer systems and specialized software for managing payroll, accounts, and operations. As the industry comes to rely more and more on online services, being comfortable with technology will help workers advance in their careers.

Teamwork Skills   Teamwork is key to nearly every job in business management and administration. Regardless of the position, individuals are required to cooperate with coworkers and various departments in the company to get the job done. Teamwork requires leadership skills, communication skills, responsibility, and respect for others.

9-4 • Education and Training for Business Management & Administration Opportunities

Social Skills Interacting with coworkers, customers, and suppliers is a requirement of all jobs in Business Management & Administration. Managers might interact with individuals from various levels of the company in their daily work. They need to interact with customers or suppliers, either over the phone or face-to-face. They should keep an open mind and learn from others.

> **9-4 Essential Question Reflection**
>
> **So, let us revisit our essential question:**
>
> *What training & education is needed for a job in Business Management & Administration?*
>
> Based on what you learned in this section, please answer this question in detail.

Practice 9-4

Skills Practice

Some calculations in the Business Management & Administration industry may require using conversions and formulas. An operations manager for an international company may need to convert currencies to calculate shipping costs, for example. **Practice this skill!**

1. As a mailroom clerk, you sell postage stamps to employees for personal mail. At the end of the day, you must record the dollar value of all stamps sold that day. If you have 7 quarters, 5 dimes, 8 nickels, and 6 pennies to record, how much money do you have?

   A. $2.71
   B. $2.95
   C. $3.08
   D. $3.75
   E. $4.15

2. In your job as a data entry technician, you work 390 minutes per day to enter all accounting transactions into the computer. The timecard you fill out requires you to enter the amount of time you worked using hours. How many hours do you enter?

   A. 3.5
   B. 4
   C. 5.25
   D. 6
   E. 6.5

To access more problems that will help you grow professional skills and are real-world examples in Business Management & Administration, go online.

9-5 Working Conditions in the Business Management & Administration Industry

The Business Management & Administration industry often offers the opportunity for remote work. This shifts the responsibly for the work environment to the employee. The efficiency and comfort of an environment (ergonomics) is important to help employees with their overall health and productivity.

9-5 Essential Question

As you read this section, keep this question in mind:

What are typical work environments in Business Management & Administration?

Physical Environment

The physical work environment for many Business Management & Administration positions is still an office. Most offices and reception areas are clean, and well lit. Private offices are typically reserved for managers.

Some jobs require working with noisy office equipment, including copiers, printers, computers, and fax machines. Although most new equipment is quieter than older equipment, some equipment is still noisy when in use. Some tasks in business and administration, such as inputting data and filing, can be monotonous. Employers today, however, are more aware of the need for variety in an individual's work.

Since the global COVID pandemic began in 2020, more employees work remotely than ever before. For remote workers, the environment is designed by the workers, and may be heavily individualized.

Work Hours

The work hours for jobs in Business Management & Administration can vary. Most employees work a standard nine-to-five day. However, larger companies may require two or three shifts so the companies can operate around the clock. Credit card and online retail companies, which provide around-the-clock customer service, are two examples of businesses that hire shift workers.

Some companies offer flextime options to their employees. Flextime allows workers to choose the hours and days they work, if they maintain a standard total number of hours per week. Workers may adjust their hours to suit their needs. For example, an employee may choose to work ten hours a day on four days a week. Flextime is especially convenient for workers who have young children or other family commitments. Flextime is not practical for all positions. Some workers who adopt flextime schedules include budget analysts, data entry clerks, and auditors.

Many workers in this industry deal with tight deadlines. A deadline might specify that all budgets be prepared and approved by a specific date. This deadline would affect bookkeepers and financial support employees. It would also affect managers who must submit budgets for their departments. Managers feel the stress of deadlines because they are responsible for making sure the work gets done on time. Auditors and accountants face tight deadlines during tax season. As deadlines approach, employees may work long hours to make sure everything is completed on time.

Essential Physical Activities

Most jobs in Business Management & Administration do not involve heavy lifting or much physical exertion. However, they can be a source of physical discomfort on your body's alignment when sitting for long periods can be stressful. Looking at a computer screen for long periods of time can cause eyestrain and headaches.

9-5 • Working Conditions in the Business Management & Administration Industry

You can make minor adjustments for better health by considering the efficiency and comfort (ergonomics) of your work environment. Excessive work at a keyboard can put a strain on arms, wrists, and fingers. Filing paperwork sometimes involves lifting heavy file boxes, stooping, reaching, and standing for long periods of time. It is important that workers are trained to handle equipment properly. Workspaces must be set up to reduce strain and avoid injury.

Injuries and Illnesses

Most on-the-job impairments are either occupational injuries or occupational illnesses. Occupational injuries are injuries that occur at work. They may include cuts, fractures, and sprains. Occupational illnesses are caused by on-the-job exposure to harmful substances. They may include rashes and skin diseases, respiratory problems, or poisoning.

Stress Stress at work can be caused by physical factors, such as heavy workloads, few breaks, or long work hours. It can also result from poor communication, job insecurity, and unpleasant working conditions. Managers and data clerks may feel similar levels of stress despite having different job requirements. Periodic stress is part of any job, and usually it does not harm a person's health. However, prolonged stress can lead to fatigue, mood, and sleep problems, upset stomach, and headaches.

9-5 Essential Question Reflection

So, let us revisit our essential question:

What are typical work environments in Business Management & Administration?

Based on what you learned in this section, please answer this question in detail.

9-6 Trends in Business Management & Administration

The Business Management & Administration industry continues to change, along with the rest of the economy. Technology has changed work processes throughout the industry. Laptops, tablets, and smartphones allow workers to communicate from just about anywhere. Making buildings more energy efficient and creating less waste and pollution are important sustainable business practices that help companies cut costs.

9-6 Essential Question

As you read this section, keep this question in mind:

What factors affect trends in Business Management & Administration?

Technology in the Industry

It is difficult to imagine a time when offices operated without computers and e-mail, especially when you consider today's widespread use of videoconferencing.

As new technologies emerge, large companies are often among the first to use them to communicate with customers and make office work more efficient. Businesses are always looking for ways to save money. Videoconferencing and other communication technologies help avoid costs associated with traveling. All workers, even interns and entry-level employees, are expected to work with common computer hardware and software.

In a business environment, new technology affects everyone in an organization. Following are some ways technology has changed the industry.

Office Technology

The pandemic widened the opportunities for remote work. Businesses began with gigantic mainframe computers to do simple tasks. Remote work has created technology to overcome the challenges that flexibility causes in business.

Videoconferencing

Remote work has become more widespread because the COVID-19 pandemic forced many organizations to create work-from-home opportunities. Remote workers collaborate with their coworkers through various videoconferencing applications.

The Business Management & Administration industry offers many remote work opportunities. For example, operations research analysts use technology to allow them to physically be onsite in one place while conferencing with others at different sites to improve efficiencies. In addition, accountants use videoconferencing to host meetings with their clients.

Many businesses have adopted videoconferencing to increase business and sales opportunities. Videoconferencing is available for many jobs and will continue to grow as technology improves.

Technology in Business Information Management

As computing power grows, more devices are becoming smarter to help with more tasks. Quantum computing will be a trillion times more powerful than what we get from today's advanced supercomputers.

Improvements in financial software products have affected all areas of business. Accounting software enables businesses to:

- Manage their accounting and payroll systems
- Allow users to set up account records to track inventory
- Generate financial statements and print electronic checks
- Customize software for specific kinds of businesses, such as churches, restaurants, and farms

Web-based accounting software allows businesses to use accounting programs that are stored on the Internet. Web-based software is particularly useful for small companies and start-up companies. Instead of buying expensive software, a company simply needs a computer and an Internet connection to get their accounting records in order.

Market Trends in the Industry

Businesses are always looking for better, cheaper, and faster ways to satisfy their customers. The pace of change is rapidly increasing, and the side effects of the rapid change are to be determined.

Cybersecurity With increases in identity theft and online scams, businesses must go to great lengths to reassure their customers. Customers need to know that a company's website is secure and that personal and credit card information will remain confidential. Methods of protecting this information must stay ahead of identity thieves' ability to access them.

Other security problems are posed by hackers and computer viruses. To protect against these threats, companies use a variety of techniques. Most companies establish security systems known as firewalls. A firewall is a hardware and software checkpoint at which all data, both incoming and outgoing, are stopped to make sure the data are acceptable.

Workplace Trends in the Business Management & Administration Industry

Changes taking place in the U.S. workforce affect the Business Management & Administration industry. The popularity of consultants, the increased need for information management workers, and the rise of the global economy are some of today's major trends.

Improving Work Environments Traditionally, businesses calculated goals the same way they counted profits. Increasingly, employers offer their employees the opportunity to work remote as a way to improve their work environment. Mental health strategies teach how the efficiency and comfort of an environment (ergonomics) affect people's overall health. Employees, therefore, gain an essential skill set for life.

Businesses need to make their workforce as productive as possible. Many employees now work from home. These individuals have a greater opportunity to control their environment at home than on the job site.

One way to increase productivity is to improve the work environment. Lighting, air quality, and ease of communication are all critical to worker productivity. These efforts increase employee satisfaction and productivity.

9-6 • Trends in Business Management & Administration 269

Knowledge Workers Advances in computer technology have led to the automation of many jobs that were once done by people. However, it has led to an increased demand for knowledge workers, particularly those who are experts in information technology and information systems management. Operations research analysts, who set up, analyze, and manage computer systems and databases, are also in high demand.

> **9-6 Essential Question Reflection**
>
> **So, let us revisit our essential question:**
>
> *What factors affect trends in Business Management & Administration?*
>
> Based on what you learned in this section, please answer this question in detail.

Chapter 10

Finance

Chapter Topics

10-1 Finance Today

10-2 Finance Jobs

10-3 Building a Career in Finance

10-4 Education and Training for Finance Opportunities

10-5 Working Conditions in the Finance Industry

10-6 Trends in Finance

Essential Questions

By the end of the chapter, you will be able to answer the following questions:

- **10-1** What types of opportunities are available in Finance?
- **10-2** Which opportunities may be right for you?
- **10-3** How can I match my skills & interests with the right job?
- **10-4** What training & education is needed for a job in Finance?
- **10-5** What are the typical work environments in Finance?
- **10-6** What factors affect trends in Finance?

10-1 Finance Today

For thousands of years, people used a system of trade and exchange for goods and services. As civilized society developed, so did financial systems such as paper money, banks, and stock markets. Over time, financial systems grew more complex. They eventually evolved into the financial system we know today.

When you think of workers in the Finance industry, you may envision a worker sitting at a desk interpreting data on computer screens. Or perhaps you picture a Wall Street stockbroker shouting orders to buy and sell stocks.

Workers in the Finance industry are quite varied. Treasurers and controllers at a hospital ensure that funds are available to pay salaries and to buy medicine and equipment. Insurance agents help people protect themselves against losses. Financial services sales agents help people buy and sell securities. All these activities are part of Finance—obtaining, investing, and managing money.

If you choose a career in Finance, you will be part of a global, dynamic, technology-driven industry.

10-1 Essential Question

As you read this section, keep this question in mind:

What types of opportunities are available in Finance?

Career Journeys in Finance

People commonly move into and out of different financial paths. Each contains a group of careers requiring similar skills. This industry is divided into five main career paths:

- Banking Services
- Business Finance
- Securities & Investments
- Insurance
- Accounting

Finance firms range from self-employed individuals to huge global corporations with divisions that employ thousands of workers. Whether large or small, all firms in the Finance industry can be divided into these five paths.

272 Chapter 10 • Finance

Banking Services

The basic business of banking is quite simple: a bank accepts deposits from customers (depositors) and pays interest to these customers. Then it loans money to other customers (debtors), to whom it charges a greater rate of interest. The bank's profit is the difference between the interest it pays to depositors and the interest it receives from debtors.

Banks offer a wide array of products and services. They issue debit and credit cards, extend loans, store valuables, cash checks, and issue money orders.

There are several types of banks, and each type caters to a different market and offers different services. They are:

Commercial Banks These banks offer services to individuals, businesses, and governments. They provide loans, mortgages, checking accounts, and savings accounts.

Savings Banks These banks accept customer savings deposits and make mortgage loans. Their customers are usually individuals. Savings banks may offer services such as safe-deposit boxes and auto loans, but they often do not issue credit cards. Savings banks are generally small and serve a specific geographic area.

Credit Unions These banks are started by a group of people who share a common link. These people may belong to the same labor union, or they may be employed at the same company. Credit unions charge low service fees and often lend money at fairly low interest rates.

Federal Reserve Banks These banks provide services to other banks and to the federal government. They also ensure that all bank consumers receive information they need and that they are treated fairly in their dealings with banks.

The Banking Services career path includes a variety of jobs. Some of them are bank tellers, bill and account collectors, and statement clerks. Bank tellers handle customers' withdrawals and deposits. They change money, sell money orders and traveler's checks, and accept payment for loans and utility bills. Bill collectors contact customers who are behind on payments. Statement clerks handle the everyday, behind-the-scenes banking tasks. These include canceling checks, taking orders for printing new checks, and filing paperwork.

Workers in the Banking Services path must have excellent math and computer skills, good analytical skills, and good communication skills. Clerks and tellers need no advanced training, but a high school diploma is usually required. More senior positions require at least a bachelor's degree, preferably in math, accounting, or business.

Business Finance

Workers in the Business Finance path direct a company's investment policies. They prepare financial documents for regulatory agencies, such as the Securities and Exchange Commission (SEC). Jobs in this path include treasurers, controllers, and financial analysts.

Treasurers and controllers guide the preparation of a company's financial documents. They manage the company's accounting, auditing, and budgeting. They oversee investments and set financial goals. They may make decisions about raising or setting aside money to support growth.

Financial analysts research publicly owned companies. They analyze their financial statements and business practices and produce reports recommending whether customers should buy or sell a company's stock.

Workers in the Business Finance path must have at least average math, analytical, and communication skills. They must have good computer skills and be able to use spreadsheets and accounting software. A bachelor's degree is required for most positions. Financial analysts often have master's degrees in business administration, data analytics, or accounting.

Securities and Investments

Securities and investments firms buy and sell investments for clients. They manage their clients' money and offer financial advice. Securities are financial assets, such as stocks, bonds, and commodities. Stocks are shares of ownership in a corporation. Bonds are written pledges made by a government or a corporation to repay a certain amount of money with interest after a set period. Commodities are papers giving ownership of a quantity of basic goods, such as sugar, coffee, lumber, and oil.

Jobs in the Securities and Investments career path include personal financial advisors, securities and commodities traders, and investment underwriters.

Personal financial advisors advise clients on investments, retirement planning, tax management, and other money matters. They may buy and sell stocks, bonds, mutual funds, and insurance for their clients. Securities and commodities traders buy and sell securities and commodities for their customers. Investment underwriters work with companies that issue stocks as well as with people interested in investing. Their companies underwrite, or guarantee financial support, to back the stock so that the stock can be issued.

A bachelor's degree (and ideally a master's degree) is required for many jobs in the Securities and Investments path. Many personal financial advisors earn certification in their field. Securities, commodities, and financial services sales agents must be licensed to buy and sell securities. All workers in this path need good communication and organizational skills, along with good math skills.

Insurance

Insurance companies agree to pay for losses that result from events such as a fire or a car accident. Life insurance provides funds to the person named in an insurance policy when the policyholder dies. Disability insurance pays for a policyholder's expenses if that person is unable to work.

Insurance sales agents sell policies to individuals, groups, or corporations. Actuaries analyze statistics to calculate insurance risks. The risk determines the premiums, or the amount customers pay for their policies.

All workers in this path need very good analytical and problem-solving skills. Computer skills and an understanding of statistics are helpful. A college degree is required for most insurance adjusters, agents, underwriters, and actuaries. Agents must get a license in the state or states where they plan to sell insurance.

Accounting

Accounting firms oversee the finances of businesses, institutions, and individuals. They prepare a company's public financial records. They file tax forms and fees. They make sure companies are run in a cost-effective way. A bachelor's or a master's degree is required for most jobs in this path.

Accountants and auditors are higher-level employees who have expertise in financial operations. They provide services including public, management, and government accounting.

Some are responsible for internal auditing, a company's own review of its financial records. Accountants may be responsible for tax preparation. They may work on budgeting and cost-and-asset management.

Finance Future Outlook

The outlook for the Finance industry is mixed. Jobs in market research are expected to increase faster than average. Moderate growth is expected in computer and information systems. The Business Finance path is likely to see mixed results.

Table 10.1: Job Forecast for a Sample of Occupations in the Finance Industry over the Next Ten Years

Occupation	Expected Growth Rate
Market Research Analysts	15%+
Insurance Sales Agent/Claims Clerks	5%–10%
Computer and Information Systems Managers	10%–15%
Personal Finance Advisors	15%+
Financial Managers	15%+
Fundraisers	10%–15%
Actuaries	15%+
Accountants and Auditors	5%–10%

Source: *Bureau of Labor Statistics*

10-1 Essential Question Reflection

So, let us revisit our essential question:

What types of opportunities are available in Finance?

Based on what you learned in this section, answer this question in detail.

Practice 10-1

Skills Practice

When reading documents, such as new tax laws, workers in the Finance industry need to be able to identify the main idea. They must also find details supporting the main idea. The main idea tells what the document is about. Details provide more information that helps explain the main idea. **Practice this skill!**

NOTICE FROM THE INTERNAL REVENUE SERVICE: PAST-DUE RETURNS

The integrity of our tax system and well-being of our country depend, to a large degree, on the timely filing and payment of taxes by each individual, family, and business in this country. Those choosing not to file and pay their fair share increase the burden on the rest of us to support our schools, maintain and repair roadways, and continue the many important programs that use our tax dollars to make life easier for all citizens.

Some people don't know they should file a tax return; some don't file because they expect a refund; and some don't file because they owe taxes. Encourage your family, neighbors, friends, and coworkers to do their fair share by filing their federal tax returns and paying any taxes due on time.

1. As a tax preparer, you must file timely returns for your clients. What is the main idea of this Internal Revenue Service (IRS) notice regarding past-due returns?

    A. The U.S. tax system has integrity.

    B. Every individual, family, and business must pay taxes.

    C. Citizens should report people who do not pay their taxes.

    D. Some people do not know that they must file a tax return.

    E. Not paying taxes creates a burden for others.

2. Schools and roadways are details in the IRS notice that support which of the following ideas?

    A. People need encouragement to pay their taxes.

    B. Some people do not want to pay taxes.

    C. Taxes should be paid on time.

    D. Everyone benefits from our tax dollars.

    E. Life is easy for U.S. citizens.

To access more problems that will help you grow professional skills and are real-world examples in Finance, go online.

10-2 Finance Jobs

There are many kinds of jobs in the Finance industry. You can find jobs at all skill levels, from entry level to managerial. You may be interested in working with customers at a bank branch as a teller. Perhaps you would enjoy helping people set up their financial plans by becoming a personal financial advisor. Or you might enjoy the fast-paced buying and selling required of an accountant. Here are some common Finance industry jobs and the skills they require.

10-2 Essential Question

As you read this section, keep this question in mind:

Which opportunities may be right for you?

Fastest-Growing Occupations:

Financial Managers

- Analyze market trends to maximize profits and find expansion opportunities
- Prepare financial statements, business activity reports, and forecasts

Fast Facts:

Employment: 730,800 employees
Annual Openings: 71,300
Median Annual Wage: $63.32 hourly, $131,710 annually
Education Needed: Bachelor's degree

Market Research Analysts

- Monitor and forecast marketing and sales trends
- Devise and evaluate methods for collecting data, such as surveys, questionnaires, and opinion polls

Fast Facts:

Employment: 792,500 employees
Annual Openings: 99,800
Median Annual Wage: $30.73 hourly $63,920 annually
Education Needed: Bachelor's degree
Other: Some analysts influence the artists who create charts, graphs, and infographics summarizing their research and findings.

Great Jobs! – High School Diploma Needed:

Bank Tellers

- Answer questions from customers about their accounts
- Record all transactions electronically

Fast Facts:

Employment: 378,000 employees

Annual Openings: 35,100

Median Annual Wage: $17.46 hourly $36,310 annually

Other: Working as a bank teller provides opportunities to advance in the Finance industry.

Insurance Sales Agents

- Interview prospective clients to get information about their financial resources and discuss existing coverage
- Customize insurance programs to suit individual clients

Fast Facts:

Employment: 215,400 employees

Annual Openings: 22,100

Median Annual Wage: $18.13 hourly $37,700 annually

Other: This occupation may offer some travel and a flexible schedule, including evenings and weekends off!

Bill and Account Collectors

- Find consumers and businesses who have overdue bills
- Inform debtors that they have an overdue bill and try to negotiate a payment

Fast Facts:
   Employment: 215,400 employees
   Annual Openings: 22,100
   Median Annual Wage: $18.13 hourly $37,700 annually
   Other: Many people in this occupation have the ability to work remotely.

Highest-Wage Occupations:

Accountants and Auditors

- Examine financial statements to ensure that they are accurate and comply with laws and regulations
- Inspect account books and accounting systems for efficiency and use of accepted accounting procedures and identify potential risks for fraud

Fast Facts:
   Employment: 1,449,800 employees
   Annual Openings: 8,180
   Median Annual Wage: $37.14 hourly $77,250 annually
   Education Needed: Bachelor's degree and additional certification
   Other: To become a certified public accountant (CPA), you must pass an exam.

Actuaries

- Estimate the probability and likely economic cost of an event such as death, sickness, an accident, or a natural disaster
- Design and test insurance policies, investments, and other business strategies to minimize risk and maximize profitability

Fast Facts:
   Employment: 28,300 employees
   Annual Openings: 2,400
   Median Annual Wage: $50.91 hourly $105,900 annually
   Education Needed: Bachelor's degree and passing scores on actuarial exams
   Other: Actuaries use their mathematical skills on a daily basis and have the ability to make a huge impact on the companies they work for.

Finance Jobs Related to Other Industries:

Computer and Information Systems Managers

- Direct daily operations of department, analyze workflow, establish priorities, develop standards, and set deadlines
- Meet with department heads, managers, supervisors, vendors, and others to solicit cooperation and resolve problems

Fast Facts:
  Employment: 482,000 employees
  Annual Openings: 4,240
  Median Annual Wage: $76.45 hourly, $159,010 annually
  Education Needed: Bachelor's degree or some college

Fundraisers

- Organize campaigns or events to solicit donations
- Train volunteers in fundraising procedures and practices

Fast Facts:
  Employment: 105,800 employees
  Annual Openings: 11,400
  Median Annual Wage: $29.17 hourly $60,660 annually
  Education Needed: Bachelor's degree
  Other: Employers may prefer candidates who have studied public relations, communications, English, or business.

10-2 Essential Question Reflection

So, let us revisit our essential question:

Which opportunities may be right for you?

Based on what you learned in this section, what 2 or 3 opportunities are the most interesting? Explain your answer.

Case Study: Personal Financial Advisors

What do they do?

- Advise clients on financial plans using knowledge of tax and investment strategies, securities, insurance, pension plans, and real estate
- Assess clients' assets, liabilities, cash flow, insurance coverage, tax status, and financial objectives
- Buy and sell financial assets for clients

What would you do?

- Interview clients to determine their current income, expenses, insurance coverage, tax status, financial objectives, risk tolerance, or other information needed to develop a financial plan
- Recommend strategies in cash management, insurance coverage, investment planning, or other areas to help clients achieve their financial goals
- Manage client portfolios, keeping client plans up-to-date

What do you need to know?

Business
Customer service
Accounting and economics

Arts and Humanities
English language

Math and Science
Arithmetic, algebra, geometry, calculus, or statistics
Psychology

Safety and Government
Law and government

What skills do you need?

Basic Skills
Listen to others, do not interrupt, and ask good questions
Read work-related information

Problem Solving
Notice a problem, and figure out the best way to solve it

People and Technology Systems
Think about the pros and cons of different options, and pick the best

Figure out how a system should work and how changes in the future will affect it

What abilities must you be good at?

Verbal
Communicate by speaking
Communicate by writing

Math
Add, subtract, multiply, or divide
Choose the right type of math to solve a problem

Ideas and Logic
Make general rules or come up with answers from lots of detailed information
Use rules to solve problems

Who does well in this occupation?

People interested in this work like activities that include leading, making decisions, and business.

They do well at jobs that need:
Integrity
Dependability
Attention to detail
Analytical thinking
Concern for others
Achievement/effort

What educational level is needed?

- Bachelor's degree or certificate

Practice 10-2

Skills Practice

The details in workplace documents are not always clearly stated. For example, an investment fund manager may have to draw conclusions about what a client wants from a brief description in their stock portfolio. It may sometimes be necessary to make a logical guess, when a detail is suggested rather than stated. **Practice this skill!**

MEMO

To: All Tax Advisors

From: K. Allen, Supervisor

The Village of Sunnyville has levied a 2.5 percent income tax on all residents of the Village (anyone who lives within the Village boundaries of Sunnyville), workers, and business owners operating within the Village limits. All employers will be responsible for withholding the 2.5 percent tax on employee wages and remitting, or paying, the tax to the Village. Employers may pay this withheld tax to the Village on a monthly or quarterly basis. Residents who did not have the tax withheld by an employer must file a Village tax return.

1. As a tax advisor for a tax preparation firm, you receive the above memo. Based on the memo, who or what is a **resident** of Sunnyville?

   A. an employer within the village
   B. someone who lives in the village
   C. someone who works in the village
   D. a business that operates within the village
   E. a business with taxable income

2. Employers are responsible for **remitting** withheld taxes. What do you infer the word "remitting" means?

   A. paying
   B. investing
   C. keeping
   D. withholding
   E. saving

Skills Practice

When reading workplace graphics, such as a chart showing the benefits of various insurance plans, finance workers must know what information to look for. The key information may be in one or more graphics. Workers must be able to sift through unimportant or distracting information to find what is needed. **Practice this skill!**

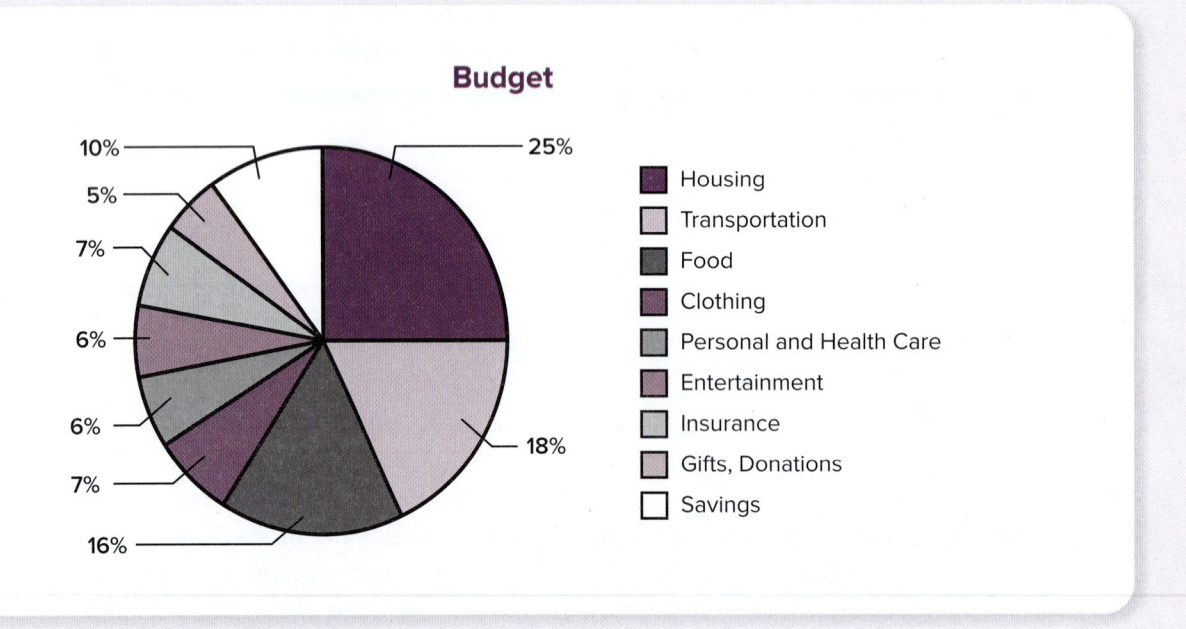

Budget

- Housing — 25%
- Transportation — 18%
- Food — 16%
- Clothing — 7%
- Personal and Health Care — 6%
- Entertainment — 6%
- Insurance — 7%
- Gifts, Donations — 5%
- Savings — 10%

3. You work as a credit counselor for an agency that helps people get their personal finances in order. This graph shows a client's budget. What is her biggest expense?

    A. entertainment
    B. food
    C. housing
    D. clothing
    E. transportation

4. What percentage of her budget is spent on entertainment?

    A. 5%
    B. 6%
    C. 7%
    D. 10%
    E. 16%

To access more problems that will help you grow professional skills and are real-world examples in Finance, go online.

10-3 Building a Career in Finance

If you are interested in obtaining a job in the Finance industry, think about the path you must take to reach your ultimate career goal.

For example, if you are interested in a career in banking but do not have a college degree, you may start out as a teller. Bank tellers deal with the public. They take deposits, make withdrawals, and accept payments to credit lines. If you do well, you may be promoted to head teller. Then you will supervise other tellers and have added responsibilities.

You may then move up to be a customer service representative, where you will answer questions about the bank's products and services and make sure the branch is meeting its customers' needs.

Next, you may become an associate branch manager and help the branch manager run the bank branch. From there, you may be promoted to branch manager and later to executive positions in the bank's administration.

Don't worry if you change your mind about your career path. This happens to many people. It often takes time to find the right path.

10-3 Essential Question

As you read this section, keep this question in mind:

How can I match my skills & interests with the right job?

Are You More Interested in Working With Data, People, or Things?

Almost all careers in the Finance industry offer the opportunity to work with a combination of data, people, and things. Working with data involves the evaluation of information. Working with people requires building human relationships. Working with things involves using objects, such as tools and machines. Most jobs focus mainly on one of these. Accountants, for example, work mainly with data. Financial planners work primarily with people. Insurance claims adjustors work mostly with things. When thinking about a career in Finance, consider what balance of data, people, and things you want.

Careers That Involve Working With Data

Working with data means working with words, ideas, and numbers. Examples of working with data include preparing financial statements and drawing up budgets, analyzing sales figures and planning investment strategies, and analyzing insurance risks.

If you decide to pursue a Finance career that involves working mostly with data, your days will be spent calculating, gathering facts, and analyzing data. For example, as a financial analyst, you will study a broad array of financial and economic data before creating and suggesting investment strategies. As a controller of a corporation, you will work with company funds, prepare budgets, and monitor your company's financial standing.

Careers That Involve Working With People

Many Finance jobs focus on human relationships. Working with people can include meeting one-on-one with clients to assess their investment needs, talking to witnesses to determine the level of fault in a car accident, or helping a customer open a new checking account. All of these activities require strong communication skills.

For everyone from bank tellers to personal financial advisors, contact with clients is a daily part of the job. Many Finance jobs involve working as part of a team. For example, as part of a portfolio management team, you would be required to work together with the rest of the group to produce one final product. All information must be shared, and common strategies must be developed.

Careers That Involve Working With Things

Working with things includes all jobs in the Finance industry that are related to the design, creation, use, and repair of machines, tools, and instruments. In Finance, working with things might involve checking a damaged car to assess the cost of repairs. It might mean opening lockboxes at a bank so customers can access their valuables. It could mean keeping the office copier or other machines running smoothly.

Although most careers in Finance involve working primarily with data and people, some positions require employees to work with things. If you work at a bank branch, you may find yourself counting dollar bills and coins, securing clients' valuables in safe-deposit boxes, and collecting receipts from registers.

> **10-3 Essential Question Reflection**
>
> **So, let us revisit our essential question:**
>
> *How can I match my skills & interests with the right job?*
>
> Based on what you learned in this section, please answer this question in detail.

10-4 Education and Training for Finance Opportunities

Jobs in the Finance industry require varying levels of education and training. Some jobs in this industry require little or no formal training. For other jobs, it is necessary to have specific education and experience.

10-4 Essential Question

As you read this section, keep this question in mind:

What training & education is needed for a job in Finance?

Training and Education for the Industry

The level of training to succeed in Finance varies by job and by field. Jobs can be divided into three groups—those requiring little or no training, those requiring some training, and those requiring advanced training.

Jobs Requiring Little or No Training

Some jobs in the Finance industry do not call for a great deal of education or training. Most do require at least a high school diploma. They also call for strong math skills.

In Banking Services path, many workers are not required to have much previous training. These occupations include tellers, bill and account collectors, and statement clerks. Workers in these jobs usually get on-the-job training provided through the company they are hired by.

Similarly, in the Insurance path, a variety of entry-level jobs are available to high school graduates. These include insurance claims clerk, insurance policy processing clerk, and office machine operator.

In the Accounting path, you can become a tax preparer or an office clerk with very little training.

Jobs Requiring Some Training

Most jobs in Finance do require specialized training after high school. After getting experience in an entry-level job, you can sometimes move up to a job such as a customer service specialist in a bank or insurance agency. The same is true for becoming an insurance adjuster, examiner, or investigator.

You can complete an internship, which will be discussed later in this chapter, to prepare for many of the skilled positions in Finance. A formal education gives you a chance to learn specialized skills. Community colleges offer courses in fields such as economics, business administration, and computer technology. Some programs offer an associate degree after you complete a two-year program.

Other programs combine study with onsite training to meet the requirements for specific types of certification. Trade organizations, or organizations representing a specific industry or type of job, often offer certification programs. These programs give thorough training for a specific job. Certification programs often require a minimum number of hours on the job and a minimum score on a standardized test created by the trade organization.

Jobs Requiring Advanced Training

Are you interested in working as a securities and commodities trader, a financial analyst, a personal financial advisor, or an auditor? If your answer is yes, you'll need a bachelor's degree, a specialized degree, or certification.

Some jobs, such as an actuary, require several years' work experience in the field and a license to practice.

Financial analysts need at least a bachelor's degree. They receive years of onsite training after being hired. Financial analysts delve into a company's records. Their goal is to forecast, or predict, whether the company's stock is likely to go up or down. Analysts' forecasts can sway the direction of a stock price. Analysts must understand accounting, finance, marketing, and business.

Many finance managers have undergraduate degrees in finance and graduate degrees in business management. Treasurers and controllers are also likely to have advanced degrees.

Table 10.4: Training Required for Finance Jobs

Level of Training	Job Title
Little or No Training	Tellers Bill and Account Collectors Insurance Claims Clerks/Sales Agents Tax Preparers
Some Training	Customer Service Specialists Insurance Adjusters, Examiners, or Investigators Insurance Sales Agents Insurance Claims Clerks
Advanced Training	Accountants and Auditors Actuaries Financial Managers Market Research Analysts Treasurers and Controllers Investment Bankers

Job and Workplace Skills

Securing a position in the Finance industry can be difficult, even for someone who has many years of experience and education. When considering job candidates, employers look for someone with well-developed job-specific skills and general workplace skills. Job-specific skills are the skills necessary to do a particular job. They may include balancing a budget or programming a computer. General workplace skills can be used in a variety of jobs.

Finance Skill Standards

Both educational and professional organizations have developed knowledge and skill standards for the Finance industry. The National Council on Economic Education (NCEE) and the National Business Education Association (NBEA), for example, have compiled basic standards that specify what students should know about economics and finance. For example, the NBEA's accounting standards include understanding the steps in the accounting cycle, determining the value of assets, and preparing financial statements.

The National Association of Securities Dealers (NASD) and the Institute of Certified Bankers (ICB) have also developed standards for workers in their fields. The SEC requires licensed securities professionals to undergo ongoing training. This training teaches securities traders to conduct business professionally and to avoid unethical practices.

Core Skills

Regardless of the career that you choose in Finance, you will find that certain core skills are needed. Core skills differ from academic or job-specific skills. They are learned both inside and outside the classroom. They are transferable from job to job. Developing these skills will make you more marketable in Finance jobs and in any job situation.

Communication Skills   Communication skills include the ability to speak and write clearly. In Finance, managers need to instruct the people they supervise. Workers also need to explain financial information to clients.

Listening Skills   Active listening involves paying attention and checking for understanding by restating what has been said. A customer service representative must listen well in order to give customers the responses they need. Listening skills are needed to carry out instructions safely and precisely. Active listening helps create a safe working environment.

Problem-Solving Skills   All employees in Finance must solve problems that arise. A bill collector needs to figure out how to help people meet their financial commitments. Solving problems requires creativity, ingenuity, and thinking skills.

Technology Skills   In the Finance industry today, nearly all workers use computers and other office technology. Bank tellers use computers to input deposits and withdrawals and to find consumer data. Sales agents in securities and commodities use computers to enter orders to buy and sell. They track investment performance online and keep records of their transactions.

Decision-Making Skills The ability to gather and analyze information rapidly and to think clearly under pressure is required in most Finance jobs. For example, as a securities and commodities trader, you will need to make quick decisions about buying and selling in order to get the best price.

Organizing and Planning Skills Being organized and planning carefully enable financial professionals to keep track of their work. These skills help them meet deadlines and work with clients. People employed in financial support positions are required to effectively track invoices, payments, or payroll.

Teamwork Skills In this industry, most people work on teams. Sometimes the teams are made up of people from different departments. Leading a team requires the ability to identify and make use of the strengths of coworkers.

Social Skills Interacting with coworkers, clients, and colleagues in other industries is a requirement of many jobs in Finance. Social interaction with coworkers makes for a more enjoyable work atmosphere, and coworkers can learn from one another. A personal financial advisor may need to ask clients probing questions to understand their financial situations.

Adaptability Skills Job descriptions, work environments, and work processes are constantly changing along with technology and economic shifts. Statement clerks had to adapt when banks shifted from returning checks to customers to storing electronic checks. Workers must be ready to acquire new skills.

10-4 Essential Question Reflection

So, let us revisit our essential question:

What training & education is needed for a job in Finance?

Based on what you learned in this section, please answer this question in detail.

Practice 10-4

Skills Practice

It may be necessary at times to add information to graphics as part of a job in the Finance industry. A financial services sales agent may need to fill out a checklist every time they make a sale. Knowing how to correctly add information to graphics is an important skill in this industry. **Practice this skill!**

Automotive Sales Figures for May 2023

	May 2023 Sales	Percent Change from May 2022	YTD 2023 Sales	Percent Change from YTD 2022
Cars				
Midsize	242,532	26.1	423,859	15.8
Small	174,987	23.8	314,200	18.0
Luxury	66,380	12.4	126,480	10.1
Large	7,095	14.9	14,082	11.8
Light-duty trucks				
Pickup	130,919	36.4	244,297	30.0
Cross-over	215,145	30.8	401,096	27.9
Minivan	56,247	21.8	102,914	36.7
Midsize SUV	56,201	43.2	102,176	42.2
Large SUV	17,748	26.0	33,694	13.6
Small SUV	15,195	33.2	28,213	33.8
Luxury SUV	10,938	8.6	22,181	10.5

1. As an investment analyst specializing in the Automotive industry, you follow sales figures for different kinds of cars. Which category saw the greatest percentage of change from YTD 2022 to YTD 2023 and also from May 2022 to May 2023?

   A. midsize cars
   B. luxury cars
   C. pickups
   D. midsize SUVs
   E. luxury SUVs

2. What is the best way to describe the change in automotive sales between YTD 2022 and YTD 2023?

   A. Sales mostly stayed flat, with few categories having increased or decreased sales.
   B. Most categories had a significant decrease in sales by at least 10 percent.
   C. Most categories had a slight decrease in sales, but no more than 5 percent.
   D. Few categories had sales increases, but some categories increased dramatically.
   E. All categories saw a sales increase of at least 10 percent.

Skills Practice

When reviewing workplace graphics, it may be necessary to compare information in one or more graphics. An actuary might compare the rate of insurance claims for people living in different locations. Workers must know how different graphics relate to each other and be able to compare information and trends within them.
Practice this skill!

Travel Packages

	Option 1	Option 2	Option 3
Departure Date	May 1	April 30	May 1
Return Date	May 5	May 4	May 6
Includes	Airfare and hotel	Airfare and hotel	Airfare, hotel transfer, hotel
Price	$633	$612	$635

Travel Specials

	Special 1	Special 2
Valid Dates	April 1 through May 30 (Valid for four- night stay only)	May 10 through June 30 (Valid for four- night stay only)
Includes	Airfare, hotel transfer, hotel, and breakfast	Airfare, hotel transfer, hotel, and breakfast
Price	$651	$628

3. As a personal financial advisor, you help your clients stay on budget. A client wants to take her family on a four-night trip. They need to travel before the second week of May, and the airfare and hotel must cost less than $630. Which of the following packages or specials best meets the client's needs?

   A. option 1
   B. option 2
   C. option 3
   D. special 1
   E. special 2

4. If the client has a change in plans and needs to travel after the first week of May and wants to stay for five nights, which package or special is the best deal?

   A. option 1
   B. option 2
   C. option 3
   D. special 1
   E. special 2

To access more problems that will help you grow professional skills and are real-world examples in Finance, go online.

10-5 Working Conditions in the Finance Industry

When choosing a career path, it is important to know what it is like to work in the industry. Understanding the work environment, hazards, and benefits of a job can help you make informed decisions.

> **10-5 Essential Question**
>
> **As you read this section, keep this question in mind:**
>
> *What are typical work environments in Finance?*

Work Environment

Work environment refers to factors that affect workers' health and satisfaction on the job. Remote work and flexible schedules create opportunities and challenges. Planning your schedule gives you a greater chance of meeting your personal and professional goals. Professionals in the Finance industry work in cities across the United States and around the world. Some workers sit in offices and talk to clients on the phone from the early in the morning until late in the evening. Other workers stand on their feet all day in a noisy and stressful environment. Many jobs in Finance involve long hours of work, with a high level of stress and great mental exertion. However, workers in this industry are usually well paid.

Physical Environment

The physical environment in the Finance industry varies by occupation. Some people work in comfortable, well-lit offices. They often spend much of their time working on computers, talking on phone, in person, and in virtual reality environments. Offices may be sectioned off into workstations. These cubicles provide each worker with a small amount of privacy. Employees have their own desks, filing cabinets, and computers. Managers and executives often have their own offices.

Traders spend much of the day standing. Typically, the trading floor is crowded, chaotic, and loud. It is packed with traders buying and selling large blocks of securities. Floor traders must find buyers who are willing to buy their seller's stock at a specific price. Traders are under pressure to complete deals quickly. Brokerage houses (companies that buy and sell stocks) tend to be active. So are the offices of sales agents, who work in noisy call centers.

Work Hours

Work hours for careers in Finance vary greatly. Most positions require employees to work a typical 40-hour week. Bank workers who deal with the public generally do not work more than 40 hours in a week. However, as bank branches open in grocery stores and malls, some employees need to work evenings or weekends. Workers in Finance may need to make and maintain business contacts by going to conferences, meetings, and other social gatherings. This requires spending extra time outside the office.

Customer service departments in some financial institutions offer 24-hour assistance to clients. To keep these departments staffed, most employees work in shifts. This allows a business to operate around the clock. It also allows workers to select the hours they want to work. Shift work is common for customer service representatives and technical service providers.

Flextime allows workers to choose the hours and days they work, as long as they work a certain number of hours per week. Workers may adjust their hours to suit their needs. One employee may choose to work four days a week for 10 hours a day. Another may work six days a week for six-and-a-half hours a day. Flextime is helpful for workers with young children or other family commitments. Since most financial positions involve working in companies that are open to the public during regular business hours, flextime is not always appropriate.

Positions in areas such as portfolio management (managing the investments of a person or a firm), investment banking, and corporate and public finance may require workers to put in long, irregular hours. A financial analyst may need to make last-minute, final adjustments to an earnings report that require them to work nights or over the weekend.

Many positions in Finance require workers to deal with tight deadlines. All publicly owned companies must file financial statements with the SEC on certain dates. Other companies have strict deadlines for preparing budgets. Everyone working on the budget will feel the stress created by the deadline. This includes budget analysts, who provide advice and technical help to financial managers, and department heads, who supply the analysts with estimated costs and expenses.

Essential Physical Activities

Most workers in the Finance industry are not subjected to difficult physical activity. Finance professionals generally work in comfortable offices. They may work remotely. Offices may be in high-rise buildings that hold hundreds of offices or in small buildings with just a few employees.

Although most careers in Finance do not require workers to lift heavy objects, work with hazardous materials, or operate dangerous machinery, the workday can be strenuous. Traders and bank tellers stand for hours at a time. Most people in Finance work on computers for extended periods. These factors may cause fatigue, eye strain, or repetitive-stress injuries.

Some employees, such as investment underwriters, often travel. Work schedules for departments with international clients may require employees to work abroad for weeks, months, or perhaps years at a time.

Injuries and Illnesses

Most workers in Finance face a much-lower-than-average risk of being hurt or becoming ill on the job. They are, however, exposed to certain health risks. Musculoskeletal disorders are a particular concern. The U.S. Department of Labor defines a musculoskeletal disorder (MSD) as an injury or disorder of the muscles, nerves, tendons, joints, cartilage, and spinal discs. MSDs do not include disorders caused by an accident on the job, such as a slip, trip, fall, or motor vehicle accident.

Finance workers can take steps to protect themselves against MSDs. Customer service representatives, bill and account collectors, and sales agents who spend most of their time on the phone should use headsets. Making this change will help them to avoid neck strain from holding a receiver.

Repetitive stress injuries (RSIs) are musculoskeletal disorders that can develop when the same motions are performed over and over. Spending many hours working at a keyboard, for example, can hurt the tendons of the wrist. Over a long period of time, injuries from these repetitive actions can cause pain and disability.

10-5 Essential Question Reflection

So, let us revisit our essential question:

What are typical work environments in Finance?

Based on what you learned in this section, please answer this question in detail.

10-6 Trends in Finance

The Finance industry is constantly changing due to the ups and downs of the economy. Advances in technology affect the way business is conducted. America's aging population, diversity in the workplace, and sustainability also heavily impact this industry.

> **10-6 Essential Question**
>
> As you read this section, keep this question in mind:
>
> *What factors affect trends in Finance?*

Technology in the Finance Industry

The Internet and e-mail enable people to communicate rapidly, which is necessary for someone to be successful in the Finance industry. Laptops, tablets, and smartphones give workers the ability to communicate across continents at any time. Computers have transformed the way business is transacted and the kinds of business that finance companies can conduct.

Technology in Banking Services

The Banking Services path was disrupted in the early 2000s by the global financial crisis. To remain strong and reduce their risk, banks adapted and began to offer more services. These include products formerly available only from insurance companies or from securities and investments firms. Banks are getting their message out through more channels than ever before. They use tools such as social networking sites and other online networks.

In addition, by improving online banking, banks can cut costs and serve more consumers. Online banking allows customers to open and close accounts, pay bills, transfer funds between accounts, and use online personal finance-management software.

One key to the successful use of the Internet for financial transactions is encryption. Encryption is technology that scrambles electronic data, such as a person's account information, into code. The code can be read only by the intended receiver, who has the decryption key.

Encryption technology is used in banking and throughout the Finance industry to protect corporate information and customers' account information and to transmit information safely over the Internet. However, companies must work constantly to ensure that their files and databases are secure from tampering because encryption protects only data in transit.

Technology in Business Finance

The Internet offers financial organizations new opportunities to improve company profits. Instead of having to rely on print or TV advertisements to market a new product, companies now rely on technology to spread information. For example, social media and email advertisement campaigns. It now takes less time than ever for people to learn about new products, which can lead to an increase in sales and profit for a company.

Information does not just flow in one direction, though. Some companies are calling for feedback through online surveys. This feedback is used to improve products and services. By observing how consumers spend, companies have access to vast quantities of market data that they never had before. They also have more access to their competitors' data, making it easier to stay competitive.

Software continues to evolve and expand into new areas, giving financial analysts additional tools that help them strategize for the future. Artificial Intelligence (AI) will support humans to create affordable personalized financial portfolios for businesses or individuals.

Technology in Securities and Investments

In the past, individuals placed orders to buy and sell stocks by calling their sales agent. Now, people use electronic brokerage accounts on their cellphones to trade online securities. Online brokerage services give people control over their own accounts. This is convenient for the customer. It is also cheaper for the brokerage firm. Discount brokerage firms offer lower commission rates, the fee charged for making a trade, than rates offered by traditional sales agents.

The growth of online investing, especially with discount brokers, has brought many new investors into the stock market. The Internet has not eliminated the need for sales agents, however, even at online brokerage firms. Most brokerage services will provide help for customers who need assistance with trades or complicated transactions. Customers who use this service are often charged a fee.

The pace of trading has sped up in recent years, and this trend is expected to continue. The trader who can make the fastest bid has an advantage. No matter how fast transactions take place, though, there must still be a record of each sale and purchase. This record-keeping can slow the pace of trading.

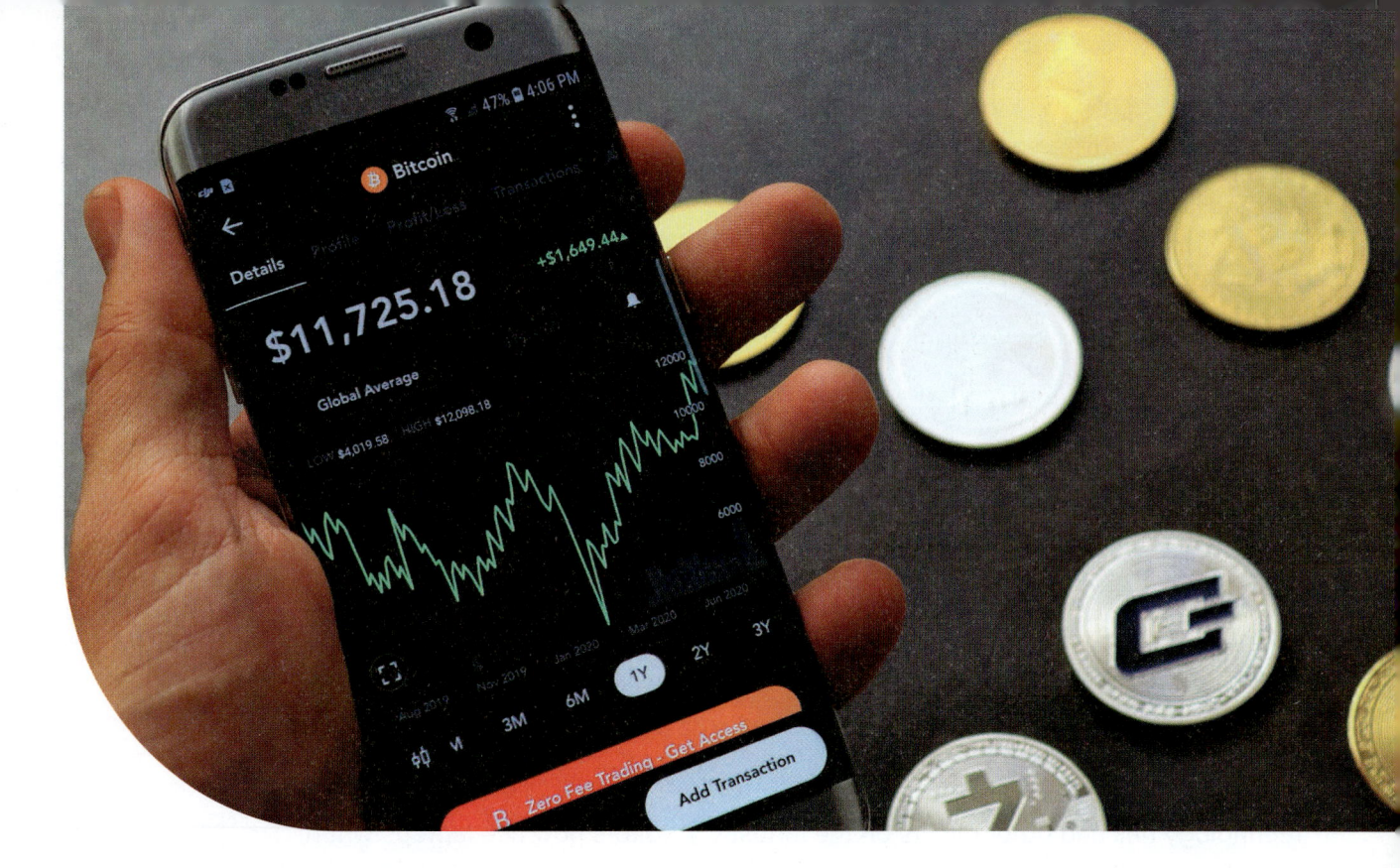

Technology in Insurance

Insurance companies have had to rethink their traditional strategy of relying on agents to sell policies. All major insurance companies now have websites that allow customers to compare the products offered by different companies. Customers can buy insurance and review their account information online. New technologies are good for customers because they make everything easier and more accessible. However, as more and more functions become automated, new technologies may lead to a reduction in jobs.

The job outlook may improve as insurance companies expand into new products, such as securities and mutual funds. More workers may be needed to make sure companies comply with new government regulations. Keeping a close eye on a company's risk is a growing challenge as well. New software should make these jobs more manageable. For example, insurance claims adjusters may no longer need to visit sites to look at damage. Instead, they will be able to use satellite imagery. This will allow them to handle more cases.

Technology in Accounting

In recent decades, technology has revolutionized the Accounting career path. Computers perform the calculations that were once done by hand. The availability of tax software means that many individuals no longer must rely on accountants to complete their tax forms. New regulations were designed to prevent the kind of problems that led to the economic downturn of the late 2000s. These new rules will require more corporate accountants and auditors in the Finance industry. These accounting professionals make use of ever-improving software to handle their growing responsibilities and keep their companies strong.

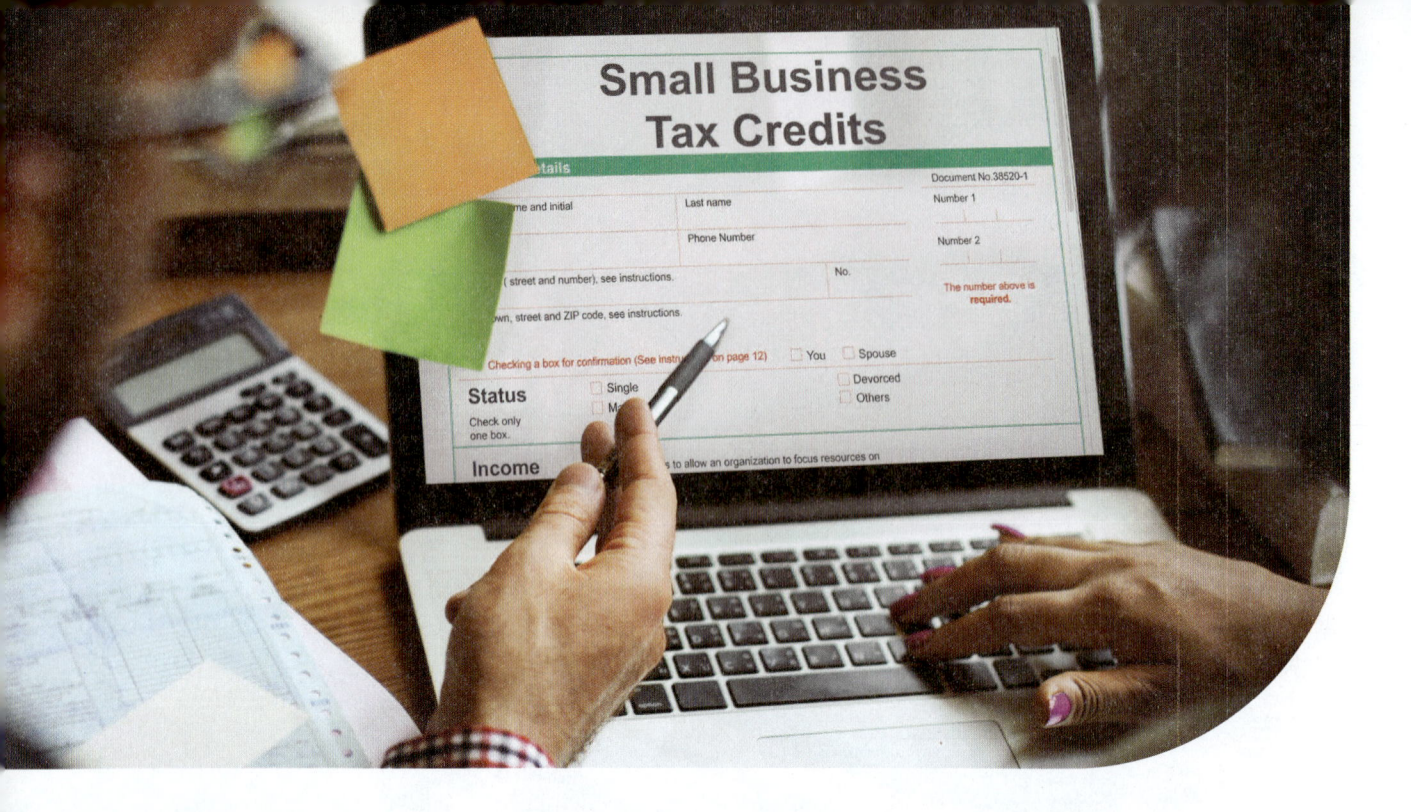

Technology has had other effects on the industry. Auditors now use laptops when they visit companies for an audit. People use computers, not pencils, to take the CPA exam. If they like, they can use e-books to study for the CPA exam. For the first time, thanks to technology, people living outside the United States can take the CPA exam without traveling from their home countries.

Demographics in the Industry

The demographics of the United States are changing. One of today's most significant demographic changes is the aging of the American population. Another major change is the changing patterns of women and ethnic minorities in the workplace. These and other changes will have important effects on every path of the Finance industry.

Aging Populations

Baby boomers, those Americans born between 1946 and 1964, are starting to reach retirement age. This generation has invested heavily in stocks to save for retirement. Their demand for investment services and personal finance advisors is expected to increase. They have also increased the demand for life insurance and for annuities, which are insurance products that provide the policyholder with a set amount of money for the rest of their life.

Diversity in the Workplace

Like other industries, the Finance industry is working to increase diversity in the workplace by encouraging women and people of color to pursue positions. Banks have been especially conscious of this issue, and many have started diversity, equity, and inclusion (DE&I) initiatives to address the need for diversity in the workplace.

Sustainability in the Industry

In recent years, the Finance industry has become increasingly sustainable. For example, online communication reduces the need for travel. Businesses can now hold meetings with workers in other countries via videoconferencing applications instead of meeting in person. In addition, there has been a push for banks and other financial institutions to make the transition to paperless communication and billing. These solutions are more cost-effective and environmentally friendly.

The Economy and the Finance Industry

On January 20, 2020, the Center for Disease Control and Prevention (CDC) reported the first Coronavirus case in the United States. The resulting COVID-19 pandemic and subsequent economic fallout caused significant hardship in the Finance industry. In the early months of the crisis, many small businesses closed or were reorganized due to nationwide shutdowns. In addition, the Finance industry also worked with large and small businesses to manage the challenging financial environment the pandemic created.

A recent bright spot may be the globalization, or the creation of a shared worldwide market. People in some other parts of the world now have more money to invest. Some are eager to purchase U.S. securities and commodities. This will create greater demand and rising values. Recent mergers make it easier for people in the United States to invest abroad. This broadening of their assets may strengthen their financial position.

10-6 Essential Question Reflection

So, let us revisit our essential question:

What factors affect trends in Finance?

Based on what you learned in this section, please answer this question in detail.

Chapter 11: Marketing

Essential Questions

By the end of the chapter, you will be able to answer the following questions:

- **11-1** What types of opportunities are available in Marketing?
- **11-2** Which opportunities may be right for you?
- **11-3** How can I match my skills & interests with the right job?
- **11-4** What training & education is needed for a job in Marketing?
- **11-5** What are typical work environments in Marketing?
- **11-6** What factors affect trends in Marketing?

Chapter Topics

11-1 Marketing Today

11-2 Marketing Jobs

11-3 Building a Career in Marketing

11-4 Education and Training for Marketing Opportunities

11-5 Working Conditions in the Marketing Industry

11-6 Trends in Marketing

11-1 Marketing Today

Marketing is the way manufactured goods are presented to the public. Without this industry, we would have few product choices and poor, disorganized customer service. The marketing industry is responsible for promoting benefits and greatly enhancing sales of products and services. This involves influential messaging in the form of text, graphics, and other formats. It also involves providing customer support and service. In the last 25 years, the Internet has revolutionized how marketing takes place.

Many manufacturers do not have the marketing and sales staff necessary to sell their products to individual customers or retail stores. Instead, they sell their products to wholesalers. Acting as the middle person, a wholesaler buys products from the manufacturer and then resells them to retailers. A retailer then sells these products to the public and provides related services, such as installation and repair. Online stores, pharmacies, electronics stores, gift shops, jewelers, automobile dealerships, and grocery stores are all retailers. This system simplifies the process of buying and selling for both manufacturers and retailers.

Diagram 11.1: How Marketing Helps a Product or Service Reach You

Manufacturer → Wholesaler → Retailer

When a product or service is launched, marketing is the process that makes users aware of it. The product or service is created and moved to where the consumer can buy it, use it, or access it.

Even though wholesalers sometimes sell to individuals, such as farmers and businesspeople, they are different from retailers because they sell merchandise for commercial and institutional use rather than for personal or household use.

Chain stores, or groups of retail stores that have the same owners and sell the same line of products, are becoming increasingly popular. When customers go to a chain store, they know what products, services, and prices they can expect.

More products and services are being retailed to the public through direct marketing rather than through stores. For example, telemarketers sell products by telephone. Influencers sell products through ad campaigns on social media. Real estate agents do much of their selling over the phone and Internet. Some companies mail catalogs to promote and sell their products.

More and more retailers are using e-commerce, the buying and selling of goods and services on the Internet. The growth of online platforms like Amazon and app stores are examples of how retail stores have been replaced by more efficient options. Online retailing allows customers to purchase goods 24 hours a day from their homes or offices.

Career Journeys in Marketing

The Marketing industry is divided into five main career paths. Each path contains a group of careers requiring similar skills as well as similar certifications or education. Job opportunities are available in each of these areas. They are:

- Merchandising
- Professional Sales
- Marketing Management
- Marketing Communications
- Marketing Research

Each area helps different types of products reach the public. These products include clothing, electronics, appliances, food, furniture, gasoline, health items, motor vehicles, books, and many other items as well.

11-1 Essential Question

As you read this section, keep this question in mind:

What types of opportunities are available in Marketing?

Merchandising

Merchandising includes careers related to buying goods from businesses and promoting and selling goods to the public and to businesses. Retail buyers, for example, are responsible for the planning and purchasing of product lines for retail stores. A department store buyer might concentrate on women's fashion goods or on fine jewelry.

Salespeople may work in small local shops or in large international businesses. Cashiers and checkers are responsible for scanning items and for handling transactions with customers. Stock clerks ensure that items in each product line are regularly available, both on the floor and in stock rooms. Demonstrators and product promoters show customers how products work. Merchandise displayers and window trimmers are responsible for creating attractive product displays that will spark consumer interest.

Entry-level jobs, such as cashier, sales assistant, or window dresser, do not require extensive education. Employers usually provide on-the-job training for these positions. More advanced positions, such as display coordinator or product manager, usually require an undergraduate degree. Merchandisers often need specific product knowledge in a particular area. Examples might include knowledge of power tools or women's footwear.

Professional Sales

Sales is an area where people with knowledge of a product or service educate and influence people who should use the product or service. Employees in this career path specialize in a particular area of retailing. For example, real estate agents and rental clerks deal with property. They help clients sell, buy, or rent homes or commercial spaces. Buying a house is very often the largest single investment an individual makes. Specialized real estate agents use their unique expertise to make the process go smoothly.

Another area requiring specialized knowledge and training is insurance. Homeowners who have mortgages are usually required to insure their homes. Auto insurance is required in almost every state. Life, health, and disability insurance policies are popular ways to guard against personal risk. The insurance industry is highly competitive. Insurance policies are often lengthy and contain technical language. In addition, laws relating to insurance differ from state to state. For these reasons, retailers in the industry must acquire a specialized understanding of numerous aspects of the field.

Marketing Management and Entrepreneurship

An entrepreneur is a person who takes business risks with the hope of making a profit. Entrepreneurs often manage all aspects of their stores, including finances, displays, sales, and service. However, in larger retail stores a variety of managers may be needed. Managers also work in marketing departments, merchandising and buying departments, advertising, public relations firms, and in wholesale distribution. E-commerce specialists follow online sales trends. These managers help businesses market their goods on the Internet. Although large businesses have more money to spend on more staff, small business owners can manage the same tasks by paying for professional services that affordably meet their needs.

Managers must have good people skills and strong organizational abilities. Entrepreneurs must be forward-thinking and creative. They must have a strong grasp of all the factors involved in running a business. Although a bachelor's degree is necessary for most management positions, entrepreneurship skills can begin at any age or level of education. Work experience and good business sense are important for success in this path.

Marketing Communications

Employees in this path "spread the word" about products. Workers in Marketing Communications include sales representatives, marketing managers, and employees in advertising and public relations. The ability to speak and write persuasively is a key skill in these jobs.

For example, advertising managers create and manage advertising campaigns to raise the public's awareness of a product or company. Marketing managers create plans to showcase a company's products and services. These methods might include advertising campaigns and public-relations events. Public-relations specialists work to enhance the reputation of stores and brands. To do this, they may use unique events, newspaper articles, television coverage, and in-store promotions.

Entry-level jobs in this path include marketing assistant, public relations assistant, and advertising copywriter. These jobs generally require at least a bachelor's degree in a relevant field. Individuals interested in public relations (PR), for example, can choose a degree program in communications, marketing, or public relations. To succeed in this competitive career path, employees must be creative, driven, and have strong people skills. They must thoroughly know the company, organization, and product they represent.

Marketing Research

Companies want to bring products and services to market efficiently to make a sale for profit. Marketing employees most often work behind the scenes researching how to better serve the customer. The better you understand your target customer/market, the more likely your business is to succeed.

Social media influencers gain followers through shared interests. A market research analyst will explore market conditions for a particular product on a local, regional, or national level. An analyst will gather information and prepare a report of the findings on a company's competitors and analyze their prices, sales, and distribution methods. Another important task of a market research analyst is to uncover information about the public. What are the likes and dislikes of the company's prospective customers? Do they have favorite colors, textures, or tastes? What are they likely—or not likely—to buy?

Employees in Marketing Research must have good numerical skills. Training in mathematics and statistical survey methods is highly desirable. Jobs in this path can be extremely technical. Students can begin their journey toward this career by seeking out situations in which they can help solve a community problem. The problem can be complicated or minor. Critical thinking skills will help students gain strength in any career field.

Marketing Future Outlook

Industry outlook refers to the projected growth or decline in a particular industry. According to the Bureau of Labor Statistics (BLS), growth will be slow but steady in the Marketing industry in the years up to 2032. The greatest growth will be in the demand for market research analysts and marketing specialists ocuppations.

Table 11.1: Forecast for Marketing Occupations over the Next 10 Years

Occupation	Expected Growth Rate
Advertising and Promotions Managers	10%–15%
Market Research Analysts and Marketing Specialists	15+%
Models	10%–15%
First-Line Supervisors of Retail Sales Workers	0– -5%
Property, Real Estate, and Community Associate Managers	1%–5%
Fundraising Managers	10%–15%
Cashiers	0– -5%
Public Relations Specialists	10%–15%

Source: O*Net

11-1 Essential Question Reflection

So, let us revisit our essential question:

What types of opportunities are available in Marketing?

Based on what you learned in this section, please answer this question in detail.

Practice 11-1

Skills Practice

It may be necessary to follow multi-step instructions in a variety of situations, such as when learning how to manage incoming calls within a large organization or dealing with a customer who wants to order merchandise that is not currently in stock. Workers must read carefully to know when to take each step and be able to apply the same instructions in a variety of situations. **Practice this skill!**

FOLDING SWEATERS

Lay the sweater facedown on a flat surface to prevent it from slipping out of your hands. Smooth the wrinkles out as much as possible. Fold the right side of the sweater lengthwise to the neckline. Flatten the fold to ensure a smooth line. Fold the sleeve down so that it runs along the length of the fold you created in your first step. Repeat the same process on the other side. Fold the bottom of the sweater up halfway to the middle of the sweater. Finally, fold the sweater up again to the top of the sweater.

1. As a stock clerk on the sales floor of a men's clothing store, you are folding sweaters for a display. According to the instructions, at what point should you smooth the sweater to prevent wrinkles?

   A. after you fold the sleeves down
   B. before you begin folding
   C. before you turn the sweater over
   D. after you fold up the bottom of the sweater
   E. after you finish folding

2. Which part of the folding process uses the neckline of the sweater as a reference point?

   A. folding in the side of the sweater
   B. smoothing out the sweater
   C. turning the sweater over
   D. folding up the bottom of the sweater
   E. folding down the sleeves

To access more problems that will help you grow professional skills and are real-world examples in Marketing, go online.

11-2 Marketing Jobs

You can find jobs at all skill levels in the Marketing industry. You might want to manage corporate accounts. You might work on the road as a salesperson for a wholesaler. You may want to research customer needs and wants. Perhaps working behind the scenes in inventory control, visual merchandising, or telemarketing intrigues you. Here are some common industry jobs and the skills they require.

Table 11.2: Marketing Skills You Can Build Starting Now

Skill	Marketing Job	Example of Skill Building
Creativity	Copywriters and Social Media Coordinators	Producing short, innovative videos for a new social media campaign
Research	Market Research Analysts and Marketing Specialists	Considering social media methods to best persuade/influence as a volunteer for your favorite nonprofit or other worthy cause
Listening	Public Relations Specialists	Paying attention to the comments customers post on social media
Communication	First-Line Supervisors of Retail Sales Workers	Leading a presentation to community stakeholders who support your career journey
Analytical and Critical Thinking	Fundraising Managers	Reviewing previous marketing campaigns and identifying what could be improved in the future

11-2 Essential Question

As you read this section, keep this question in mind:

Which opportunities may be right for you?

Occupation With the Most People Employed:

Public Relations Specialists

- Create and maintain a positive public image for the client or company they represent
- Write press releases and prepare information for the media
- Evaluate advertising and promotion programs to determine whether they are compatible with the client or company they represent

Fast Facts:

Employment: 276,800 employees
Annual Openings: 27,400
Median Annual Wage: $30.19 hourly, $62,800 annually
Education Needed: Bachelor's degree
Other: You can gain experience for this position in high school by working on the school newspaper or social media platforms.

Highest-Wage Occupations:

Advertising, Promotions, and Marketing Managers

- Plan and prepare advertising and promotional material to increase sales of products or services while collaborating with customers, company officials, sales departments, and advertising agencies
- Inspect layouts and advertising copy; edit scripts, audio, video, and other promotional material for adherence to specifications

Fast Facts:

Employment: 23,200 employees

Annual Openings: 2,500

Median Annual Wage: $61.13 hourly, $127,150 annually

Education Needed: Bachelor's degree

Other: People in this occupation can use new applications and technology to be creative and design material to promote events.

Fundraising Managers

- Oversee campaigns and events intended to bring in donations for their organization
- Assign, supervise, and review the activities of fundraising staff
- Compile or develop materials to submit to granting or other funding organizations

Fast Facts:

Employment: 89,000 employees

Annual Openings: 8,900

Median Annual Wage: $48.47 hourly, $100,810 annually

Occupation Where Most Work for Themselves:

Professional Models

- Use their physical appearance to promote a company or advertise a product
- Walk down a runway to introduce a fashion designer's latest clothing line
- Pose for artists and photographers
- Record rates of pay and durations of jobs on vouchers

Fast Facts:

Employment: 2,700 employees

Annual Openings: 500

Median Annual Wage: $113.73 hourly, $236,556 annually

Education Needed: High school diploma, or equivalent

Other: There are many different types of models: fashion, runway, commercial, promotional, etc. Becoming a professional model may take many years.

Great Jobs! – High School Diploma Needed:

Property, Real Estate, and Community Association Managers

- Manage and oversee operations, maintenance, administration, and improvement of commercial, industrial, or residential properties
- Meet with prospective renters and show them properties
- Prepare budgets and financial reports

Fast Facts:

Employment: 392,900 employees

Annual Openings: 11,100

Median Annual Wage: $28.47 hourly, $59,230 annually

Education Needed: High school diploma, or equivalent

Other: When owners of commercial, industrial, or residential properties lack the time or expertise needed for the management of their properties, they often hire a property or real estate manager or a community association manager.

First-Line Supervisors (Managers) of Retail Sales Workers

- Provide customer service by greeting and assisting customers and responding to customer inquiries and complaints
- Direct and supervise employees engaged in sales, inventory-taking, reconciling cash receipts, or in performing services for customers

Fast Facts:

Employment: 1,143,260 employees

Annual Openings: 13,180

Median Annual Wage: $22.54 hourly, $46,890 annually

Education Needed: High school diploma, or equivalent

Other: You can start working toward this career in high school by becoming a retail sales worker!

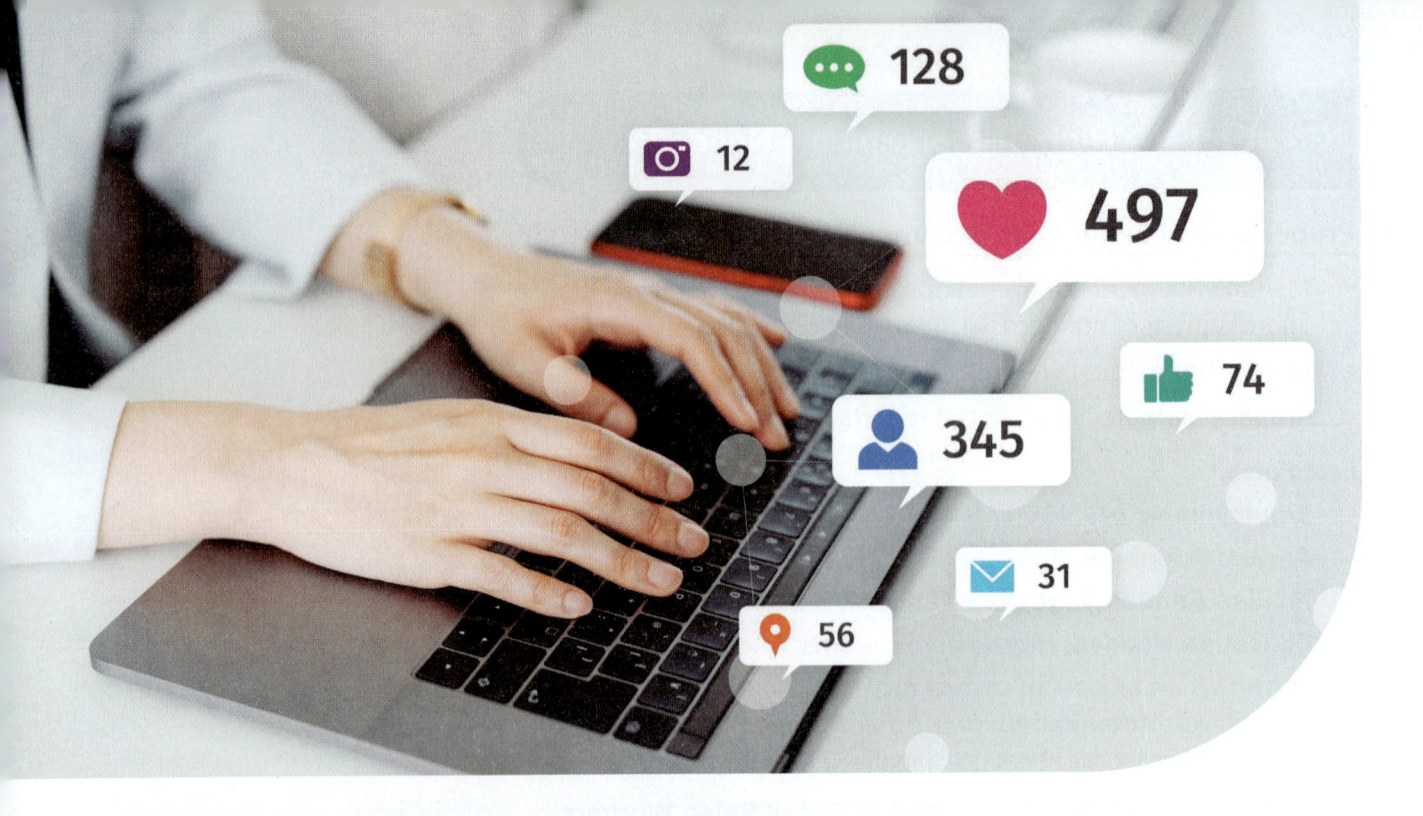

Emerging Occupation in Marketing:

Social Media Marketing Specialists

- Plan, post, and promote online content through their company's social media platforms
- Share content from outside sources, comment on posts, and moderate guest or member posts
- Work to drive traffic to a company website

Fast Facts:

Employment: 52,308 employees

Median Annual Wage: $24.80 hourly, $51,584 annually

Education Needed: Bachelor's degree

Other: Experience with social media as a post planner, media manager, content creator, or community builder may be beneficial to securing this position.

11-2 Essential Question Reflection

So, let us revisit our essential question:

Which opportunities may be right for you?

Based on what you learned in this section, please answer this question in detail.

Case Study: Market Research Analysts and Marketing Specialists

Also called: Market Analyst, Market Research Analyst, Market Research Consultant, Market Research Specialist

What do they do?

- Prepare reports of findings, illustrating data graphically and translating complex findings into written text
- Collect and analyze data on customer demographics, preferences, needs, and buying habits to identify potential markets and factors affecting product demand
- Conduct research on consumer opinions and marketing strategies while collaborating with marketing professionals, statisticians, pollsters, and other professionals

What do you need to know?

Arts and Humanities
English language

Business
Customer service
Sales and marketing

Math and Science
Arithmetic, algebra, geometry, calculus, or statistics
Sociology and anthropology

Communications
Multimedia

What skills do you need?

Basic Skills
Read work-related information
Think about the pros and cons of different ways to solve a problem

Problem Solving
Notice a problem, and figure out the best way to solve it

People and Technology Systems
    Think about the pros and cons of different options, and pick the best one
    Figure out how a system should work and how changes in the future will affect it

What abilities must you be good at?

Verbal
    Communicate by speaking
    Communicate by writing

Ideas and Logic
    Make general rules or produce answers from a variety of detailed information
    Produce many ideas

Math
    Choose the right type of math to solve a problem
    Add, subtract, multiply, or divide

Who does well in this occupation?

People interested in this work like activities that include ideas, thinking, and figuring things out.

They do well at jobs that need:

    Analytical thinking
    Attention to detail
    Dependability
    Integrity
    Initiative
    Adaptability/flexibility

What educational level is needed?

- Bachelor's or master's degree

Practice 11-2

Skills Practice

Marketing workers must sometimes analyze graphics to identify trends. They might search for data that has increased or decreased over time. A store manager or assistant manager might study a graph to find trends in sales for the past year. Being able to identify common trends from several pieces of data can help with a variety of jobs in this industry. **Practice this skill!**

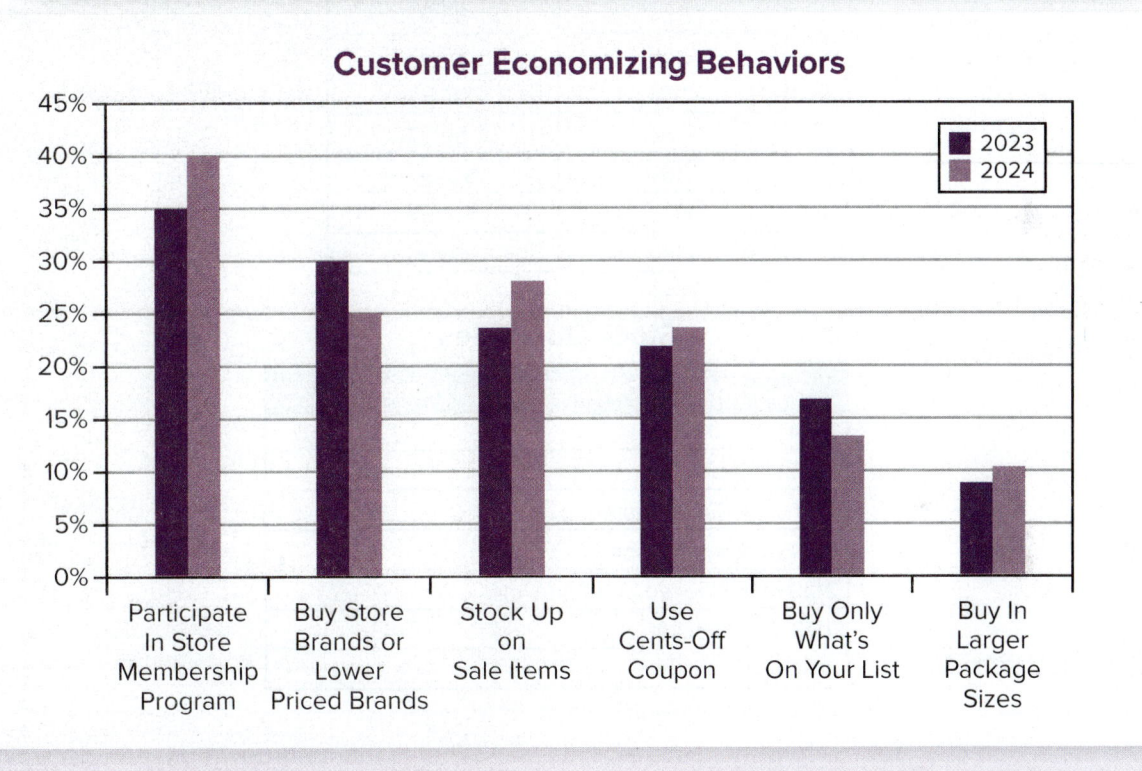

Customer Economizing Behaviors

Behavior	2023	2024
Participate In Store Membership Program	35%	40%
Buy Store Brands or Lower Priced Brands	30%	25%
Stock Up on Sale Items	24%	28%
Use Cents-Off Coupon	22%	24%
Buy Only What's On Your List	17%	14%
Buy In Larger Package Sizes	9%	11%

1. As the research manager of a grocery store chain, you are investigating the ways your customers try to economize. You plan to use this information to guide your upcoming promotions. According to the graph, which behavior shows the greatest increase from 2023 to 2024?

    A. use cents-off coupons
    B. buy store brands or lower-priced brands
    C. stock up on sale items
    D. buy in larger package sizes
    E. participate in store membership program

2. Which of the following behaviors has decreased according to the graph?

    A. use cents-off coupons
    B. buy in larger package sizes
    C. stock up on sale items
    D. participate in store membership program
    E. buy only what's on your list

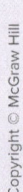

Skills Practice

When reviewing workplace graphics, it may be necessary to compare information in one or more graphics. A regional sales manager, for example, might compare maps of sales regions to graphs of top-selling products in each area. Workers must know how different graphics relate to each other and compare information and trends within them. **Practice this skill!**

May Markdowns

Lot Number	Markdown Price
2154	$6.97
2156	$6.97
2161	$14.97
2164	$9.97
2169	$12.97
2173	$14.97
2180	$9.97

Stock Quantities

Lot Number	Quantity
2154 striped polo	21
2156 solid polo	16
2161 cable-knit sweater	11
2164 dark wash jeans	18
2169 long-sleeved button down	4
2173 denim jacket	13
2180 twill pants	0

3. As a marking clerk for a department store, you are marking down clearance items in the boys' department. How many total items should you mark down to $9.97?

   A. 11
   B. 13
   C. 16
   D. 18
   E. 21

4. What is the markdown price of denim jackets?

   A. $6.97
   B. $9.97
   C. $12.97
   D. $14.97
   E. $19.97

To access more problems that will help you grow professional skills and are real-world examples in Marketing, go online.

11-3 Building a Career in Marketing

Marketing is natural to humans as a form of belonging. We "market" our ideas daily using persuasion skills to communicate our beliefs and opinions to others. You have already taken an entry-level position in marketing the brand that identifies who you are to the world around you. This industry offers a unique opportunity for you to build your skills as you take steps toward reaching your ultimate career goal.

11-3 Essential Question

As you read this section, keep this question in mind:

How can I match my skills & interests with the right job?

Are You More Interested in Working With People, Data, or Things?

Marketing decisions affect every aspect of business. Social media influencers are a good example of how marketing oneself affects others who decide to follow and share the information. As you consider your ultimate career goal and the steps you must take to reach it, it is important to reflect on what balance of data, people, and things you want to work with.

Careers That Involve Working With Data

Market research analysts focus on data and may not spend as much time face-to-face with potential buyers. The research they do provides insight to understanding how potential customers think. The data created from their research are used to persuade others toward an opinion or idea that is believed best to meet the goal. The work people in these occupations do helps when making a marketing plan to secure a sale.

Jobs in the Marketing industry may involve working with and analyzing numbers. Cashiers count money and accept checks and credit cards several times a day. Wholesale and retail inventory clerks maintain detailed records of items that enter or leave a stockroom. Clerks mark items with identifying codes and other inventory data, sometimes using handheld scanners.

Buyers frequently study sales records and inventory reports, negotiate prices, and make purchases. Each of these activities involves analyzing data to ensure that a good decision is made. Real estate agents, store managers, district managers, and administrative employees work with data as they set goals and analyze sales results.

Careers That Involve Working With People

All careers in Marketing seek to better understand human thinking. Knowing what customers want and what makes them happy is crucial to the success of a retail or wholesale company. Therefore, it is vital that employees in the Marketing industry possess good people skills.

Examples of working with people include serving and advising customers, training employees, giving presentations, and negotiating prices with suppliers. All these activities require effective communication skills.

Stock clerks, inventory clerks, and department managers may be asked to assist customers. However, they are not likely to spend most of their time communicating with customers. Telemarketers, order clerks, and online customer service representatives do not have face-to-face contact with customers, but they must be patient and friendly when they work with customers online or by phone. Other positions such as supervisors, buyers, and administrative workers require frequent interaction with coworkers and suppliers.

Careers That Involve Working With Things

In the Marketing industry, many jobs involve working with things. These jobs typically involve designing, creating, and showing products to market them to consumers. Some examples of working with things include arranging merchandise on racks or shelves, creating merchandising displays in retail stores, crafting an advertising campaign, and demonstrating products for customers.

Salespeople and cashiers work with merchandise and operate cash registers. Stock and inventory clerks count the products they are tracking. Clerks might use hand trucks to move stock from one location to another. Store designers use objects to create spaces that are attractive and effective. A graphic designer who is working on an advertising campaign may use photo editing or layout software to create an advertisement that targets the company's audience. Workers in nearly all behind-the-scenes positions in Marketing work with phones, computers, and other electronic equipment.

11-3 Essential Question Reflection

So, let us revisit our essential question:

How can I match my skills & interests with the right job?

Based on what you learned in this section, please answer this question in detail.

11-4 Education and Training for Marketing Opportunities

Jobs in the Marketing industry require varying levels of education. Many jobs in the Marketing industry can require little or no formal training. For others, it is necessary to have specific education and experience.

11-4 Essential Question

As you read this section, keep this question in mind:

What training & education is needed for a job in Marketing?

Training and Education for This Industry

The level of education and training necessary for success in the Marketing industry varies by career. Jobs can be categorized into three groups—those requiring little or no education, those requiring some education, and those requiring advanced education.

Jobs Requiring Little or No Education

Positions such as cashier, stock clerk, demonstrator, shipping clerk, and retail salesperson usually require little to no education. An experienced supervisor usually will lead you through your training once you have been hired. While a traditional degree can help you get your foot in the door, experience and knowledge in the Marketing industry can be just as valuable. To get a job in Marketing without a degree, you need to demonstrate the skills and knowledge you would bring to a role. For example, a social media specialist, model, or graphic designer who does not have a degree would need to present to potential employers a portfolio with their previous work to showcase their knowledge and skills. However, it is always important to get at least a high school diploma, or equivalent, to show employers that you are dedicated and can finish what you start.

Jobs Requiring Some Education

Many jobs in Marketing require some specialized training or education. Sales and Marketing Executives International (SMEI), a worldwide association of sales and marketing managers, has developed several online sales and marketing certification programs. Obtaining nationally recognized certification or even an associate degree in marketing can help you prosper in this industry.

326 Chapter 11 • Marketing

If you're interested in working as a manager in the Marketing industry, you'll need to complete business courses, including those on accounting, administration, marketing, and management. Managers must be computer literate so they can work with databases and inventory control systems.

You may need both classroom hours and in-store training to prepare yourself for some jobs. Customer service representatives, for example, may need four weeks of training or more before they interact with clients.

Some jobs require a license. Real estate agents must obtain a special state license before they can sell property. To obtain a real estate license, prospective agents must complete special course work and pass a test.

Jobs Requiring Advanced Education

Jobs in Marketing that require extensive training usually involve management or specialized skills such as advertising design or product research and development. Common managerial roles include president, director of operations, general manager, inventory control manager, marketing and sales manager, and customer service manager. Such jobs generally require at least a bachelor's degree, and some require a master's degree.

Some large firms prefer to hire managers who have experience in business management and sales. Running a retail or wholesale company requires that management personnel understand all aspects of the company.

Many managers have bachelor's degrees in sales, marketing, or business, and they may also have master's degrees in business management. There are specialized college programs in consumer merchandising and retail management. These programs train students in market research, consumer behavior, product sourcing and distribution, and running promotional campaigns. Other programs focus on purchasing and contracts management, customer service management, and e-commerce.

Many companies recruit college graduates to join their management training programs. These programs offer a wealth of on-the-job experience. Such programs can help an employee advance quickly from an entry-level position.

Table 11.3: Education Required for Marketing Jobs

Level of Education	Job Title
Little Education	Cashiers Models Merchandise Displayers and Window Trimmers Office Clerks Order Clerks Retail Salespersons Stock Clerks Telemarketers Social Media Influencers
Some Education	Fashion Designers Social Media Specialists Real Estate Agents Real Estate Brokers Sales Representatives Wholesale and Retail Buyers Social Media and Digital Marketers
Advanced Education	Appraisers, Real Estate Market Research Analysts Sales Engineers Sales Representatives Social Media and Digital Marketing Directors

Job and Workplace Skills

Employers in the Marketing industry look for both job-specific skills and general workplace skills such as the skill to forecast or to write promotional copy. General workplace skills are skills that can be used in a variety of jobs.

Marketing Skill Standards

The National Retail Federation (NRF) has formed the Sales and Service Voluntary Partnership to establish skill standards across all areas of the retail industry. This set of standards applies to all careers in the Marketing industry, including careers in wholesale trade. Basic skills essential for success in sales and service include the following:

- Providing personalized customer service
- Selling and promoting products, including determining customer needs
- Monitoring inventory
- Maintaining the appearance of the department or store

Professional Skills

Communication Skills   Good communication is central to Marketing. Employees communicate to satisfy the needs of customers and to promote products and services. Instructing the people they manage and discussing their company's products over the phone, by e-mail or in person, requires good communication skills. Productive relationships with coworkers rely on good communication.

Listening Skills   Listening is important for successful interaction with customers. Good listening skills help workers understand customers' ideas and points of view. Employees need active listening skills when they interact with coworkers and managers.

Problem-Solving Skills   Customer service representatives, for example, must be able to deal with customers' requests and complaints. Managers need to troubleshoot problems in all areas of store operations.

Technology Skills   Buyers and district managers often work with spreadsheet programs to set budgets and track sales progress. Familiarity with bar codes and bar code readers is essential in many areas of Marketing. Almost every item in a grocery store, department store, or mass merchandise outlet carries a bar code, or universal product code (UPC).

Decision-Making Skills   Competition is intense in Marketing. Employees in this industry need the ability to gather and analyze information rapidly and to think clearly under pressure. These skills can often mean the difference between making and losing a sale. A real estate agent, for example, might be faced with a last-minute negotiation problem. A successful agent must make effective decisions quickly.

Organizing and Planning Skills   Many jobs in Marketing involve keeping track of large amounts of information. Organization is crucial. Planning requires the ability to set goals and visualize the sequence of steps leading to those goals. Service sales representatives need to effectively track all calls to and from prospective customers. In addition, they need to organize call reports to evaluate how effective their calls have been.

Teamwork Skills   Teamwork is key to nearly every job in Marketing. Regardless of the position, coworkers and people from various departments in the company must work together to get the job done.

Social Skills   Interacting with coworkers and with customers is a requirement of nearly all jobs in Marketing. Social interaction with coworkers can make for an enjoyable work atmosphere. Individuals from various levels of the company interact with each other, from managers to interns. Many marketing workers interact with customers, either over the phone, by e-mail, or in person. When dealing with others, employees should keep an open mind and use each opportunity to learn.

Adaptability Skills Job descriptions, work environments, and sales procedures are changing constantly as technology changes. For instance, the Internet has had an extraordinary impact on Marketing in a relatively brief period. One example is the innovative approaches to marketing pioneered by online companies. Workers should be ready to acquire new skills and to build on the skills they already have.

11-4 Essential Question Reflection

So, let us revisit our essential question:

What training & education is needed for a job in Marketing?

Based on what you learned in this section, please answer this question in detail.

Practice 11-4

Skills Practice

Many jobs in the Marketing industry require workers to calculate costs and discounts. A retail sales associate at a clothing store, for example, may need to calculate the discount applied to items to be placed on the clearance rack. **Practice this skill!**

1. You are a manager at a furniture store. You have finished taking inventory and have decided to clear some older items to make room for new items. You announce a 50 percent clearance sale for the weekend only. A customer comes in and is interested in a couch that usually costs $2,500. The delivery charge, which is not discounted, is $137. How much does the customer pay for the couch and delivery?

    A. $1,250
    B. $1,387
    C. $2,500
    D. $2,000
    E. $2,637

2. You are a shoe store manager. During the holidays, you offered a 20 percent storewide discount. The discount expired on December 31st. If a pair of shoes cost $80 during the holidays, how much do they cost in January?

    A. $60
    B. $80
    C. $96
    D. $128
    E. $140

To access more problems that will help you grow professional skills and are real-world examples in Marketing, go online.

11-5 Working Conditions in the Marketing Industry

When choosing a career path, it is important to know what it is like to work in the industry. Understanding the work environment, hazards, and benefits of a job can help you make informed decisions in your career journey.

> **? 11-5 Essential Question**
>
> **As you read this section, keep this question in mind:**
>
> *What are typical work environments in Marketing?*

Physical Environment

The physical work environment in the Marketing industry varies by job and by employer. Retail stores should be clean and comfortable so that customers will want to return, but workers such as cashiers or salespeople may spend long hours on their feet assisting customers.

Marketing employees may work both indoors and outdoors, loading and unloading trucks of merchandise. Managers in merchandising and marketing work in comfortable offices but may face tight deadlines and high stress.

Work Hours

The working hours of people in this industry correspond to the times when customers are available. Salespeople must be on the sales floor and available for customers. Employees who unload deliveries and create displays often work while stores are closed. Customer service representatives who respond to customers by e-mail or online might work evening shifts.

Shift work is common in marketing sales and service. Shift work divides the day into blocks of time, generally eight hours. Shift work allows a company to operate around the clock. It also allows workers to select hours to meet their needs. Shift work is common for employees in large wholesale and retail warehouses where work often begins before 9 a.m. and extends beyond 5 p.m. Because supermarkets may be open 24 hours a day, employees may need to work late at night and early in the morning.

Flextime allows workers to choose the hours and the days they work if they meet the required total number of hours for the week. One employee, for example, may choose to work four days a week for ten hours a day. Another may work six days a week for six-and-a-half hours a day. Flextime is especially convenient for workers who have young children or other family commitments.

Not all companies offer flextime, and it is not practical for all retail jobs. People who manage employees may not be able to work flextime hours. However, salespeople and employees of retail stores can create their own schedules. Employees who do not work on the selling floor are more likely to be offered flextime schedules.

Customer service departments and computer apps offer 24-hour assistance to clients. Employees may work in shifts. Artificial Intelligence (AI) options replace the human response to clients' concerns and questions. This allows a business to operate around the clock. It also allows workers to select the hours they want to work. Shift work is common for customer service representatives and technical service providers.

Although most employees in the Marketing industry work during standard hours, employees may work from home or work overtime. Employees in retail may need to work overtime during holidays and other peak periods. Retail businesses typically operate during evenings and weekends, when their customers are most likely to be available. Workers in marketing and public relations must often adjust their schedules to meet their clients' needs. If a project is nearing completion, longer hours and overtime may be necessary.

Essential Physical Activities

Most workers in marketing sales and service must be in good physical condition. Sales workers, cashiers, and demonstrators are on their feet. Stock clerks and baggers lift and carry objects weighing as much as fifty pounds.

Customer service representatives, telemarketers, and public relations specialists spend a great deal of time at a computer. They must be careful to avoid arm, back, and eye injuries.

Hazards and Environmental Dangers

Wholesale trade jobs may involve operating heavy equipment and machinery that can be dangerous if used improperly. Retail positions may require lifting and moving heavy objects, such as merchandise boxes and product displays. Employees must be careful to avoid injuries, especially back injuries.

Proper training and common sense are necessary for tasks involving machinery. Workers must follow all safety procedures. They should take advantage of breaks to rest tired muscles. They should vary their work when possible and notify managers if they feel pain or stiffness.

11-5 Essential Question Reflection

So, let us revisit our essential question:

What are typical work environments in Marketing?

Based on what you learned in this section, please answer this question in detail.

11-6 Trends in Marketing

Our globalized economy continues to affect how businesses market their products or services. The virtual world leads the way in Marketing trends. Human control in our real world is essential to develop and monitor the software we create. We must be responsible users. Regardless of the Marketing trends, professional skills never go out of style.

11-6 Essential Question

As you read this section, keep this question in mind:

What factors affect trends in Marketing?

Technology in the Marketing Industry

Think of how technology affects your daily life. Then consider how technology might affect an entire office, factory, or industry. The Internet, email, laptop computers, innovative software, and cellular phones enable people to communicate rapidly and effectively.

Today, computers are vital to nearly every aspect of the Marketing industry. Real estate agents, for example, use laptop computers and smartphones. They send customers online listings, which show virtual tours of homes. Technology helps realtors serve more customers than in the past.

It is hard to imagine how retailers and wholesalers ever operated without the benefit of today's technological advances. Retailers and wholesalers once depended on computers for only sales transactions and inventory control. Now they use computers to conduct a large portion of their daily business.

Just-in-time (JIT) inventory systems are computerized methods of tracking inventory needs. JIT systems have reduced the amount of inventory a wholesaler or retailer must keep on hand. This saves money and space needed to store the inventory. How do the systems do this? When stock falls low, JIT systems write purchase orders. They ensure that products arrive on the day they are needed. JIT systems cut down on overstock because products are delivered only as they are needed.

336 Chapter 11 • Marketing

Retailers also use computers for assortment management. This method organizes information to forecast consumer preferences, buying patterns, and buying trends. Thorough computer analysis allows retailers to offer the right amount of product at the right time.

Technology in Online Sales and Service

Brick-and-mortar retail stores may use the same methods as online retail stores through building relationships in the online and real world. Traditional brick-and-mortar retail stores understand that if they are not participating in the online world, they might be ignoring more than 50 percent of their potential customers.

Wholesalers once purchased products from manufacturers face-to-face. They used to sell products to retailers face-to-face. Now they use the Internet to do the same job faster and with less travel. Retailers once relied on customers to visit their stores. They can now invite customers to shop on their website 24 hours a day.

Technology enables retailers to display their entire inventory on a website. Handwritten or phone orders have been replaced by more efficient online orders. Customer service questions and problems are managed efficiently with computer software. Products that were once available only through local representatives can now be purchased online. Online buying and selling have proven to be efficient for companies and convenient for customers.

Technology in Online Marketing

The world of online marketing has become nearly an industry in itself. Strategies are constantly changing as the habits of online consumers change. There are a wide variety of ways to reach consumers online.

Internet Advertising

The market for online advertising has exploded as the Internet overtakes print media. Advertisers have found more sophisticated ways of attracting the attention of Internet users. Ads can include text, images, video, and sound. Pop-up ads open in a new browser window. Additional ads "float" across a page, while other ads expand while you are on a web page. Interstitial ads are full-page ads that appear before a new page can be opened. Ads are being targeted to the interests of the viewer. When a consumer uses a search engine, for example, advertisements related to the search terms appear on the page.

Email

Companies are always looking for ways to collect e-mail addresses from customers and potential customers. These addresses are often sold from one company to another. Companies use these email lists to send advertisements, coupons, and other offers to customers.

Social Media

Social networking sites have become one of the most popular uses of the Internet. As a result, companies are looking for ways to use social networks to promote their products. Companies may have their own pages on social networking sites. They also use social networking tools to send targeted messages to potential consumers. Companies may even partner with social media influencers in hopes that they will share product information with friends in their social networks.

Search Engine Optimization

Online shoppers may use search engines to find the products they are looking for. A company whose site appears at the top of a list of sites is much more likely to be visited than a company whose site appears further down the list. Search engine optimization is a way of designing a site that is more likely to appear high on a search list. This can be done by using keywords on a web page or by revising the site's structure.

Viral Marketing

It is fun to consider how a funny video clip of a cat or a dog can "go viral" through people sharing the video online. You may have participated in a video or picture going viral by sharing something interesting with friends and family on social media.

Companies try to draw interest in their products cheaply and effectively through viral marketing. Viral marketing is any type of marketing that is likely to be passed on from one consumer to another. This can be less expensive than traditional marketing because the message is passed on without further effort from an advertiser.

One form of viral marketing comes from online video ads. If an ad is humorous or unusual, people may share it with their friends. The company may rely on free video-sharing sites rather than television advertising. Other examples of viral marketing include public stunts or mysterious billboards that create media interest.

Viral advertisements can travel around the world faster than the speed of light. They can live on social media for an indefinite period of time. Make sure your viral push represents the person you wish to be, because at any time in the future your viral contribution can become controversial. You may be asked to defend your participation. Make sure you build your brand with positive social media input. It may follow you for life.

Sustainability in the Marketing Industry

As more consumers become environmentally conscious, marketers look for ways to demonstrate that their companies care about the environment. This means designing products that create less waste, use less fossil fuels, and are safer for wildlife. In addition, some companies contribute to environmental groups or partner with them.

Companies are eager to promote their "green" credentials. Advertising campaigns are focused on portraying the company as responsible citizens. This is particularly important for businesses that have caused harm to the environment. By creating an eco-friendlier image, marketing groups hope to improve a company's public perception and, as a result, boost sales.

The Economy and the Marketing Industry

The changes taking place in the U.S. workplace and in the global economy directly affect the Marketing industry. The 2020 pandemic continues to affect our global economy. More people work from home. Therefore, more people participate in the virtual world. Marketing works to encourage customers to make a profit. Our economy affects the amount of money a person must spend on certain products or goods. The Marketing industry directly affects consumer spending. Marketing and economy are partners that go hand-in-hand, working to create the right balance of consumer spending and profits.

Consulting

A marketing consultant or team is a valuable resource to a variety of businesses, depending upon the person's or team's skills and experience.

Companies may need workers only during certain times of year. At peak periods, however, they may hire consultants. A consultant provides specialized services for clients. Companies sometimes hire consultants when a new project begins. Wholesale and retail consultants specialize in areas such as e-commerce, forecasting, training, and inventory control. Consultants may become highly specialized—for example, in merchandising for grocery stores or in sales forecasting for the clothing industry.

Megastores

Walmart, Amazon, Costco, and The Home Depot are among a growing number of megastores around the country. Megastores are large retail stores that offer an enormous variety of merchandise at low prices. They are usually part of a national chain. They buy products from wholesalers and manufacturers in large quantities. This purchase power lets them charge low prices.

The Global Economy

The global economy is the worldwide linkage of national economies. In a global economy, companies purchase resources, including labor, anywhere in the world.

Globalization is a related development. People and groups have established worldwide communication with one another. Wholesalers and retailers may buy products internationally. They can also sell their products to customers all over the world.

11-6 Essential Question Reflection

So, let us revisit our essential question:

What factors affect trends in Marketing?

Based on what you learned in this section, please answer this question in detail.

Chapter 12
Transportation, Distribution, & Logistics

Chapter Topics

12-1 Transportation, Distribution, & Logistics Today

12-2 Transportation, Distribution, & Logistics Jobs

12-3 Building a Career in Transportation, Distribution, & Logistics

12-4 Education and Training for Transportation, Distribution, & Logistics Opportunities

12-5 Working in the Transportation, Distribution, & Logistics Industry

12-6 Trends in Transportation, Distribution, & Logistics

❓ Essential Questions

By the end of the chapter, you will be able to answer the following questions:

- **12-1** What types of opportunities are available in Transportation, Distribution, & Logistics?
- **12-2** Which opportunities may be right for you?
- **12-3** How can I match my skills & interests with the right job?
- **12-4** What training & education is needed for a job in Transportation, Distribution, & Logistics?
- **12-5** What are typical work environments in Transportation, Distribution, & Logistics?
- **12-6** What factors affect trends in Transportation, Distribution, & Logistics?

12-1 Transportation, Distribution, & Logistics Today

Did you take a bus to get somewhere today? Did you buy food at the supermarket? If you did, workers in the Transportation, Distribution, & Logistics industry provided these services.

What exactly are transportation, distribution, and logistics? These terms are closely related. Transportation is moving people, goods, and services from one place to another. Distribution is coordinating the shipment and delivery of goods and services. Logistics is planning the movement of people, goods, services, information, and money.

Goods being moved are known as freight or cargo. Millions of workers keep the transportation system moving along a wide network of roads, airports, railroads, and waterways. They operate or repair planes, trains, and other vehicles. They supervise airports, warehouses, and shipyards. Without them, everyday life could not function. Without them, the U.S. economy would collapse.

12-1 Essential Question

As you read this section, keep this question in mind:

What types of opportunities are available in Transportation, Distribution, & Logistics?

Career Journeys in Transportation, Distribution, & Logistics

There are seven major paths along which your journey in Transportation, Distribution, & Logistics might be shaped. People commonly move into and out of different paths. Each path contains a group of careers requiring similar skills as well as similar certifications or education. This industry is divided into seven main career paths:

- Transportation Operations
- Logistics Planning and Management Services
- Warehousing and Distribution Center Operations
- Sales and Services
- Facility and Mobile Equipment Maintenance
- Health, Safety, and Environmental Management
- Transportation/Infrastructure Planning

Transportation Operations

The Transportation Operations path involves the operation and support of all transportation vehicles. It includes people who drive or help operate the vehicles, such as truck drivers and flight attendants. It also includes people who work behind the scenes, such as air traffic controllers and taxi dispatchers.

Workers in this career path may be employed by the government (public sector) or by a private company (private sector). They may transport passengers, freight, or both. Bus drivers carry passengers. Many bus drivers work for the public school system, transporting students to and from school. Other bus drivers operate the publicly owned buses used to transport commuting workers and other passengers around large cities or between cities and suburbs. Mass transit also employs workers who help operate passenger trains and subways.

Many operators of rail transportation carry freight for private railroad companies. Truck drivers usually work for private companies. These drivers include truckload (TL) carriers, who transport a shipment to its destination, and less-than-truckload (LTL) carriers, who combine small shipments from different customers to create a larger load.

Some airline pilots fly planes for the U.S. military. But many pilots work in the private sector. They pilot passenger planes. They also pilot planes that carry freight, such as packages and express mail. Similarly, in water transportation, many captains, pilots, and mates work for the merchant marine or the navy. Others, however, help operate privately owned boats and ships. These include tugboats, cruise ships, and sightseeing boats.

Logistics Planning and Management Services

The Logistics Planning and Management Services path involves planning, managing, and controlling the movement of people and freight. It includes issues such as strategy, budgeting, resource usage, facilities layout, inventory control, personnel, and scheduling.

Logistics analysts, engineers, and managers collect and analyze data related to the movement of people and freight. They then provide the most efficient solution for each transportation situation.

Warehousing and Distribution Center Operations

Warehouses and distribution centers are large buildings in which general merchandise and refrigerated goods are stored until they are ready to be shipped to their destination. Some of these facilities provide special atmospheres, where temperature, humidity, and gases in the air are carefully controlled to minimize food spoilage and extend storage times.

Jobs in this career path involve packaging, loading, and tracking goods that are ready for transport. Operations managers oversee the facilities. Material movers load and unload freight. Shipping, receiving, and traffic clerks make sure that orders are filled and that documents and records are correct.

Sales and Service of Transportation Services

Jobs in the Sales and Service path involve marketing and selling transportation services for people or freight. Ticket and reservations agents, for example, make reservations and sell and exchange tickets for passenger travel. Travel agents help plan people's trips. Customer service representatives assist passengers and address the special needs that customers may have. Sales managers help sell the services of transportation companies, including companies that ship freight. Billing clerks send out bills and record payments. Marketing managers perform market research, identify potential markets, and create a company's marketing strategy.

Facility and Mobile Equipment Maintenance

Those who work in the Facility and Mobile Equipment Maintenance path maintain and repair transportation vehicles and related equipment. They are also responsible for maintenance and repairs of warehouses and other facilities.

Many workers specialize in a particular type of repair. For example, some aircraft mechanics specialize in an airplane's electrical system. Railroad track workers specialize in maintaining and repairing tracks. Diesel mechanics repair buses and large trucks that run on diesel fuel. Automotive mechanics repair smaller trucks and other small motor vehicles. Service technicians make sure that vehicles and equipment are in working order.

Health, Safety, and Environmental Management

Workers in the Health, Safety, and Environmental Management path identify and manage safety risks and possible environmental hazards. They address dangers to the health and safety of workers, passengers, and communities. Often, they help develop company safety practices. They may also run training sessions to improve on-the-job safety and help workers avoid accidents.

Environmental protection specialists check to be sure that food, water, and air meet government standards. They suggest ways to stop or clean up pollution.

Transportation/Infrastructure Planning

The Transportation/Infrastructure Planning path focuses on the planning, management, and regulation of the public transportation infrastructure. This includes roads, bridges, rail lines, and all other transportation facilities needed for the operation of the economy. Many workers in this path are employed by a federal, state, or local government transportation agency. Those in the private sector often work for architectural and engineering firms.

Urban and regional planners look for the best ways to meet the transportation needs of communities. Civil engineers design and maintain parts of the transportation infrastructure. Government regulators and inspectors develop transportation safety rules and make sure those rules are followed.

Transportation, Distribution, & Logistics Future Outlook

The outlook for the Transportation, Distribution, & Logistics industry is average overall. International and cross-country shipping will continue to increase. This will create job growth in transportation as well as in warehousing and logistics. Increases in online ordering will also help increase jobs in trucking and warehousing. All these jobs, however, are linked to the economy's health.

Opportunities for military jobs are expected to be excellent. Government jobs overall, however, are expected to decline due to decreasing budgets. Population growth and higher fuel costs will mean some growth in jobs for mass transit. Health, safety, the environment, and the decaying infrastructure all remain key public concerns. Both government and private sector jobs that address these concerns should continue to grow.

Table 12.1: Forecast for Occupations in the Transportation, Distribution, & Logistics Industry over the Next 10 Years

Occupation	Expected Growth Rate
Bus Drivers, School	15% or higher
Truck Drivers, Heavy and Tractor-Trailer	5%–10%
Transportation Planners	1%–5%
Industrial Truck and Tractor Operators	5%–10%
Taxi Drivers and Chauffeurs	15% or higher
Locomotive Engineers	5%–10%
Bus Drivers, Transit and Intercity	15% or higher
Railroad Conductors and Yardmasters	5%–10%
Logistics Analysts	15% or higher
Laborers and Freight Movers, Hand	5%–10%
Supply Chain Managers	5%–10%
Bus/Truck Mechanics and Diesel Engine Specialists	5%–10%
Automotive Body Repairers	5%–10%
Truck Drivers, Light or Delivery Services	5%–10%

Source: *O*NET*

12-1 Essential Question Reflection

So, let us revisit our essential question:

What types of opportunities are available in Transportation, Distribution, & Logistics?

Based on what you learned in this section, please answer this question in detail.

Practice 12-1

Skills Practice

It may be necessary to follow multi-step instructions in a variety of situations. A bicycle repairer may need to follow a list of posted instructions when performing a tune-up. Workers must read carefully to know when to take each step and be able to apply the same instructions in a variety of situations. **Practice this skill!**

TRAINING MANUAL: PLAN OF ACTION FOR FIRST-AID AND EMERGENCY TRANSPORT

The following points summarize the course and plan of action in rendering effective first-aid to ill and injured persons and transporting them for specialized medical care:

1. Evaluate the scene, and collect all information possible on the cause of the injury or illness and the circumstances surrounding it.

2. Evaluate the injuries, and establish the order that should be followed in caring for them.

3. Identify your resources, and make them available for use.

4. Decide on a plan for the most effective use of available communication and transportation resources.

The school bus driver must remember that breathing, heartbeat, bleeding of a profuse nature, and shock are the four most important conditions to evaluate, and these must be cared for immediately if the person is to survive. Prevention of further injury in moving and transporting the victim is also extremely important.

1. School bus drivers are trained in basic first-aid procedures. According to the training manual, what is the first step in developing a course of action in an emergency?

   A. Decide on a plan.
   B. Transport the victim.
   C. Identify resources.
   D. Evaluate the injuries.
   E. Evaluate the scene.

2. When should a school bus driver collect information on the cause of an injury or illness?

   A. after evaluating the injury
   B. while transporting the victim
   C. after deciding on a plan
   D. after identifying resources
   E. while evaluating the scene

To access more problems that will help you grow professional skills and are real-world examples in Transportation, Distribution, & Logistics, go online.

12-2 Transportation, Distribution, & Logistics Jobs

The Transportation, Distribution, & Logistics industry offers a great variety of jobs. You can find jobs at all skill levels, from entry level to managerial. Do you want to make transportation more efficient? Would you like to fly an airplane? These job profiles will introduce you to some professions in the industry.

12-2 Essential Question

As you read this section, keep this question in mind:

Which opportunities may be right for you?

Occupation With the Most People Employed:

Hand Laborers and Freight, Stock, and Material Movers

- Move freight, stock, or other materials to and from storage or production areas, loading docks, delivery vehicles, ships, or containers, by hand or using trucks, tractors, or other equipment
- Sort cargo before loading and unloading
- Attach identifying tags to containers, or mark them with identifying information

Fast Facts:
Employment: 2,821,700 employees
Annual Openings: 34,275
Median Annual Wage: $15.02 hourly, $31,230 annually
Education Needed: No high school diploma or GED required

Fastest-Growing Occupation:

Flight Attendants

- Verify that first-aid kits and other emergency equipment, including fire extinguishers and oxygen bottles, are in working order
- Announce and demonstrate safety and emergency procedures, such as the use of oxygen masks, seat belts, and life jackets
- Monitor passenger behavior to identify threats to the safety of the crew and other passengers

12-2 • Transportation, Distribution, & Logistics Jobs 349

- Direct and assist passengers in emergency procedures, such as evacuating a plane following an emergency landing

Fast Facts:
Employment: 102,500 employees
Annual Openings: 1,760
Median Annual Wage: $39 hourly, $61,640 annually
Education Needed: Bachelor's degree

Highest-Wage Occupation:

Airline Pilots, Copilots, and Flight Engineers

- Use instrumentation to guide flights when visibility is poor
- Start engines, operate controls, and pilot airplanes to transport passengers, mail, or freight, adhering to flight plans, regulations, and procedures
- Work as part of a flight team with other crew members, especially during takeoffs and landings
- Respond to and report in-flight emergencies and malfunctions
- Inspect aircraft for defects and malfunctions, according to preflight checklists

Fast Facts:

Employment: 74,700 employees
Annual Openings: 960
Median Annual Wage: $202,180 annually
Education Needed: Bachelor's degree and certification

Great Job! - High School Diploma Required:

Transit and Intercity Bus Drivers

- Drive vehicles over specified routes or to specified destinations according to time schedules, complying with traffic regulations to ensure that passengers have a smooth and safe ride
- Park vehicles at loading areas so that passengers can board
- Inspect vehicles and check gas, oil, and water levels prior to departure

Fast Facts:

Employment: 165,200 employees
Annual Openings: 2,460
Median Annual Wage: $23.37 hourly, $48,620 annually
Education Needed: High school diploma and commercial driver's license (CDL)

12-2 Essential Question Reflection

So, let us revisit our essential question:

Which opportunities may be right for you?

Based on what you learned in this section, please answer this question in detail.

Case Study: Heavy and Tractor-Trailer Truck Drivers

What do they do?

- Drive a tractor-trailer combination or a truck with a capacity of at least 26,001 pounds gross vehicle weight (GVW)
- Unload truck
- Possess a CDL

What would you do?

- Check all load-related documentation for completeness and accuracy
- Inspect loads to ensure that cargo is secure
- Check vehicles to ensure that mechanical, safety, and emergency equipment is in good working order

What do you need to know?

Transportation
Movement of people or goods by air, rail, sea, or road

Safety and Government
Public safety and security
Law and government

Business
Customer service

Arts and Humanities
English language

What skills do you need?

Basic Skills
Keep track of how well people and/or groups are doing in order to make improvements
Read work-related information

Problem Solving
Notice a problem, and figure out the best way to solve it

What abilities must you be good at?

Controlled Movement
Change when and how fast you move based on how something else is moving
Quickly change the controls of a machine, car, truck, or boat

352 Chapter 12 • Transportation, Distribution, & Logistics

Spatial Awareness
    Know where objects are around you

    Imagine how something will look after it is moved around or changed

Vision
    See details that are far away

    Decide which object is closer or farther away from you, or decide how far away it is from you

Attention
    Pay attention and avoid distractions

Who does well in this occupation?

People interested in this work like activities that include practical, hands-on problems and solutions.

They do well at jobs that need:

    Attention to detail

    Dependability

    Self-control

    Stress tolerance

    Cooperation

    Integrity

What educational level is needed?

- No degree, but a CDL is required

Practice 12-2

Skills Practice

Transportation, Distribution, & Logistics workers must sometimes analyze graphics to identify trends. They might search for data that have changed over time. A warehouse manager might note that shipments from a certain location are being delivered more slowly than previously. Being able to identify common trends from several pieces of data can help with a variety of jobs in this industry. **Practice this skill!**

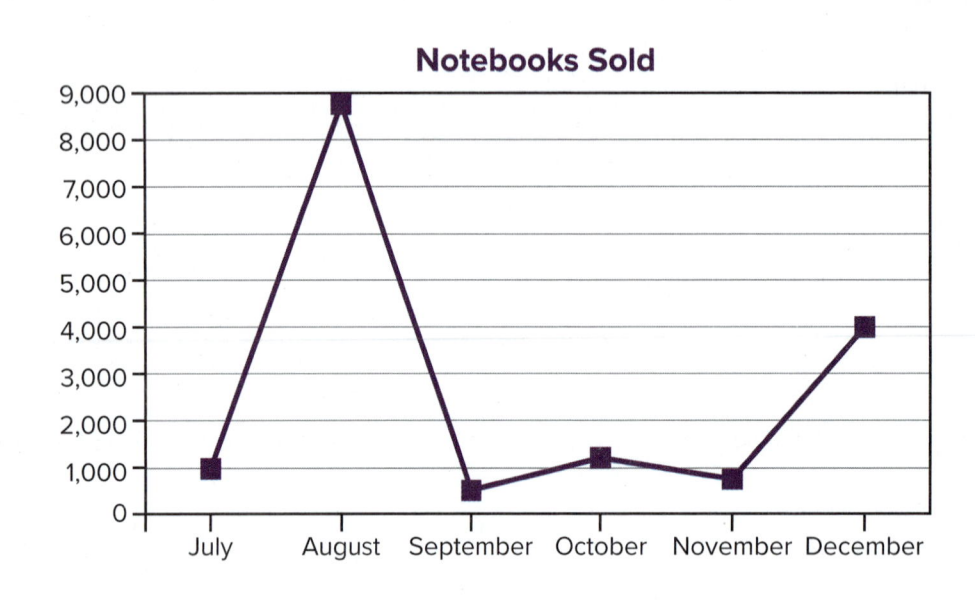

Notebooks Sold

(Line graph showing notebook sales from July through December: July ~1,000; August ~8,750; September ~500; October ~1,250; November ~750; December ~4,000)

1. As an inventory control analyst, you are looking at notebook sales to predict inventory needs for next year. What conclusions can you draw from the sales data?

   A. Notebook sales are relatively consistent throughout the year.

   B. Notebook sales increase dramatically before school starts in September.

   C. Notebook sales fluctuate unpredictably year-round.

   D. Notebook sales are highest in October.

   E. Notebook sales are lowest in December.

2. Which two months would require prioritizing the restocking of notebooks?

   A. October and November

   B. July and August

   C. September and November

   D. August and December

   E. October and December

354 Chapter 12 • Transportation, Distribution, & Logistics

Skills Practice

When reviewing workplace graphics, it may be necessary to compare information in one or more graphics. A home delivery driver might compare a schedule of truck maintenance with his own delivery schedule. The driver must know how different graphics relate to each other and be able to compare information and trends within them. **Practice this skill!**

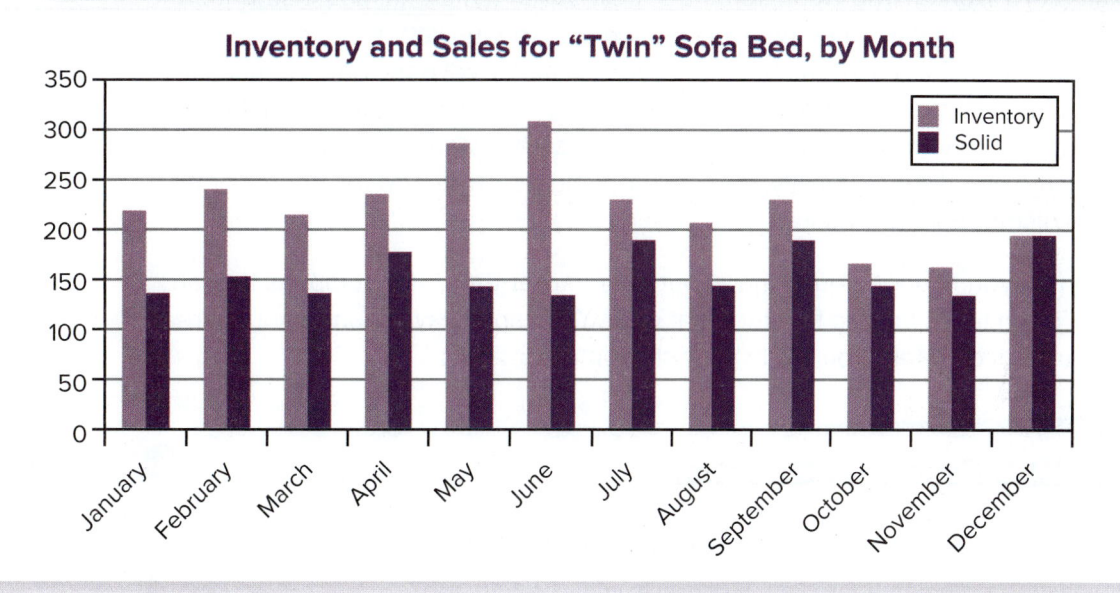

Inventory and Sales for "Twin" Sofa Bed, by Month

3. You work as a supply chain manager for a national retail furniture store. You are reviewing last year's sales and inventory data for a specific sofa bed. You try to avoid having inventory levels that are too high. In which month were inventory levels at least twice as high as sales?

   A. February
   B. June
   C. July
   D. August
   E. November

4. What is the trend in the relationship between inventory levels and sales?

   A. Inventory and sales figures were close to each other year-round.
   B. Inventory and sales figures were never close at any time of year.
   C. Inventory and sales figures were very different early in the year but were close late in the year.
   D. Inventory and sales figures differed greatly part of the year but were closest in January.
   E. Inventory and sales figures were about the same during much of the year but were very far apart in the last three months.

To access more problems that will help you grow professional skills and are real-world examples in Transportation, Distribution, & Logistics, go online.

12-3 Building a Career in Transportation, Distribution, & Logistics

Once you have chosen a field that interests you, look ahead and consider your career path. This path is made up of the job experiences and career moves that lead you toward your career goal. You may take several steps before reaching your goal. You will likely spend time in an entry-level position. This will help you gain the professional experience needed to move ahead in your career.

For example, a worker who wants to be a supervisor of a material and distribution operation might begin in an entry-level position as a manual laborer in the distribution center. More experience may lead to a mid-level position as a machine operator. The next step may be an advanced job repairing and maintaining the equipment, and that might lead to a promotion as an assistant supervisor in charge of maintenance and repair. Finally, the worker could be promoted to supervisor of the entire distribution operation.

Don't worry if you change your mind about your career path. This happens to many people. It often takes time to find the right path. You can always change your career path regardless of where you are in your chosen profession.

12-3 Essential Question

As you read this section, keep this question in mind:

How can I match my skills & interests with the right job?

Are You More Interested in Working With Data, People, or Things?

Most jobs focus mainly on working with data, people, or things. Billing clerks, for example, work mainly with data. Flight attendants work primarily with people. Mechanics work mostly with things. When planning your career path, consider what balance of data, people, and things you want.

Careers That Involve Working With Data

Working with data means working with words, ideas, concepts, and numbers. Compiling packing lists, preparing budgets, and scheduling are examples of working with data. These tasks require good math, verbal, and organizational skills. The tasks often involve using computers.

Several jobs in the Transportation, Distribution, & Logistics industry focus on working with data. Cargo and freight agents, for example, record orders, provide payment methods, and prepare documents that list data about shipments. Billing clerks compile and list services performed and the costs of those services. Transportation planners collect and analyze data to make decisions about the design of highways, airports, and bus systems.

As an airline dispatcher, you might keep track of flight data for as many as 12 planes at a time. You need to track each plane's route, speed, and changes in altitude; keep records of the weight of the plane's cargo and amount of fuel; and know the amount of time each member of the crew has flown. In addition, you need to keep track of landing plans and weather conditions.

Careers That Involve Working With People

Working with people refers to jobs dealing mainly with human relationships. Examples of working with people include serving passengers, training or supervising employees, and advising customers. All these activities require strong communications skills.

Many jobs in Transportation, Distribution, & Logistics focus on working with people. They include many jobs in passenger transportation. Taxi and bus drivers, railroad conductors on passenger trains, flight attendants, and reservations and ticket agents work with passengers for most of the day. They often interact during busy travel times when passengers' tempers may be short.

Other Transportation, Distribution, & Logistics jobs require working with coworkers in teams. Managers or supervisors must effectively lead teams of workers. Workers in teams must be able to follow directions and communicate ideas to one another.

Careers That Involve Working With Things

Working with things refers to jobs dealing with goods, machinery, tools, and other objects. Examples of working with things include operating vehicles, loading freight, and repairing equipment. All these activities require strong mechanical skills.

Diesel, automotive, boat, and airline mechanics spend most of their days working with tools, parts, and electronic testing equipment. Rail-track layers use tools and equipment to lay, maintain, and repair the tracks that trains travel on. Material movers at docks, warehouses, and distribution centers use special vehicles and other equipment to load and unload freight.

> ### 12-3 Essential Question Reflection
>
> **So, let us revisit our essential question:**
>
> *How can I match my skills & interests with the right job?*
>
> Based on what you learned in this section, please answer this question in detail.

12-4 Education and Training

Jobs in the Transportation, Distribution, & Logistics industry require varying levels of education. Many jobs in this industry require little or no formal training. For others, it is necessary to have specific education and experience.

12-4 Essential Question

As you read this section, keep this question in mind:

What training & education is needed for a job in Transportation, Distribution, & Logistics?

Training and Education for This Industry

The level of training necessary to succeed in the Transportation, Distribution, & Logistics industry varies by career. Jobs can be categorized into three groups—those requiring little or no training, those requiring some training, and those requiring advanced training.

Jobs Requiring Little or No Training

Many jobs in this industry require little or no education or pre employment training. Dock and marina workers and material movers at distribution centers can often begin work without training. They usually get informal training on the job. Workers such as ticket and reservations agents may have workplace training programs after they are hired.

However, getting at least a high school education or the equivalent is important. Many employers look for workers who earned solid grades in high school. Failing to complete high school may hurt your chances for advancement.

Table 12.2: Training Required for Transportation, Distribution, & Logistics Jobs

Level of Training	Job Title
Little or No Training	Automotive Body Repairers Bus and Taxi Drivers Cargo and Freight Agents Flight Attendants Industrial Truck and Tractor Operators Railroad Signal and Switch Operators Railroad Conductors and Yardmasters Shipping, Receiving, and Traffic Clerks
Some Training	Air Traffic Controllers Aircraft and Airfield Mechanics Automotive Master Mechanics Automotive Specialty Technicians Avionics Technicians Material Movers Ship and Boat Captains Ship Engineers
Advanced Training	Airline Pilots and Flight Engineers Freight and Cargo Inspectors Industrial Safety Engineers Storage and Distribution Managers Supply Chain Managers Transportation Managers

Jobs Requiring Some Training

Some jobs in Transportation, Distribution, & Logistics require some training. Technical schools and community or junior colleges offer programs that can prepare you for jobs that demand specialized training, such as auto mechanics.

Training may also be obtained through trade organizations, such as the Professional Truck Driver Institute (PTDI). Such groups offer certification programs that provide training for a specific occupation. The program may require a minimum number of hours on the job and a minimum score on a test.

Jobs Requiring Advanced Training

Some jobs in Transportation, Distribution, & Logistics require more extensive training or formal education. To become a manager, you usually need at least a bachelor's degree from a four-year college. Experience may substitute for lack of higher education, but most managers have college degrees in business administration, organizational management, or marketing.

Many of the fastest-growing careers in this industry require college degrees. Logistics managers, for instance, are usually required to have at least a bachelor's degree in logistics or business management. Industrial safety and health engineers and environmental managers need advanced degrees. Professionals who manage the public transportation infrastructure often have a master's and even a doctoral degree.

Certain jobs require a great deal of experience in addition to college degrees. Airline pilots, for instance, must have a minimum of 1,500 hours of flying time before they can captain a passenger plane. Deck officers on merchant vessels must accumulate thousands of hours of experience at sea.

Job and Workplace Skills

Employers are looking for both job-specific skills and general workplace skills. Both are highly valuable to complete day-to-day tasks. Job-specific skills are needed for a particular job. Examples of job-specific skills include knowing how to operate a forklift or the ability to drive a bus. General workplace skills are skills that can be used in a variety of positions, such as the ability to write an email.

Transportation, Distribution, & Logistics Skill Standards

Skills standards in the Transportation, Distribution, & Logistics industry vary depending on the occupation. Many states have their own skill standards for some jobs. Federal agencies and nonprofit groups also maintain skill standards.

For example, the Federal Aviation Administration (FAA) sets skill standards for pilots. The FAA requires all pilots to pass a series of practical tests. They must demonstrate their ability to prepare for flight, to fly and maneuver, and to handle emergencies.

The U.S. Coast Guard sets skill standards for merchant marines. Specific standards govern all merchant-vessel jobs, such as able seaman and marine radio operators. Able seamen, for example, must have a certain number of days at sea and basic safety training. They also must pass either a coast guard exam or a coast guard-approved course.

Some nonprofit organizations focus on providing standards for training programs. These standards play a key role in turning out top-quality workers. For example, the National Automotive Technicians Education Foundation (NATEF) maintains standards for automotive mechanic training programs. These standards ensure that students who complete programs certified by NATEF have the skills to perform tasks expected of an automotive mechanic.

Professional Skills

Professional skills are critical to perform in transportation and logistics. They differ from academic or job-specific skills. They are learned both inside and outside the classroom. They are also transferable from job to job. Developing these skills will make you more marketable in the Transportation, Distribution, & Logistics industry, and in any job situation.

Communications Skills Communication skills are very important in the Transportation, Distribution, & Logistics industry. Safety, on-time deliveries, and business success all depend on the ability to communicate clearly with customers and coworkers.

Problem-Solving Skills Problem-solving is essential to many jobs in Transportation, Distribution, & Logistics. For example, a railroad conductor inspecting a train before a trip may be called on to troubleshoot problems related to defective cars. A logistics manager may need to deal with unexpected delays caused by a flood or a blizzard.

Technology Skills Modes of transportation, as well as distribution and logistics systems, involve increasingly complex technology. Workers must be able to keep up with these cutting-edge advances. In addition, many industry jobs require computer skills. Billing clerks, for example, use computer software to prepare invoices. Logistics managers use computers to prepare flow-charts that help in planning the flow of goods.

Decision-Making Skills Being able to gather and analyze information quickly and to think clearly under pressure are skills required in many jobs in the Transportation, Distribution, & Logistics industry. Railroad engineers, ship captains, and other transportation operators often face problems that require them to make quick decisions.

Organizing and Planning Skills Since efficient transportation involves so many steps, organization and planning are crucial. Planning requires setting goals and mapping out the steps needed to achieve these goals. This is the main function of logistics. It is also a central function of jobs such as freight forwarding and transportation management.

Teamwork Skills Teamwork is key to getting passengers or freight from point to point, especially if a variety of transportation methods is used. A complex vehicle or a vessel such as a plane, train, or ship can function only when every crew member works toward a common goal.

Social Skills Social interaction is basic to the customer service that must be provided in jobs dealing directly with clients or passengers. Social interaction with coworkers also makes for a better work atmosphere and happier workers.

12-4 Essential Question Reflection

So, let us revisit our essential question:

What training & education is needed for a job in Transportation, Distribution, & Logistics?

Based on what you learned in this section, please answer this question in detail.

Practice 12-4

Skills Practice

Some jobs in the Transportation, Distribution, & Logistics industry require workers to calculate costs and discounts. A billing clerk, for instance, may need to calculate a discount for a purchaser shipping a big order of items to one location. **Practice this skill!**

1. You are the fleet supervisor for a distribution company. You want to replace your diesel delivery vans with hybrid fuel delivery vans. Operation costs are $0.55 per mile for your current diesel delivery vans. You will save 20 percent per mile by switching to the hybrid van. What is the operation cost of the hybrid van?

   A. $0.11 per mile
   B. $0.20 per mile
   C. $0.38 per mile
   D. $0.44 per mile
   E. $0.53 per mile

2. The price of gasoline directly impacts profits. Gasoline averages $3.368 per gallon but is expected to increase 18 percent next year. What will the average cost of gasoline be next year?

   A. $3.135
   B. $3.368
   C. $3.498
   D. $3.974
   E. $4.066

Skills Practice

Some calculations in transportation, distribution, and logistics may require using conversions and formulas. As a rail-track layer, you may need to calculate the length of track that has been laid based on different lengths of track that have been used. You may also need to convert minutes into hours to find out how long the job has taken. **Practice this skill!**

3. You are a document delivery driver, and you bring a letter from a lawyer's office to the client's office. The client gives you six quarters, two dimes, and a penny for the balance due on her delivery. How much money did she give you?

   A. $1.21
   B. $1.46
   C. $1.61
   D. $1.71
   E. $1.75

4. As a shipping clerk, it takes you 240 minutes to enter shipping information into the computer for 48 packages. After completing this task, how many hours remain in your eight-hour shift?

   A. 1
   B. 2
   C. 3
   D. 4
   E. 5

To access more problems that will help you grow professional skills and are real-world examples in Transportation, Distribution, & Logistics, go online.

12-5 Working in the Transportation, Distribution, & Logistics Industry

When choosing a career path, it is important to know what it is like to work in the industry. Understanding the work environment, hazards, and benefits of a job can help you make informed decisions.

> **12-5 Essential Question**
>
> As you read this section, keep this question in mind:
>
> *What are typical work environments in Transportation, Distribution, & Logistics?*

Physical Environment

People in the Transportation, Distribution, & Logistics industry work in a variety of settings. Some are employed in comfortable offices. Others spend long periods of time in small spaces, noisy areas, or wet places. Material movers in ship and rail yards are outdoors in all weather conditions. Truck and bus drivers must drive in bad weather or heavy traffic. Ship pilots and able seamen often must work in damp and cold conditions.

Workplace conditions have improved because of new workplace laws. Modern equipment, safety precautions, and exhaust systems have also cut down on the dangerous and unpleasant conditions that were once more common in the industry.

Work Hours

Many employees in the Transportation, Logistics, & Distribution industry work irregular hours. Ships, trains, buses, and other means of transportation often operate day and night, so employees must work in shifts. Shift work divides the day into blocks of time. Some workers start their shifts early in the morning. Others work night shifts. Many workers do not have weekends or holidays off.

366 Chapter 12 • Transportation, Distribution, & Logistics

The U.S. Department of Transportation regulates the maximum number of hours that many industry employees can work. Transportation operators may work any time of day, but for safety reasons, they cannot work overtime. Workers in warehouses and distribution centers, however, often work overtime to meet delivery demands. In the delivery business, late deliveries mean disappointed clients and a potential loss of business.

Essential Physical Activities

Work in the Transportation, Distribution, & Logistics industry can be very physically demanding. Many workers perform heavy lifting or handle heavy equipment. Others drive or travel long hours under sometimes grueling conditions. Workers making repairs may need to crawl into confined spaces in or under vehicles.

Hazards and Environmental Dangers

According to the U.S. Bureau of Labor Statistics, transportation and warehouse workers have a high risk of injury at work. The leading cause of on-the-job injuries are motor vehicle accidents. In fact, deaths from highway incidents were the most frequent kind of job-related fatality in 2019.

In warehouses and distribution centers, serious injuries often occur when equipment like forklifts tip over or harm workers. Other common injuries include muscle strain from lifting heavy objects and bruises and broken bones from tripping and falling.

In addition to on-the-job-injuries, transportation workers risk chronic health dangers. Irregular schedules and frequent travel may cause exhaustion from lack of sleep. Airline personnel often experience jet lag, fatigue caused by traveling across several time zones. Those who work near engines and other noisy equipment face the danger of hearing loss.

12-5 Essential Question Reflection

So, let us revisit our essential question:

What are typical work environments in Transportation, Distribution, & Logistics?

Based on what you learned in this section, please answer this question in detail.

12-6 Trends in Transportation, Distribution, & Logistics

The Transportation, Distribution, & Logistics industry is constantly evolving. New technology affects the way business is run. Changes in society affect how goods are shipped and how people travel. In a global economy, even events overseas can affect the way things are done at home.

? 12-6 Essential Question

As you read this section, keep this question in mind:

What factors affect trends in Transportation, Distribution, & Logistics?

Technology in the Industry

During the past few decades, technological advances have drastically changed the Transportation, Distribution, & Logistics industry. Clients now contact companies through websites and e mail. Companies use computers to keep track of freight, workers, schedules, and payments. Logistics managers use special software to compare costs, times, and routes in order to choose the best means of getting goods to their destinations.

Smartphones and Wi-Fi

Mobile computer devices are very useful in an industry that focuses on moving people and goods. Devices such as smartphones and computer tablets allow drivers to keep track of delivery locations, times, and other details. Navigation devices can direct drivers to their destination. Wi-Fi, or wireless service, allows passengers and workers to use their laptop computers as they travel. The service is now being offered on more buses and trains.

E-Ticketing and Passenger Information Display Systems

Technology is making passenger travel easier. E-ticketing, or electronic ticketing, lets passengers buy tickets electronically, with no need for a physical ticket. Most airlines are moving toward a completely paperless system. Many cruise lines, train lines, and bus companies have followed their lead.

Airports and some other transportation centers now gather and display information electronically. A passenger information display system (PIDS) provides arrival and departure times, gate or track numbers, and other real-time information. At transportation centers, the information is displayed on large boards and on small screens or touchscreens that passengers use. The system can display data in vehicles themselves. For example, an overhead monitor on a train might indicate the next stop and estimated arrival time. Real-time information may be accessible online by using a computer or a smartphone.

Engine Analyzers

Computer technology is now standard in motor vehicle repair. An engine analyzer, for example, is an electronic device that helps mechanics assess an engine's performance. The device looks like a large hand held computer. It can be hooked up to various parts of a vehicle to test whether the parts are working.

Motor vehicles also have internal engine analyzers. The analyzers attach directly to the engine. They gather information about engine condition and performance. They often include an oscilloscope, which evaluates the ignition system, and a tachometer, which monitors the engine's speed.

Conveyor Systems and Robotics

In warehouses and distribution centers, computer controls have helped conveyor systems move goods more quickly. Robots are also increasing efficiency in warehouses. Stationary robots are used to fill orders. Gantry robots work from overhead to select cases of goods and move them to the shipping area. Robotic arms can grab specific items identified by bar-code scanning. Mobile robots, which may use lasers or floor wires to move around, do many of the tasks a person used to do.

Global Positioning and Intelligent Transportation Systems

The U.S. government plays a role in key transportation advances. The Global Positioning System (GPS), a project of the Department of Defense, is a group of satellites that pinpoint locations on earth. Today, GPS receivers aid water navigation and help taxi and delivery truck drivers find their way. GPS allows shippers to track vehicles and better manage their fleets.

Also useful in vehicle tracking are advances in telemetry, in which sensors on vehicles collect data and transmit the information wirelessly. Such sensors are likely to play a big role in the Intelligent Transportation System (ITS) program. This joint effort between the U.S. Department of Transportation and private industry uses technology to improve the nation's surface transportation system. Its future includes the use of wireless telemetry to create "smart" highways that provide data directly to the vehicles that travel on them.

Environmental Issues in Transportation, Distribution, & Logistics

Sustainability is another trend in business today. Sustainability refers to economic activity that does not harm the environment. The issue is of special concern to the Transportation, Distribution, & Logistics industry, which traditionally has run on petroleum-based fuels that harm the environment.

Alternative Fuels and Lower Fuel Consumptions

Efforts to make transportation "greener," or more sustainable, include the use of alternative fuels. Alternative fuels are not petroleum based. Ethanol, a kind of alcohol made from corn and other grains, may be used to fuel buses, boats, and trucks. Solar power may be used to run water vessels such as ferries. Biodiesel, diesel engine fuel made from non petroleum oils, can be used in vehicles with diesel engines. Engines that run on electricity reduce pollution, but they have a limited range because they need recharging. A possible solution is the use of fuel cells, devices that change hydrogen and oxygen into electricity in the vehicles themselves.

Shifting to alternative fuels can be costly. By contrast, efforts to cut down on fuel use have the advantage of immediate cost savings. New technology often helps companies reduce fuel use. GPS systems on truck fleets, for instance, help avoid idle time and route errors, which waste fuel. New vehicle design features take fuel savings into account. For example, some companies are creating special truck tires that improve fuel efficiency.

Greener Transportation Systems

Some forms of transportation are greener than others. A big barge or a long freight train carrying cargo uses less fuel than individual trucks. A city's workforce commuting on mass transit uses less fuel than individual commuters driving to work. Today, many people and businesses are making greener transportation choices, especially when those choices save time or money. For example, rising fuel costs and traffic have increased the use of mass transit and intercity buses and trains.

Regional planners recognize these trends. Many have proposed new commuter rail systems to connect cities and suburbs. Others are considering high-speed rail between cities. Private companies are offering low-cost intercity buses.

Economic Trends in Transportation, Distribution, & Logistics

In the global economy, many goods made overseas are shipped to U.S. markets. This increases the need for workers in the Transportation, Distribution, & Logistics industry. Companies providing the services become more international. As a result, industry workers may find themselves in contact with workers in other countries when placing orders or scheduling deliveries.

Intermodal Transportation

One important trend in the global economy is the use of intermodal transportation. Intermodal transportation is a method of shipping freight through a combination of trucks, trains, planes, or ships. Goods manufactured in Asia, for example, may be placed into containers and shipped to Seattle. The containers may then be moved to freight trains and carried to a distribution center in the Midwest. There, the goods may be unloaded onto trucks and delivered to regional stores.

E-Commerce

E-commerce is the buying and selling of goods over the Internet. It is popular with both businesses and individuals. Once goods are bought, they are shipped straight to customers from warehouses or factories. E-commerce increases the demand for carriers that can deliver small loads to individual consumers. Package delivery, air-freight express, and less-than-truckload (LTL) carriers have seen business increase as a result of e-commerce.

Amazon.com is one of the most well-known e-commerce sites. As their logo implies, Amazon sells everything from A-to-Z and has developed such an efficient logistics department that in some areas, they offer same day delivery. You can now order from your phone from the comfort of your living room and have the item at your doorstep within hours. Amazon's efficiency has set the standard in the e-commerce industry.

Outsourcing and Consultants

Two ongoing workplace trends are outsourcing and the use of consultants. When companies outsource, they turn over control of some tasks to other companies. For example, manufacturers may outsource warehousing tasks. This decision can be cost-effective because not owning warehouse space saves real-estate costs. A growing trend in the global economy is to outsource certain tasks to workers abroad who work for lower pay. Such outsourcing is most likely to affect office jobs, such as phone or computer sales.

Consultants are people who provide special services. They are often hired when a project starts or when a project is being reexamined. For example, when new transportation systems are being planned, environmental consultants may be hired because of their technical knowledge.

12-6 Essential Question Reflection

So, let us revisit our essential question:

What factors affect trends in Transportation, Distribution, & Logistics?

Based on what you learned in this section, please answer this question in detail.

Chapter 13

Hospitality & Tourism

❓ Essential Questions

By the end of the chapter, you will be able to answer the following questions:

- **13-1** What types of opportunities are available in Hospitality & Tourism?
- **13-2** Which opportunities may be right for you?
- **13-3** How can I match my skills & interests with the right job?
- **13-4** What training & education is needed for a job in Hospitality & Tourism?
- **13-5** What are typical work environments in Hospitality & Tourism?
- **13-6** What factors affect trends in Hospitality & Tourism?

Chapter Topics

13-1 Hospitality & Tourism Today

13-2 Hospitality & Tourism Jobs

13-3 Building a Career in Hospitality & Tourism

13-4 Education and Training for Hospitality & Tourism Opportunities

13-5 Working Conditions in the Hospitality & Tourism Industry

13-6 Trends in Hospitality & Tourism

13-1 Hospitality & Tourism Today

Every time you go on vacation or eat out, you use services provided by workers in the Hospitality & Tourism industry. Some plan dream vacations. Others help businesspeople travel to meet customers. Still others help families enjoy eating simple meals out.

People regularly come into contact with workers in the industry, such as hotel desk clerks, restaurant servers, and flight attendants. Other workers, such as hotel cleaning staff, restaurant chefs, and airline caterers, work behind the scenes. Whatever their job, all these people work toward the same goal: providing good service to their customers.

Millions of people are employed in Hospitality & Tourism. In fact, a single segment of the industry—the Restaurant segment—accounts for 8.7 million service jobs in the United States. Another 1.8 million people work in hotels, motels, and other lodging establishments. These people and the millions of others in the industry work to ensure that traveling, staying at lodging establishments, and dining out are enjoyable experiences.

13-1 Essential Question

As you read this section, keep this question in mind:

What types of opportunities are available in Hospitality & Tourism?

Career Journeys in Hospitality & Tourism

Each of the four paths in the Hospitality & Tourism industry contains a group of careers requiring similar skills as well as similar certifications or education. This industry is divided into four main career paths:

- Lodging
- Restaurant and Food/Beverage Services
- Recreation, Amusements, and Attractions
- Travel and Tourism

Companies in this industry are highly dependent on each other. Lodging facilities depend on travel and tourism to bring in guests. As a result, when one part of the industry flourishes, the others flourish, too.

Lodging

The Lodging path includes workers at hotels, motels, inns, bed-and-breakfasts, time-share arrangements, and hostels. Each type of place serves a slightly different purpose:

- Many **hotels** provide lodging to people staying overnight for brief trips. Hotels are often located in cities or near airports.
- **Resort hotels** offer more than a place to stay. They also provide a variety of recreational services.
- **Motels** are aimed at travelers looking for an inexpensive place to sleep while on the road.
- **Inns** and **bed-and-breakfasts** are quaint places geared toward tourists.
- In **time-share arrangements**, people can purchase days or weeks at a vacation spot over many years.
- **Hostels** offer dormitory-style accommodations to budget travelers.

Responsibilities vary in lodging jobs. Hotel or lodging managers oversee the building and staff and handle problems that come up. Front desk clerks check guests in and help them with questions. Custodial workers keep lodging grounds tidy. They tend the lawns, clean pools and spas, and make sure interiors are kept clean.

Housekeepers prepare rooms for the arrival of new guests. Housekeepers and cleaning service attendants also maintain rooms during guests' stays, providing clean linens and towels. Room service workers deliver meals, pick up laundry, and deliver requested items. A concierge manages guest services and might offer recommendations for local attractions and restaurants.

Workers in the Lodging career path must enjoy working with people. Most of their day is spent interacting with coworkers and guests. Many jobs in lodging, such as housekeeper, janitor, and hotel desk clerk, require little training. However, hotel managers may need a college degree in business or hotel administration and experience working in a hotel.

Restaurant and Food/Beverage Services

The Restaurant and Food/Beverage Services path includes work in all types of places that provide food and drinks. Businesses from food trucks to gourmet restaurants are included. So are fast-food restaurants, diners, cafeterias, bars, and sandwich shops.

Restaurant and Food/Beverage Services is the largest path in the Hospitality & Tourism industry. Food service employs a great number of employees in a variety of settings.

The work in these businesses varies, but most of it is fast-paced and team oriented. Food service providers, such as servers and bus persons, serve food and set up and clear place settings. At bars, a bartender prepares drinks. A host greets guests, takes reservations, and seats diners. Food and beverage managers are responsible for the restaurant. Restaurant managers ensure that their restaurants operate smoothly and make a profit. Chefs, cooks, bakers, and others plan menus and prepare the food.

Some positions in this path, such as chef, food technologist, and nutritionist, require education beyond high school. Most, however, are entry-level jobs that include training. Entry-level jobs can eventually lead to managerial positions.

Recreation, Amusements, and Attractions

The Recreation, Amusements, and Attractions path includes work in places that provide entertainment and amusement. These include zoos, museums, sports stadiums, and gaming places, among others.

Each of these establishments requires different types of workers. Animal trainers can be found at zoos, while projectionists play films at movie theaters. Curators, administrators, and exhibit designers keep museums up to date. Sports stadiums are the workplace of athletes, umpires, and concessions workers, among others. Visitors to casinos will find dealers, cashiers, managers, and others.

Most careers in this path do not require more than a high school diploma. Some workers, however, such as exhibit designers and technicians at museums, generally must earn college degrees.

Travel and Tourism

Workers in the Travel and Tourism path plan for everything from rental cars to honeymoon vacation packages. Travel planning services are provided for businesses, groups, and individuals. Travel agents and guides require training at vocational schools, related on-the-job experience, or an associate degree. Tour guides may require a license.

Business Travel Planning The most common travel services used by business travelers are booking reservations for flights, hotels, and rental cars. Travel agents and ticket agents provide these services.

About half of all business travel involves conferences, conventions, or trade shows. People may work in convention halls and for convention planning services.

Vacation Travel Planning People use the Internet to book their own travel. However, others use travel agents to help with planning. Travelers may book tours with tour companies. These companies may offer deals that include airfare, hotel accommodations, and other services. Tour companies may offer guided tours to different attractions. Others specialize in educational or athletic tours, such as theater tours or mountain-climbing trips. Other tour guides work at historic sites or parks, leading groups of visitors.

Hospitality & Tourism Future Outlook

Industry outlook refers to the projected job growth or decline in a particular industry. Even though the Hospitality & Tourism industry experienced a decline during the pandemic, the outlook for the Hospitality & Tourism industry has recovered and is increasing overall.

The strongest job growth will be in the Lodging path. Smaller, limited-service hotels will open. However, most jobs will be in larger hotels. In the Restaurant and Food/Beverage Services path, demand for places offering quick but healthful meals will grow faster than traditional fast-food restaurants. Inexpensive restaurants will grow more quickly than fine-dining restaurants. The greatest demand will be for cooks, servers, and combined food-preparation staff and servers.

In the Recreation, Amusements, and Attractions path, the number of gaming establishments, museums, and historical sites are all expected to grow, offering the most job opportunities. The Travel and Tourism path will grow, as technology makes travel planning easier for individuals to do on their own.

Table 13.1 Job Forecast for a Sample of Hospitality & Tourism Opportunities

Occupation	Expected Growth Rate
Amusement and Recreation Attendants	10%–15%
Animal Trainers	10%–15%
Food Preparation Workers	1%–5%
Baggage Porters and Bellhops	10%–15%
Chefs and Head Cooks	10%–15%
Concierges	10%–15%
Transportation, Storage, and Distribution Managers	5%–10%
Cooks, Restaurants	10%–15%
Hosts	10%–15%
Meeting and Convention Planners	10%–15%
Travel Agents	10%–15%
Janitors and Cleaners	5%–10%
Housekeepers	5%–10%
Interpreters and Translators	10%–15%
Food Servers	5%–10%
Food Preparation Workers	1%–5%
Recreation Workers	5%–10%
Tour Guides	10%–15%

Source: O*Net

13-1 Essential Question Reflection

So, let us revisit our essential question:

What types of opportunities are available in Hospitality & Tourism?

Based on what you learned in this chapter, please answer this question in detail.

Practice 13-1

Skills Practice

It may be necessary to follow multi step instructions in a variety of situations, such as when learning how to enter a restaurant patron's order into a computerized system or how to check in a new hotel guest. Workers must read carefully to know when to take each step and be able to apply the same instructions in a variety of situations. **Practice this skill!**

PROCEDURES FOR ADDRESSING GUEST COMPLAINTS REGARDING INTERNET CONNECTION PROBLEMS:

- Verify the room number.
- Ask about the problem, and take notes.
- If the problem is the loss of Internet connection, verify that you still have an Internet connection at the front desk, and then find out when the guest lost connectivity.
- If the problem seems to be limited to the guest's room, offer to have another cable sent to the room.
- If the problem persists, send the hotel technician to the guest's room.
- If the problem seems not to be limited to the room (no Internet connection in the entire hotel), apologize and promise the guest that the problem will be fixed as soon as possible.
- Call the hotel technician immediately.

1. You are a guest services agent working in a hotel. A guest reports that he is unable to connect to the Internet. According to the procedures, what is the first thing you should you do after the guest has explained that he does not have Internet access in his room?

   A. Verify the room number.
   B. Promise the guest that the problem will be fixed.
   C. Send another cable to the room.
   D. Check the Internet on your computer.
   E. Call the hotel technician immediately.

2. What should you do if a new cable does not solve the guest's problem?

   A. Check the Internet connection in the entire hotel.
   B. Promise that you will fix the problem.
   C. Send a technician to the guest's room.
   D. Find out when the guest lost connectivity.
   E. Send a different cable to the guest's room.

To access more problems that will help you grow professional skills and are real-world examples in Hospitality & Tourism, go online.

13-2 Hospitality & Tourism Jobs

The Hospitality & Tourism industry offers a vast variety of jobs. Workers may get paid to fly all over the world or lead tour groups. Others work in fast-paced restaurant kitchens. This section highlights common industry jobs and the skills they require.

> **13-2 Essential Question**
>
> As you read this section, keep this question in mind:
>
> *Which opportunities may be right for you?*

Great Jobs! – No Degree Required:

Baggage Porters and Bell Hops

- Handle baggage for travelers at transportation terminals or for guests at hotels
- Greet incoming guests and lead them to their rooms
- Receive and mark baggage by completing and attaching claim checks

Fast Facts:
Employment: 21,700 employees
Annual Openings: 410
Median Annual Wage: $14.00 hourly, $29,120 annually
Other: This job requires being reliable and great people skills.

Food Preparation Workers

- Clean and sanitize work areas, equipment, utensils, dishes, or silverware
- Store food in designated containers and storage areas to prevent spoilage
- Prepare a variety of foods, such as meats, vegetables, or desserts, according to customers' orders or supervisors' instructions

Fast Facts:
Employment: 817,400 employees
Annual Openings: 145,800
Median Annual Wage: $13.84 hourly, $28,780 annually
Other: This is a fast-paced job that requires strong organizational skills.

Occupations With a Bright Outlook:

Animal Trainers

- Train animals for riding, harness, security, performance, or obedience, or for assisting persons with disabilities
- Cue or signal animals during performances
- Talk to or interact with animals to familiarize them with human voices and/or contact
- Conduct training programs to develop or maintain desired animal behaviors for competition, entertainment, obedience, security, riding, or related purposes

Fast Facts:
Employment: 52,900 employees
Annual Openings: 1,060
Median Annual Wage: $15.04 hourly, $31,280 annually
Education Needed: High school diploma, or equivalent

Recreation Workers

- Conduct recreation activities with groups in public, private, or volunteer agencies or recreation facilities
- Enforce rules and regulations of recreational facilities to maintain discipline and ensure safety
- Organize, lead, and promote interest in recreational activities, such as arts, crafts, sports, games, camping, and hobbies
- Manage the daily operations of recreational facilities

Fast Facts:

Employment: 279,600 employees

Annual Openings: 6,170

Median Annual Wage: $14.27 hourly, $29,680 annually

Education Needed: High school diploma, or equivalent

Other: There are many opportunities to progress in this career by being promoted to manager or supervisor.

Great Job! – High School Diploma Required:

Concierges

- Assist patrons at hotels, apartments, or office buildings with personal services
- Make reservations for patrons, such as for dinner, spa treatments, or golf tee times, and obtain tickets to special events
- Provide information about local features, such as shopping, dining, nightlife, or recreational destinations

Fast Facts:

Employment: 35,000 employees

Annual Openings: 610

Median Annual Wage: $16.93 hourly, $35,210 annually

Education Needed: High school diploma, or equivalent

Other: Having strong communication and people skills is a must for this career.

Occupations That Offer the Opportunity to Travel for Work:

Tour Guides

- Escort individuals or groups on sightseeing tours or through places of interest, such as industrial establishments, public buildings, and art galleries
- Describe tour points of interest to group members, and respond to questions
- Monitor visitors' activities to ensure compliance with establishment or tour regulations and safety practices

Fast Facts:

Employment: 43,400 employees
Annual Openings: 960
Median Annual Wage: $14.32 hourly, $29,780 annually
Education Needed: Associate degree

Interpreters and Translators

- Interpret oral or sign language, or translate written text from one language into another
- Follow ethical codes that protect the confidentiality of information
- Translate messages simultaneously or consecutively into specified languages, orally or by using hand signs, maintaining message content, context, and style as much as possible

Fast Facts:

Employment: 69,400 employees
Annual Openings: 920
Median Annual Wage: $23.61 hourly, $49,110 annually
Education Needed: Bachelor's degree
Other: Interpreters can connect people who speak different languages.

13-3 Essential Question Reflection

So, let us revisit our essential question:

Which opportunities may be right for you?

Based on what you learned in this section, please answer this question in detail.

13-2 • Hospitality & Tourism Jobs

Case Study: Meeting, Convention, and Event Planners

Also called: Conference Planning Manager, Conference Services Manager, Convention Services Manager (CSM), Events Manager

What do they do?

- Coordinate activities of staff, convention personnel, or clients to plan for group meetings, events, or conventions

What would you do?

- Consult with customers to determine objectives and requirements for events, such as meetings, conferences, and conventions
- Review event bills for accuracy, and approve payment
- Coordinate services for events, such as accommodation and transportation for participants, facilities, catering, signage, displays, special needs requirements, printing, and event security

What do you need to know?

Business
Customer service
Administrative services

Arts and Humanities
English language

Communications
Multimedia

Engineering and Technology
Computers and electronics

What skills do you need?

Basic Skills
Listen to others, do not interrupt, and ask good questions
Read work-related information

Problem Solving
Notice a problem, and figure out the best way to solve it

Social
    Change what is done based on other people's actions

    Look for ways to help people

What abilities must you be good at?

Verbal and Written
    Communicate by speaking

    Communicate by writing

Ideas and Logic
    Notice when problems happen

    Use rules to solve problems

Attention
    Pay attention to something without being distracted

    Do two or more things at the same time

Who does well in this occupation?

    People interested in this work like activities that include leading, making decisions, and business.

What educational level is needed?

- Bachelor's degree or some college

Practice 13-2

Skills Practice

Hospitality & Tourism workers must sometimes analyze graphics to identify trends. They might search for data that indicate changes over time. A travel agent might study a graph to compare and contrast current and past travel habits to make projections about future trends. A hotel manager might look for trends in guest responses to satisfaction surveys. Being able to identify common trends from several pieces of data can help with a variety of jobs in this industry. **Practice this skill!**

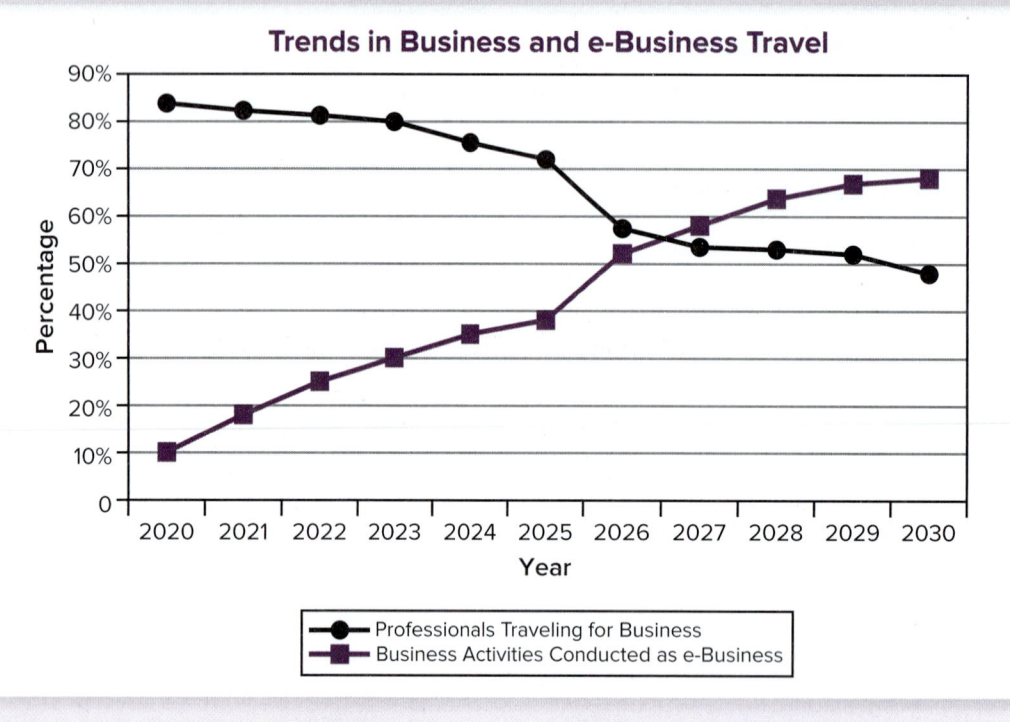

Trends in Business and e-Business Travel

- Professionals Traveling for Business
- Business Activities Conducted as e-Business

1. You are a research assistant at a travel office. You are studying how the Internet and e-business have impacted the business travel industry. What is the overall trend since 2020?

   A. Business travel has steadily decreased as e-business has steadily increased.
   B. Business travel has steadily increased as e-business has steadily decreased.
   C. Business travel and e-business have both increased.
   D. Business travel and e-business have both decreased.
   E. Business travel and e-business have both remained about the same.

2. Between which two years does the graph indicate business travel having the biggest decline?

   A. 2021–2022
   B. 2022–2023
   C. 2023–2024
   D. 2024–2025
   E. 2025–2026

388 Chapter 13 • Hospitality & Tourism

Skills Practice

When reviewing workplace graphics, it may be necessary to compare information in one or more graphics. A travel agent might compare graphics detailing the offerings of two or more cruise lines, for example. Workers must know how different graphics relate to each other and be able to compare information and trends within them. **Practice this skill!**

Late Fee Schedule

Boat Return Time	Fee
Before 5:00 p.m.	No fee
5:00 to 5:59 p.m.	$5.00
6:00 to 6:59 p.m.	$10.00
7:00 to 7:59 p.m.	$15.00
8:00 p.m. or later	$25.00

Customer Records

Customer Name	Time Boat Was Returned
Jane Smith	6:45 p.m.
Richard Johnson	5:15 p.m.
Paul Jones	4:50 p.m.
Karen Wilson	8:25 p.m.
Larry Peterson	7:00 p.m.

3. You manage a paddle boat rental service at a city park. Customers who do not return the rented boats by a certain time must pay a late fee. Of the customers listed, who returned their boat on time and avoided a late fee?

   A. Jane Smith
   B. Richard Johnson
   C. Paul Jones
   D. Karen Wilson
   E. Larry Peterson

4. How much must Larry Peterson pay for his late fee?

   A. $0.00
   B. $5.00
   C. $10.00
   D. $15.00
   E. $25.00

To access more problems that will help you grow professional skills and are real-world examples in Hospitality & Tourism, go online.

13-3 Building a Career in Hospitality & Tourism

Once you have found a field that interests you, look ahead and consider your career path. This path is made up of the job experiences and career moves that lead you toward your career goal. You may take several steps before reaching your goal. You will likely spend time in an entry-level position. This will help you gain the professional experience necessary to move ahead in your career.

People who become directors of hotel food and beverage services, for example, often start in entry-level positions. They may be dishwashers or room service order takers. From there, they move along their path and eventually into their first management position, perhaps as an assistant director in the catering, restaurant, or banquet department. Becoming a food and beverage director requires knowledge of all a hotel's food service departments. For this reason, managers who want to advance often move from department to department. It may take many years to become a director. You may also need to change employers at least once or twice.

13-3 Essential Question

As you read this section, keep this question in mind:

How can I match my skills & interests with the right job?

Are You More Interested in Working With Data, People, or Things?

Most careers in the Hospitality & Tourism industry offer opportunities to work with a combination of data, people, and things. Working with data involves the evaluation of information. Hotel auditors, for example, work mainly with data. A job that focuses on people is based on human relationships. Restaurant servers work primarily with people. Working with things involves using objects, such as tools, equipment, and machines. For example, amusement park ride attendants work mostly with machines. When planning your career path, consider what balance of data, people, and things you want in a career.

Careers That Involve Working With Data

Examples of working with data in the Hospitality & Tourism industry include drawing up a nutritional plan for a diabetic patient, analyzing guest attendance figures, and scheduling the steps required to cater a banquet.

Some jobs in the Hospitality & Tourism industry require expertise at analyzing data. Chief financial officers of large hotel chains spend most of their time reviewing statistics. Accountants who work in the Hospitality & Tourism industry also work almost entirely with numbers. Travel promoters look at tourism figures and plan marketing strategies to interest travelers in certain destinations.

Managers in the Hospitality & Tourism industry spend at least some of their time working with data. Restaurant managers and department heads, for example, spend many hours every week studying spreadsheets that detail costs, revenues, and profits. They use this data to make decisions about how to run the business cost-effectively.

Careers That Involve Working With People

Everyone in the Hospitality & Tourism industry works with people. Most employees in this industry serve customers or clients. They might deal with restaurant diners, hotel guests, amusement park visitors, casino gamblers, sports fans, or convention attendees. Managers supervise workers, ensuring that their staff work together as a team and that all job duties are carried out.

Many workers in Hospitality & Tourism—such as hotel front office staff, hotel concierges, restaurant waitstaff, and travel agents—deal directly with clients. Others, such as kitchen and housekeeping staff, deal mainly with their colleagues and supervisors.

Careers That Involve Working With Things

Many jobs in the Hospitality & Tourism industry require the ability to work with things. Examples of working with things include cooking food, setting tables, making beds, and dealing cards.

Even in jobs that deal mainly with people, you will need skills at working with things. Ride attendants at amusement parks operate the controls of rides and ensure that safety straps are properly secured on passengers before operating the ride. Adventure guides make sure that all their equipment is in working order. Lifeguards check the chlorine in pools to ensure safe levels of chemicals.

13-3 Essential Question Reflection

So, let us revisit our essential question:

How can I match my skills & interests with the right job?

Based on what you learned in this section, please answer this question in detail.

13-4 Education and Training for Hospitality & Tourism Opportunities

Jobs in the Hospitality & Tourism industry require varying levels of education. Many jobs in this industry require little or no formal training. Others require specific education and experience.

One good way to research careers in this industry is job shadowing. Job shadowing is following a worker on the job for a few days. It can help you learn whether a career matches your aptitudes and interests. You might learn how a bed-and-breakfast owner handles day-to-day operations. You could watch a camp athletic director lead sports activities for children. You might even follow a tour director who takes foreign tourists on guided tours of your hometown.

13-4 Essential Question

As you read this section, keep this question in mind:

What training & education is needed for a job in Hospitality & Tourism?

Training and Education for Hospitality & Tourism

The level of training necessary to succeed in the Hospitality & Tourism industry varies by career. Jobs can be categorized into three groups—those that require little or no training, those that require some training, and those that require advanced training.

Jobs Requiring Little or No Training

Many entry-level jobs in the Hospitality & Tourism industry do not require much training or education. Jobs such as front desk clerk or reservations agent usually require little training. The training for jobs such as these is usually provided by your employer when you are hired.

However, getting a high school education or the equivalent is important. Many employers look for workers who earned solid grades in high school. Failing to complete high school may hurt your chances for advancement in your career.

Jobs Requiring Some Training

Some jobs in Hospitality & Tourism require specialized training or education. Examples include travel agents, food and beverage managers, and hotel managers.

People can receive the education and training they need in various ways. Community colleges, junior colleges, and four-year institutions offer associate degrees and bachelor's degrees in Hospitality & Tourism and related fields. An associate degree is awarded after a two-year course of study. A bachelor's degree requires four years of study.

Trade organizations, or organizations representing a specific industry or type of job, often offer certification programs that provide training for an occupation. For instance, the American Hotel & Lodging Association certifies hotel administrators, food and beverage executives, and others. The American Culinary Federation offers various levels of certification for chefs. Certification programs may require a minimum number of hours on the job and a minimum score on a standardized test.

Jobs Requiring Advanced Training

Some Hospitality & Tourism jobs require extensive practical experience or advanced education. Others require the completion of a formal training program.

To become a professional athlete, chef, or convention or trade show specialist, candidates must generally gather years of experience. Athletes, for example, complete rigorous training in their sport.

A college education is usually necessary for managers in Hospitality & Tourism. Associate, bachelor's, and master's degrees are available in hotel management. In addition, hundreds of technical institutes, trade schools, and other institutions offer training in hotel and restaurant management. These programs cover hotel administration, general administration, and information technology (computers). They may also deal with marketing and sales, human resources (people) management, accounting, and property management. Professionals that meet certain requirements can become Certified Hotel Administrators (CHAs). Certifications such as these not only improve your skills but also make you a more attractive candidate to potential employers.

Most chefs learn their profession at culinary institutes or through one- or two-year degree programs offered by colleges. Others train through apprenticeships. Many of the best chefs in the United States trained at the Culinary Institute of America (CIA), which offers both associate and bachelor's degree programs. Others earn associate degrees in the culinary arts at community colleges or other culinary schools.

Table 13.2 Training Required for Hospitality & Tourism Jobs

Level of Training	Job Title
Little or No Training	Cleaning and Grounds Workers Fast-Food Cooks Hotel, Motel, and Resort Desk Clerks
Some Training	Animal Trainers Caterers Restaurant Cooks Recreation Workers
Advanced Training	Convention or Trade Show Specialists Interpreters and Translators Museum Technicians and Conservators Chefs Meeting and Convention Planners Professional Athletes

13-4 • Education and Training for Hospitality & Tourism Opportunities

Job and Workplace Skills

When considering job candidates, employers look for both job-specific skills and general workplace skills. Job-specific skills are the skills necessary to do a specific job. They may include balancing a budget or programming a computer. General workplace skills can be used in a variety of jobs.

Hospitality & Tourism Skill Standards

Organizations such as the American Hotel & Lodging Association and the American Culinary Federation establish skill standards for various careers. Meeting these standards often leads to certification. Skill standards are important for students because they help them pick the training programs that fit their career goals.

Food Skill Standards The American Culinary Federation has established skill standards for eight different levels of culinary professionals. To become a master chef, for example, candidates must master a variety of cooking, baking, and pastry preparation skills. They must also study food science, menu development, food service management, sanitation and safety, and other subjects.

Lodging Skill Standards The American Hotel & Lodging Association has established skill standards for many different occupations, from housekeepers to hotel administrators. Comprehensive examinations test workers' knowledge in relevant areas. Skill standards for hotel administrators, for example, include knowledge of human resources management, engineering, property management, and marketing and sales. Skill standards for lower-level jobs, such as housekeeping positions, test knowledge of specific tasks, such as bed making and cleaning.

Travel Agent Skill Standards The American Society of Travel Agents (ASTA) has established more than 100 core competencies in using computerized reservations systems. These standards include displaying and interpreting air availability and fare information, arranging airline reservations, and arranging hotel and car rental reservations.

Professional Skills

Communication Skills Being able to communicate effectively is critical in the Hospitality & Tourism industry, where many employees are in constant contact with the public. For example, front desk clerks at hotels must have strong communication skills because they deal with a wide variety of guests.

Listening Skills Listening is the foundation of learning. Developing listening skills is a vital part of being an effective communicator. Waiters and waitresses, for example, must listen carefully to understand exactly what customers want. Good listening skills also help workers understand other people's ideas and points of view.

Problem-Solving Skills Employers value workers who can spot problems and take action to find solutions. Solving problems requires creativity and self-reliance. A concierge, front desk clerk, or hotel or restaurant manager will often be called upon to solve problems that guests have.

Technology Skills Many people in the Hospitality & Tourism industry—including reservations agents, front desk clerks, and restaurant workers—use computers. Being comfortable using technology will help workers advance their career in this industry.

Decision-Making Skills The ability to gather and analyze information rapidly, and to think clearly under pressure, are important skills in any career. Travel agents and hotel managers are likely to encounter problems that will require them to make quick decisions. Being able to do so calmly and effectively is an important job skill.

Organizing and Planning Skills Planning requires the ability to set goals and to visualize the sequence of steps leading up to these goals. A convention specialist might be called on to plan a convention for 12,000 people. Doing so effectively will require excellent organization and planning skills.

Teamwork Skills Teamwork is key in Hospitality & Tourism. Most workers in this industry are required to work with many different people to get their jobs done. For example, everyone in a restaurant, from short-order cooks to hosts to managers, must work together as a team during busy times.

Social Skills In the Hospitality & Tourism industry, every job involves interacting with people, whether they are coworkers, hotel guests, restaurant patrons, or travelers. Social interaction is the foundation of customer service. Social interaction with coworkers also makes for a more enjoyable work atmosphere. In fact, studies show that between 80 and 85 percent of a person's success in the world of work is due to the person's social skills.

Adaptability Skills Job descriptions, work environments, and work processes are constantly changing along with technology and consumer preferences. People in the Travel industry, for example, must constantly adapt to the new ways that consumers plan vacations and get their travel information. They need to be ready to acquire new skills and be adaptable.

13-4 Essential Question Reflection

So, let us revisit our essential question:

What training & education is needed for a job in Hospitality & Tourism?

Based on what you learned in this section, please answer this question in detail.

Practice 13-4

Skills Practice

Many jobs in the Hospitality & Tourism industry require workers to calculate costs and discounts. A food service manager, for example, may need to calculate the cost of buying kitchen supplies from vendors offering discounts on different quantities. **Practice this skill!**

1. You are a chef in charge of preparing all the sauces used in an Asian fusion restaurant. Your restaurant makes its own fish sauce, a staple ingredient in Vietnamese cuisine. You need to purchase 200 fresh trout from a local fisherman. Normally the trout would cost $700, but you receive a 13% discount for being a frequent customer. How much does your purchase cost?

   A. $91
   B. $174
   C. $609
   D. $700
   E. $791

2. You are a hot air balloon guide. The standard price for a hot air balloon ride is $130. To give newcomers an incentive to try hot air ballooning, you offer 20% off the price of the first two rides. A new customer wants to purchase five rides. How much do you charge the customer?

   A. $52
   B. $208
   C. $572
   D. $598
   E. $650

Skills Practice

Some calculations in the Hospitality & Tourism industry may require using conversions and formulas. A travel agent may need to calculate a price by converting it from a foreign currency, for example. Other calculations require working with mixed units, such as when a cook combines quantities in a recipe. **Practice this skill!**

3. You work as an attendant at an amusement park, selling tickets to enter the park. The entry fee is $11.50, and the person buying the ticket pays with one $20 bill. How much money does the person receive back?

    A. one $5 bill, three $1 bills, and two quarters
    B. nine $1 bills and two quarters
    C. one $5 bill, four $1 bills, and two quarters
    D. one $10 bill, one $1 bill, and two quarters
    E. one $10 bill, three $1 bills, and two quarters

4. You are a recreation director, and you have organized four basketball teams. In the first game, Team A is playing Team B. Their game started at 10:00 a.m. and ended at 12:50 p.m. How long did the first game last?

    A. 1 hour 50 minutes
    B. 2 hours
    C. 2 hours 50 minutes
    D. 3 hours 50 minutes
    E. 4 hours 10 minutes

To access more problems that will help you grow professional skills and are real-world examples in Hospitality & Tourism, go online.

13-5 Working Conditions in the Hospitality & Tourism Industry

When choosing a career path, it is important to know what it is like to work in the industry. Understanding the work environment, hazards, and benefits of a job can help you make informed decisions.

> **13-5 Essential Question**
>
> **As you read this section, keep this question in mind:**
>
> *What are typical work environments in Hospitality & Tourism?*

Physical Environment

People in the Hospitality & Tourism industry work in a variety of settings. Hotel workers may spend their days in pleasant hotel lobbies. Short-order cooks work in hot kitchens. Workers at a ski resort may be in extreme cold all day. Tour guides might lead customers through challenging outdoor settings. Ride operators at an amusement park may spend all day in a small control room.

Work Hours

The work hours of jobs in Hospitality & Tourism vary as widely as the physical environment. In some jobs, people work weekdays from 9 a.m. to 5 p.m. In many others, employees work weekends and evenings.

Lodging

Hotels and motels are usually open year-round. To keep these facilities staffed, many employees work irregular hours. Most housekeeping, maintenance, and activities staff work during the day. At some hotels, housekeeping and maintenance workers work at night, too. Restaurant, room service, front desk, and management workers often work during the day and at night. People from all lodging occupations are needed on weekends.

Restaurants and Food/Beverage Services

Many people in this path work irregular hours. They may start work early in the morning, finish late at night, or work night shifts. Because some restaurants operate 24 hours a day, shift work is common. Shift work divides the day into blocks of time, often eight hours per shift. This allows food-service companies to operate continuously. In addition, many workers do not have weekends or holidays off.

Restaurant managers regularly work 50 to 60 hours a week. They are often the first to arrive at a restaurant in the morning and the last to leave at night. But not everyone in food service works irregular hours. People who serve or prepare food in schools, hospitals, and corporations may not work nights or weekends. Many other people in the restaurant business work part-time or on a flexible schedule.

Some people in the path also work fewer than 12 months a year. Food service workers at resorts are sometimes only needed seasonally. A seasonal worker is a worker who works only during certain months of the year.

Recreation, Amusements, and Attractions

Workers in this path have a variety of work hours and situations. Stadium workers often work evenings and weekends when games are played, as do umpires and sports officials. Workers at most recreation and amusement parks are on a seasonal schedule, as many of these facilities close when the weather gets colder.

Travel and Tourism

Most travel agents work regular business hours. Some work weekends or early evening hours to accommodate clients. Other travel agents work part-time. Meeting and convention planners may spend long evening hours setting up conventions. They may also work weekends and evenings to handle any problems that arise during the convention. Tour directors often work regular hours, although they are often on call after hours. They must be prepared for any emergencies that arise with their group.

Essential Physical Activities

Most jobs in the Hospitality & Tourism industry do not require physical strength or conditioning. However, some of them can be physically demanding. For example, professional athletes must continuously train to excel in their sport. Some food service jobs require lifting supplies and equipment in the kitchen. In addition, food service jobs usually require workers to spend most of their time standing. This can make the jobs tiring. Cleaning jobs, such as dishwashing, may also be strenuous. In the Lodging career path, baggage porters must carry heavy bags, while housekeepers and janitors do taxing cleaning work.

Hazard and Environmental Dangers

Because accidents can happen at any job, safety must be a priority. The federal government protects workers by creating workplace safety standards and laws through the agency Occupational Safety and Health Administration (OSHA). These rules help prevent accidents and ensure that accident victims are helped.

Injuries and Illnesses

People in the Hospitality & Tourism industry face above-average risks of occupational illnesses and injuries. In fact, workers in Lodging face a higher rate of illness or injury than most other workers in this industry. About 5 percent of these workers become sick or injured on the job each year.

In the food industry, burns, cuts, slips, falls, and back problems are relatively common. Nevertheless, restaurants are safer places to work now than they have ever been.

In the Recreation, Amusements, and Attractions path, athletes face a high risk of injury, especially in contact sports, during a game or during practice. Sun exposure may be a risk for amusement park workers, who spend many hours in the sun. Cruise ship workers, tour directors, and other workers who travel abroad need vaccinations to prevent infectious diseases.

Workers in the Travel Services path frequently work at computers and may suffer from repetitive stress injuries. Repetitive stress injuries (RSIs) can develop when the same motions are performed repeatedly. One of the most common RSIs is carpal tunnel syndrome, a swelling of tendons in the wrist. This injury can result from frequently repeated tasks such as typing. Travel agents and other workers who use computers extensively may suffer from this disorder.

13-5 Essential Question Reflection

So, let us revisit our essential question:

What are typical work environments in Hospitality & Tourism?

Based on what you learned in this section, please answer this question in detail.

13-6 Trends in Hospitality & Tourism

The Hospitality & Tourism industry is constantly evolving. People's travel, dining, and lodging needs and wants change over time. Advances in technology affect the way business is conducted. The makeup of the customer base also changes over time.

> **13-6 Essential Question**
>
> As you read this section, keep this question in mind:
>
> *What factors affect trends in Hospitality & Tourism?*

Technology in the Hospitality & Tourism Industry

The Internet has changed the way the Hospitality & Tourism industry operates. More and more people book their travel plans online. Customers can visit hotel or restaurant websites to make reservations. They can also visit third-party sites to find reviews from other customers. More travelers have turned to the Internet to book their own flights and car reservations, too.

These changes have streamlined how the industry serves the customer's needs. Using the Internet, customers can compare different options at once. They can quickly compare the menus and prices of different Italian restaurants in one town, for instance. They can learn which hotels have the best service or the most comfortable beds through online review websites. Smartphone and tablet computer applications allow people to find nearby hotels and restaurants at any time or place and compare their services.

These developments increase competition. They make it more important for workers in this industry to satisfy the customer every time. One bad online review can drive customers away. However, a few good reviews can give business a boost.

Technology in Lodging

Increasingly, hotels are using online training, or instruction transmitted over the Internet or intranet, to train employees. This technology is used to provide information on basic hotel functions, company policies, and how to best serve customers. Hotel chains may use e-learning (electronic learning) to teach employees more sophisticated tasks, such as selling hotel services.

Customer demand for access to technology has also increased for lodging facilities. Hotels may offer free wireless Internet, either in the lobby or within individual rooms. Workers with strong technology skills will be in increasing demand to help maintain onsite wireless access.

Technology in Restaurant and Food/Beverage Services

Most restaurants now use point-of-sale (POS) systems, or computerized ordering machines. Servers keep track of diners' bills by using a computer with a touchscreen button or numeric code for each menu item. This software allows restaurants to easily keep track of sales, orders, and inventory.

The increased use of wireless technology has also streamlined food and beverage services. Wireless headsets allow waitstaff, cooks, and hosts to communicate with one another. This helps to prevent backups. Managers also use wireless technology to track orders and make sure that timely service is provided.

Technology in Recreation, Amusements, and Attractions

All professional sports teams have websites for ticket information, merchandise, and statistics. Many stadiums are equipped with advanced fiber-optic networks. These networks handle data from voice and data links, concession stands, scoreboards, and other sources. The data are used in many ways, including to measure attendance, improve services, and support modern sound systems.

Many stadiums have been equipped with large high-definition (HD) video screens that can be seen anywhere in the stadium. In some areas, HD video displays show different games and other content. Digital menu boards allow operators to provide real-time information about concessions or special merchandise offers.

Technology in Travel and Tourism

Technology has changed the role of transportation attendants and ticket agents. In the past, all airline passengers used ticket agents to check baggage, confirm reservations, and receive tickets. Today, most travelers reserve and print their tickets online. Other travelers use self-service kiosks at airports to print their tickets.

As a result of online bookings, travel agents are no longer needed for most basic travel. Instead, many agents focus on vacation packages. Most people still look to professionals to help plan all inclusive trips.

Sustainability in the Hospitality & Tourism Industry

One growing trend in the Hospitality & Tourism industry is sustainability. Sustainability refers to economic activity that does not harm the environment. Sustainable activities may use renewable energy. Sustainable practices may also reduce waste and use recycled or reusable materials.

Within the Restaurant and Food/Beverage Services path, more businesses are selling food produced in sustainable ways. This includes produce from organic farms. Locally grown foods are also popular. Restaurant food recycling programs are also becoming more prevalent.

Sustainability is also a growing trend in Lodging. Many hotels are being built to be more energy efficient. Hotels also encourage visitors to reuse towels rather than having them washed after each use.

Ecotourism, which strives to have a minimal impact on the environment, has also grown. Ecotourism trips are designed to avoid disturbing the wildlife of an area. Tourists may even volunteer to help preserve the environment. Money raised from ecotourism is often spent to help sustain the local wildlife and help the local population care for the land.

The Economy and the Hospitality & Tourism Industry

When the economy is strong, the Hospitality & Tourism industry is strong. Low unemployment and rising wages allow more people to eat out, travel, and enjoy recreational activities. On the other hand, when the economy is weak, more people stay home, and the industry suffers. These downturns make workers especially vulnerable to layoffs.

However, those least likely to lose their jobs are workers who have a variety of skills, a strong work ethic, and a willingness to be flexible. Working hard to improve your skills, gaining diverse experience, and building strong relationships will help you succeed in good times and bad.

13-6 Essential Question Reflection

So, let us revisit our essential question:

What factors affect trends in Hospitality & Tourism?

Based on what you learned in this section, please answer this question in detail.

Chapter 14

Health Science

Chapter Topics

14-1 Health Science Today

14-2 Health Science Jobs

14-3 Building a Career in Health Science

14-4 Education and Training for Health Science Opportunities

14-5 Working Conditions in in the Health Science Industry

14-6 Trends in Health Science

Essential Questions

By the end of the chapter, you will be able to answer the following questions:

- **14-1** What types of opportunities are available in Health Science?
- **14-2** Which opportunities may be right for you?
- **14-3** How can I match my skills & interests with the right job?
- **14-4** What training & education is needed for a job in Health Science?
- **14-5** What are typical work environments in Health Science?
- **14-6** What factors affect trends in Health Science?

14-1 Health Science Today

The Health Science industry, including both medical science and health care, provides an extensive range of services, such as preventive care, surgery, counseling, and rehabilitation services. Workers in these occupations help clients maintain and improve well-being. Through vaccines, screenings, and medications, Health Science has nearly eradicated out diseases such as polio and measles. It has also helped treat illnesses such as cancer and AIDS. Our lives are enriched by Health Science in other ways, too. Research on nutrition and human development has improved human health. Research on common diseases, such as diabetes, has led to discoveries about healthy lifestyles. The Health Science industry accounts for more than 14.3 million jobs. It is one of the largest industries in the United States. Employment in this industry will increase as the baby boom population ages and develops health problems associated with getting older. In spite of health care reform efforts, national spending on health care is expected to climb. The current spending is over $2.5 trillion.

14-1 Essential Question

As you read this section, keep this question in mind:

What types of opportunities are available in Health Science?

Career Journeys in Health Science

There are five major paths along which your career in Health Science might be shaped. People commonly move into and out of different paths. Each contains a group of careers requiring similar skills as well as similar certifications or education. The Health Science industry is divided into five main career paths:

- Diagnostic Services
- Therapeutic Services
- Support Services
- Health Informatics
- Biotechnology Research and Development

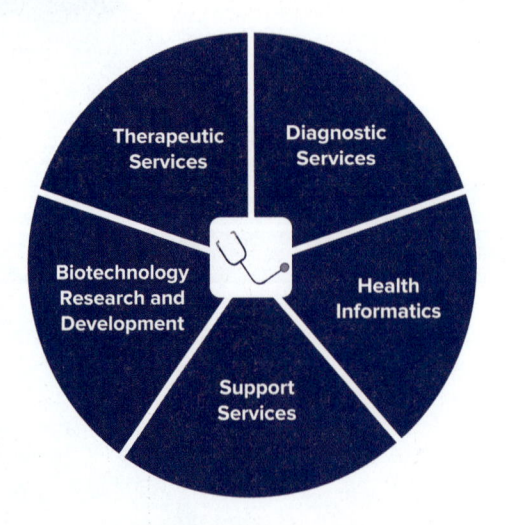

The traditional health care setting is a hospital or a private practice. A private practice is a small medical business owned by one or more doctors. They may work in partnership with a hospital. But health care is being delivered in a wide range of locations. These facilities include clinics, treatment centers, diagnostic centers, nursing homes, and assisted-living facilities. In addition, home health agencies are bringing health care directly to patients' homes. People in this industry have more options than ever before in deciding where they will work.

Diagnostic Services

Jobs in the Diagnostic Services path focus on diagnosing, or identifying, illness and disease. This is done by studying a patient's symptoms. Many workers in this path are technicians or technologists. They use X-rays, magnetic resonance imaging (MRIs), ultrasound, and other means to diagnose a patient. Others work as laboratory technicians.

Lab technicians draw blood and show patients how to collect other samples themselves. In a medical lab, the technicians analyze tissue and bodily fluids. They may check blood sugar, cholesterol, and hormone levels. In medical research facilities, laboratory technicians help scientists investigate diseases.

Careers in Diagnostic Services require excellent observation skills for detecting and diagnosing symptoms. Workers must have outstanding listening skills so they can interpret patients' descriptions of their symptoms. They must have compassion so they can calm and comfort patients.

Nearly all workers in this path use high-tech equipment. They need both technical training and on-the-job training. Math and science skills are critical for success in most of these jobs. The ability to read and interpret printouts, charts, and gauges is important. Workers must be able to produce reports that give the results of the procedures they perform.

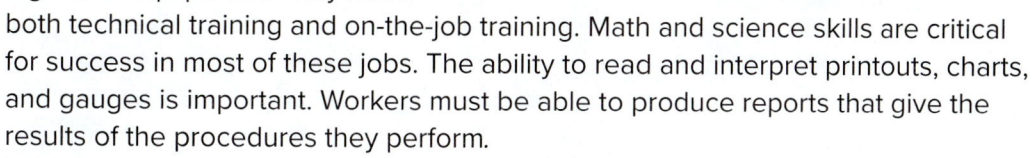

Therapeutic Services

Jobs in this career path focus on providing treatment and therapy. Workers treat both physical and emotional problems. Success in this path requires a desire to help people heal. It also requires patience and compassion.

Many workers in this path are doctors and nurses. However, there are many other career options. These include jobs as physical therapists, home health aides, and emergency medical technicians (EMTs). Dietitians, dental hygienists, athletic trainers, and acupuncturists are also a part of this field.

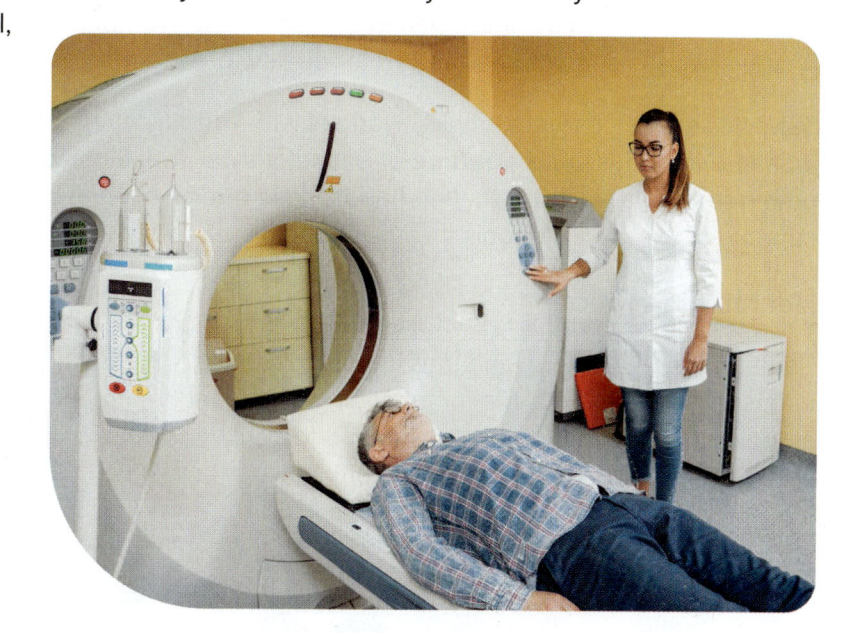

Almost all workers in this path need postsecondary education. The exact level of education varies according to the worker's responsibilities. Home health aides and dental hygienists need less formal education than nurses. Nurses must earn at least an associate degree in nursing or a diploma from an accredited nursing school. Many nurses earn bachelor's and master's degrees so they can specialize within the path. Physicians and dentists must complete intensive postgraduate education and on-the-job training. They must also pass an exam to acquire a license to practice

Support Services

Workers in this career path create a positive, helpful environment for patients and health care workers. Some workers in this path work closely with patients. Patient representatives help patients get the health care services they need. Social workers help people cope with mental health and substance abuse problems.

Others work in a variety of areas. For example, medical equipment technicians repair and maintain medical equipment. Occupational safety and health specialists work to prevent and minimize health hazards in the workplace. Environmental health specialists monitor air and water quality to ensure safety.

Support services careers employ workers with various levels of education. Some jobs require an associate degree or bachelor's degree. Most workers in this career path need to be skilled with their hands, have good observation skills, and be capable of using all the tools they need to do their jobs.

Health Informatics

Some of the fastest-growing jobs in this industry are in Health Informatics. Workers in this path are responsible for managing important health information. Some pass along health information to patients and the public. Others handle behind-the-scenes duties, from accounting to staffing.

412   Chapter 14 • Health Science

Medical coders, medical billers, and medical claims processors make sure that health care providers are paid for their services. Educators share information that helps people manage or prevent health problems. Many workers focus on community-wide health and safety issues such as sexually transmitted diseases, smoking, and weight loss.

The level of education needed for careers in this path varies greatly depending on the job. Admitting clerks and patient service representatives must often have some college or technical training.

Those in public health education typically have advanced degrees. A career in Health Informatics requires an exceptional memory, considerable organizational skills, and strong communications skills. Those who spend time working with the public and with patients should have good people skills. Workers who manage records and information should be detail-oriented.

Biotechnology Research and Development

Jobs in this path focus on the research and development of biotechnology, pharmaceuticals, and medical devices. Biotechnology is the application of science to create new medical advances, including the development of new drugs, vaccines, tests, and tissue-replacement procedures.

Biotechnology researchers work with the genetic materials of plants and animals. They may try to create new technologies and new treatments for disease. Geneticists, for example, study DNA and develop new techniques such as gene therapy. Pharmaceutical scientists focus on developing new medicines to treat diseases.

Workers in this path must have advanced scientific training, especially in biology and chemistry. They must also have good computer skills and be able to adapt to new technologies. Jobs in this path require attention to detail, excellent math skills, and analytical abilities.

Health Science Future Outlook

Overall employment in healthcare occupations is projected to grow 13 percent from 2021 to 2031, much faster than the average for all occupations; this increase is expected to result in about 2 million new jobs over the decade. In addition to new jobs from growth, opportunities arise from the need to replace workers who leave their occupations permanently. About 1.9 million openings each year, on average, are projected to come from growth and replacement needs.

The median annual wage for healthcare practitioners and technical occupations (e.g., registered nurses, physicians, surgeons, and dental hygienists) was $75,040 in May 2021, which was higher than the median annual wage for all occupations of $45,760; healthcare support occupations (e.g., home health and personal care aides, occupational therapy assistants, and medical transcriptionists) had a median annual wage of $29,880 in May 2021, which was lower than the median annual wage for all occupations.

Table 14.1: Forecast for Occupations in Health Science over the Next 10 Years

Occupation	Expected Growth Rate
Biomedical Engineers	5% – 10%
Home Health Aides	10% – 15%
Respiratory Therapists	10% – 15%
Cardiovascular Techs	5% – 10%
Radiologists	5% – 10%
Family Medicine Physicians	1% – 5%
Registered Nurses	5% – 10%
Athletic Trainers	10% – 15%
Social Workers	10 – 15%
Medical Transcriptionists	0% – 5%
Medical/Health Services Managers	10% – 15%

Source: *U.S. Department of Labor*

14-1 Essential Question Reflection

So, let us revisit our essential question:

What types of opportunities are available in Health Science?

Based on what you learned in this section, please answer this question in detail.

Practice 14-1

Skills Practice

When reading a workplace graphic such as a patient's medical record, Health Science workers must know what information to look for. The key information may be in one or more documents. Workers must be able to sift through irrelevant or distracting information to find what is needed. **Practice this skill!**

Prescription Form:

Doctor John Smith, M.D.
Family Medicine
23 Street, Township City
(tel): 555-222-3343

Patient Name: Emile Jones
Date: 2/12/24

Tests requested: Lipid profile (HDL, LDL, cholesterol total, cholesterol ratio, triglycerides)
Glucose
PSA
CBC (WBC, RBC, urinalyses)

Signature: John Smith M.D.

Lab Facility Information Form:

Medical Lab
456 Main Street, Township City
(tel): 555-333-4566

Hours: 7:30 AM - 4:00 PM, Monday - Friday
Some Insurance Accepted

1. Your job as a nurse is to make sure your patients understand the next steps they must take before they leave the doctor's office. Your patient has two forms in his hand: (1) a prescription form with the blood tests he is required to have performed and (2) is a form with information regarding the blood test laboratory. What's the name of the facility where the patient must go for his blood tests?

   A. Medical Lab
   B. Dr. John Smith
   C. Township City
   D. 456 Main Street
   E. Family Medicine

2. The doctor requests a series of tests based on the patient's exam. What are two of the lipid tests the doctor has requested?

   A. HDL, RBC
   B. triglycerides, LDL
   C. HDL, glucose
   D. urinalyses, WBC
   E. LDL, PSA

To access more problems that will help you grow professional skills and are real-world examples in Health Science, go online.

14-2 Health Science Jobs

The Health Science industry offers an extensive variety of jobs. Many health care professionals work hands-on diagnosing, treating, counseling, and comforting patients. Some of them work in medical research laboratories, investigating diseases and developing new medicines. Others work behind the scenes, managing hospitals, processing health claims, and updating records. Here are some of the fastest-growing jobs in the Health Science industry and the skills they require.

14-2 Essential Question

As you read this section, keep this question in mind:

Which opportunities may be right for you?

Occupation with the Most People Employed:

Registered Nurses

- Record patient medical information and vital signs
- Administer medications to patients, and monitor patients for reactions or side effects
- Maintain accurate, detailed reports and records

Fast Facts:

Employment: 3.13 million in 2021, expected to grow to 3.33 million in 2031

Openings: 203,200

Median Annual Wage: $77,600

Education Needed: Bachelor's degree and certification

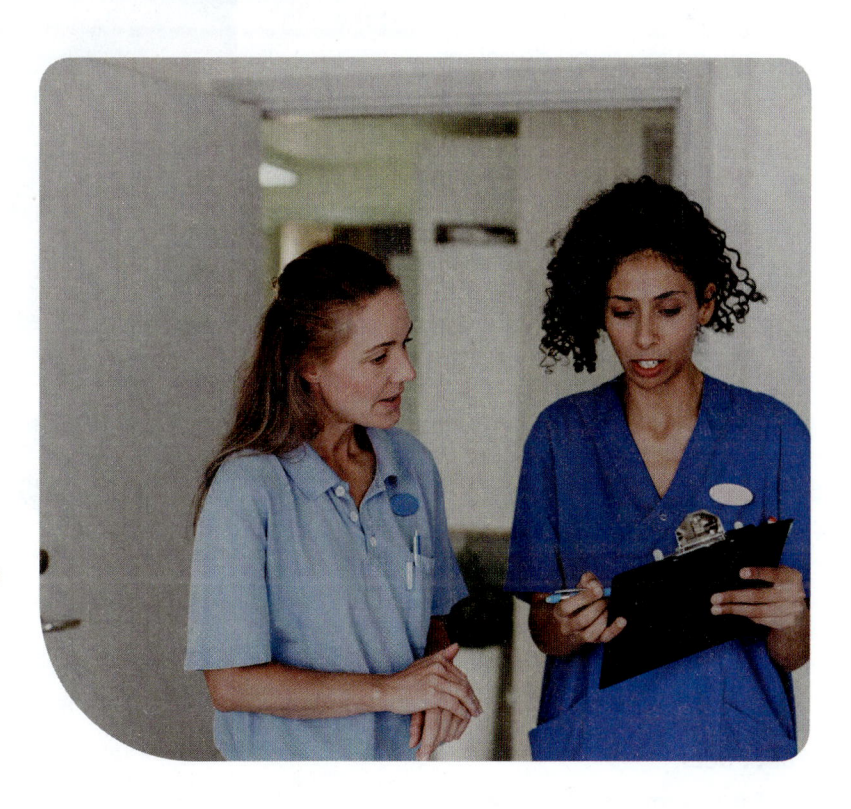

Fastest-Growing Occupation:

Nurse Practitioners

- Maintain complete and detailed records of patients' health care plans and prognoses
- Develop treatment plans, based on scientific rationale, standards of care, and professional practice guidelines
- Provide patients with information needed to promote health, reduce risk factors, or prevent disease or disability

Fast Facts:
Employment Change: 45.7%
Openings: 112,700
Median Annual Wage: $120,680
Education Needed: Master's degree and certification

Health Care Social Workers

- Advocate for clients or patients to resolve crises
- Educate clients about end-of-life symptoms and options to assist them in making informed decisions
- Collaborate with other professionals to evaluate patients medical or physical conditions and to assess client needs

Fast Facts:
Openings: 173,860
Median Annual Wage: $62,310
Education Needed: Bachelor's degree

Great Job! - High School Diploma Needed:

Opticians

- Assist clients or patients with finding the right fit of eyeglasses or contact lenses
- Follow prescriptions from ophthalmologists and optometrists
- Maintain sales records, organize prescriptions, maintain inventory

Fast Facts:
Employment Change: 4%
Openings: 74,800
Median Annual Wage: $37,570
Education Needed: High school diploma and on-the-job training

Highest-Wage Occupation:

Physicians and Surgeons

- Perform physical exams according to individual patient's medical history
- Document patient information on charts to update findings and treatments
- Design and implement treatment plans
- Review test results to identify trends or abnormalities

Fast Facts:
Employment Change: 3%
Openings: 761,700
Median Annual Wage: $208,000
Education Needed: Medical Doctor (MD) degree or Doctor of Osteopathic Medicine (DO) degree

Great Job! - Associate Degree Needed:

Radiation Therapists

- Protect all patients and clients from improper exposure to radiation
- Operate and calibrate machines necessary to administer radiation treatment
- Maintain detailed records of treatment, and explain treatment plans to patients

Fast Facts:
Employment Change: 6%
Openings: 16,400
Median Annual Wage: $82,790
Education Needed: Associate degree and certification

14-2 Essential Question Review

So, let us revisit our essential question:

Which opportunities may be right for you?

Based on what you learned in this section, please answer this question in detail.

Case Study: Home Health Workers

Also called: Certified Home Health Aide (CHHA), Certified Nurses Aide (CNA), Home Care Aide, Home Health Aide (HHA)

What do they do?

- Monitor and address the health status and concerns of individuals with disabilities or illnesses
- Perform important medical tasks under the direction of licensed nursing staff
- Aid with health care tasks and activities of daily living

What would you do?

- Maintain records of patients' condition, care, problems, and progress
- Provide patients with help moving in and out of beds, baths, and wheelchairs
- Provide patients with daily living activities such as grooming and dressing

What do you need to know?

Business
Customer service

Arts and Humanities
English language

Health
Medicine

What skills do you need?

Communication
Listen to others, do not interrupt, and ask good questions
Read work-related information

Social Skills
Empathy and ability to change what is done based off of other people's actions
Understand people's reactions

Problem Solving
Notice a problem, and create an appropriate solution
Think about the pros and cons of different options, and pick the best one

What abilities must you be good at?

Verbal
　Listen and understand what people say
　Read and understand what is written

Ideas and Logic
　Notice when problems happen
　Use rules to solve them

Visual Understanding
　See hidden patterns
　Quickly compare groups of letters, numbers, pictures, or other symbols

Attention
　Multi-task

Who does well in this occupation?

People interested in this work like tasks that include helping people, teaching, and talking with others.

They do well at jobs that need:
　Integrity
　Dependability
　Self-Control
　Concern for Others
　Attention to Detail
　Cooperation

What educational level is needed?

- High school diploma, or equivalent

Practice 14-2

Skills Practice

Health Science workers must sometimes analyze graphics to identify trends. They might search for data that have increased or decreased over time. A physician's assistant might study graphics to find trends in patients' lab results. A clinical data manager might look for trends in clinical trial data. Being able to identify common trends from graphics can help with a variety of jobs in this industry. **Practice this skill!**

Estimated Number of Serious Sports Injuries Among Persons 25-54 Years of Age, Associated with 16 Popular Sports Categories, 2010 and 2020

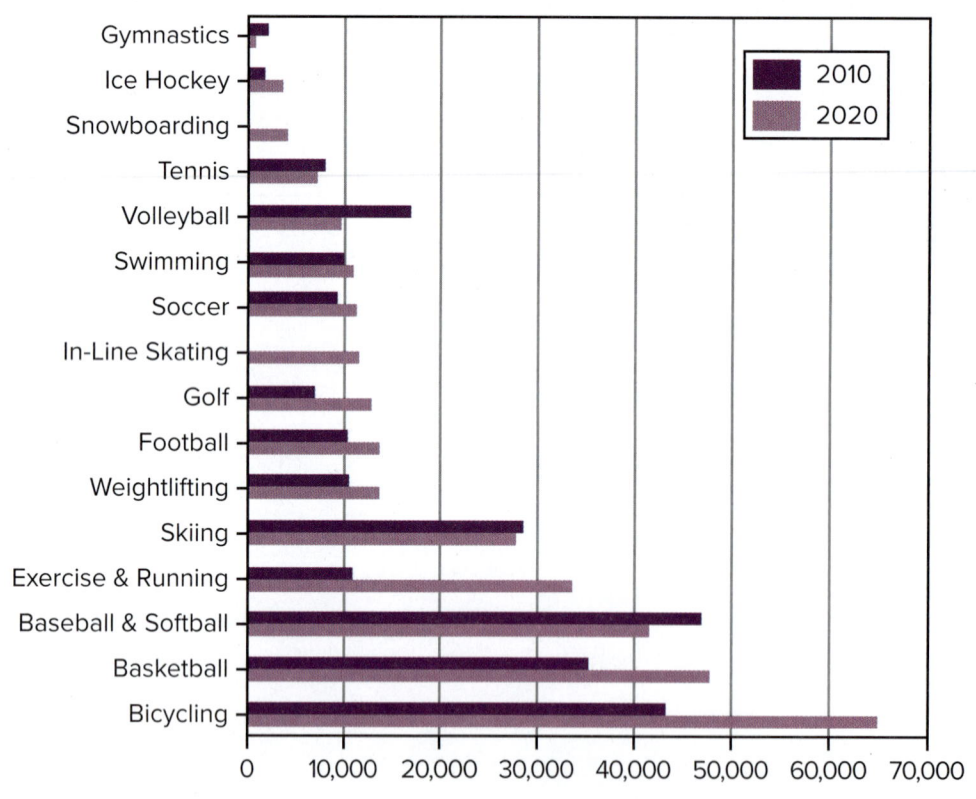

1. As a sports clinical specialist in an injury rehabilitation center, you treat sports injuries in people of all ages. Which of the following lists includes only sports that showed an increase in serious sports injuries from 2010 to 2020?

    A. tennis, skiing, golf
    B. soccer, running, basketball
    C. volleyball, football, baseball
    D. gymnastics, skiing, football
    E. tennis, baseball, softball

2. Which of the following lists includes sports that had at least 20,000 serious injuries in 2020?

    A. gymnastics, ice hockey, skiing
    B. tennis, weightlifting, golf
    C. running, basketball, bicycling
    D. tennis, soccer, softball
    E. in-line skating, golf, basketball

Percent of Obese Adults in 2010

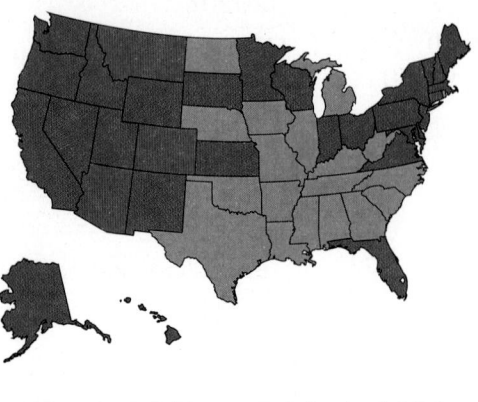

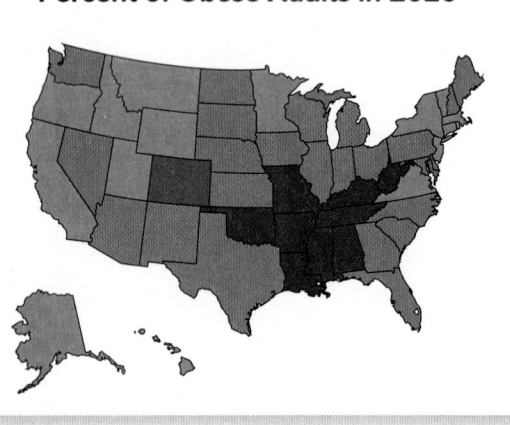

Percent of Obese Adults in 2020

- ☐ No Data
- < 10%
- 10% – 14%
- 15% – 19%
- 20% – 24%
- 25% – 29%
- ≥ 30%

3. You are a nutritionist working at a weight clinic for severely obese patients. According to the maps for 2010 and 2020, what national trend do you see?

   A. Obesity rates have increased in most U.S. states.

   B. Obesity rates have increased in every U.S. state.

   C. Obesity rates have remained about the same.

   D. Obesity rates have decreased in most U.S. states.

   E. Obesity rates have decreased in every U.S. state.

4. Which statement best describes the obesity rates in the United States in 2020?

   A. Obesity rates are 10% or higher in every state but one.

   B. Obesity rates are 15% or higher in every state but one.

   C. Obesity rates are 20% or higher in every state but one.

   D. Obesity rates are 25% or higher in every state but one.

   E. Obesity rates are 30% or higher in every state but one.

To access more problems that will help you grow professional skills and are real-world examples in Health Science, go online.

14-3 Building a Career in Health Science

In many occupations in Health Science, you may take several steps before reaching your goal. With experience, you may move ahead.

For example, many nurses start out as nursing assistants. As an assistant, you get a first-hand look at nursing as a career. You learn how to interact with patients and how to do tasks such as moving patients and taking blood pressure. Nurses often get their training at a community college. After completing a two-year program, you would take a test that qualifies you to be a registered nurse. Finally, if you continued your education, you might decide to do advanced study to become a nurse practitioner. Nurse practitioners often have specialties such as public health or pediatrics.

14-3 Essential Question

As you read this section, keep this question in mind:

How can I match my skills & interests with the right job?

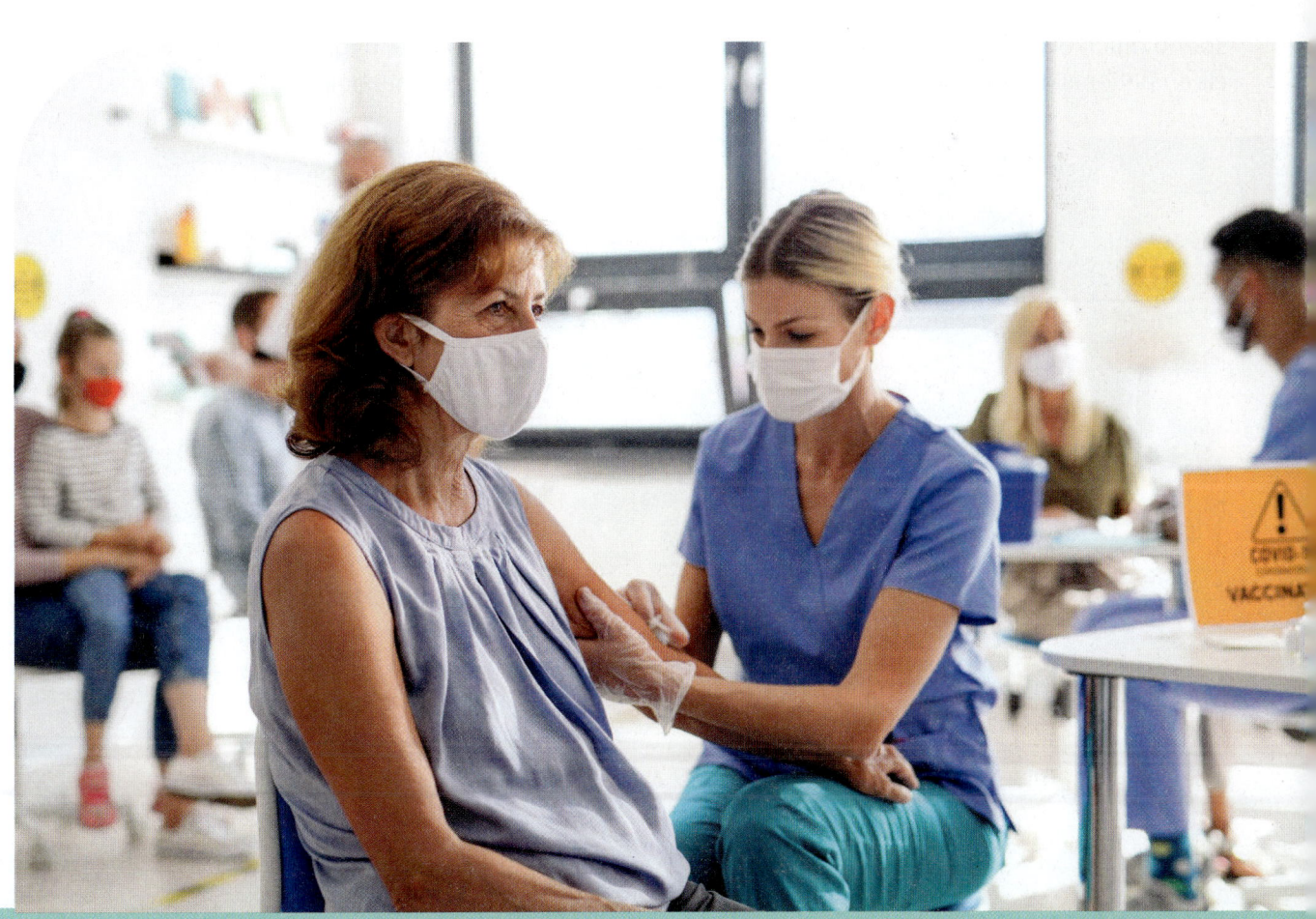

Are You More Interested in Working With Data, People, or Things?

When planning your career path, consider what balance of data, people, and things you want in a career. Many online resources can help you determine which opportunities match your skills and interests.

Careers That Involve Working With Data

Examples of working with data include organizing medical records, analyzing X-rays, and reporting the results of lab experiments.

Almost all jobs in Health Science involves working with data. Medical transcriptionists maintain patients' medical records and transcribe, or write down, information from doctors' recorded notes. Health care managers work with spreadsheets to analyze costs and profits. Doctors, nurses, and therapists work with patient histories and medical information, read X-rays and charts, and keep records of their work.

Careers That Involve Working With People

All jobs in Health Science involve working with people—coworkers, managers, administrators, technicians, patients, and patients' families. Because everyone needs health care at some time, Health Science workers interact with people from every possible cultural, economic, and language background.

You need strong people skills to succeed in a Health Science career. Pediatricians spend much of their days diagnosing and treating sick children. Dental hygienists clean patients' teeth, take X-rays, and assist dentists. Nursing assistants help patients bathe, eat, and get dressed. Home health care workers provide emotional support to homebound patients. Registered nurses examine patients, arrange treatment plans, and provide follow-up evaluations. Public health workers speak at conventions, meetings, and clinics to educate the public about timely health care issues. Physical therapists devise treatment plans for injured patients working on recovery. In short, nearly everyone employed in Health Science works with people.

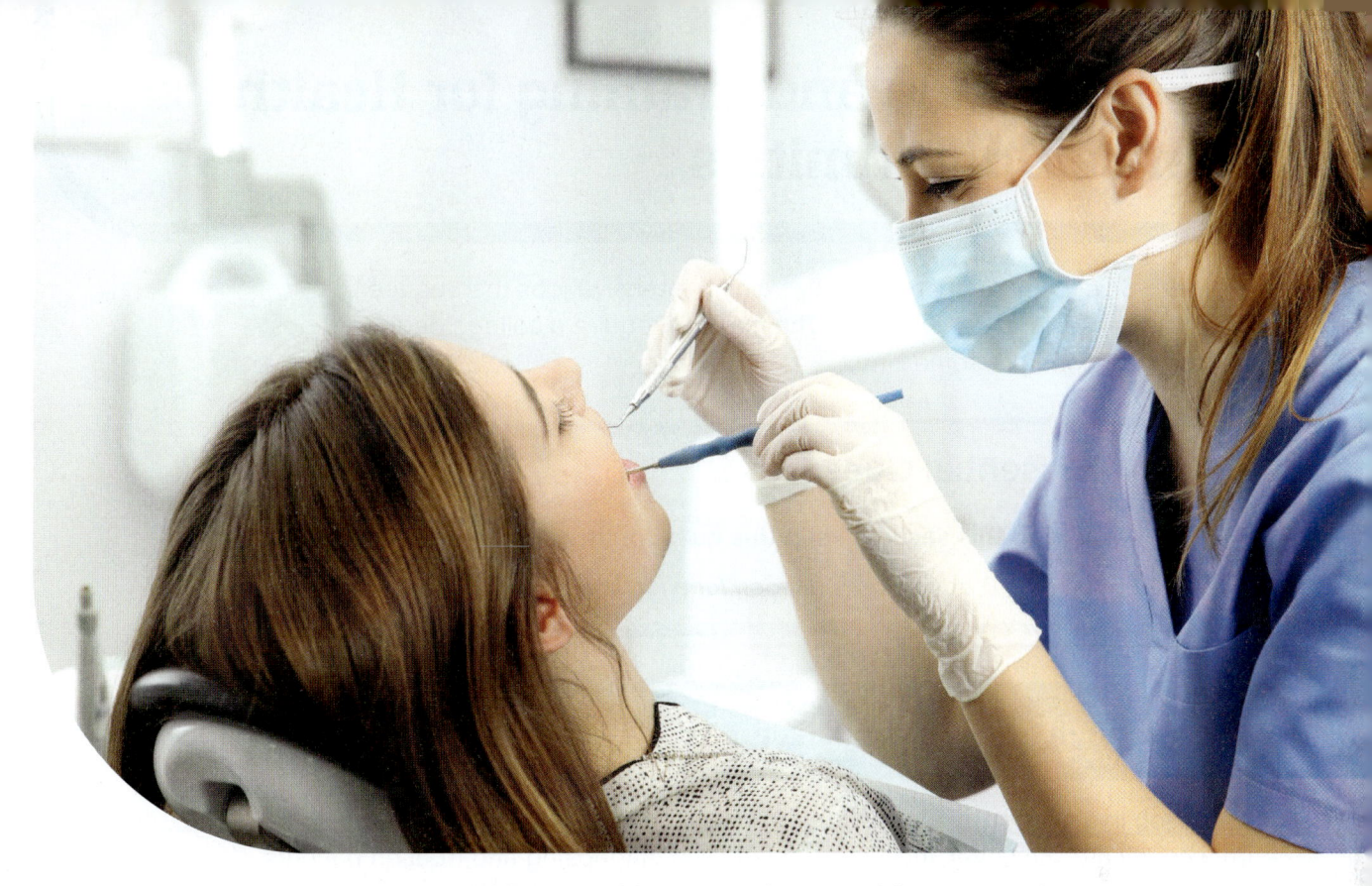

Careers That Involve Working With Things

In Health Science, working with things might involve dispensing medicine, operating and repairing medical equipment, and using precision tools, such as scalpels and drills.

Many careers in Health Science involve extensive work with things. Laboratory technicians use centrifuges (devices used to separate fluids, gas, or liquid), microscopes, and other equipment. Patient care assistants handle thermometers, specimen collection tools, and blood pressure cuffs.

14-3 Essential Question Reflection

So, let us revisit our essential question:

How can I match my skills & interests with the right job?

Based on what you learned in this section, please answer this question in detail.

14-4 Education and Training for Health Science Opportunities

The Health Science industry has mostly training-intensive jobs that require additional licenses and certifications. The majority require a college degree or post-secondary education of some kind.

14-4 Essential Question

As you read this section, keep this question in mind:

What training & education is needed for a job in Health Science?

Training and Education for Health Science

To get a job in a support position, you may need to complete a training program or earn a certificate. However, most jobs that involve diagnosing and treating patients require a college degree.

Jobs Requiring Specific Training or Certification

Almost all jobs in Health Science deal with complex problems. Virtually all of them require a high school diploma as well as additional training after high school. Training consists of education in a specific job skill or professional area that leads to a license or certification.

Careers such as hospital receptionist, orderly, patient care, housekeeper, and ambulance drivers require training after high school. Training for jobs such as nursing assistant, home health aide, and physical therapy assistant is usually provided by the employer when you are hired.

Where Health Science workers are in shorter supply, people with little previous experience or training may be able to work as aides. Nursing homes, psychiatric care facilities, and home health care services often provide on-the-job training. Some also offer classroom instruction.

Jobs Requiring an Associate Degree

Not all jobs in Health Science require advanced degrees. Technologists and technicians assistants in several Health Science fields may need only an associate degree. An associate degree is a degree awarded after two years of successful study.

Medical Sonographers and Cardiovascular Technologists and Technicians, for example, generally requires only an associate degree. Many colleges and universities over associate's programs in sonography and cardiovascular technology. Some colleges and hospitals even offer one-year certificate programs. Sonography and cardiovascular education programs include courses such as anatomy, medical terminology, and applied sciences.

Jobs Requiring a Bachelor's, Master's, or Doctoral Degree

Many jobs in Health Science require an advanced education. If you want to become a dietician, an exercise physiologist, or a recreational therapist, you will need at least a bachelor's degree in your field. Physicians, pharmacists, and Genetic Counselors obtain a master's and often a doctoral degree. These advanced degrees lead to far more job opportunities and higher pay.

Audiologists, who specialize in hearing-related problems, must obtain a state license. To be a licensed audiologist, you need a bachelor's degree and an audiology (AuD) degree. AuD programs typically take four years.

Table 14.2: Training Required for Health Science Jobs

Level of Training or Education	Job Title
Specific Training or Certification	Dietetic Technicians Dental Laboratory Technicians Home Health Aides Medical Equipment Preparers Nursing Assistant/Aides/Orderlies and Attendants Medical Receptionists Opticians Pharmacy Aides
Associate Degree	Dental Assistants Dental Hygienists Emergency Medical Technician Medical Assistants Medical Equipment Repairers Medical Laboratory Technicians Medical Transcriptionists Medical Sonographers Nurses, all areas Paramedics Pharmacy Technicians
Bachelor's, Master's, or Doctoral Degree	Athletic Trainers Biologists Biomedical Engineers Clinical Data Managers Dietitians and Nutritionists Dentists Medical and Public Health Social Workers Mental Health and Substance Abuse Social Workers Nurse Practitioners Occupational Therapists Orthotists Physicians, all areas Pharmacists Radiologists

Source: *U.S. Department of Labor*

Job and Workplace Skills

When considering job candidates, employers look for people who have both job-specific skills and general workplace skills. Job-specific skills are the skills necessary to do a particular job. For example, operating a medical device or understanding the human body. General workplace skills are the skills that workers use in most jobs, such as communication skills.

Health Science Skill Standards

The National Consortium for Health Science Education has a list of skill standards for the Health Science industry. Here are some skills that relate to specific career paths:

- **Therapeutic Service** Workers in this path should have strong communication skills and be able to work well with a team. They must be able to create and implement a treatment plan. They should be able to monitor patients and evaluate their progress.

- **Diagnostic Services** Workers in this path should have strong communication skills. They should be able to assess the health of patients. They should be able to conduct, evaluate, and report on procedures that are requested.

- **Health Informatics** Health Informatics workers should be able to manage the flow of communication. They should be able to analyze and interpret health information and records. They must develop processes for sharing information and understand what information is private.

- **Support Services** These workers should be able to implement department goals and policies and coordinate activities with other departments. They should be able to monitor the quality of care and make sure all regulations are being met. Workers must help keep a clean workplace and ensure that resources are being used effectively.
- **Biotechnology Research and Development** Workers in this path should understand the importance of research in improving people's quality of life. They should be highly skilled in math, genetics, chemistry, and biology. Workers should understand specific biotechnology processes and lab procedures. They should know how new products are designed. Finally, they should understand the ethics involved in their work.

Other skills relate generally to the Health Science industry. Some of these skills include the following:

Academic Foundations Health Science workers need well-developed academic skills. These include knowledge of the human body and its functions and understanding of diseases and disorders. They also include basic math skills related to health care procedures.

System Knowledge Health Science workers need to know their role within the health system. This means understanding their contribution to their department and the entire workplace. They must understand how various Health Science professionals work together to provide care. They should also have a basic understanding of how health care is delivered and how it is paid for.

Legal Responsibilities Health Science workers must understand the legal responsibilities and limitations of their job. They must be aware of the possible consequences of their actions. They must follow workplace and legal regulations, policies, and laws. This includes reporting accidents, keeping patient records private, and following workplace safety standards and laws.

Ethics Ethics are the values that help people know right from wrong. All Health Science workers must understand accepted ethical practices in the industry. They must respect the ethical standards of different cultures and ethnicities. Additionally, they need to understand and accept differences between their own personal ethics and the ethics of their organization.

Safety Practices Health Science workers must understand potential health and safety hazards. Infection-control and work-safety procedures are in place to protect them, other workers, and patients from injury and illness. They need to follow all health and safety recommendations and use safe work practices.

Health Maintenance Practices Health Science workers must know the fundamentals of wellness and disease prevention so they can encourage healthy living. They need to learn about behaviors that promote good health, including routine health screenings, regular checkups, and alternative medicine.

Technical Skills Health Science workers must have the necessary technical skills to perform their workday duties. This means they must learn how to measure and record vital signs, recognize "normal" ranges, and perform cardiopulmonary resuscitation (CPR).

Information Technology Applications Health Science workers must understand the information technology used in their careers. They should be able to identify records and files, access and distribute data, and recognize technology applications in Health Science settings.

> ### 14-4 Essential Question Reflection
>
> **So, let us revisit our essential question:**
>
> *What training & education is needed for a job in Health Science?*
>
> Based on what you learned in this section, please answer this question in detail.

Practice 14-4

Skills Practice

Many jobs in the Health Science industry require workers to calculate costs and discounts. A certified dietary manager, for example, may need to calculate the cost of buying foods including discounts for bulk items for a hospital cafeteria. These skills are important for budgeting and collecting payments. **Practice this skill!**

1. You are an office assistant for a periodontist. The office is running out of its brochure on proper gum care. Your local printer charges $0.25 for 1 brochure and offers a 15% discount if you place an order over 1,000. How much will 1,500 brochures cost?

    A. $300.25
    B. $318.75
    C. $350.00
    D. $356.25
    E. $375.00

2. As an ophthalmic medical technologist, you just received a notice from the laboratory that makes contact lenses that they need to increase their prices by 20%. You normally charge $255 for a pair of contact lenses. If you raise your prices by the same percentage as the lab's increase, how much will your customers be paying for contact lenses?

    A. $270
    B. $272
    C. $274
    D. $298
    E. $306

Skills Practice

For some calculations in the Health Science, a formula may need to be manipulated to solve a problem. For example, a family practitioner or nurse practitioner may need to use a formula to calculate the correct dosage of a medication based on the patient's weight. Health Science workers should be able to work with formulas to find the information required. **Practice this skill!**

3. You are a laboratory assistant preparing a solution of a liquid chemical. You need to measure out 50 grams of a chemical whose density is 2 grams. What is the volume of the chemical needed for your solution?

   Formula for mass:
   $mass = density \times volume$

   A. 10 milliliters
   B. 25 milliliters
   C. 50 milliliters
   D. 100 milliliters
   E. 150 milliliters

4. As a maintenance engineer at a hospital that is exploring green technology, you are asked to provide information about the energy usage of some of the devices in the hospital. One device uses 120 volts of electricity and draws 5 amps of current during its use. It runs on an AC current that cycles at 60 hertz (Hz). How much power does the device use?

   Formula for finding watts:
   $watts = (volts)(amps)$

   A. 0.04 watts
   B. 10 watts
   C. 24 watts
   D. 600 watts
   E. 36,000 watts

To access more problems that will help you grow professional skills and are real-world examples in Health Science, go online.

14-5 Working Conditions in the Health Science Industry

When choosing a career in the Health Science industry, it is important to know what it is like to work in the industry. Understanding the work environment, hazards, may benefits of a job can help you make informed decisions.

> **? 14-5 Essential Question**
>
> As you read this section, keep this question in mind:
>
> *What are typical work environments in Health Science?*

Physical Environment

People in Health Science work in a variety of settings. Surgeons, physicians, and nurses may work in busy hospitals or private practices. Medical and dental technicians spend their days in clean, sterile laboratories. Paramedics and emergency medical technicians spend their days in ambulances or fire trucks, driving to medical emergencies. They must treat patients in all types of weather, indoors or outdoors. Health Science workers may also be at greater risk and exposure to contagious diseases.

In most cases, however, workers in this industry work in clean, well-lit, and well-supplied environments.

Work Hours

The work hours of Health Science jobs also vary greatly. Some health workers, such as dentists and doctors, often run their own practices and can set their own hours. However, they may need to be on call to treat emergencies. For example, surgeons are often asked to be on call to treat patients in hospital emergency rooms. If someone needs surgery while the surgeon is on call, the surgeon must leave for the hospital immediately.

Many people in the Health Science industry work long hours. Emergency medical technicians often work 50 hours a week. Doctors may work even more hours.

Since hospitals and medical care facilities must always be available to the public 24 hours a day, many workers in Health Science work in shifts. Shift work is common for medical personnel such as doctors, nurses, and paramedics. Shift work divides the day into blocks of time, generally eight-hour blocks. But it is not uncommon for health professionals to work 12-hour or even 24-hour shifts.

Many Health Science employees may need to work overtime. Overtime is work beyond 40 hours a week. Because hospitals are open around the clock, most doctors, nurses, specialists, and staff such as admitting clerks work some nights, weekends, and holidays. Most health care managers often work overtime. They may spend time traveling.

Essential Physical Activities

Many occupations in the Health Science industry require hands-on activities. Some are unique to this industry. For example, doctors, nurses, and some technicians must draw blood from patients. They must handle specimens safely and carefully. These duties require the workers to be skilled with their hands.

Many workers in Health Science spend all day on their feet. Nurses spend most of their shifts standing and walking. They perform many physical activities such as moving patients, moving medical equipment, and changing bedding.

Other health care workers may move patients or heavy equipment. These include home health aides, paramedics, ambulance drivers, physician assistants, doctors, and radiologic technologists. These workers must be physically fit and trained in the proper procedures to avoid injuring patients.

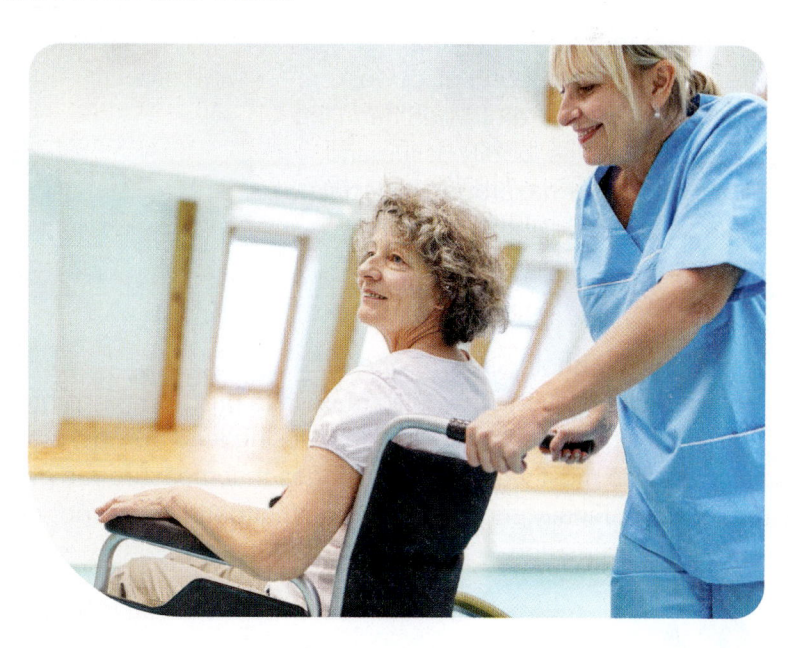

Ambulance drivers, EMTs, and home health care workers must drive carefully to protect themselves and patients from accidents and injuries. Surgeons must have very steady hands and excellent vision, and they must be able to work with extreme care and precision for many hours. Dentists must be able to work carefully within the confines of a person's mouth.

Hazards and Environmental Dangers

Because accidents can happen at any job, safety must always be a priority. The federal government protects workers by creating workplace safety standards and laws. These rules help prevent accidents and ensure that accident victims are helped.

Injuries and Illnesses

Most on-the-job impairments are either occupational injuries or occupational illnesses. An occupational injury is any injury that occurs at work. Injuries include cuts, fractures, and sprains. An occupational illness is caused by on-the-job exposure to harmful substances. These illnesses include rashes and skin diseases, respiratory problems, and poisoning.

Workers in Health Science face uncommon dangers. They must take special precautions to avoid catching or spreading infectious diseases. Workers in this industry often encounter blood and other bodily fluids. They are also in contact with patients who may have contagious diseases.

Workers may be exposed to illnesses as minor as the common cold or as dangerous as AIDS, hepatitis, and tuberculosis. Workers wear latex gloves, masks, and gowns to help protect themselves and patients from disease.

To ensure that they do not prick themselves or someone else, workers must always be careful when handling needles. Needles, bodily tissue and fluids, and other hazardous materials must always be disposed of properly disposed of to prevent spreading diseases.

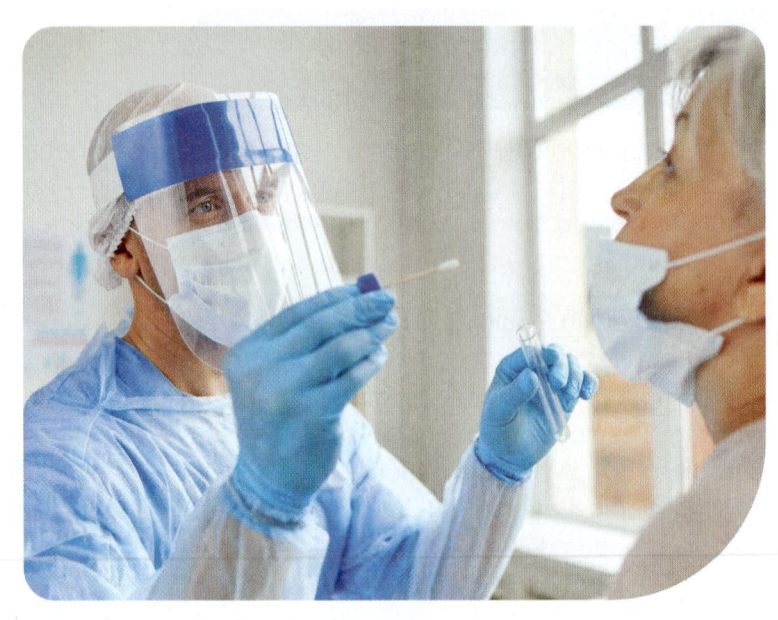

Radiologic technologists are often exposed to radiation. They also must take precautions to protect themselves. Radiation exposure can be limited by using lead aprons, gloves, and shields. These workers also must wear special badges that measure radiation levels while they are at work. Finally, they must ensure that patients are not exposed to excessive amounts of radiation.

14-5 Essential Question Reflection

So, let us revisit our essential question:

What are typical work environments in Health Science?

Based on what you learned in this section, please answer this question in detail.

14-6 Trends in Health Science

The Health Science industry is constantly evolving. Advances in technology affect how health care can be provided to people. The changing population and its needs also create new trends in the industry.

> **14-6 Essential Question**
>
> As you read this section, keep this question in mind:
>
> *What factors affect trends in Health Science?*

Technology in the Health Science Industry

Technology has changed the Health Science industry in many ways. Such changes have led to new and better ways to diagnose, treat, and prevent illness. Doctors now use technology to communicate with paramedics to assess patients' conditions before the ambulance arrives at the hospital. Tests that were once done in labs can now be run in an ambulance or even at home.

Certain changes have also made Health Science more environmentally friendly. For example, electronic health records, accessible through computers and hand-held devices, have reduced the amount of paper used. The increase in health care done through the Internet has reduced the need to drive to doctors' offices. Hospitals have begun using "green information technology" such as cloud computing, or virtual servers, to reduce the amount of computer hardware used.

Smartphones

Most doctors now routinely use smartphones and tablet computers in their work. These devices allow doctors to access and convey information from anywhere. They may look up information about drugs and procedures, play instructional videos for patients, or write electronic prescriptions. Doctors can instantly receive test results and immediately change patient treatment.

Using a smartphone or a desktop computer is more convenient than using a computer. Hospital health workers can keep these small devices in their pockets as they move from room to room. Hundreds of smartphone applications have been developed for medical workers.

Medical Informatics

Medical informatics is the study of using medical information, such as patient records and research data, for decision-making and problem-solving. Workers in this field try to make patient care, medical research, and health care administration more effective. As technology advances, medical informatics is becoming increasingly important in Health Science.

One important application of medical informatics is the use of computerized systems for storing patient information. Patient medical records are now compiled and stored electronically at many hospitals and practices.

Patients' records are updated whenever patients seek medical treatment. Information, such as lab test results, allergies, prescriptions, and vital signs, is added to the record. This gives a comprehensive portrait of the patient's health. Some doctors use smartphones or computers to input information directly into a patient's record during a consultation. Some computerized devices, such as MRI machines, can even feed data directly into the patient's record.

Many electronic record systems have multimedia capabilities. They can store photographs, voice recordings, and videos. They can also organize information, suggest ways of assessing patients, and provide alerts to health workers. Some systems are connected to many hospitals.

These record systems give health professionals immediate access to patient information. They can help doctors diagnose patients by showing them the patient's full medical picture. They can learn about recurring symptoms and past illnesses. The systems can also help administrators manage patient records, set up appointments, and verify insurance information.

Telemedicine

Another growing field in Health Science technology is telemedicine. Telemedicine is the use of technology to connect patients with medical services and information.

Telemedicine is being used in many settings. It allows school nurses to consult with physicians. It helps homebound patients to communicate with doctors, and it allows prisons to provide health services to inmates who cannot be transported.

Telemedicine consultations are based on three types of technology. The first method, known as store and forward, enables the transfer of digital images from one location to another. In this system, the doctor and patient exchange information but don't hold live virtual meetings. A worker might use e-mail to send images and sounds of an abnormal heart to a cardiologist for a diagnosis. Store and forward are used in situations when a diagnosis is necessary but not urgent.

The second type involves monitoring a patient remotely. Devices at a patient's home might record data, such as blood pressure or glucose levels. That information is then automatically sent to a physician, nurse, or other health worker.

The third type of telemedicine is interactive services. Health workers and patients can hold virtual meetings, using video or web-based conferences.

Minimally Invasive Surgical Techniques

Today's surgical technologies focus on making surgery less invasive and less traumatic to the body. Using lasers or high-intensity focused ultrasound instead of scalpels, surgeons can operate on patients without cutting tissue. Surgeons can even perform noninvasive surgery on brain tumors by using radiation to kill unwanted cells.

Minimally invasive surgeries are faster and less risky than regular surgeries. They are less painful, require less healing time, and often do not require anesthesia. Two techniques gaining in popularity are laser surgery and robotic surgery.

Laser surgery is the use of a laser instead of knife to cut tissue or remove bleeding blood vessels. Unlike a scalpel, a laser heats cells in tissue until they burst. The laser works by breaking the bonds of molecules that hold the tissue together, without damaging the tissue. Laser surgery has numerous applications, including the removal of tumors, varicose veins, and even tattoos. Surgeons use different kinds of lasers to perform different types of surgery.

Robotic surgery is surgery performed by remote-controlled robotic devices. Surgeons use remote controls and voice-activated software to guide robotic devices through specific surgical tasks. One of the most important benefits of robotic surgery is that it is minimally invasive. Because only tiny cuts are required, healing time is much faster. Surgical robots can be steadier and more precise than even the best surgeon.

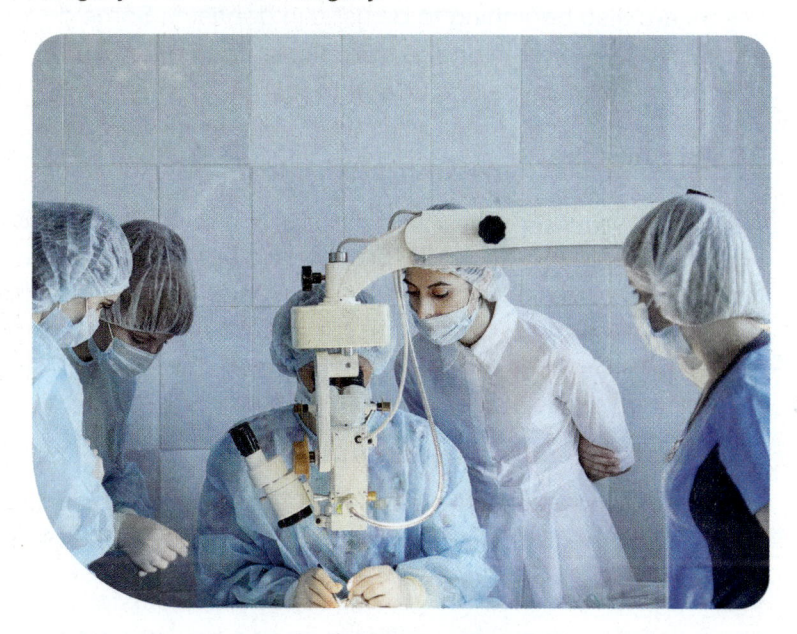

Dental Technologies

In many dental offices, traditional dental tools are being replaced with high-tech equipment. This equipment is often designed to be more effective and less painful for patients. Tools using air abrasion are increasingly used in place of dental drills. Air abrasion is the use of compressed air to blow tiny particles onto teeth. It gets rid of tooth decay as well as stains on tooth enamel. Air abrasion is less painful than traditional drilling procedures. It is silent, and it produces no vibration.

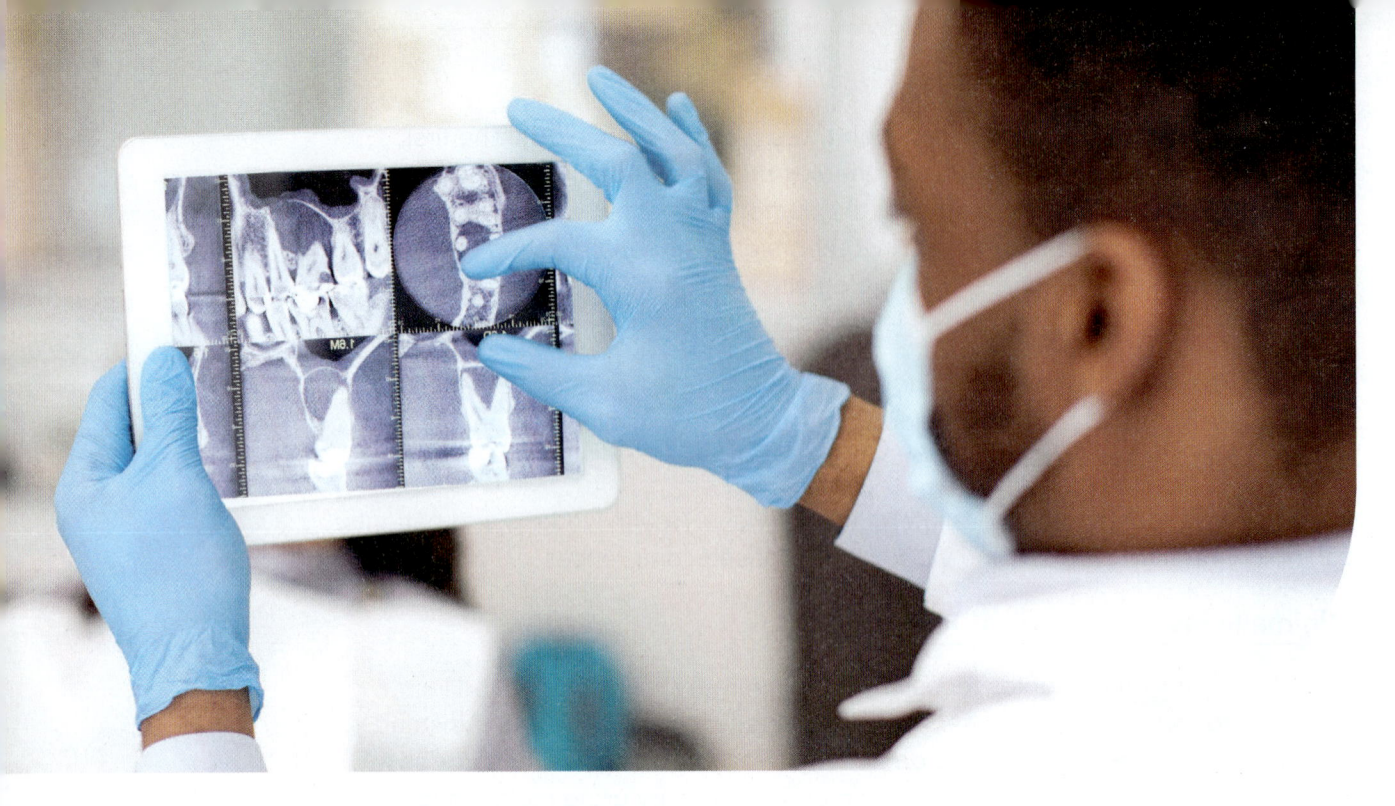

Lasers are also beginning to be used in dentistry. Some dentists use lasers to remove decay in teeth and remove tissue to test for cancer. Lasers can also be used to reshape gums and whiten teeth.

3D Printing

The Health Science industry is utilizing 3D printers as they become more accessible and affordable. 3D printers can be used to create necessary medical tools, patient-specific models of organs, and individual prosthetics.

Workplace Trends in Health Science

Workplace trends affecting the Health Science industry include the use of consultants, medical consultations, and temporary workers.

Consultants A consultant provides specialized services for one or more clients. Consultants are sometimes called in when a new project starts, or a system is re-evaluated. Some consultants work for one client on a long-term project. Others work for several clients simultaneously. A health care manager, for example, may be called in to establish new hospital procedures. As a result of a recent dramatic increase in medical malpractice lawsuits, medical expert witnesses are in growing demand.

Medical Consultations Perhaps the most common form of consultation, or meeting of professionals, is the interaction between specialists. Doctors specializing in one area of medicine consult with doctors in another area. They work together to determine the best course of action for a patient. This form of consultation gives doctors access to a broad range of knowledge and helps improve patient care.

Temporary Workers Temporary workers work for a short time at a company, but they are hired and paid by independent employment agencies. Temporary workers are used often in health care. If a home health care agency has a sudden increase in clients, for example, a temporary worker might be called in to fill a position.

In health care, temporary workers might serve as medical secretaries or home health care aides. They may fill clerical positions in a hospital or clinic. Hospitals even call in temporary registered nurses to maintain full staffing.

> ### 14-6 Essential Question Reflection
>
> **So, let us revisit our essential question:**
>
> *What factors affect trends in Health Science?*
>
> Based on what you learned in this section, please answer this question in detail.

Chapter 15

Human Services

❓ Essential Questions

By the end of the chapter, you will be able to answer the following questions:

- **15-1** What types of opportunities are available in Human Services?
- **15-2** Which opportunities may be right for you?
- **15-3** How can I match my skills & interests with the right job?
- **15-4** What training & education is needed for a job in Human Services?
- **15-5** What are typical work environments in Human Services?
- **15-6** What factors affect trends in Human Services?

Chapter Topics

15-1 Human Services Today

15-2 Human Services Jobs

15-3 Building a Career in Human Services

15-4 Education and Training for Human Services Opportunities

15-5 Working Conditions in the Human Services Industry

15-6 Trends in Human Services

15-1 Human Services Today

Human Services improve people's quality of life and help build safe, healthy communities. Workers in this industry tend to people's physical, social, and mental health needs. These workers—from child care providers to social workers to hair stylists—do very different kinds of work. But they all care for the people they serve.

One major part of this industry is social services. These services help people with basic needs such as housing, nutrition, health, and education. Government agencies do much of this work, so many workers are employed by government. Nonprofit groups meet some of these needs as well. Nonprofits are organizations that serve the public and do not earn profits, although some may receive funding from the government. However, most nonprofits rely on donations from individuals, businesses, and foundations. Nonprofit groups in Human Services include the Red Cross and neighborhood community centers.

15-1 Essential Question

As you read this section, keep this question in mind:

What types of opportunities are available in Human Services?

Career Journeys in Human Services

There are five major paths along which your journey in Human Services might be shaped. People commonly move into and out of different paths. Each path contains a group of careers requiring similar skills as well as similar certifications or education. This industry is divided into five main career paths:

- Early Childhood Development and Services
- Counseling and Mental Health Services
- Family and Community Services
- Personal Care Services
- Consumer Services

Early Childhood Development and Services

Childhood development refers to the physical, emotional, and intellectual growth of children. It includes a child's ability to understand and use language, to learn new concepts, to cope with emotional issues, and to interact with others. Some workers in this path study the development of children from birth to age four or five. Others work directly with children in day care centers.

Some childhood development services are mainly educational. In preschools, children learn social, personal, and academic skills. Young children learn best through playing, so preschool teachers build lessons around activities, games, and interactive play, such as storytelling and painting.

Child care workers care for children. They may work in the child's home, in their own home, or at child care centers. These centers may be stand-alone businesses, or they may be day care centers that employers provide for their workers. Nonprofits such as social service organizations and religious institutions run many child care centers.

Working with young children demands patience, kindness, and a positive attitude. Workers must be responsible and attentive. Since working with parents is a large part of the job, workers in this path need excellent interpersonal and communication skills as well. Entry-level workers in child care need at least a high school diploma. Preschool teachers must have a high school diploma and experience working with children. Many states require an associate or bachelor's degree. Most states also require early childhood workers to have training in health, first aid, and child-abuse detection and prevention.

Counseling and Mental Health Services

Workers in Counseling and Mental Health Services path aim to help people with emotional or mental problems. Some problems, such as job stress, grief over the loss of a loved one, and marriage difficulties, are temporary. Other problems are chronic, or long term. These include depression, substance abuse, and eating disorders. Problems such as schizophrenia are very serious. Major fields in this path include psychology and counseling.

Psychology is the scientific study of the mind and human behavior. Psychologists are professionals who work with people facing psychological problems. They are not trained in medicine, and they do not administer drugs. They help people by using various therapy techniques. There are many forms of therapy. Professionals choose the approach they think is most suitable for a particular person.

Counseling is offering advice on troubling personal issues. Trained mental health counselors help individuals who have mental health issues. Substance abuse and behavioral disorder counselors help people who have problems with drugs or alcohol abuse. Sometimes these counselors work with people who are affected by the problems of family members.

Counselors work in a variety of settings, including schools, hospitals, clinics, prisons, private practices, and residential facilities. Residential facilities provide housing and counseling for people in crisis, such as runaway teens, AIDS patients, and teenage mothers.

Most careers in Counseling and Mental Health Services require extensive training. Psychologists usually need a doctoral degree. Counselors typically need a master's degree. In addition to their training, workers in this path must have patience, compassion, and a strong desire to help others.

Family and Community Services

Workers in the Family and Community Services path provide a wide variety of services that help strengthen family and community life. Services include job counseling, adult day care, emergency relief, nutritional and housing help, and spiritual guidance.

A critical field in this path is social work. Social work aims to improve the conditions of a community by counseling and giving help to those in need. Much social work focuses on helping under-served populations, such as people with low income or who are jobless. Government agencies employ some social workers. Other social workers work for businesses, schools, hospitals, or nursing homes. Social workers are active in a wide range of family and community issues, including child welfare, family services, substance abuse, and care for older people.

Training required for careers in this area varies. Most social workers need a bachelor's or master's degree. On the other hand, adult daycare workers and home health aides generally need only a high school diploma. Most employers prefer to hire workers with some related work experience.

All workers in this path must have a desire to help others. Maturity and emotional stability as well as respect for their clients are essential for building strong relationships. Volunteering for a charitable organization is one way to test your interest in Family and Community Services.

Personal Care Services

Personal Care Services help people feel better or look better, or they help make people's lives more convenient. Fitness trainers and aerobics instructors help people remain physically fit. They might lead exercise classes or coach an individual in weight training. Hairstylists are experts at hair cutting, hair coloring, permanent waving, and chemical relaxing.

Success in this path requires excellent interpersonal skills and a positive view of customer service. Hairstylists must have a creative flair and an eye for trends, and they must be able to communicate with their customers. Some workers in this path, such as cosmetologists, need a license to practice. Many workers in this path run small businesses. This requires knowledge of business practices, including marketing and accounting.

Consumer Services

Consumers have an enormous variety of goods and services to choose from. They shop for everything from health insurance plans to cars. The variety of possibilities can make it difficult to choose wisely. Workers in the Consumer Services path help consumers to learn about their options, to make wise purchasing decisions, and to understand their legal rights.

Workers in this path include loan counselors and managers of property, real estate, and community associations. Loan counselors work with people who wish to borrow money but have difficulty qualifying for loans. The borrowers might have poor credit histories or low incomes. Loan counselors help borrowers find the best loan, and they clearly explain the terms of the loan. Managers of property, real estate, and community associations operate apartment buildings or run neighborhood associations. They respond to problems and make sure regular maintenance work is performed.

Workers in Consumer Services, as in the other career paths in Human Services, need above-average interpersonal and communication skills. Because they often deal with financial information, they must be willing to keep information private. Consumer Services workers need knowledge of law, business, product manufacturing, and finance.

Human Services Future Outlook

Industry outlook refers to the projected growth or decline in a particular industry. The industry outlook for many careers in the Human Services industry is overall positive. According to the Bureau of Labor Statistics, jobs in social assistance are expected to grow by as much as 30 percent from 2021 to 2031. Personal care is also expected to grow rapidly. The number of jobs in this area should grow by about 15 percent from 2021 to 2031. Personal home care aides are expected to be the fourth fastest-growing job in the entire country. The number of jobs in child day care services is projected to grow only moderately, by about 15 percent. However, economists expect many job openings each year because job turnover is very rapid in this career.

Table 15.1: Forecast for Human Services Occupations over the Next 10 Years

Occupation	Expected Growth Rate
Child Care Workers, Including Nannies	5% – 10%
Rehabilitation Counselors	10% – 15%
Mental Health Counselors	10% – 15%
Substance Abuse and Behavioral Disorder Counselors	10% – 15%
Marriage and Family Therapists	10% – 15%
Sociologists	5% – 10%
Social and Human Service Assistants	10% – 15%
Child, Family, and School Social Workers	5% – 10%
Personal and Home Care Aides	15+%
Hairdressers, Hairstylists, and Cosmetologists	10% – 15%
Exercise Trainers and Group Fitness Instructors	10% – 15%
Funeral Attendants	5% – 10%
Skin Care Specialists	10% – 15%
Property, Real Estate, and Community Association Managers	0% – 5%
Loan Counselors	5% – 10%

Source: *O*Net*

15-1 Essential Question Reflection

So, let us revisit our essential question:

What types of opportunities are available in Human Services?

Based on what you learned in this section, please answer this question in detail.

Practice 15-1

Skills Practice

It may be necessary to follow multi-step instructions in a variety of situations, such as when social and Human Services assistants must follow government-set procedures in filling out forms. Workers must read carefully to know when to take each step and be able to apply the same instructions in a variety of situations. **Practice this skill!**

PROCEDURES FOR GREETING PATIENTS

The receptionist is responsible for making clients feel welcome and setting a tone of high-level service. As a receptionist, you should greet a patient as soon as possible after they enter the office. If you are on the phone, ask for a break in the conversation, tell the patient that you will serve them shortly, and conclude the call as soon as possible.

Ask the patient if they have an appointment. If the patient has an appointment, find out with whom and at what time. Consult the schedule to confirm this. Ask the patient to wait, and then inform the physical therapist assistant that the patient has arrived. Find out how soon the professional will be ready, and convey that information to the customer. Invite them to sit and read while waiting. Offer a beverage or snack.

For walk-in patients, welcome them and ask what services are desired. Consult the schedule for the next opening for that service. Check with the next available professional before estimating wait time. Then, provide that information to the customer, and make them feel welcome.

1. As the receptionist in a physical therapy office, you greet patients entering the business and prepare them to receive services. What should you do when a patient tells you they have an appointment with the physical therapist at 2 p.m.?

    A. confirm the appointment before doing anything else
    B. call the physical therapist
    C. bring the patient to the therapist
    D. tell the patient how long he will have to wait
    E. ask the patient for proof of the appointment

2. What should you do with a walk-in patient before estimating the time that they may need to wait for service?

    A. offer a beverage or snack
    B. ask him or her to sit down
    C. confirm the wait time with the needed specialist
    D. warn him or her that the wait will be long
    E. explain that people with appointments come first

To access more problems that will help you grow professional skills and are real-world examples in Human Services, go online.

15-2 Human Services Jobs

You can find jobs at all skill levels, from entry level to managerial, in the Human Services industry. You might be interested in a career in child care. Perhaps you'd like to help people by becoming a social worker, psychologist, or counselor? Maybe working in a salon appeals to you? The following job profiles will introduce you to some of the professions in this industry.

15-2 Essential Question

As you read this section, keep this question in mind:

Which opportunities may be right for you?

Occupations That Make a Big Impact:

Credit Counselors

- Calculate clients' available monthly income to meet debt obligations
- Create debt management plans, spending plans, or budgets to assist clients to meet financial goals
- Prioritize client debt repayment to avoid dire consequences, such as bankruptcy or foreclosure or to reduce overall costs
- Assess clients' overall financial situations by reviewing income, assets, debts, expenses, credit reports, or other financial information

Fast Facts:

Employment: 35,300 employees
Annual Openings: 3,200
Median Annual Wage: $22.87 hourly, $47,580 annually
Education Needed: High school diploma, or equivalent
Other: People in this occupation must have excellent people skills and some knowledge of finances.

Mental Health and Substance Abuse Social Workers

- Counsel clients in individual or group sessions to assist them in dealing with substance abuse, mental or physical illness, poverty, unemployment, or physical abuse
- Collaborate with counselors, physicians, or nurses to plan or coordinate treatment, drawing on social work experience and patient needs
- Monitor, evaluate, and record client progress with respect to treatment goals

Fast Facts:

Employment: 119,800 employees
Annual Openings: 12,700
Median Annual Wage: $23.62 hourly, $49,130 annually
Education Needed: Master's degree and certification

Occupations With a Bright Outlook:

Hairdressers, Hairstylists, and Cosmetologists

- Provide beauty services, such as cutting, coloring, and styling hair, and massaging and treating scalp
- Keep workstations clean and sanitize tools, such as scissors and combs
- Schedule client appointments
- Update and maintain customer information records, such as beauty services provided

Fast Facts:

Employment: 558,700 employees
Annual Openings: 87,200
Median Annual Wage: $14.26 hourly, $29,670 annually
Education Needed: High school diploma and certification

Health-Care Social Workers

- Provide individuals, families, and groups with the psychosocial support needed to cope with chronic, acute, and terminal illnesses
- Advocate for clients or patients to resolve crises
- Educate clients about end-of-life symptoms and options to assist them in making informed decisions
- Collaborate with other professionals to evaluate patients' medical or physical condition and to assess client needs

Fast Facts:
Employment: 179,500 employees
Annual Openings: 19,700
Median Annual Wage: $29.25 hourly, $60,840 annually
Education Needed: Master's degree
Other: This is a fulfilling career that allows you to connect with patients throughout their care, sometimes from diagnosis to death.

Great Jobs! – Associate Degree Required:

Morticians, Undertakers, and Funeral Arrangers

- Obtain information needed to complete legal documents, such as death certificates and burial permits
- Consult with families or friends of the deceased to arrange funeral details, such as obituary notice wording, casket selection, and plans for service

- Perform embalming duties as necessary
- Oversee the preparation and care of the remains of people who have died
- Contact cemeteries to schedule the opening and closing of graves

Fast Facts:

Employment: 27,400 employees

Annual Openings: 4,300

Median Annual Wage: $23.53 hourly, $48,950 annually

Residential Advisors

- Communicate with other staff to resolve problems with individual students
- Observe students to detect and report unusual behavior
- Supervise, train, and evaluate residence hall staff, including resident assistants, participants in work-study programs, and other student workers
- Make regular rounds to ensure that residents and areas are safe and secure

Fast Facts:

Employment: 99,300 employees

Annual Openings: 18,900

Median Annual Wage: $15.01 hourly, $31,220 annually

Other: Employers usually pay for room and board, along with a salary.
This is the perfect position for someone who may be interested in obtaining a bachelor's degree but needs financial assistance.

15-2 Essential Question Reflection

So, let us revisit our essential question:

Which opportunities may be right for you?

Based on what you learned in this section, please answer this question in detail.

Case Study: Neuropsychologists

Also called: Neurologists, Psychiatrists

What do they do?

- Apply research to evaluate and diagnose disorders of higher cerebral functioning, often in research and medical settings
- Study the human brain and the effect of physiological states on human cognition and behavior
- Conduct neuropsychological evaluations such as assessments of intelligence, academic ability, attention, concentration, sensorimotor function, language, learning, and memory
- Design or implement rehabilitation plans for patients with cognitive dysfunction
- Diagnose and treat conditions involving injury to the central nervous system, such as cerebrovascular accidents, neoplasms, infectious or inflammatory diseases, degenerative diseases, head traumas, and various forms of dementing illnesses

What do you need to know?

Arts and Humanities
English language

Business
Customer service
Sales and marketing

Math and Science
Arithmetic, algebra, geometry, calculus, and/or statistics
Sociology and anthropology

Communications
Multimedia

What skills do you need?

Basic Skills
Read work-related information
Think about the pros and cons of different ways to solve a problem

Problem-Solving
Notice a problem, and figure out the best way to solve it

People and Technology Systems
Think about the pros and cons of different options, and pick the best one
Figure out how a system should work and how changes in the future will affect it

What abilities must you be good at?

Verbal and Written
Communicate by speaking
Communicate by writing

Ideas and Logic
Make general rules or produce answers from a range of detailed information
Produce several ideas

Math
Choose the appropriate type of math to solve a problem
Add, subtract, multiply, and divide

Who does well in this occupation?

People interested in this work like activities that include ideas, thinking, and figuring things out.

They do well at jobs that need:
Analytical thinking
Attention to detail
Dependability
Integrity
Initiative
Adaptability/flexibility

What educational level is needed?

- Bachelor's or master's degree

Practice 15-2

Skills Practice

When workers look at a graphic such as a diagram or a bar graph, they need to analyze and make sense of the information. It may be necessary to summarize the information or boil it down to the most important facts. For example, directors of youth activities may need to summarize attendance information to report on the success of a summer camp program. Being able to summarize allows workers to make sense of varying information. **Practice this skill!**

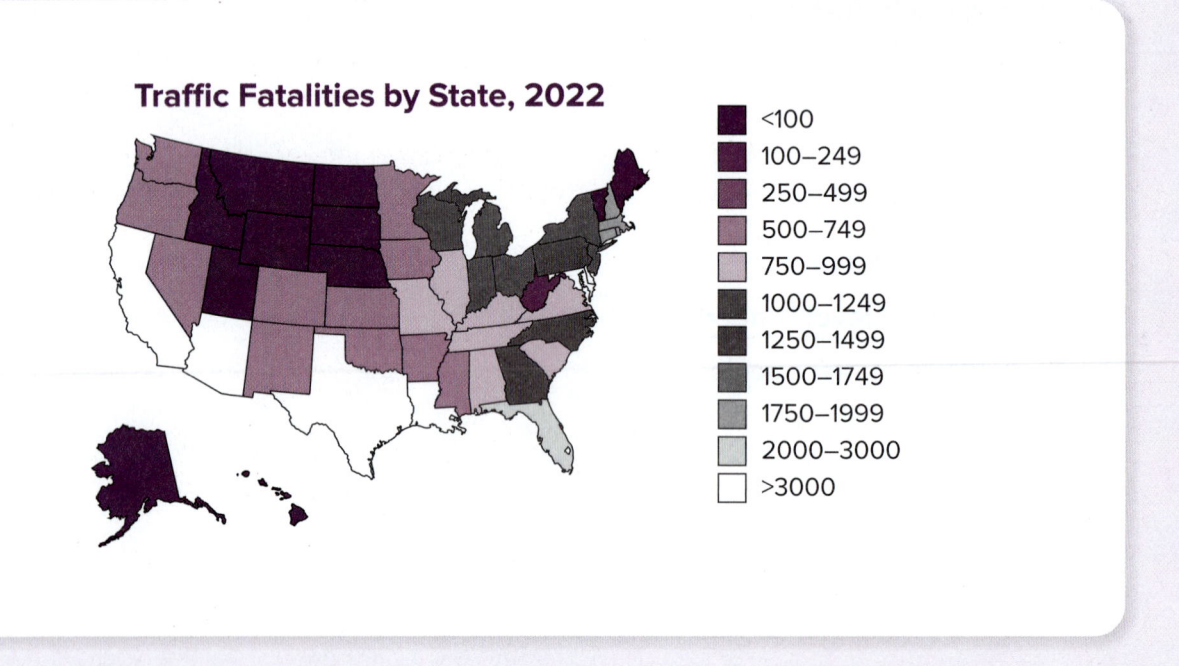

Traffic Fatalities by State, 2022

Legend:
- <100
- 100–249
- 250–499
- 500–749
- 750–999
- 1000–1249
- 1250–1499
- 1500–1749
- 1750–1999
- 2000–3000
- >3000

1. As a consumer research department representative, you conduct research to help businesses find markets for their products. A car company has developed a new car-safety product that can make the most difference in areas with the most traffic fatalities. In which states should the car company introduce its product first?

    A. Maine, Vermont, North Dakota, Montana

    B. Louisiana, Texas, Arizona, California

    C. New Mexico, Colorado, Kansas, Oklahoma

    D. Florida, Connecticut, Rhode Island, Massachusetts

    E. Wisconsin, Michigan, Pennsylvania, New York

2. Which of the following group of states has the lowest traffic fatalities by state?

    A. Maine, Vermont, North Dakota, Montana

    B. Louisiana, Texas, Arizona, California

    C. New Mexico, Colorado, Kansas, Oklahoma

    D. Florida, Connecticut, Rhode Island, Massachusetts

    E. Wisconsin, Michigan, Pennsylvania, New York

To access more problems that will help you grow professional skills and are real-world examples in Human Services, go online.

15-3 Building a Career in Human Services

For a career in social work, you may begin as a caseworker, working directly with a few clients. As you gain experience, you may take on more clients. With more education, such as a master's degree in social work, you may become a supervisor or a program manager of a service center. As you learn more on the job and gain more experience, you might be promoted to executive director of your agency or move into private practice.

15-3 Essential Question

As you read this section, keep this question in mind:

How can I match my skills & interests with the right job?

Are You More Interested in Working with People, Data, or Things?

Most careers in Human Services offer opportunities to work with a combination of data, people, and things. Working with data involves the evaluation of information. Credit counselors work with data by analyzing their clients' financial information. Working with people requires building human relationships. Psychologists counsel their clients and use various therapy methods to address their clients' problems. Working with things involves using objects, such as tools and machines. Massage therapists may use balls, rollers, and hot stones in combination with techniques to relieve tension in their clients' bodies. Which area are you most interested in?

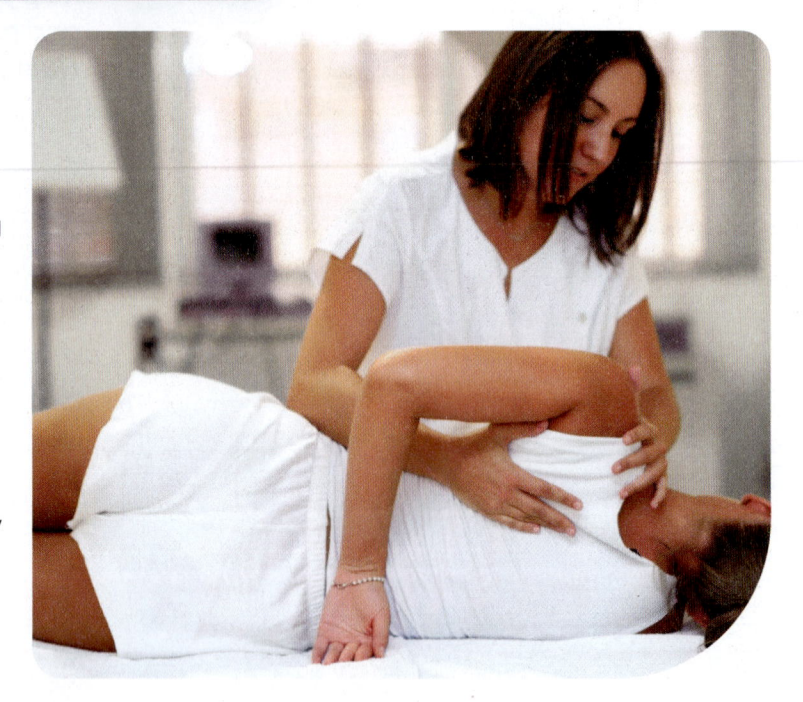

Careers That Involve Working With Data

Examples of working with data include comparing the features of various service agreements or planning the activities for the week at a day care center.

Few careers in Human Services focus entirely on data, but many careers have a data component. Consumer credit counselors, for example, must be able to draw up budgets and compute interest rates. They must make sense of credit reports, tax returns, bills, and other financial statements. Psychologists who perform research work with data to test their ideas.

Careers That Involve Working With People

All Human Service jobs focus on human relationships. Examples of working with people include a counselor advising a troubled teen, a massage therapist giving a client a massage, and a nanny teaching life skills and supervising children. All these activities require strong communication and interpersonal skills.

Jobs in schools, hospitals, and churches involve working with people. Preschool teachers, child care workers, and preschool teacher aides all interact with children at day care centers or preschools. Counselors, clergypersons, mental health aides, and psychologists help patients with problems such as substance abuse, mental illness, grief, and family crises. Working with people who are disadvantaged, ill, very young, or much older requires social workers to have compassion, patience, and dedication.

Employment counselors aid people in choosing careers and finding jobs, while housing specialists may work with families experiencing homelessness and in need of shelter. Personal care workers develop relationships and provide support and assistance for clients in hair salons, day spas, and gyms.

Careers That Involve Working With Things

Although most careers in Human Services involve working primarily with people, some jobs require employees to work with things as well. If you work at a community food bank, you may move cases of food and stock food shelves. As a skin care specialist, you will use a variety of cleansers, creams, and other skin care products.

> **15-3 Essential Question Reflection**
>
> **So, let us revisit our essential question:**
>
> *How can I match my skills & interests with the right job?*
>
> Based on what you learned in this section, please answer this question in detail.

15-4 Education and Training for Human Services Opportunities

Jobs in the Human Services industry require varying levels of education and training.

15-4 Essential Question

As you read this section, keep this question in mind:

What training & education is needed for a job in Human Services?

Training and Education for Human Services

The level of training needed to succeed in this industry varies by career. Human Services jobs can be grouped into three broad categories—those requiring little or no training, those requiring some training, and those requiring advanced training.

Jobs Requiring Little or No Training

Some jobs in Personal Care Services and Early Childhood Development Services require only a little training. Hair salons may hire stylists with no experience to work as shampooers or receptionists. Day care centers, nursing homes, home health-care services, and psychiatric care facilities often hire aides with no experience.

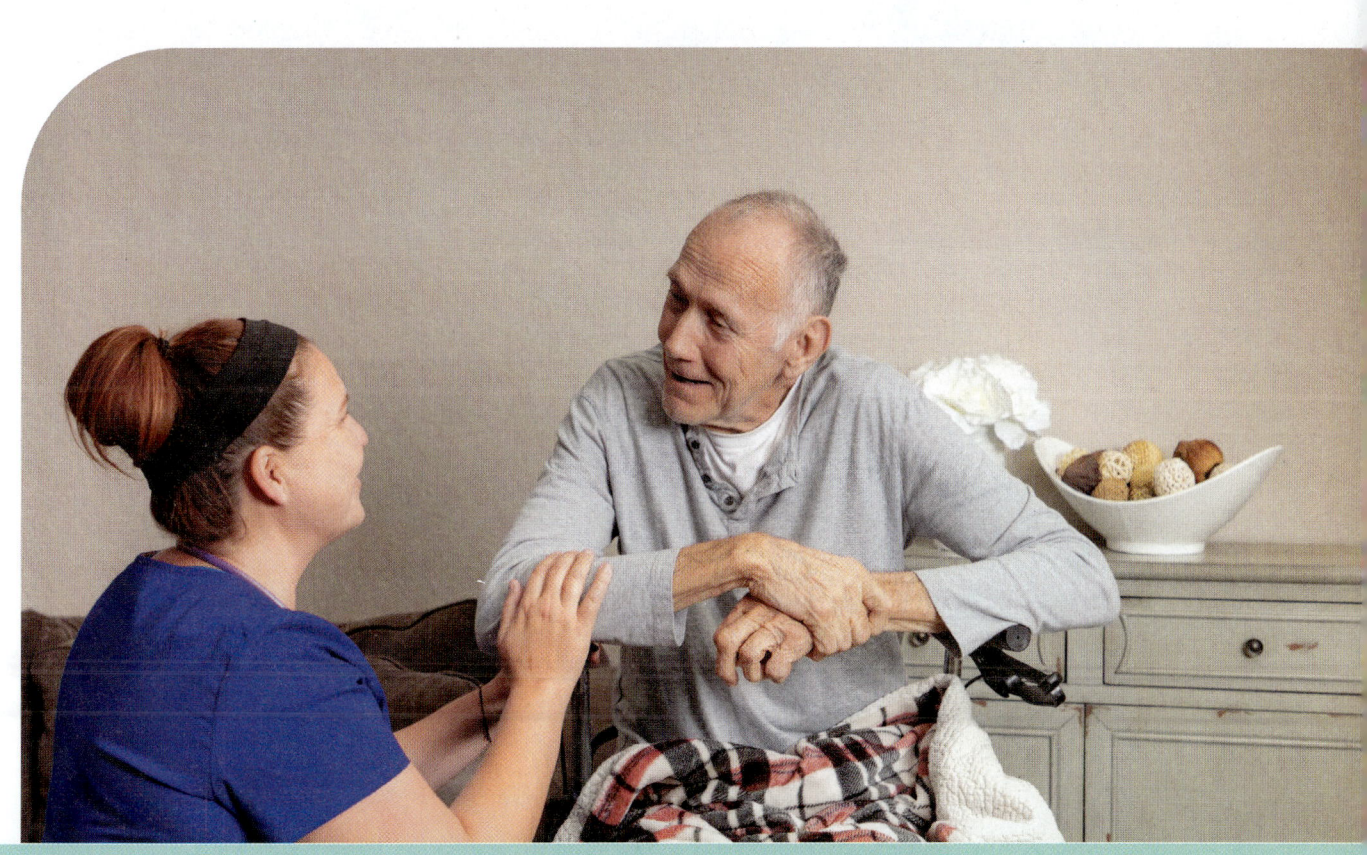

However, getting a high school education or the equivalent is important. Failing to complete high school may hurt your chances for advancement.

Jobs Requiring Some Training

Many jobs in Human Services require either an associate degree or a certificate. An associate degree is earned by completing a two-year program at a community college. A technical certificate is the result of finishing a training program offered at a technical school, trade school, or career preparation institute. Certificates are often required in personal care services.

Community colleges and some universities offer two-year, associate degree programs that can qualify you to work in child development, social services, massage therapy, and consumer services. Some programs offer courses online.

Cosmetologists often receive formal training at a cosmetology school or technical school. Completion of such a program is usually necessary before applying for a license, which is required in every state. To receive a license, applicants must demonstrate their knowledge of cosmetology by passing both a written test and a hands-on presentation.

Jobs Requiring Advanced Training

Many jobs in Counseling and Mental Health Services require at least a bachelor's degree. The same is true in family and community services. Social workers need a bachelor's degree in social work (BSW) for an entry-level position. A master's degree in social work (MSW) or clinical social work is usually needed to advance in the field. Occupational therapists must have a bachelor's degree, and they must be licensed by their state to work.

Counselors usually have a master's degree. Degree programs in counseling include both course work and experience in treating patients. Experienced counselors supervise this work with patients.

Most psychologists need a doctoral degree in psychology (PhD or PsyD). PhD programs are generally more research oriented than PsyD programs. Both PhD and PsyD candidates must complete an internship approved by the American Psychological Association (APA). Before they can practice, psychologists must be licensed by their state.

Table 15.2: Training Required for Human Services Jobs

Level of Training	Job Title
Little or No Training	Child Care Workers Receptionists Costume Attendants Funeral Attendants Laundry and Dry-Cleaning Workers Personal and Home Care Aides
Some Training	Substance Abuse and Behavioral Disorder Counselors Nannies Residential Advisors Social and Human Services Assistants Hairdressers, Hairstylists, and Cosmetologists
Considerable Training	Industrial Organizational Psychologists Mental Health Counselors Sociologists Clergies Medical and Public Health Social Workers

Job and Workplace Skills

When considering job candidates, employers look at several factors. Two important areas include job-specific skills and general workplace skills. You need job-specific skills to do a particular job. For example, knowing how to cut hair and how to help an older person into a wheelchair. General workplace skills can be used in a variety of jobs. Developing these skills will make you more marketable in any job situation.

Human Service Skill Standards

The Human Services Research Institute, in cooperation with the U.S. Department of Education, has developed national skill standards for Human Services. These standards apply especially to entry-level jobs in this field. They focus on professional responsibility, subject knowledge, and positive client interaction. Although these standards apply mainly to jobs in family, community, and mental health services, many of these skills are also suitable to jobs in personal care and consumer services.

The skill standards fall into 12 main categories. Skilled Human Services workers are expected to meet these standards.

- Empower clients to master their own lives
- Possess strong communication skills to build a solid relationship with clients
- Assess clients' abilities in ways that fit their needs, desires, and interests
- Know social services available in the community and help clients access them
- Plan treatments that consider clients' work, home environments, and support networks
- Help clients build life skills
- Pursue self-improvement and continuing education, and share knowledge with others
- Understand the wide range of social problems and ways to overcome them
- Help clients identify and reach education and career goals
- Know how to prevent, intervene, and resolve crises

- Understand an employer's mission and practices, and contribute to their employer's success
- Manage written data and records effectively

Professional Skills

Communication Skills Communication is essential for forming relationships with clients, coworkers, and supervisors. Counselors and psychologists must be able to explain diagnoses and treatment options in a clear, sensitive, and caring way. Child care workers must be able to speak effectively to both parents and children.

Listening Skills Good listening skills are essential for psychologists, counselors, and social services workers because they must understand their clients' problems. They are also needed by personal care workers so they can serve their clients. Child care workers must be able to listen to what children say and to interpret children's body language. Listening skills are necessary for following instructions safely and making a safe working environment.

Problem-Solving Skills A Human Services worker helps clients with their problems. Problems might be as serious as a mental health problem and as fleeting as a "bad hair" day. Creativity, mental flexibility, and analytical skills help these workers approach and solve problems from various angles.

Technology Skills Even traditionally "low-tech" fields like Human Services are making greater use of technology. Research psychologists use advanced imaging techniques to track areas of the brain that feel sadness or pain. Workers in all areas file reports by computer and communicate with colleagues by e-mail. Having strong technology skills are crucial to a successful career in Human Services.

Decision-Making Skills Being able to gather information and analyze it rapidly and to think clearly under pressure are important skills for Human Services workers. A social worker or counselor must intervene in crises and provide help. A manager of a social service organization must make effective decisions, sometimes with little advance notice.

Organizing and Planning Skills Planning is the ability to set goals and figure out the steps needed to reach those goals. Therapists must be able to plan treatments for their clients. Child care workers must think ahead to plan activities to keep children occupied throughout the day at a day care center. They must also be sure to have needed supplies and equipment ready. Strong organization and planning skills are required for success in this industry.

Teamwork Skills Teamwork is key to nearly every job in Human Services. Regardless of the position, workers in Human Services are required to work with others to get the job done. To be a good team player, they need to place the team's goal above their own personal goals and be willing to put in their share of the work.

Social Skills Interacting with supervisors, coworkers, and clients is essential in all Human Services jobs. Social services workers are likely to interact with people from all walks of life and from various kinds of backgrounds. They need to keep an open mind and use the opportunity to learn from others.

Adaptability Skills Job descriptions, work environments, and office procedures are constantly evolving as community needs change. Welcome this as an opportunity to acquire new skills and make the job more interesting.

15-4 Essential Question Reflection

So, let us revisit our essential question:

What training & education is needed for a job in Human Services?

Based on what you learned in this section, please answer this question in detail.

Practice 15-4

Skills Practice

Many jobs in the Human Services industry require workers to calculate costs and discounts. For example, a massage therapist may want figure out how much of a discount they can offer a loyal client while maintaining a profit. **Practice this skill!**

1. You are a manicurist working at a nail salon. You must purchase 2,000 artificial nail tips. Your supplier will sell you a box of 500 artificial nail tips for $21 and offers you a 5% discount. How much do you spend on 2,000 artificial nail tips?

   A. $19.50
   B. $39.90
   C. $79.80
   D. $84.00
   E. $42.00

2. In your job as an embalmer, you are responsible for purchasing the necessary amount of embalming fluid. The type of embalming fluid you need costs $85.99 per bottle. However, since you are making such a large purchase, you receive a 9% discount. How much does one bottle of embalming fluid cost?

   A. $7.74
   B. $51.90
   C. $78.25
   D. $88.49
   E. $93.79

Skills Practice

Some calculations in the Human Services industry may require using conversions and formulas. A nanny who is planning a birthday party may need to use a formula to adapt a recipe to serve many children. In addition, the nanny may need to convert a recipe with measurements in metric units to standard units.
Practice this skill!

3. In your job as a benefits advisor, you estimate that it will take you 90 minutes to enter new benefit changes into the computer. You have a meeting at 10 a.m. and want to ensure that you start entering the benefits early enough to be finished before your meeting. If you started entering benefits at 8 a.m., what time would you finish?

    A. 9:15 a.m.
    B. 9:30 a.m.
    C. 10:30 a.m.
    D. 11:10 a.m.
    E. 11:45 a.m.

4. You are a community food service director. Today you decide to try a new recipe for lunch. The recipe states, "Cook turkey for 15 minutes per pound." If the turkey weighs 9 pounds, you need to cook it for 135 minutes. How much time is this in hours and minutes?

    A. 1 hour, 30 minutes
    D. 1 hour, 55 minutes
    C. 2 hours, 15 minutes
    D. 3 hours, 0 minutes
    E. 3 hours, 10 minutes

To access more problems that will help you grow professional skills and are real-world examples in Human Services, go online.

15-5 Working Conditions in the Human Services Industry

When choosing a career path, it is important to know what it is like to work in the industry. Understanding the work environment, hazards, and benefits of a job can help you make informed decisions.

> **15-5 Essential Question**
>
> As you read this section, keep this question in mind:
>
> *What are typical work environments in Human Services?*

Physical Environment

The physical work environment in Human Services varies greatly. Psychologists and clinical social workers usually work in a clinic or a private office. Some, however, work at mental hospitals, prisons, or halfway houses—places that can be stressful. Mental health counselors may work in a residential facility, or an institution where patients live. Sometimes mental health counselors even live at the facility to provide around-the-clock guidance and supervision. Social service assistants work in offices. Their jobs can be stressful when clients outnumber the staff. Personal service workers such as hairstylists typically work in pleasant settings that are clean and well lit.

Work Hours

Like the working conditions, the work hours in Human Services vary greatly. Because some social service workers need to work through the night, shift work is vital in this industry. Shift work divides the day into blocks of time, generally into eight-hour blocks. Shift work allows residential programs and shelters to be open around the clock. Workers might have some ability to choose hours to meet their needs.

Many workers in Human Services work evenings, weekends, and holidays. Hairstylists, for instance, are often busiest at these times.

Some workers in this industry work a regular eight-hour shift and a 40-hour week. Although they do most of their work during standard working hours, they may need to work overtime to handle emergencies. Overtime is work done in addition to an employee's regular schedule. Working some nights, weekends, and holidays is not uncommon.

The hours of most child care workers can be very irregular. Child care centers are open 12 or more hours a day to suit the work schedules of parents. However, traffic jams or late meetings can cause even the most punctual parents to be late on occasion. Child care workers must stay at work until the last child has been safely picked up.

Essential Physical Activities

Most workers in Human Services must be in good physical condition. Although psychologists, counselors, and consumer scientists spend a good deal of time in offices or clinics, other workers in this industry are on their feet much of the day. This includes most social workers and home care aides.

Child care workers have a very active work environment. They spend their days playing, leading activities, cleaning up spills, putting supplies in order, and running after children. People who work with babies and infants often lift and carry the children. Child care requires frequent bending and stooping.

Hairstylists spend long days on their feet. Most salon chairs can be adjusted to a height that is comfortable for the stylist, but long hours of standing can be tiring to the legs and back. When cutting hair, hairstylists repeatedly extend their arms, a motion that can cause shoulder pain. These workers should wear comfortable shoes and take frequent breaks.

Hazards and Environmental Dangers

Federal laws and rules set workplace safety standards aimed at preventing accidents. Other laws ensure that accident victims receive help. The Occupational Safety and Health Administration (OSHA) sets job standards and inspects job sites. OSHA inspectors visit companies to ensure that working processes and conditions are safe. Twenty-six states also run job safety programs.

Injuries and Illnesses

According to the U.S. Bureau of Labor Statistics (BLS), about 71,000 injuries and illnesses occurred among social assistance workers in 2021. This represented less than 3 percent of all workers in this field. Another 24,000 injuries and illnesses affected workers in personal and laundry services. Injuries and illnesses affected less than 2 percent of these workers. These rates are about the average for all service industries. Most workplace injuries involve cuts, bruises, sprains, and back pain. Other common injuries are fractures and burns.

To prevent injury, workers must follow safety procedures. It helps to take breaks so overworked muscles can rest and to vary work tasks when possible. Workers should notify managers if they feel pain or stiffness. Some workers, such as adult day care aides and nursing home aides, need to lift people or heavy equipment. The law requires that these workers must be given proper training.

Ergonomics is the study of creating and adjusting work equipment and practices to make workplaces and processes safer and more comfortable. Increased attention to ergonomics is helping to create a healthier work environment in the Human Services industry. For instance, hairstylists can now choose brushes with comfortably styled handles and lightweight hair dryers. One main goal of ergonomics is to reduce the occurrence of musculoskeletal disorders (MSDs). Social service assistants and program directors, who spend a good deal of time using the computer, are among those most likely to suffer from MSDs. These workers use the same tools and motions every day. Cosmetologists must also be careful to vary their activities to avoid MSDs.

15-5 Essential Question Reflection

So, let us revisit our essential question:

What are typical work environments in Human Services?

Based on what you learned in this section, please answer this question in detail.

15-6 Trends in Human Services

People have been caring for one another since the beginning of time. They have taken care of the young, helped people with disabilities, and counseled people through mental health crises. Technology has changed the way some services are provided. Changing family structures have spurred an increase in need for certain services. However, smaller government budgets are forcing some services to be cut.

> **15-6 Essential Question**
>
> As you read this section, keep this question in mind:
>
> *What factors affect trends in Human Services?*

Technology in the Human Services Industry

Technology has changed work processes and working conditions for jobs in every industry. Even Human Services—care provided for people by people—is affected by advances in technology.

Assistive Technology

Assistive technology makes it easier for people with disabilities to live on their own, and it has been life changing. A wide variety of products helps people get around and carry out everyday activities. Stair glides, which move a person safely up or down a flight of stairs, can enable an older person or someone with a disability to live in a two-story home. Special keys enable people with arthritic hands to open locks. Applications can be installed on mobile phones, tablets, or laptops that allow a person who is nonverbal to communicate their needs with their caregiver. New telephones help people who are deaf communicate. Other devices make it possible for stroke victims and children who suffer from speech impairments to communicate.

Smart home technology is another type of assistive technology that enables a central computer to monitor various functions in a home. This technology gives people with physical impairments more control over their living space.

Automated Case Management Systems

Social workers can have trouble keeping track of clients, many of whom receive help through several aid programs. Multiply that problem by 300 clients and you can see the difficulty that these workers face. Automated case management systems, now used by almost all social workers, allow them to assist more clients.

An automated case management system is a computer database of clients. The database keeps track of case histories and the services used by the clients. The system helps social workers quickly determine what aid clients are eligible for. It allows for the tracking of benefits from more than one program. It can be used to provide automated reports to state and federal agencies.

Videoconferencing

Videoconferencing allow people to work by computer from any location without having to go to the workplace. In the Human Services industry, videoconferencing has been growing in use. Counselors and psychologists are increasingly connecting with clients via online consultations. Family therapists can use videoconferencing applications to connect with their clients who might be in different cities. Social workers, who usually spend more than half of their time outside the office, are also part of this trend. They use computers to complete paperwork at home rather than commuting to the office every day. The ability to work remotely has allowed for more productivity in this industry.

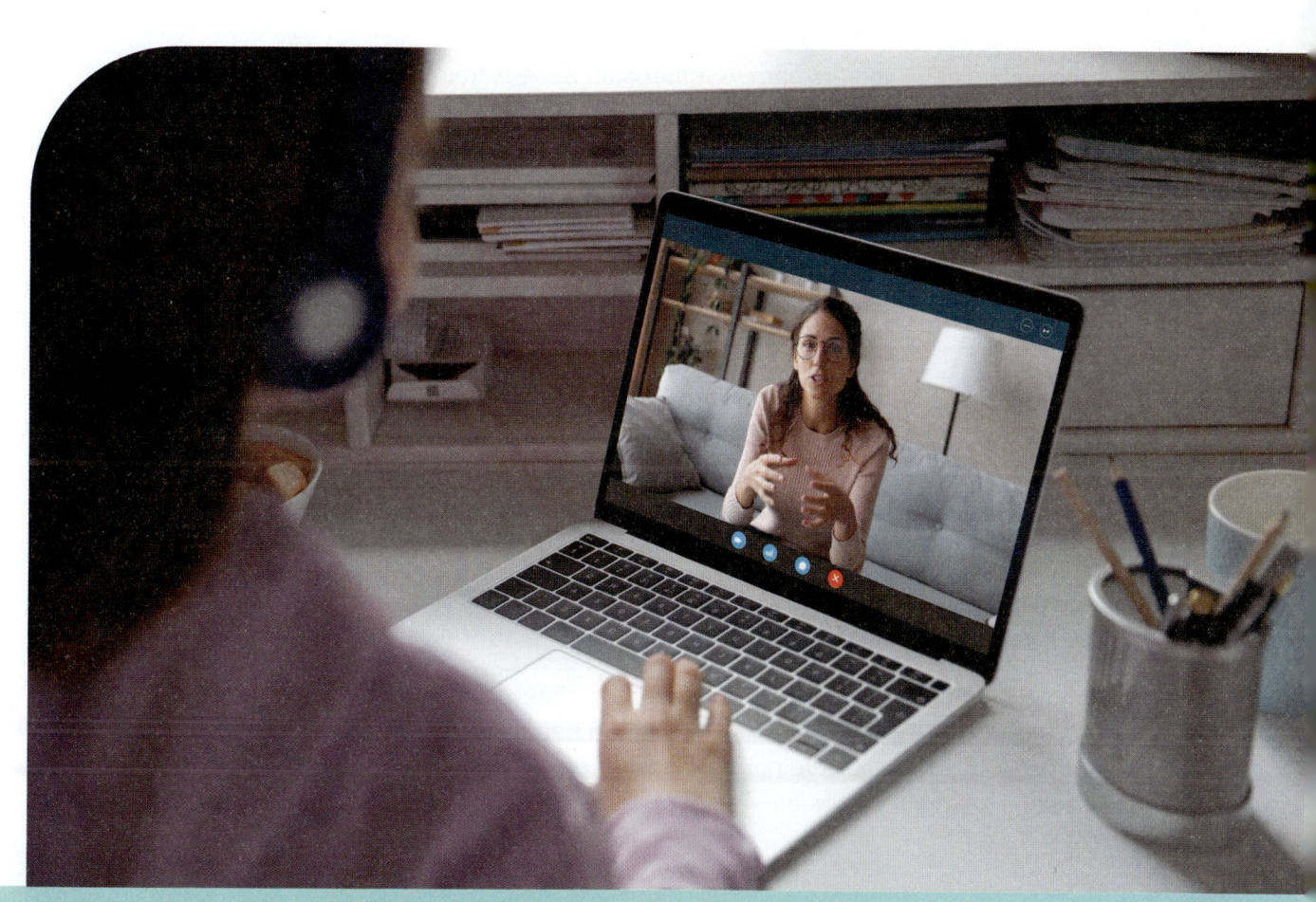

Contemporary Issues in the Human Services Industry

Many social issues affect the Human Services industry. The increased demand for child care, government budgetary problems, and an aging population will continue to shape the industry for years to come.

Issues in Early Childhood Development and Services

Many studies have shown that children can get a head start by going to preschool. As a result, many people have asked for more access to preschool. Some say that preschool is particularly important for children from low-income homes, who are at high risk for having difficulty in school. The federal government has two federally funded programs, Early Start and Head Start, which provide funds to address these issues. These programs provide preschool for children in under-served communities.

While the demand for quality child care is rising, child care centers have many problems. A key issue is the lack of staff. This is caused in part by the low wages most child care workers earn. Another staff issue is training. In the past, these workers were not required to have academic degrees or even certification. This has led to calls for upgrading the training of these workers.

Issues in Counseling and Mental Health Services

The importance of mental health is receiving increased attention. More people are seeking treatment for psychological disorders than before. Obtaining this care is often difficult, however.

Online counseling is a new option in this field. Counselors and psychologists may use text messages, e-mail, or other forms of Internet communication. This form of counseling helps people who have difficulty getting to a counselor's office. The American Counseling Association accepts online counseling as a useful approach for some clients. Its code of ethics tells counselors to advise a client if they think online counseling is not the right approach for that person.

Issues in Personal Care Services

One key issue in the Personal Care path is the growing interest in environmentally friendly products. Today, more people are demanding beauty products that do not harm the environment and that have not been tested on animals. Many cosmetics, skin care, and hair care companies have begun selling organic products.

476 Chapter 15 • Human Services

Issues in Consumer Services

Workers in the Consumer Services path have felt the tremendous impact of the Internet's rising popularity. Use of the Internet has created new social, economic, and legal issues. The ease of access to personal information has increased the number of identity theft victims. Identity theft is the illegal use of personal information gathered from sources such as bank accounts and credit cards. The Federal Trade Commission reports that more than 33 percent of Americans have faced an identity theft attempt, which is nearly three times higher than in other countries.

Another consumer issue relates to electronic health-care records. Consumer Services workers are responsible for safeguarding patients' records from hackers trying to obtain personal information for illegal use.

Demographic Trends in Human Services Industry

Many jobs in the Human Services industry—from cosmetologist to child care worker to social worker—are held mainly by women. Some women have chosen these professions because they offer flexible schedules and the chance to work with other women. Some organizations are seeking to attract more men to this industry. They believe that bringing more male workers into the Human Services industry will provide young boys with strong male role models in nontraditional professions. Some community colleges offer programs for men in nontraditional careers to promote gender equity in the industry.

15-6 Essential Question Reflection

So, let us revisit our essential question:

What factors affect trends in Human Services?

Based on what you learned in this section, please answer this question in detail.

Chapter 16: Education & Training

❓ Essential Questions

By the end of the chapter, you will be able to answer the following questions:

- **16-1** What types of opportunities are available in Education & Training?
- **16-2** Which opportunities may be right for you?
- **16-3** How can I match my skills & interests with the right job?
- **16-4** What training & education is needed for a job in Education & Training?
- **16-5** What are typical work environments in Education & Training?
- **16-6** What factors affect trends in Education & Training?

Chapter Topics

- **16-1** Education & Training Today
- **16-2** Education & Training Jobs
- **16-3** Building a Career in Education & Training
- **16-4** Education and Training for Education & Training Opportunities
- **16-5** Working Conditions in the Education & Training Industry
- **16-6** Trends in Education & Training

16-1 Education & Training Today

How did you learn to read a book or a map? Who taught you to solve addition problems or drive a car? You learned most of what you can do from a teacher.

A teacher can be anyone who passes on skills or knowledge to someone else. A father can teach his daughter to ride a bike. A computer systems manager at a corporation can teach a CEO how to use a computer program. People can even teach themselves through self-study.

Education is the process of teaching and learning. It can be formal and take place inside a classroom, or it can be informal and take place outside a classroom. Training is also a part of education. Training is education in a specific skill or professional area, such as computer programming or auto repair. Students in training courses are usually adults.

Educators and trainers serve students from infancy all the way to adulthood. Most children and adults learn in a school or home classroom. It is also common for students to learn online or to participate in distance learning.

16-1 Essential Question

As you read this section, keep this question in mind:

What types of opportunities are available in Education & Training?

Career Journeys in Education & Training

There are three major paths where your journey in the Education & Training industry might be shaped. People often move in and out of different paths. Each path contains a group of careers requiring similar skills as well as similar certifications or education. This career cluster is divided into three main career paths:

- Teaching and Training
- Professional Support Services
- Administration and Administrative Support

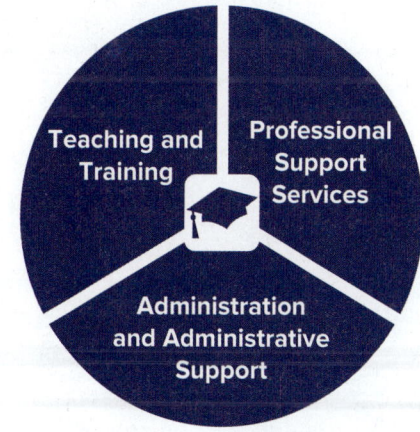

Education and training could not take place without teachers and teacher assistants. However, many other people contribute to the Education & Training industry. Principals lead and oversee teachers and school communities. Superintendents put educational policies and standards into place for entire districts. Education researchers study teaching and learning methods and make suggestions to improve schools. All these educators depend on one another to make education and training successful.

Teaching and Training

The Teaching and Training path includes teachers, trainers, teacher assistants, and child care workers in a variety of settings:

- **Early Childhood Education:** Preschools, nursery schools, and day care institutions
- **K–12 Education:** Public, charter, home, and private schools from kindergarten through grade 12
- **Postsecondary Education:** Public and private colleges and universities
- **Athletic Education:** School and community athletic programs
- **Corporate Education:** Corporate training departments or programs
- **Adult Education:** Trade/technical schools and adult education institutions

While these settings share many features, they each require somewhat different workers. Child care workers and nursery schoolteachers care for and instruct young children in day-care centers and nursery schools. Their directors lead these centers and schools. Child life specialists help families at clinics and hospitals to cope with medical treatment.

Classroom teachers and teacher assistants at all levels provide knowledge and understanding to their students. In kindergarten, they teach the basics of letters and numbers, as well as important life skills. In college or trade schools, they teach complex academic and skill-related subjects. Coaches train athletes in sports fundamentals, and they help build teamwork and good sporting behavior. Human resources trainers work for companies. They provide workshop sessions to improve workers' job skills and conduct new employee orientation. Corporate trainers instruct workers in everything from time management and teamwork to specialized computer use.

Most jobs in this path require patience, organization, and the ability to explain topics and problems in various ways. Teachers and teacher assistants must usually be certified, or licensed, to work with students. At high schools, colleges, or corporate/career training schools, teachers need expertise in a subject area, such as art or math.

Child care workers usually need a minimum of a high school diploma. Those who work with young children should understand child development, behavior, and nutrition. They must have the energy and ability to interact with children and maintain a positive attitude.

Everyone in a classroom setting should know safety and first-aid procedures. Finally, teachers, trainers, aides, and child care workers must first and foremost enjoy interacting with students.

Professional Support Services

The Professional Support Services path includes the widest variety of jobs in the Education & Training industry. It includes many services that are essential for student success. These services are provided to schools, teachers, students, and parents. They can be loosely grouped into three main categories:

Student support professionals work directly with students and their families to provide special services. Speech pathologists, for example, provide speech or language therapy to students who have difficulty speaking. Social workers act as links between educators, parents, and students. They identify and address personal and family issues that may affect a student's school performance.

Program advisors coordinate support services available to students. For example, financial aid advisors help students or their families determine how they will pay for education. Career counselors help students evaluate various career paths and the schools where they get the education these career paths require. Placement counselors help students find jobs.

Support administrators run programs that serve students and teachers. They may coordinate training programs. They may oversee a school's media and technical equipment. For example, they may make sure that computers or sound systems are available to students and teachers.

Professional support services workers in the Education & Training industry need empathy, patience, and interpersonal skills. Most support professionals are highly specialized. Many have advanced education or training. School psychologists, for example, generally complete master's or doctoral degrees. These degrees combine study with several hundred hours of experience with patients. Social workers, speech pathologists, and counselors must be able to deal with difficult problems. Program advisors and coordinators must know the specific language and features of their program. For example, a distance-education coordinator must be skilled at using technology. A financial aid advisor must know about bank loans as well as government aid programs.

Administration and Administrative Support

Like companies, schools need someone to manage them. The Administration and Administrative Support path includes a great variety of jobs related to this type of management.

School principals and superintendents coordinate staff and policy within a school or a school district. These administrators oversee the use and maintenance of school buildings. They decide how to spend funds. Academic deans and department chairs work for colleges or universities. They coordinate administrative duties and assist school presidents in shaping policies.

Instructional media designers create learning materials for print and for electronic media. Curriculum developers work with educational planners to create a curriculum. The curriculum must meet the learning objectives required by state education standards. Assessment and test-measurement specialists figure out the best way to test students' skills and knowledge.

Skills necessary for success in education administration vary by job. But all these jobs require an understanding of the teaching and learning process. Higher-level administrators often have a master's or doctoral degree in their field or in educational administration. Curriculum developers, instructional media designers, and test specialists need excellent analytical skills. They need the ability to work with large amounts of data. Instructional media designers need well-developed technical skills. Principals, deans, and other administrators must have excellent communication and interpersonal skills to deal with students, parents, and staff.

Education & Training Future Outlook

With more children and adults enrolling in school, the outlook for the Education & Training industry is strong. The large number of people retiring will create many opportunities for workers in this industry.

Table 16.1: Job Forecast for a Sample of Education & Training Opportunities

Occupation	Expected Growth Rate
Elementary School Teachers	1 – 5%
Teacher Assistants	5 – 10%
Preschool Teachers	15% or higher
Special Education Teachers	1 – 5%
High School Teachers	5 – 10%
Coaches and Scouts	15% or higher
Child, Family, and School Social Workers	5 – 10%
Educational, Vocational, and School Counselors	10 – 15%
Instructional Coordinators	5 – 10%
Distance-Learning Coordinators	5 – 10%
Administrative Services and Facilities Managers	5 – 10%
Instructional Coordinators, Curriculum Developers, Test Specialists	5 – 10%
Administrative Assistants	-5 – 10%
Principals	1 – 5%
Superintendents	5 – 10%
Postsecondary Education Administrators	5 – 10%

Source: *O*Net*

16-1 Essential Question Reflection

So, let us revisit our essential question:

What types of opportunities are available in Education & Training?

Based on what you learned in this section, please answer this question in detail.

Practice 16-1

Skills Practice

When reading documents, such as an article about trends in special needs education, workers in the Education & Training industry need to be able to identify the main idea. They must also find details supporting the main idea. The main idea tells what the document is about. Details provide more information that helps explain the main idea. **Practice this skill!**

From: District Superintendent's Office

To: All District 108 Personnel

In light of recent events and increasing concerns from parents, students, and staff members, this Friday's upcoming in-service will focus on crisis response and prevention planning. ALL DISTRICT 108 PERSONNEL are required to attend this training, with no exceptions.

Training will begin at 8:00 a.m. and last until 4:00 p.m., with a lunch break scheduled from 12:00–1:00 p.m. Training will be held at the south campus high school in the main auditorium. Lunch will be provided, but attendees will also have the option to leave campus to eat.

We will have two scheduled presenters, both of whom specialize in preparation and planning for disasters and crises. If you are unable to attend the training for any reason, please contact Laura in the District Office immediately.

1. You are an administrative assistant at a large urban high school in District 108. You receive this e-mail in your inbox Monday morning. What is the main idea of this e-mail?

    A. Parents, students, and staff are concerned about crisis planning.

    B. All district employees are required to attend the in-service training on Friday.

    C. Training will run from 8 a.m. to 4 p.m., with a one-hour break.

    D. There will be two presenters at the training who specialize in disasters.

    E. Laura is the appropriate contact for anyone unable to attend the training on Friday.

2. You had planned to go out to lunch with a friend this Friday. You want to coordinate the details so you can use your lunch break to meet. Where will you be on that day?

    A. the Superintendent's office

    B. the north campus high school

    C. the south campus high school

    D. off-campus

    E. the District Office

To access more problems that will help you grow professional skills and are real-world examples in Education & Training, go online.

16-2 Education & Training Jobs

There are jobs at all skill levels in the Education & Training industry. If you pursue a career in this industry, you might find yourself assisting a teacher in a classroom, training workers, or managing an entire school district.

> **16-2 Essential Question**
>
> **As you read this section, keep this question in mind:**
> *Which opportunities may be right for you?*

Fastest-Growing Occupation:

Coaches and Scouts

- Work together to teach and evaluate amateur or professional athletes
- Need extensive knowledge of their sport

Fast Facts:
> **Annual Openings:** 39,900
> **Median Annual Wage:** $38,970
> **Education Needed:** Bachelor's degree – although some positions may not require formal education
> **Other:** Extensive knowledge of the sport is often necessary and salary may vary greatly.

Occupation Making a Difference With Young Students:

Preschool Teachers

- Educate and care for children younger than five years old
- Work in a fun and fast-paced environment
- Are creative and hands-on during daily activities.

Fast Facts:
> **Employment:** 483,000
> **Annual Openings:** 63,100
> **Median Annual Wage:** $30,000
> **Education Needed:** Varies based on each state — typically requires an associate degree or higher
> **Other:** On-the-job training and other certifications are often necessary.

Occupation Where You Develop Instructional Material:

Instructional Coordinators

- Oversee school curriculums and the standards that need to be taught
- Provide support to classroom teachers by instructing them on classroom management strategies
- Create materials that are then implemented into classrooms

Fast Facts:
> **Employment:** 205,700
> **Annual Openings:** 20,900
> **Median Annual Wage:** $63,740
> **Education Needed:** Master's degree and teaching experience

Occupation Where You Oversee School Operations and Activities:

Elementary, Middle, and High School Principals

- Oversee all school operations
- Counsel staff, students, and parents to ensure a productive learning environment
- Hire and evaluate teachers, and provide support when needed

Fast Facts:
Employment: 292,200
Annual Openings: 23,500
Median Annual Wage: $98,420
Education Needed: Master's degree and certifications
Other: The position may also require previous teaching experience.

Great Job! – High School Diploma Needed:

Paraeducators or Teaching Assistants

- Assist the licensed teacher by giving students additional attention or instruction as needed
- Translate content for students to understand better
- Help teacher keep record of attendance and grades
- Monitor students' comprehension of lessons

Fast Facts:

Employment: 1,235,100

Annual Openings: 62,100

Median Annual Wage: $29,360

Did You Know: Paraprofessionals are the backbone of the classroom and can make a huge impact on students.

> ### 16-2 Essential Question Reflection
>
> **So, let us revisit our essential question:**
>
> *Which opportunities may be right for you?*
>
> Based on what you learned in this section, please answer this question in detail.

Case Study: School and Career Counselors

Also called: Advisors, College Admissions Advisors

What do they do?

- Work in public and private schools to help students build their academic and social skills
- Advise people on how to choose a career path

What would you do?

- Help students in high school decide their next step into a new career or higher education
- Advise someone who is deciding to change career paths
- Discuss social or academic concerns with students, and help them to develop a plan to address them
- Collaborate with families and teachers to build student plans and goals

What do you need to know?

Communications
Family communication
Interpersonal communication

Business
Customer service

Arts and Humanities
English language
Learning and behavior development

What skills do you need?

Analytical Skills
Be able to interpret data and student records
Evaluate data and assessments to help match interests with new career opportunities

Compassion
Be patient and empathetic with your students and clients

Listening and Speaking Skills
Give your full attention to the speaker
Practice active listening to help your clients find solutions to their problems
Communicate effectively with clients and students
Be able to express information and new ideas in a way that your audience fully understands

490 Chapter 16 • Education & Training

What abilities must you be good at?

Verbal
    Listen to and understand what people say
    Read and understand what is written
    Effectively communicate new ideas

Ideas and Logic
    Observe cilents' behavior and identify problems
    Follow procedures when interacting with clients and students

Attention
    Give your full attention to the issue at hand

Who does well in this occupation?

People interested in this work like activities that include practical, hands-on problems and solutions.

What educational level is needed?

- Master's degree, most often in counseling or psychology

Practice 16-2

Skills Practice

The details in workplace documents are not always clearly stated. For example, a career counselor may have to draw conclusions about what a student's interests and abilities are from a brief survey. It may sometimes be necessary to infer, or make a logical guess, when a detail is suggested rather than stated. **Practice this skill!**

TODAY'S ACTIVITY: MAKING A WOVEN PLACEMAT

1. Select one piece of large, pre-cut paper in any color you want. Choose eight to ten different colored strips to weave into your pre-cut paper.
2. Push the first strip into the first open space on your large paper so that it disappears behind the pre-cut paper.
3. Pull the paper back through the next cut space so that it is now in front of the large paper.
4. Repeat all the way from one side to the other so that the strip alternates going behind the large paper, then in front, then behind.
5. Weave a second strip of colored paper next to the first strip, but this time start from below the large paper. Continue going over and under to create a pattern opposite that of the first strip.
6. Remember to push your colored strips close together so there are no gaps. This will help strengthen your placement.
7. Repeat until all the strips have been woven into the large paper with alternating patterns.

1. In your job as a living history interpreter, or guide, you lead activities with students who are coming to visit the historical farmhouse where you work. Today, you are helping visitors with a weaving project. Based on this handout, how many large pieces of paper will each student need for one placemat?

   A. 1
   B. 2
   C. 5
   D. 8
   E. 18

2. Which step alerts you to check to make sure students have not woven their strips too far apart?

   A. step 1
   B. step 3
   C. step 4
   D. step 6
   E. step 7

Skills Practice

When reading workplace graphics, such as a flow chart to determine eligibility for special education services, education and training workers must know what information to look for. The key information may be in one or more graphics. Workers must be able to sift through unimportant or distracting information to find what is needed. **Practice this skill!**

Nutrition Facts

Serving Size: 1 ounce   Servings in bag

Amount Per Serving

Calories 155   Calories from Fat 93

% Daily Value*

Total Fat 11g	16%
Staurated Fat 3g	15%
Trans Fat	
Cholesterol 0mg	0%
Sodium 148 mg	6%
Total Carbohydrate 14g	5%
Dietart Fiber 1g	5%
Sugars 1g	
Protein 2g	

Vitamin A	0%	☐ Vitamin C		9%
Calcium	1%	☐ Iron		3%

*Percent Daily Values are based on a 2,000 calorie diet. Your daily values may be higher or lower depending on your calorie needs.

3. As a family and consumer sciences teacher in a high school, you always include a unit on reading food labels for nutritional information. According to this label that you have provided to your students, how many grams of sugar does this food contain per serving?

   A. 1
   B. 4
   C. 14
   D. 93
   E. 148

4. Which nutritional component makes up 6% of this food's daily value?

   A. total fat
   B. cholesterol
   C. sodium
   D. dietary fiber
   E. vitamin C

494   Chapter 16 • Education & Training

16-3 Building a Career in Education & Training

An elementary school teacher may begin their career by student teaching. After years of classroom teaching, they may become a principal or another kind of administrator. Some teachers gain specialized training and move into careers such as special education or instructional design.

16-3 Essential Question

As you read this section, keep this question in mind:

How can I match my skills & interests with the right job?

Are You More Interested in Working With Data, People, or Things?

When considering the journey you will take to reach your career goals, it is important to consider your skills & interests. Most careers offer the opportunity to work with a combination of data, people, and things. Working with data involves the evaluation of information. A job that focuses on people will be based on human relationships. Working with things involves using objects, such as tools, equipment, and machines. Most jobs focus mainly on one of these. Education researchers work with data. Teachers work with people. Media specialists work mostly with things. When planning your career path, consider what balance of data, people, and things you want in a career.

Careers That Involve Working With Data

Examples of working with data in the Education & Training industry include preparing lesson plans, grading tests and essays, and planning school activities.

Most jobs in education require you to handle large amounts of data, such as attendance records, student grades, or research results. School administrators work with data when they create and manage school budgets. They must be able to account for all the money spent. Coaches keep track of their team's statistics for the season. They keep team records, such as games won and lost. They also keep individual player records, such as the number of home runs per season. Teachers and trainers evaluate their students' data to make informed decisions on the curriculum they teach to improve learning. All teachers, regardless of what subject they focus on, work with data in the form of concepts and ideas.

Careers That Involve Working With People

Every job in the Education & Training industry requires interacting with others. Examples of working with people as a teacher include leading a class or a training session, holding conferences with parents or students, and working one-on-one with a student, a coworker, or an employee. All these activities require strong communication skills.

Most Education & Training jobs enable you to spend a great deal of time working with people. For example, corporate trainers usually work for large corporations and instruct employees in-person and virtually on skills needed to promote their growth and development. Principals spend time meeting with staff members to help them with personnel issues. College professors teach classes, mentor graduate students and less-experienced faculty members, and meet with colleagues in their discipline. Child care workers interact with both children and parents.

Careers That Involve Working With Things

Working with things involves designing, creating, using, and repairing objects such as machines, buildings, cameras, art projects, and musical instruments. Examples of working with things in the Education & Training industry include setting up and operating a computer system, organizing library materials, and conducting laboratory experiments.

Some careers in Education & Training involve working with things. A corporate trainer who teaches computer classes works with computer hardware and equipment. Physical education trainers show people how to use sports equipment. Paraeducators or teacher assistants help with student instruction and keep supplies in order. Biology teachers work with plants and other objects from the natural world.

> **16-3 Essential Question Reflection**
>
> So, let us revisit our essential question:
>
> *How can I match my skills & interests with the right job?*
>
> Based on what you learned in this section, please answer this question in detail.

16-4 Education and Training for Education & Training Opportunities

Jobs in the Education & Training industry include a wide variety of different levels of education. Some jobs require higher levels of education and certificates. Some jobs in the field require more hands-on experience or training.

One good way to research careers is job shadowing. Job shadowing is following a worker on the job for a few days. This can help you learn whether a career matches your abilities and interests. When you shadow someone, observe closely and ask questions. What academic and workplace skills do you need for this job? Can you acquire these skills in school or through on-the-job training?

16-4 Essential Question

As you read this section, keep this question in mind:

What training & education is needed for a job in Education & Training?

Training and Education for the Education & Training Industry

The level of training necessary to succeed in the education and training industry varies by career. Jobs can be categorized into three groups—those requiring little or no training, those requiring some training, and those requiring advanced training.

Jobs Requiring Little or No Training

Most jobs in the Education & Training industry require a college degree. However, there are a few exceptions. Some schools, such as those with a high number of at-risk students, require that paraeducators or teacher assistants have some college experience. Other schools might accept a paraeducator or teacher assistant with a high school diploma and experience working with children. Requirements vary by school and by job. Paraeducators must often pass a background check. Many states also require first-aid and safety training for people who work with children.

Many employers look for employees who have completed at least some college. You can find courses and even associate degree programs for teacher assistant training at many community colleges. Some teacher assistants pursue a degree while gaining on-the-job experience.

Jobs Requiring Some Training

Most jobs in Education & Training require at least a bachelor's degree. For example, in most states, teachers need a bachelor's degree. They must also complete a teacher-training program and pass a certification exam approved by the state. These programs include classes in educational methods and in an academic subject area. This means that a high school French teacher takes courses in educational theory and practice. They also take advanced courses in the French language.

Teacher-training programs may include a supervised period of student teaching. Student teachers work with experienced, licensed teachers. They observe the teacher in the classroom. The mentor teacher helps them to design lesson plans before teaching a class on their own.

Many states are becoming more flexible in their requirements. Some states have programs where teachers can take ownership of a classroom while they continue to work on their certifications and licenses. Private school teachers are usually not subject to state requirements.

Corporate trainers usually have a bachelor's degree. Many employers look for candidates with degrees in human resources or personnel administration.

Employers may also hire experienced candidates who have only a high school diploma or an associate degree. Corporate trainers usually receive considerable on-the-job training. A background in human resources, instructional technology, or education is also useful.

Jobs Requiring Advanced Training

Some jobs in Education & Training require a master's or doctoral degree. School counselors, reading specialists, school administrators, and college faculty, for example, almost always have master's or doctoral degrees. Many teachers attend graduate school after teaching for several years. For example, a special education teacher may pursue a master's degree to become a reading specialist.

A master's or doctoral degree in educational administration helps teachers advance to administrative positions such as department head, assistant principal, principal, or superintendent. License requirements for administrators vary from state to state.

To teach at the college or university level, you need to have at least a master's degree. Most college and university faculty, however, have a PhD in their field of specialization, such as English literature or biology. To earn a PhD, students complete an average of six to eight years of course work and independent research after completing college. After passing a series of exams, doctoral candidates write a lengthy paper based on original research.

Table 16.2: Training Required for Jobs in This Industry

Level of Training	Job Title
Little or No Formal Training	Child Care Workers Nannies Paraeducators or Teacher Assistants Tutors
Some Training	Coaches and Scouts Preschool Teachers Elementary School Teachers Middle School Teachers Secondary School Teachers Corporate Trainers
Advanced Training	Education Administrators Instructional Coordinators Librarians School Psychologists Postsecondary Teachers Graduate Teaching Assistants

Licensing

All teachers in the public school system must have a teaching license in addition to an undergraduate or graduate degree. A license is official recognition by a state government that an individual meets state teaching requirements.

Licensing requirements vary from state to state. Most states require thorough knowledge of the subject to be taught and minimum scores on various standardized tests. Some states require that candidates have completed an education program at an accredited school and a supervised period of teaching practice. Most states require teachers to renew their licenses regularly. To do so, teachers must prove that they have completed a minimum number of hours in professional development courses.

For the most part, teachers are licensed to teach specific age groups. Secondary teachers are usually certified in their subject area as well. For example, an elementary school teacher is licensed to teach all subjects of the primary grades. A secondary school teacher may be licensed to teach a specific content area, such as social studies, for grades 7 to 12.

When there are teacher shortages, some school systems hire teachers who have bachelor's degrees in needed subjects but not licenses. Such teachers are typically granted temporary licenses, but they must complete a state certification program within a certain period. Sometimes schools require teachers to teach subjects they are not certified in. For example, unusually high enrollment in science courses may prompt a school's administration to ask a math teacher to teach a science class for a semester.

Teachers who meet all their state's requirements for a particular teaching field can obtain national certification. Certification recognizes that an individual has qualifications beyond licensing. It helps teachers move from school to school because most states and districts allow certified teachers to carry over their license from another state. Some districts help teachers pay for the course work they need to complete for certification. Fully licensed, certified teachers and those with advanced degrees may earn higher salaries.

Professional Skills

Communication Skills Being able to communicate effectively is important in the Education & Training industry. For example, teachers rely on communication every day and must have well-developed communication skills. They must teach their daily lessons and inform their students of upcoming due dates. They may be required to send weekly emails or reach out to parents if one of their students is failing their class. Being able to effectively communicate is critical to a teacher's success. Strong relationships with coworkers and fellow educators are founded on good communication. A principal must work to develop strong relationships with their staff members to keep the school morale high.

Listening Skills Listening is the foundation of learning. Teachers and other educators must listen carefully to student questions. Good listening helps educators and trainers understand other people's ideas and points of view.

Problem-Solving Skills Employers value workers who can spot problems and take action to find solutions. Solving problems requires creativity and self-reliance. A teacher, career counselor, or college president will be called upon to solve problems. For example, a career counselor at a high school may be asked to study data-related to graduation rates and provide a solution to address the number of students who do not earn their high school diploma.

Technology Skills Many workers in the Education & Training industry use computers. For example, teachers may post assignments and feedback for students. They may communicate with students, parents, and other teachers by e-mail. They may conduct research or use classroom computers to present information. As the industry comes to rely more and more on distance learning and instructional technology, being comfortable with technology will help teachers advance in their career.

Decision-Making Skills The ability to gather and analyze information rapidly is important to careers in the Education & Training industry. It's also important to think clearly under pressure. Teachers, coaches, resource coordinators, and labor relations managers are likely to encounter problems that require them to make quick decisions. Being able to do so calmly and effectively is an important job skill.

Organizing and Planning Skills Planning requires the ability to set goals and to visualize the sequence of steps leading up to these goals. A social worker needs to guide students and families through various processes. Doing so effectively requires excellent organization and planning skills.

Teamwork Skills Teamwork is key in the Education & Training industry. Most workers in this industry collaborate with a wide variety of people. For example, everyone in a school or college, from the principal to technology administrators, must work together as a team. This is the only way to deliver top-quality education to students.

Social Skills In the Education & Training industry, almost every job involves interacting with people. Education workers must interact with coworkers, students, families, and members of the community. Social interaction is more than just a simple necessity. The foundation of education is building trusting relationships. Social interaction with coworkers also makes for a more enjoyable work atmosphere. Studies show that between 80 and 85 percent of a person's success in the workforce is due to their social skills.

Adaptability Skills Job descriptions, work environments, and work processes are constantly changing along with technology and consumer preferences. People in the Education & Training industry must constantly adapt to the new ways that students access information. They must incorporate the expanding ways that instruction can be delivered.

16-4 Essential Question Reflection

So, let us revisit our essential question:

What training & education is needed for a job in Education & Training?

Based on what you learned in this section, please answer this question in detail.

16-4 • Education and Training for Education & Training Opportunities

Practice 16-4

Skills Practice

It may be necessary at times to add information to graphics as part of a job in the Education & Training industry. A school counselor may need to fill out student schedules, for example. Knowing how to correctly add information to graphics is an important skill in this industry. **Practice this skill!**

WEEKLY SHOP SAFETY CHECKLIST

Date: _____   Room: _____

Inspection performed by: _____

Questions to Answer	YES	NO	Additional Comments
Are all work areas in the shop in neat and orderly condition?			
Are emergency numbers and procedures clearly posted?			
Is a first aid kit available and stocked?			
Are all rags, oily clothes, and flammable waste items stored in metal, lidded containers?			
Does all equipment with moving parts (belts, sanders, blades, fans) have safety guards in place?			
Is the floor clean, swept, and free of oil spills?			

1. As an industrial technology teacher at a high school, you require your students to conduct weekly safety checks of the shop area. At the start of the school year, you explain the checklist to the class. How would a student note the presence of oil on the floor?

   A. by checking YES for question 1
   B. by checking NO for question 2
   C. by checking NO for question 4
   D. by checking YES for question 5
   E. by checking NO for question 6

2. What should students do if there are items missing from the first aid kit?

   A. check NO and add comments for question 1
   B. check NO and add comments for question 2
   C. check NO and add comments for question 3
   D. check NO and add comments for question 4
   E. check NO and add comments for question 5

To access more problems that will help you grow professional skills and are real-world examples in Education & Training, go online.

16-5 Working Conditions in the Education & Training Industry

When choosing a career path, it is important to know what it is like to work in the industry. Understanding the work environment, hazards, and benefits of a job can help you make informed decisions.

> **16-5 Essential Question**
>
> As you read this section, keep this question in mind:
>
> *What are typical work environments in Education & Training?*

Physical Environment

The physical work environment in Education & Training varies by career and by location. Most school employees spend their days in clean buildings with good lighting and ventilation. Some schools, however, are in older buildings that are too small or that need extensive repairs. In crowded districts, schools may hold some classes in trailers or other temporary buildings. As distance learning expands, education workers may have more workspace options.

Education administrators and many support professionals have private offices. This gives them a space for confidential meetings with staff and students. Corporate trainers generally work in office buildings. Coaches may work outdoors in all kinds of weather.

Work Hours

The work hours for jobs in the Education & Training industry vary greatly. Many teaching jobs offer attractive work hours and generous vacation time during the summer. However, educators are also required to make a substantial commitment of personal time.

Public School Teachers

Most public school employees work ten months per year and enjoy two months off during the summer. Day care workers usually work year-round. Most schools in the United States operate between August and June. Some school districts now use a year-round school calendar. These schools take short breaks every few months. Other schools offer optional summer school programs for some of their students.

Most teachers work more than 40 hours a week. They spend the hours during the school day working with students. Additional hours are spent working at home or at school on other tasks. Teachers spend time on administrative duties such as correcting papers, creating lesson plans, and contacting parents. They may spend time doing research or continuing their education. The working hours of distance learning teachers can be very flexible.

Other School Staff

Nearly half of all paraeducators or teacher assistants work part-time. Adult educators may frequently work part-time, often in the evenings. Some of these teachers hold other full-time jobs during the regular workday. Administrators and their assistants, even at schools on ten-month schedules, usually work year-round. University and college faculty may teach classes for 12 to 16 hours a week. They also attend staff or department meetings and hold regular office hours. Most professors spend many hours each week on research.

Human Resources and Corporate Trainers

Most workers in human resources and corporate training work a standard 40-hour work week. Those who travel to lead training sessions at various locations may work longer or unusual hours. Those who recruit and interview job candidates may need to travel to a variety of locations for job fairs. If a job involves conflict resolution, unusually long hours can be required. Technology is making some of these tasks easier to accomplish at a distance or on flexible schedules.

Distance-Learning Coordinator

Along with database administrators and technology support administrators, education workers with responsibility for technology may need to work unusual hours. Students, faculty, and staff may ask for assistance with technology systems or equipment at all hours. Support workers may need to answer questions or provide that support, regardless of the time of day.

Essential Physical Activities

Little strenuous physical activity is required in most Education & Training careers. Physical education teachers and coaches, however, often perform strenuous activities. Many paraeducators or teacher assistants work with special education students who need help moving around the classroom and the school.

Elementary school teachers and paraeducators may spend time watching their students play at recess in all kinds of weather. All classroom teachers spend most of their school day on their feet. They stand in the front of the room or walk around the classroom to check students' work and answer questions.

Hazard and Environmental Dangers

Job safety must be a priority in any industry, including Education & Training. The Occupational Safety and Health Administration (OSHA) is the agency of the federal government that sets job safety standards and inspects job sites. Twenty-six states also run their own OSHA programs. OSHA inspectors check that all safety laws are being followed. They make sure that working processes and conditions are safe.

Injuries and Illnesses

Overall, the education and training industry is a safe industry to work in. The average number of cases of work-related injuries and illnesses in education was 5 per 100 workers in 2020. This means that 5 percent of workers reported on-the-job injuries or illnesses.

16-5 Essential Question Reflection

So, let us revisit our essential question:

What are typical work environments in Education & Training?

Based on what you learned in this section, please answer this question in detail.

16-6 Trends in Education & Training

The Education & Training industry is constantly evolving. New approaches to teaching, methods of delivery, and contemporary issues all contribute to these changes.

16-6 Essential Question

As you read this section, keep this question in mind:

What factors affect trends in Education & Training?

Technology in the Education & Training Industry

Technology such as the Internet, messaging tools, computers, smartphones and tablets, and social media have dramatically expanded the learning environment. These new technologies bring real-world information into the classroom. They allow learners and teachers to communicate more effectively. Presentation equipment, such as collaborative cloud-based applications and video recording software, gives teachers and trainers more ways to present material. In addition, more and more students and teachers are taking advantage of distance learning.

Internet and Computers in the Classroom

Technology has had a huge impact on education, and it will have an increasing impact in the future. School districts may provide students with laptop computers, classroom computers, or even provide computer labs. Students can use the computers to take notes, generate reports or multimedia presentations, complete coursework, and do research on the Internet.

The Internet has provided teachers and students with easy access to a wealth of information. There is an ever-expanding variety of educational software and applications available.

Lesson plans, assignments, and schedules can be posted for students and parents on school websites and virtual classrooms. Homework can be started at school and completed at home. Students who are absent can upload their work for their teachers. Families and schools can exchange questions and send updates about things such as weather-related closings. Teachers can engage students through social media, e-mail, and video chat sites. Groups can collaborate on team projects from home.

Smartphones and Tablets

Smartphones perform many functions of a computer. Tablet computers offer these functions on screens that are larger than smartphone screens. These devices allow students and teachers more portable Internet access. They expand the classroom and the teaching experience. Software companies are producing more and more applications, or "apps," for mobile computing. An increasing number of apps are educational.

Distance Learning

Distance learning occurs when the students and the teacher are at different locations. This type of learning has taken place for decades through correspondence courses. Today, however, the Internet has by far become the most common delivery method of this form of education.

Students across the country and across the globe gain equal access to educational opportunities through distance learning. A student in New Jersey, for example, can take a class from a university in California without leaving home. Students who live in isolated rural areas can access distant resources by taking a virtual museum tour. Families who choose to home school can access course work and instruction through distance learning. Students with disabilities that challenge physical attendance can gain greater access to education. At the postsecondary level, distance learning can help learners balance work and school.

In difficult economic times, distance learning offers school districts ways to cut costs and manage crowding. Many states report spending significantly less per pupil for distance learners than for students in brick-and-mortar schools. In schools where teacher or building shortages lead to overcrowding, distance learning can help.

Contemporary Issues in the Education & Training Industry

In the twenty-first century, the concept of a school is changing. Education now takes many forms, from online learning to home schooling. Schedules vary from the traditional ten-month school year to different forms of year-round schooling. Sustainable buildings have changed what brick-and-mortar schools look like and how they function.

School Options

Families and communities are redefining schools and school calendars. Some are choosing to homeschool. Others have formed charter schools. Still others have chosen year-round schooling or schools with a special focus for their children. At traditional schools, green buildings have brought about changes.

Many families choose homeschooling because they feel they can improve the quality of their local schools or offer their children a safer environment. For families with special-needs students, homeschooling offers greater flexibility.

Charter schools are publicly funded schools created by educators and members of the community. At charter schools, educators have the freedom to try new ideas and policies. Some charter schools—and some private schools—have a special focus, such as science or the performing arts.

A growing number of traditional public-school districts now operate on a year-round basis. Supporters argue that year-round schooling is more effective.

Many students will be attending green schools. These schools use resources efficiently and focus on providing productive and healthy learning environments.

Alternative Methods

New teaching methods are changing education. Teachers are incorporating technology into lessons. They are also using technology to support collaborative learning. This approach allows teachers to group students in various ways. Students may work across ability levels, areas of expertise, or geographic locations. Students can video chat and virtually collaborate on the same assignment at the same time. Teachers can collaborate to team-teach or to support one another.

The Law in the Education & Training Industry

Because most schools are publicly funded, local, state, and federal governments make laws related to education. Laws determine the number of days students spend in school, the amount of tuition charged at community colleges, and what curriculum is taught.

In 2015, the government took more action. The next federal K-12 education law implemented was ESSA (Every Student Succeeds Act). ESSA replaced the previous education law, No Child Gets Left Behind. ESSA's focus was to make sure that public schools provide a quality education for all students. Through ESSA, states can form their own education plans which must include detailed descriptions of their set of academic standards, annual testing, goals for academic achievement, as well as a variety of other strategies for supporting and improving struggling schools.

Demographics in the Education & Training Industry

One of today's most significant demographic changes is the increased percentage of Hispanics and Latinos in the U.S. population. According to the U.S. Census Bureau, US residents speak more than 350 languages. Of those who reported that they speak a language other than English, almost two-thirds speak Spanish. Workers in all segments of the Education & Training industry will need to serve the growing Hispanic population. Knowing Spanish will be increasingly useful in all segments of the industry.

Another change is the flexibility in certification that many districts are offering their prospective teachers. With a growing teacher shortage, schools are relaxing their requirements to entice those interested in the education field. Some states are allowing educators to begin teaching once they pass a skills test that measures their knowledge of math, reading, and writing. Other states are allowing people to work on short-term licenses while they are still working within teacher preparation programs.

These factors all improve the job outlook for new workers in the Education & Training industry.

16-6 Essential Question Reflection

So, let us revisit our essential question:

What factors affect trends in Education & Training?

Based on what you learned in this section, please answer this question in detail.

Chapter 17: Law, Public Safety, Corrections, & Security

Chapter Topics

17-1 Law, Public Safety, Corrections, & Security Today

17-2 Law, Public Safety, Corrections, & Security Jobs

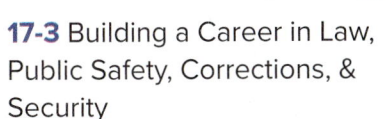

17-3 Building a Career in Law, Public Safety, Corrections, & Security

17-4 Education and Training for Law, Public Safety, Corrections, & Security Opportunities

17-5 Working Conditions in the Law, Public Safety, Corrections & Security Industry

17-6 Trends in Law, Public Safety, Corrections, & Security

Essential Questions

By the end of the chapter, you will be able to answer the following questions:

- **17-1** What types of opportunities are available in Law, Public Safety, Corrections, & Security?
- **17-2** Which opportunities may be right for you?
- **17-3** How can I match my skills & interests with the right job?
- **17-4** What training & education is needed for a job in Law, Public Safety, Corrections, & Security?
- **17-5** What are typical work environments in Law, Public Safety, Corrections, & Security?
- **17-6** What factors affect trends in Law, Public Safety, Corrections, & Security?

513

17-1 Law, Public Safety, Corrections, & Security Today

The law, public safety, corrections, and security industry affects nearly every part of our lives. It provides the foundation of law and order that is needed for a healthy society. We rely on the availability and quick response of law enforcement officers, paramedics, and other public safety workers to help and protect us. We count on lawyers and other judicial workers to defend the innocent and bring the guilty to justice.

Think about the many ways law and public safety officials have affected your life. Perhaps there was a fire in your home and firefighters, police, and paramedics came to your aid. Maybe one day you will serve on a jury and be able to witness lawyers and judges working on a trial? Maybe you felt reassured when you saw the security guards at your local bank? The people of the law, public safety, corrections, and security industry are present throughout the community.

17-1 Essential Question

As you read this section, keep this question in mind:

What types of opportunities are available in Law, Public Safety, Corrections, & Security?

Career Journeys in Law, Public Safety, Corrections, & Security

There are five major paths along which your journey in Law, Public Safety, Corrections, & Security might be shaped. The paths are:

- Law Enforcement Services
- Legal Services
- Correction Services
- Emergency and Fire Management Services
- Security and Protective Services

Each of these paths is related. Legal Services and Correction Services relate primarily to the justice system. Emergency and Fire Management Services focus mainly on public safety. Law Enforcement Services and Security and Protective Services include a combination of justice system and public safety services.

Law Enforcement Services

The Law Enforcement Services path includes employees in a variety of federal, state, county, and city agencies across the United States. Most of these agencies have authority over a certain type of crime or a certain area. People in these occupations enforce the law and protect people in the community. Some examples of careers in this path include police and patrol officers, police detectives, sheriffs, and U.S. marshals.

- **Police and patrol officers** provide protection from theft and physical harm by patrolling neighborhoods and roadways, solving crimes, and building cases against criminals.
- **Police detectives** gather facts and collect evidence for criminal cases.
- **Sheriffs** provide county law enforcement services. They are elected by the citizens of their county. Deputy sheriffs work for the county sheriff. They perform duties like those of an officer in a city police department.
- **US marshals** provide protection for federal courts, federal judges, and federal witnesses. They transport federal prisoners and handle goods seized from criminal activities. They may track down escaped prisoners and people who violate their probation or parole.

Applicants for all jobs in this career path must meet age, education, and personal background requirements. Nearly all applicants in this path must undergo some form of background check. This may include lie-detector tests, drug tests, and criminal record and fingerprint checks. A high school degree or its equivalent is required for most jobs in this path. In addition, some police departments and federal agencies require a college degree.

Legal Services

The United States has two main systems of courts: federal courts and state courts. Both hear civil and criminal cases. Civil law involves disputes, or disagreements, between individuals, such as contract disagreements and divorce.

Occupations in the Legal Services path involve working with the court system. Careers in this path include lawyer, judge, paralegal, and legal secretary. All states require lawyers to be members of the bar, or to be licensed. To qualify for the licensing test, an aspiring lawyer must earn an undergraduate degree and a law degree.

Judges are usually lawyers who are elected or appointed to serve in a specific court. Paralegals perform many of the same functions as lawyers, with some restrictions. They are often required to have formal paralegal training through an associate or bachelor's degree program. Legal secretaries must have knowledge of legal terms and procedures.

Correction Services

The Correction Services path involves the control and treatment of convicted offenders. These careers often involve working with the jail and prison systems. Prisons house convicted offenders who are serving sentences of a year or more. Jails are primarily short-term holding facilities for those who have been arrested or are waiting for a trial. Jails are also used to house convicted offenders who are serving short sentences.

Correctional, parole, and probation officers oversee individuals who have been arrested or convicted of a crime. They also work with people who have been released from jail or prison. Correctional officers guard prisoners and maintain order in jails and prisons. Parole officers help people who have served time in prison return to society. Probation officers work with people who have been spared a jail sentence. In addition to meeting certain educational requirements, applicants for the jobs in this path often have specialized training.

Emergency and Fire Management Services

Occupations in the Emergency and Fire Management Services path include firefighters, fire protection inspectors, emergency dispatchers, and emergency medical technicians (EMTs). Many positions in this path involve working in potentially dangerous situations.

Firefighters provide protection against fires of all kinds. They use heavy equipment, water hoses, and hand tools to fight fires. To become a firefighter, you must pass a written exam along with tests of strength, physical stamina, and agility. Applicants must be at least 18 years old. They must have a high school diploma, or the equivalent. Some firefighters may be required to have a college degree. Most firefighters go through a long period of on-the-job training. With experience, firefighters may become supervisors, captains, or chiefs.

EMTs and paramedics are specially trained medical technicians. They respond to the scene of accidents or crimes. They provide life saving emergency care and quick transportation to hospitals. Formal certification and training is required for all EMTs and paramedics.

Dispatchers respond to 911 calls and send the appropriate services to an emergency scene. Some emergency dispatchers are trained in emergency medical service. These dispatchers can provide medical assistance over the telephone.

Security and Protective Services

The Security and Protective Services path includes a variety of occupations ranging from uniformed security officers (both armed and unarmed) to information security. Careers in this path include lifeguards and ski-patrol personnel. Uniformed security officers are often hired to protect people and property from robberies, fire, and vandalism. They work in public buildings such as museums and banks. They may work for private businesses.

New technology has expanded the Security and Protective Services path beyond traditional uniformed security officers. Computer security specialists and computer forensics specialists focus on the security of digital information. Information security includes careers in information technology (IT) that require expertise in computers and security technology.

Law, Public Safety, Corrections, & Security Future Outlook

The Bureau of Labor Statistics (BLS) projects employment in the Law, Public safety, corrections, and security industry to increase. The increase is expected to result in about 72,600 new jobs over the decade. In addition to new jobs from growth, opportunities arise from the need to replace workers who leave their occupations permanently. About 421,500 openings each year, on average, are projected to come from growth and replacement needs.

Table 17.1: Forecast For Occupations in the Law, Public Safety, Corrections & Security Industry

Occupations	Expected Growth Rate
Paralegals and Legal Assistants	10% – 15%
Police Officers	5% – 10%
Private Detectives and Investigators	1% – 5%
Forest Fire Inspectors and Prevention Specialists	10% – 15%
Forensic Science Technicians	10% – 15%
Fish and Game Wardens	-0 – 5%
Lawyers	5% – 10%
Legislators	1% – 5%
Firefighters	5% – 10%
Dispatchers	1% – 5%
Emergency Medical Technicians	5% – 10%
Security Guards	1% – 5%
Crossing Guards and Flaggers	5% – 10%
Lifeguards	10% – 15%

Source: *Bureau of Labor Statistics (BLS)*

17-1 Essential Question Reflection

So, let us revisit our essential question:

What types of opportunities are available in Law, Public Safety, Corrections, & Security?

Based on what you learned in this section, which field of Law, Public Safety, Security & Corrections is the most interesting to you? Explain in detail.

Practice 17-1

Skills Practice

Workers in law, public safety, corrections, and security need to understand workplace documents that use technical terms and jargon, or industry-specific language. Paralegals, for example, need to understand the terms used in legal documents, such as contracts and wills. They must be able to interpret the meanings of these terms and apply them to the situation at hand. **Practice this skill!**

JURY DUTY GUIDE

To be eligible to serve on a jury, you must be 18 years of age, a U.S. citizen, and a resident of the county for which you have been called. You are considered ineligible for the following reasons:

- You are convicted felon or are under indictment.
- You or someone in your family works for the legislative branch of the local or state government.
- You do not speak, read, or write English.

WHAT HAPPENS NEXT?

If you are found to be eligible, you will be called to the courtroom where the judge will describe the case and introduce the lawyers. You will take an oath and undergo a process called voir dire, in which you will be asked about any knowledge you have and your feelings about the case. If selected, you will be given instructions on when to report for the trial.

AM I ALLOWED TO GO HOME EACH NIGHT?

Typically, jurors are allowed to go home at night. However, in rare cases, a judge may order that a jury be "sequestered" during the trial or while the jury is deliberating. A jury may be sequestered to reduce outside influences. While sequestered, transportation and lodging are provided.

1. As a lawyer, how would you explain **voir dire** to potential jurors?

   A. The lawyers make sure all potential jurors are present.

   B. Potential jurors tell whether they can serve on the jury or not.

   C. The judge asks the jurors to leave the courtroom.

   D. The members of the jury pool promise to be fair.

   E. Potential jurors are interviewed to ensure their impartiality.

2. What is the purpose of a jury being **sequestered**?

   A. to remove jurors who may already know about the case

   B. to allow the judge and lawyers to speak without the jury hearing

   C. to prevent jurors from hearing or seeing outside information about the trial

   D. to keep the jurors close to the court so the trial takes less time

   E. to give the lawyers a chance to see how the jurors behave

To access more problems that will help you grow professional skills and are real-world examples in Law, Public Safety, Security & Corrections, go online.

17-2 Law, Public Safety, Security & Corrections Jobs

You can find jobs at all skill levels that suit a variety of interests in the law, public safety, corrections, and security industry. People interested in public safety can become a police officers, dispatchers, EMTs, or firefighters. Those interested in other paths can become lawyers, paralegals, corrections officers, or security guards. Here, are some common industry jobs and the skills they require.

17-2 Essential Question

As you read this section, keep this question in mind:

Which opportunities may be right for you?

Occupations Where You Can Save Lives:

Lifeguards and Ski Patrol Officers

- Patrol or monitor recreational areas, such as trails, slopes, or swimming areas, on foot, in vehicles, or from towers
- Rescue distressed persons, using rescue techniques and equipment
- Contact emergency medical personnel in case of serious injury

Fast Facts:

Employment: 120,800 employees

Annual Openings: 3,620

Median Annual Wage: $12.32 hourly, $25,630 annual

Education Needed: Certification, no degree required

Paramedics

- Administer drugs, orally or by injection, or perform intravenous procedures
- Administer first-aid treatment or life support care to sick or injured persons in prehospital settings
- Assess nature and extent of illness or injury to establish and prioritize medical procedures

Fast Facts:

Employment: 97,600 employees

Annual Openings: 600

Median Annual Wage: $22.48 hourly, $46,770 annually

Education Needed: Certification, no degree required

Other: To advanced in your career as a paramedic, you may need to obtain an associate degree.

Great Jobs! – High School Diploma Required:

Forest Fire Inspectors & Prevention Specialists

- Relay messages about emergencies, accidents, locations of crew and personnel, and fire hazard conditions
- Conduct wildland firefighting training
- Estimate sizes and characteristics of fires, and report findings to base camps by radio or telephone

Fast Facts:

Employment: 2,900 employees

Annual Openings: 300

Median Annual Wage: $20.48 hourly, $42,600 annually

Other: If you enjoy the outdoors and protecting the environment, you might enjoy this career.

Security Guards

- Lock doors and gates of entrances and exits to secure buildings
- Answer alarms and investigate disturbances
- Monitor and authorize entrance and departure of employees, visitors, and other persons to guard against theft and maintain security of premises

Fast Facts:

Employment: 1,077,700 employees

Annual Openings: 15,450

Median Annual Wage: $15.13 hourly, $31,470 annual

Other: There are opportunities for security guards to work around the clock.

Occupations With a Bright Outlook:

Paralegals and Legal Assistants

- Prepare legal documents, including briefs, pleadings, appeals, wills, contracts, and real estate closing statements, and organize and maintain them in paper or electronic filing systems
- Assist lawyers in preparing for trial by performing tasks such as organizing exhibits
- Investigate facts and law of cases to determine causes of action
- Meet with clients and other professionals to discuss details of case

Fast Facts:

Employment: 352,800 employees

Annual Openings: 4,580

Median Annual Wage: $27.03 hourly, $56,230 annually

Education Needed: Associate degree and certification

Other: This is a great career for those interested in law who do not want to obtain a bachelor's degree.

Private Detectives and Investigators

- Write reports or case summaries to document investigations.
- Conduct private investigations on a paid basis
- Search computer databases, credit reports, public records, tax or legal filings, or other resources to locate persons or to compile information for investigations
- Conduct personal background investigations, such as pre-employment checks, to obtain information about an individual's character, financial status, or personal history
- Expose fraudulent insurance claims or stolen funds

Fast Facts:
Employment: 37,000 employees
Annual Openings: 370
Median Annual Wage: $28.55 hourly, $59,380 annually
Education Needed: Bachelor's degree

17-2 Essential Question Reflection

So, let us revisit our essential question:

Which opportunities may be right for you?

Based on what you learned in this section, please answer this question in detail.

Case Study: Forensic Science Technicians

Also called: Crime Laboratory Analyst, Crime Scene Technician (Crime Scene Tech), CSI (Crime Scene Investigator), Forensic Scientist

What do they do?

- Collect, identify, classify, and analyze physical evidence related to criminal investigations
- Perform tests on weapons or substances, such as fiber, hair, and tissue to determine significance to investigation
- Testify as expert witnesses on evidence or crime laboratory techniques
- Serve as specialists in area of expertise, such as ballistics, fingerprinting, handwriting, or biochemistry

What do you need to know?

Safety and Government
Law and government
Public safety and security

Arts and Humanities
English language

Math and Science
Chemistry

Engineering and Technology
Computers and electronics

What skills do you need?

Basic Skills
Listen to others, do not interrupt, and ask good questions
Read work-related information

Problem Solving
Notice a problem, and figure out the best way to solve it

People and Technology Systems
Think about the pros and cons of different options, and pick the best one
Figure out how a system should work and how changes in the future will affect it

17-2 • Law, Public Safety, Security & Corrections Jobs   525

What abilities must you be good at?

Verbal
  Listen and understand what people say
  Read and understand what is written

Ideas and Logic
  Make general rules or produce answers from lots of detailed information
  Use rules to solve problems

Visual Understanding
  See hidden patterns
  Quickly compare groups of letters, numbers, pictures, or other objects

Hand and Finger Use
  Keep your arm or hand steady

Who does well in this occupation?

People interested in this work like activities that include ideas, thinking, and figuring things out

They do well at jobs that need:
  Attention to detail
  Integrity
  Self-control
  Analytical thinking
  Stress tolerance
  Adaptability/flexibility

What educational level is needed?

- Bachelor's degree or some college

Practice 17-2

Skills Practice

When reading documents, such as an article about trends in security system design, workers in the law, public safety, corrections, and security industry need to be able to identify the main idea. They must also find details supporting the main idea. The main idea tells what the document is about. Details provide more information that helps explain the main idea. **Practice this skill!**

NOTE FROM THE SUPERVISOR

Hi Bill:

I'm sure you're busy, but I need you to do a few extra things on your shift tonight. Paul called in sick, so I wasn't able to take care of everything during the day. Since you will be transitioning to the day shift, it will be good for you to start learning how to do these things anyway.

First, I need you to reset the security system with the new codes. You can find the instructions for how to do this in the top left-hand drawer of your desk. Be sure to reset the codes at the beginning of your shift, because the old codes expire at midnight.

Next, please order the tapes needed for the security cameras. First, check how many tapes we have on hand. We need a total of 28 tapes, so subtract the number we have from 28. Fill out the order form on the desk and fax the order to the number on the form.

I hope I'm not giving you too much to do. If you have an emergency, feel free to give me a call. Good luck!

1. As a mall security officer, you receive this note from your supervisor when you arrive for your shift. What is the main idea of the second paragraph?

    A. You need to do a few extra things on your shift.
    B. You need to reset the security system.
    C. You must reset the codes at the beginning of your shift.
    D. You can find the instructions in the top left-hand drawer.
    E. The old codes expire at midnight.

2. Which detail helps you understand how to order the security tapes?

    A. The instructions are in the top left-hand drawer.
    B. You will be picking up the tapes.
    C. You should fill out the order form on the desk.
    D. You can call in case of an emergency.
    E. Be sure to reset the security codes at the beginning of your shift.

To access more problems that will help you grow professional skills and are real-world examples in Law, Public Safety, Security & Corrections, go online.

17-3 Building a Career in Law, Public Safety, Corrections, & Security

A lawyer's career path begins with four years of undergraduate study followed by three years of law school. During the summer, most law students work as interns. Upon graduation, they must pass a state bar examination. Most new lawyers join law firms. After several years of experience, lawyers may become partners in law firms, or they may start their own firms. Building a career in Law, Public Safety, Corrections, & Security may take lots of hard work and dedication to your occupation.

17-3 Essential Question

As you read this section, keep this question in mind:

How can I match my skills & interests with the right job?

Are You More Interested in Working with Data, People, or Things?

Most careers offer opportunities to work with a combination of data, people, and things. Working with data involves the evaluation of information. Legal assistants, for example, work mainly with data. A job that focuses on people will be based on human relationships. Probation officers work primarily with people. Working with things involves using objects, such as tools, equipment, and machines. Firefighters work mostly with things.

Careers That Involve Working With Data

Examples of working with data in this industry include preparing financial statements and drawing up budgets, researching laws and previous decisions to prepare for court cases, and putting together clues to solve crimes.

Jobs that focus on data are often found in fire departments, police departments, and law firms. Fire investigators may need to go to fires to determine how the blaze started. This requires conducting research, running tests, and collecting and analyzing data. Crime laboratory technicians in police departments perform calculations and make predictions based on data. Security specialists may analyze a security system to make sure it is effective. Judges need to consider complex ideas, documents, and legal principles when making their decisions.

Some managers in law enforcement need to work with data. A state-trooper supervisor, for instance, will study spreadsheets that display crime rates to determine whether current methods of crime prevention are efficient and cost-effective.

Careers That Involve Working With People

Many law, public safety, corrections, and security jobs focus on working with people. Examples of working with people include training new police recruits, mediating conflicts, negotiating with hostage-takers, and counseling a prisoner on probation. All these activities require strong communication skills.

In addition, many of the jobs in this industry involve working closely with others. Paramedics, for example, must supervise and lead teams of EMTs. Firefighters must work together effectively. Police officers, lawyers, and judges must communicate with one another and with people from many different backgrounds.

Careers That Involve Working With Things

Almost all careers in law, public safety, corrections, and security involve working with things. Examples of things that people in this industry work with include crime scene evidence, crime laboratory equipment, firearms, weapons, and other kinds of equipment, such as breathalyzers and radar speed detectors. Firefighters spend time each day working with and maintaining ladders, hoses, fire trucks, and other equipment. Police, corrections, and security officers deal with a wide range of equipment on their jobs.

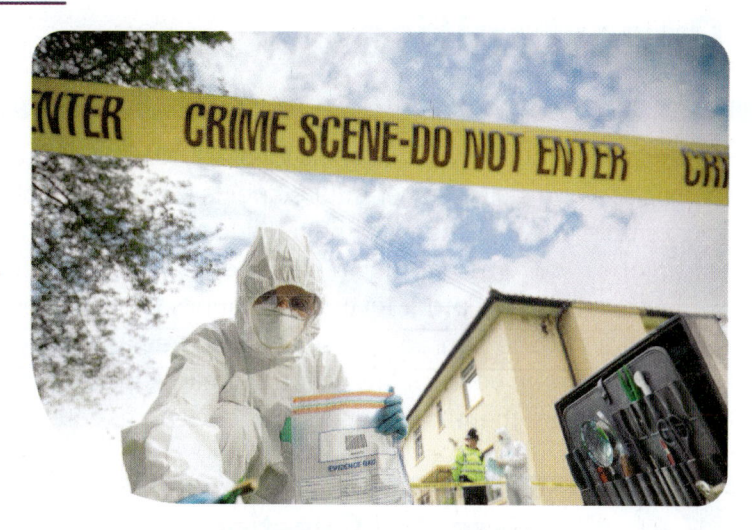

17-3 Essential Question Reflection

So, let us revisit our essential question:

How can I match my skills & interests with the right job?

Based on what you learned in this section, please answer this question in detail.

17-4 Education and Training for the Law, Public Safety, Corrections, & Security Opportunities

All jobs in law, public safety, corrections, and security require job-specific knowledge and skills. Some require specialized on-the-job training. Police officers, for example, receive intensive job training through department-run academies. Other jobs require at least some higher education. Paralegals often need to complete a two-year program at a community college. Federal agents must have a four-year college degree plus specialized training. Lawyers need four years of college and three years of law school. Criminologists and forensic scientists need PhDs to prepare them to conduct independent research.

17-4 Essential Question

As you read this section, keep this question in mind:

What training & education is needed for a job in Law, Public Safety, Corrections, & Security?

Training and Education for This Industry

The level of training and education needed varies by career. Jobs can be categorized into three groups—those requiring little or no training, those requiring some training, and those requiring advanced training.

Jobs Requiring Little or No Training

Most jobs in the industry require at least some formal training. However, there are some jobs in this industry that require less than the average amount of training. Depending on the job, this training can be obtained at a technical school, a community college, or on the job. These jobs include security guards, prison guards, police dispatchers, and 911 operators.

Jobs Requiring Some Training

Many jobs in this industry require a moderate level of education and training. For example, police officers, firefighters, and correctional officers complete a formal training program as well as on-the-job training. Police officers study federal, state, and local laws. They participate in hours of physical and practical training each day. Candidates run, lift weights, and increase their endurance. They learn how to handle firearms and cope with dangerous situations. Firefighters learn about the science of fires and how to operate fire equipment. They practice search-and-rescue techniques and receive EMT training. You do not need a college degree to enter many careers in this industry. However, a college degree improves your opportunities for promotion and higher pay.

For other jobs in this industry, certification is required. For example, you can become certified as an EMT, a firefighter, or a paralegal. Some of these jobs may require ongoing education.

Jobs Requiring Advanced Training

Some careers in this industry require a high level of training and education. This education is often in the form of a master's or a doctoral degree (PhD). A master's degree is granted after a one- to two-year program of study beyond the bachelor's degree level at a university or college. A doctoral degree is an advanced degree. A doctoral degree signifies that an individual is an expert in a particular field. Doctoral students must write and defend an original scholarly paper called a dissertation, which is an in-depth analysis on an important idea.

People who work in the science of crime and rehabilitation generally need postgraduate degrees. Criminologists, forensic scientists, and psychologists all need master's degrees, and many of these professionals hold doctoral degrees. Criminologists, for instance, usually hold master's and doctoral degrees in fields such as clinical psychology, sociology, and criminology. Parole and probation officers may benefit from pursuing master's degrees in psychology, sociology, or other related fields.

Lawyers must earn both a bachelor's degree and a juris doctor (JD) degree. In college, aspiring lawyers take courses in English, history, political science, economics, foreign languages, computer science, and social sciences. The law school application process is very selective. Admission is based on college grades and scores on the Law School Admission Test (LSAT). Law school generally lasts three years. Lawyers must pass the bar exam before they are accepted into the bar, the organization of lawyers in a state. The bar exam varies from state to state, but it is usually a two-day test.

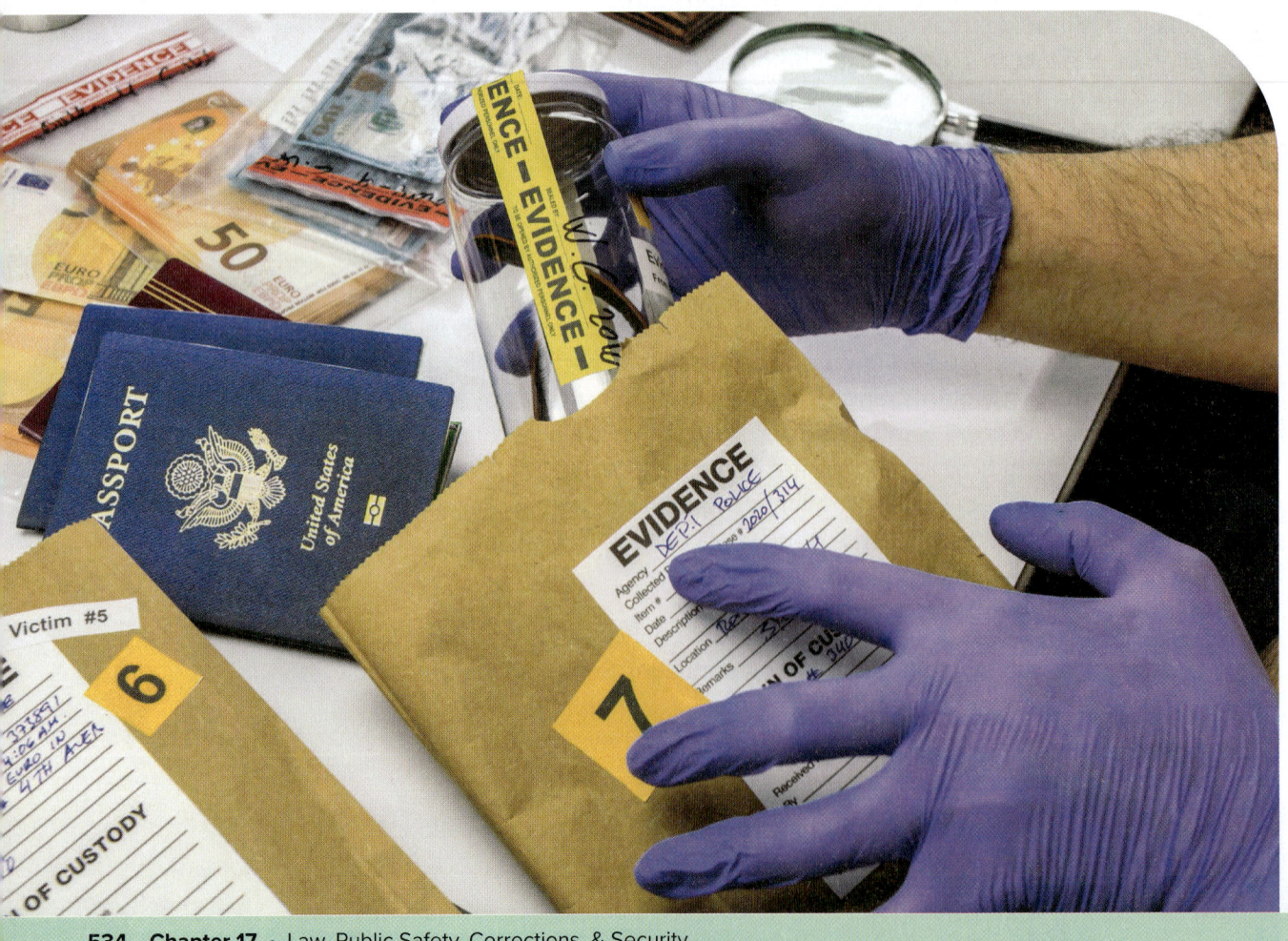

Table 17.2: Training Required for a Sample of Law, Public Safety, Corrections, & Security Occupations

Level of Training	Job Title
Little or No Training	Animal Control Workers Bailiffs Parking Enforcement Workers Police, Fire, and Ambulance Dispatchers Security Guards Transportation Security Officers
Some Training	Correctional Officers and Jailers Firefighters Paralegals and Legal Assistants Police Detectives Police Patrol Officers Private Detectives and Investigators Sheriffs and Deputy Sheriffs
Advanced Training	Arbitrators, Mediators, and Conciliators Forensic Science Technicians Intelligence Analysts Judges and Magistrates Law Clerks Lawyers Security Management Specialists

Job and Workplace Skills

When considering job candidates, employers look for both job-specific skills and general workplace skills. Job-specific skills are the skills necessary to do a particular job. They may include preparing a legal form or attaching a fire hose to a tanker truck. General workplace skills are skills that can be used in a variety of jobs.

Law, Public Safety, Corrections, & Security Skill Standards

Many positions in law and public safety require applicants to meet specific skill standards. This may include licensing, certification, or completion of a particular training program. Some positions, including police officer, federal agent, firefighter, and security guard, require applicants to pass a written examination as well as a physical test.

Some positions require certification in addition to employer training programs. For example, EMTs and paramedics must be formally certified and registered before they can work. Extensive coursework and field experience are required. In some states, security guards must be certified before they can legally work. Paralegals can become certified through a variety of exams and certification programs. Often employees must be regularly recertified.

Professional Skills

Communication Skills In the law, public safety, corrections, and security industry, effective verbal communication is of the utmost importance. Police officers and firefighters must be able to communicate clearly so they can help victims of crimes and disasters. Communication skills are also important when testifying in court and when communicating with colleagues.

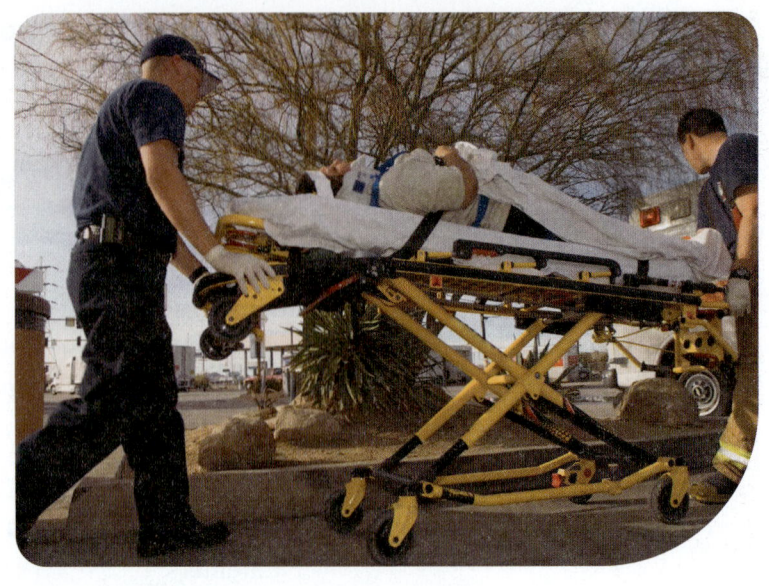

Listening Skills Listening skills are necessary for police detectives who question citizens and must get the facts straight. Lawyers need to be able to listen carefully to their clients and to judges. Emergency workers need to listen for details about a situation from a variety of sources.

Problem-Solving Skills Employers value workers who can spot problems and take action to find solutions. Solving problems requires creativity and confidence. A correctional officer might be called on to solve conflicts between inmates. Detectives use problem-solving skills to solve crimes. EMTs use problem-solving skills to assess a patient's injuries and begin treatment.

Technology Skills Most jobs in law and public safety involve the use of computer technology. Many police officers use computers in their cars to guide them from one call to another. In courtrooms, judges use computers to access the criminal and driving records of defendants. Legal secretaries use computers to produce daily work logs. Security specialists may need extensive computer knowledge to install and operate complex security systems.

Decision-Making Skills Judges, law enforcement officers, and emergency workers frequently need to make important decisions. They must be able to gather and analyze information rapidly and think clearly under pressure. Their decisions directly affect people's lives. A parole officer's decisions might make the difference between a dangerous criminal staying in prison and the prisoner being set free.

Organizing and Planning Skills Planning requires the ability to set goals and identify the steps leading to these goals. Judges and lawyers must manage their court schedules and large amounts of casework. Police chiefs must organize their staff and keep track of the cases in their department. Paralegals must perform research and organize their findings into briefs and other legal documents.

Teamwork Skills Teamwork is key in many laws, public safety, corrections, and security careers. At an accident scene, for example, police officers, EMTs, and firefighters all work together to help victims. Similarly, judges, lawyers, and parole officers work closely together. Teamwork is essential for members of federal, state, and local law enforcement agencies, who may need to work together to solve a crime.

Social Skills Some jobs do not require much social interaction with coworkers. However, social interaction makes for a more enjoyable and productive workplace. In this industry, workers interact with individuals from various levels of their organization. They can use these opportunities to learn from others.

Adaptability Skills Job requirements, work environments, and safety procedures are constantly changing along with technological innovations and changes in the law. The ability to learn new technologies and procedures is essential in today's workplace and job market.

17-4 Essential Question Reflection

So, let us revisit our essential question:

What training & education is needed for a job in Law, Public Safety, Corrections, & Security?

Based on what you learned in this section, please answer this question in detail.

Practice 17-4

Skills Practice

When reviewing workplace graphics, it may be necessary to compare information in one or more graphics. A police chief may need to review data about the frequency of different types of crimes in various areas of a city to determine the number of patrol officers to assign per shift. Workers must know how different graphics relate to each other and be able to compare information and trends within them. **Practice this skill!**

Statistics of Cold Hits and Success Rates Based on NDIS Data from CODIS

State	*Offender Profiles	*Forensic samples	*CODIS Labs	*Investigations Aided	Success Rate (= No. of Cases Aided/No of Forensic Samples)
Alabama	163,656	3,944	4	2,234	0.566430
Alaska	11,920	704	1	228	0.323864
Arizona	137,639	7,281	7	2,365	0.324818
Arkansas	92,366	2,303	1	505	0.219279
California	1,061,374	18,519	20	7,333	0.395972
Colorado	95,267	3,856	5	925	0.239886
Connecticut	43,397	2,403	1	845	0.351644
Delaware	3,557	275	1	10	0.036364
DC/FBI-Lab	63,924	1,757	4	274	0.155948
Florida	523,834	21,075	10	8,593	0.407734
Georgia	156,887	6,868	3	1,742	0.253640
Hawaii	11,527	177	1	42	0.237288

Number of*

1. As a forensic DNA analyst, you are preparing a report for your supervisor. The Combined DNA Index System, or CODIS, is a computer software program that operates databases of DNA profiles. What does this table tell you?

   A. A greater number of CODIS labs correlates to a greater success rate.

   B. A greater number of CODIS labs correlates to fewer aided investigations.

   C. A greater number of offender profiles results in a greater number of aided investigations.

   D. A greater number of forensic samples results in a lower success rate.

   E. A greater number of offender profiles results in fewer CODIS labs.

2. Which of the following states had the highest success rate using information from CODIS?

   A. Alaska
   B. California
   C. Delaware
   D. Florida
   E. Alabama

To access more problems that will help you grow professional skills and are real-world examples in Law, Public Safety, Security & Corrections, go online.

17-4 • Education and Training for the Law, Public Safety, Corrections, & Security Opportunities

17-5 Working in the Law, Public Safety, Corrections, & Security Industry

When choosing a career path, it is important to know what it is like to work in the industry. Understanding the work environment, hazards, and benefits of a job can help you make informed decisions.

17-5 Essential Question

As you read this section, keep this question in mind:

What are typical work environments in Law, Public Safety, Corrections & Security?

Physical Environment

The physical work environment in this industry varies by job. Professionals such as lawyers, judges, and paralegals who spend most of their time in offices or courtrooms enjoy a pleasant work environment.

Correctional officers often work in modern buildings, but their work environment is at times unpleasant. Prisons are often noisy. Because of the safety hazards in prisons, officers must follow complicated security procedures.

Security officers often stand or walk for most of their shift. Security officers may work in museums, banks, casinos, concert venues, stadiums, or parks.

Police officers, firefighters, and EMTs spend much of their time outside, patrolling or working at crime scenes and accidents. Firefighters must withstand extreme heat. They risk inhaling smoke, falling from ladders or buildings, and receiving severe burns. Police officers and other law enforcement professionals may risk injury when pursuing a fleeing suspect on foot or by car.

Work Hours

The work hours for careers in this industry vary greatly. While some careers follow a typical nine-to-five schedule, many others require shift work or irregular hours to ensure the safety of the population.

Law Enforcement Services   Because citizens need law enforcement officers 365 days a year, 24 hours a day, shift work is vital in this path. Shift work divides the day into blocks of time, often eight hours. Shift work allows citizens to have police services available around the clock. It also gives officers the possibility of selecting the hours they want to work. Some shifts are permanent, while others rotate on a weekly, biweekly, or monthly basis.

Legal Services   Lawyers, judges, paralegals, and mediators typically work eight to twelve hours a day. They often work overtime to meet the needs of their clients. If several court cases are pending, lawyers and paralegals must work overtime to prepare for court. They often meet with clients in the late afternoon or early evening.

Correction Services   Workers in this path have a variety of work hours and situations. Corrections officers rely on shifts to make sure prison inmates are always supervised. Parole and probation officers typically work eight to 12 hours a day.

Emergency and Fire Management Services   As in Law Enforcement path, shift work in Emergency and Fire Management Services is common. It allows citizens to have fire and emergency medical services available around the clock. Firefighters often work 24-hour shifts, with two days off between shifts. They may work longer when needed for emergency situations.

Security and Protective Services   Security professionals, such as security officers and gaming surveillance officers, work shifts to make sure a business or building is always secure. These shifts are typically about eight hours long. Part-time work is common in this path.

Essential Physical Activities

Workers must be in good physical condition for many Law, Public Safety, Corrections, & Security jobs. Law enforcement officers must be able to run and to climb fences and other barriers. They must have enough endurance for a foot pursuit. They often need to stand or walk for long periods of time. Firefighters must climb ladders, fences, and other structures. They may carry heavy firefighting equipment up many flights of stairs and wear gear that weighs up to 40 pounds.

Good vision is a must for many workers in this industry. Accurate vision is needed to fire weapons, see at night, and write and read reports and instructions. Glasses and contact lenses are usually permitted to correct vision problems.

Hazard and Environmental Dangers

Because accidents can happen on any job, safety must be a priority. The federal government protects workers by creating workplace safety standards and laws. These rules help prevent accidents and ensure that accident victims are helped.

Injuries and Illnesses

An occupational injury is any injury that occurs at work. Such injuries include cuts, fractures, and sprains. An occupational illness is an illness caused by on-the-job exposure to harmful substances. These illnesses include rashes and skin diseases, respiratory problems, or poisoning.

Many law, public safety, corrections, and security jobs involve operating heavy equipment and entering dangerous situations. Firefighters must enter burning buildings. They may be exposed to hazardous chemicals, fumes, or construction materials. Corrections and police officers may encounter dangerous situations, including those involving weapons. Security professionals also may encounter life threatening situations on the job. Guards in armored vehicles carry weapons and wear bulletproof vests. Proper training and common sense are necessary for handling dangerous situations.

Another job hazard is eye injury. Eye protection is necessary if workers come into contact with sharp objects or are exposed to chemicals. Showers and eye baths must be available to workers who are at risk for eye damage. Police officers use eye baths if they get pepper spray in their eyes while spraying a suspect.

Workers may be exposed to chemicals that are dangerous to touch or breathe. Even dust in the air can harm the lungs and prevent normal breathing. Safety shoes, gloves, and respirators must be available to all workers who are exposed to dangerous substances.

Employees who work at computers for long periods of time, such as dispatchers, may suffer from repetitive-stress injuries and eyestrain. Repetitive-stress injuries (RSIs) can develop when the same motions are performed over and over. One of the most common RSIs is carpal tunnel syndrome, a swelling of tendons in the wrist. This injury can result from frequently repeated tasks such as typing. Eyestrain can develop from reading printed material or using a computer.

Unions in Law, Public Safety, Corrections, & Security

About 10 percent of all workers in all industries nation-wide were union members in 2021. However, workers Law, Public Safety, Corrections, & Security generally have a much higher rate of union membership.

The International Association of Fire Fighters (IAFF) is the largest firefighters' labor organization in the country. With more than 298,000 members, the IAFF represents firefighters and emergency medical service providers. In addition, many states and even some cities have their own organizations for firefighters.

Most sworn police officers are members of the Fraternal Order of Police (FOP). This is the largest professional police organization in the United States. A variety of local unions for police officers exist all over the country.

Federal law enforcement officers may become members of the FOP. In addition, several associations exist for federal law enforcement officers, including the Federal Law Enforcement Officers Association and the FBI Agents Association. These organizations do not have collective bargaining powers. However, they do act as advocates for federal agents, providing publications, legal counsel, and a political voice in Washington D.C. for their members.

17-5 Essential Question Reflection

So, let us revisit our essential question:

What are typical work environments in Law, Public Safety, Corrections & Security?

Based on what you learned in this section, please answer this question in detail.

17-6 Trends in Law, Public Safety, Corrections, & Security

The law, public safety, corrections, and security industry is constantly changing. Technology has affected work processes and working conditions for jobs in this industry. In addition, new trends are affecting the practices and the workplaces of many occupations.

17-6 Essential Question

As you read this section, keep this question in mind:

What factors affect trends in Law, Public Safety, Corrections, & Security?

Technology in the Law, Public Safety, Corrections & Security Industry

It is hard to imagine how workers operated in the past without the benefit of today's technological advances. For example, law enforcement agencies could once only communicate with one another by telephone or letter. Now they use the Internet and national crime databases. Police officers used to write all reports by hand. Now they complete and file reports using a computer. It is common for officers to have laptop computers and Internet access in their patrol cars. Today computers and communication technologies are vital to nearly all functions within this industry.

Technology in Law Enforcement Services

Technological advances in Law Enforcement Services is helping officers identify, locate, and contain criminals. Criminal histories, penal codes, driving records, wanted suspect lists, and stolen property lists can be accessed easily. In addition, the ability of law enforcement agencies to share information securely can make solving crimes easier.

Biometric identification has grown in scope and accuracy over the years. Biometric identification includes any method of identification that uses unique biological features to confirm a person's identity. For example, face-recognition technologies can be used to compare the faces of criminals caught on video surveillance systems to mug shots in a police department's database.

Smartphone technology is making law enforcement more effective. For example, some cities use smartphone applications (apps) to allow citizens to report crimes. Tips can be sent quickly and easily to police departments. In addition to dialing 9-1-1 on a cellphone to request emergency assistance, some cities have also implemented a system that allows citizens to request assistance by texting 9-1-1. Language translation apps help officers communicate with a variety of people.

Advances in computer technology have allowed new analytical methods to develop. Crime mapping is the creation of detailed maps of where and when specific crimes have occurred. The maps can then be analyzed and used to track patterns of crime. In addition, analysis of evidence, including DNA, has become more reliable as better technology is available.

Technology in Legal Services

Improvements in communications systems has also helped the legal system. Real-time deposition technology allows lawyers to see depositions over the Internet. As the court reporter types the transcript, a computer automatically translates the shorthand notes into standard English. Transcribing depositions used to take several days. Now it is done instantly. This allows paralegals to prepare summaries, medical experts to prepare testimony, and lawyers to make notes, all at the same time.

Online law libraries minimize research time. Work that used to require a trip to the library can now be done by computer. Searchable online databases include legal documents and other resources.

Technology in Correction Services

The use of technology to support traditional correctional strategies is known as technocorrections. Technocorrections meets the public's demand for tougher jail sentences and greater control over offenders. At the same time, it reduces the population of overcrowded prisons.

Electronic monitoring of offenders has been used for many years. But new technologies can make these devices much more effective. GPS technology enables law enforcement officers to track and record an offender's movements. In general, those convicted of nonviolent crimes may be able to serve all or part of their sentences under house arrest. If an offender leaves their home or other approved location, an alarm goes off.

Biometric identification technology is being used to improve security in prisons. Fingerprint-recognition systems are used to allow access into and out of secure areas. Cards or passcodes, which can be lost or stolen, can now be replaced with biometric scans. Visitors and guards can move about more freely than before. Inmates have fewer opportunities for escape.

Technology in Emergency and Fire Management Services

Firefighting techniques such as fire modeling are more accurate due to advances in computer software. Fire modeling is the process of predicting the effects and behaviors of a fire. Computer programs analyze a building's layout, ventilation, and other factors to predict how and where flames will spread. These programs can predict how much heat and smoke may be produced by the fire and whether toxic gases may be present. This information can be used to fight fires.

Advanced fire safety technology allows firefighters to stay safe while fighting fires. One example is the Personal Alert Safety System (PASS). The first PASS devices contained sensors that monitored a firefighter's motion. If the firefighter stopped moving, the device would signal for help. New technologies are being developed to improve these devices. For example, heat sensors can warn a firefighter when conditions become extreme. GPS technology in the PASS devices can be used to locate a firefighter in a burning building.

Another example is new advances in drone technology. Drone technology is advancing rapidly and providing fire departments across the United States with a safer and more dependable way to fight fires. Drones give firefighters access to higher elevations than fire trucks equipped with ladders. They also take less time to deploy. This allows fire departments to survey the risk quickly and accurately from the ground before sending firefighters into the fire.

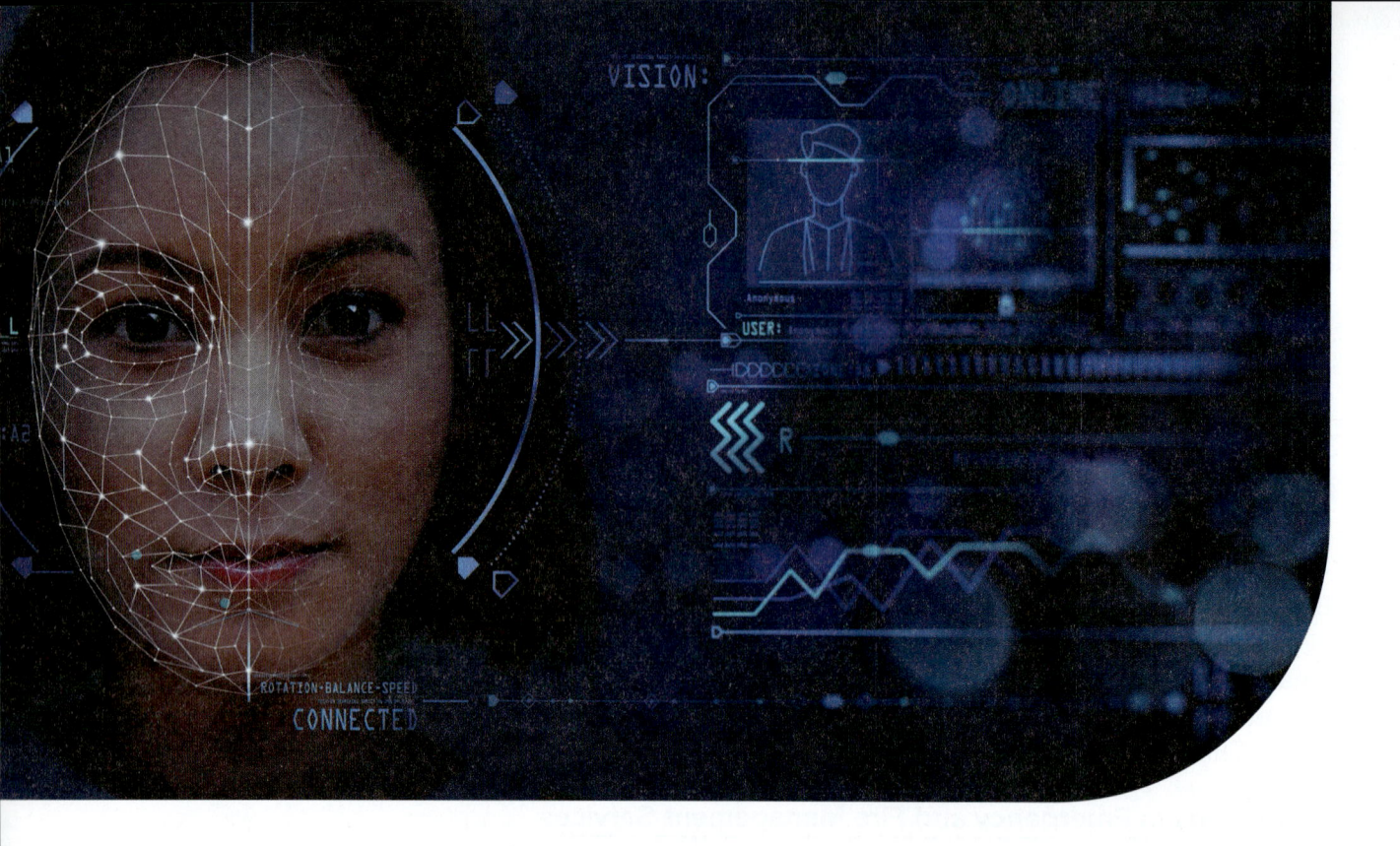

Technology in Security and Protective Services

Advances in security systems and the need for tighter information security have changed the Security and Protective Services path. The security systems in buildings are becoming more sophisticated. Computer skills are becoming more and more vital to careers in this path.

Biometric identification is affecting the practices in this pathway. Facial recognition technology can be used in areas where tight security is needed. Facial scans of travelers in an airport, for example, can be compared to photo databases of known terrorists. Fingerprint scans, iris scans, and even scans of the vein patterns in a person's hand can be used to restrict access to offices and ATMs. These technologies can be used to protect sensitive computer systems from unauthorized access.

Trends in the Law, Public Safety, Corrections, and Security Industry

This industry has seen several new trends in recent years. One trend has been the increasing effort to find methods that save money and treat suspects and convicts humanely while still protecting the public.

Less-than-Lethal Force

Technologies that allow officers to use less-than-lethal force are becoming more common. These devices allow officers to take control of difficult situations with less risk of serious injury or death. One popular less-than-lethal weapon is a stun gun. This is a handheld remote stun system. It subdues subjects with a jolt of electricity.

It is intended to cause no long-term injury, and it does not affect the heart or pacemakers. Various nonlethal firearms, such as guns that have rubber bullets and pepper ball guns, are also being used.

Alternative Sentencing

Alternative sentencing refers to sentencing options other than traditional jail or prison terms. Alternative punishments include house arrest and electronic monitoring. Work release, counseling programs, drug treatment, and community service may also be alternative sentencing options. One goal of these programs is to reduce the prison population. In addition, these programs help offenders become contributing members of society.

> **17-6 Essential Question Reflection**
>
> **So, let us revisit our essential question:**
>
> *What factors affect trends in the Law, Public Safety, Corrections, & Security Industry?*
>
> Based on what you learned in this section, please answer this question in detail.

Career Fields and Paths

A **career field** is a grouping of jobs and industries based on common characteristics. A **career path** is an area of focus within a career field. You can explore each of the following career fields and paths in McGraw-Hill's *Career Explorations*.

Agriculture, Food, & Natural Resources
Food Products and Processing Systems
Plant Systems
Animal Systems
Power, Structural & Technical Systems
Natural Resources Systems
Environmental Service Systems
Agribusiness Systems

Architecture & Construction
Design/Pre-Construction
Construction
Maintenance/Operations

Arts & Media
Audio and Video Technology and Film
Printing Technology
Visual Arts
Performing Arts
Journalism and Broadcasting
Telecommunications

Business Management & Administration
General Management
Business Information Management
Human Resources Management
Operations Management
Administrative Support

Education & Training
Administration and Administrative Support
Professional Support Services
Teaching/Training

Finance
Securities & Investments
Business Finance
Accounting
Insurance
Banking Services

Government & Public Administration
Governance
National Security
Foreign Service
Planning
Revenue and Taxation
Regulation
Public Management and Administration

Health Science
Therapeutic Services
Diagnostic Services
Health Informatics
Support Services
Biotechnology Research and Development

Hospitality & Tourism
Restaurants and Food/Beverage Services
Lodging
Travel & Tourism
Recreation, Amusement & Attractions

Human Services
Early Childhood Development & Services
Counseling & Mental Health Services
Family & Community Services
Personal Care Services
Consumer Services

Information Technology (IT)
Network Systems
Information Support and Services
Web and Digital Communications
Programming and Software Development

Law, Public Safety, Corrections, & Security
Correction Services
Emergency and Fire Management Services
Security & Protective Services
Law Enforcement Services
Legal Services

Manufacturing
Production
Manufacturing Production Process Development
Maintenance, Installation & Repair
Quality Assurance
Logistics & Inventory Control
Health, Safety and Environmental Assurance

Marketing
Marketing Management
Professional Sales
Merchandising
Marketing Communications
Marketing Research

Science, Technology, Engineering, & Mathematics (STEM)
Engineering and Technology
Science and Math

Transportation, Distribution, & Logistics
Transportation Operations
Logistics Planning and Management Services
Warehousing and Distribution Center Operations
Facility and Mobile Equipment Maintenance
Transportation Systems/Infrastructure Planning, Management and Regulation
Health, Safety and Environmental Management
Sales and Service

Index

A

Abstractors, 219
Academic foundations, 432
Accountants, 281
Account collectors, 280–281
Accounting
  Finance jobs, 275–276
  technology in, 303–304
Actors, 113–114
Actuaries, 281
Adaptability skills
  Agriculture, Food, & Natural Resource jobs, 193
  Architecture & Construction job, 158
  Arts & Media job, 126
  Education and Training Industry, 503
  Finance jobs, 294
  Government & Public Administration job, 229
  Hospitality & Tourism industry, 398
  Human Services, 468
  Information Technology job, 94
  Law, Public Safety, Corrections, & Security, 537
  Manufacturing job, 64
  Marketing jobs, 331
  STEM jobs, 33
Adaptive reuse, 166–167
Administrative support
  Business Management & Administration, 243
  Education and Training Industry, 482
Advanced manufacturing, 70
Advanced training
  Education and Training Industry, 500, 501
  Hospitality & Tourism industry, 394–395
  Human Services, 464–465
  Law, Public Safety, Corrections, & Security, 533–534

Advertising managers, 315–316
Aerospace engineering technicians, 22
Agriculture, Food, & Natural Resources
  career building, 186–188
  career paths, 170–174
  education and training, 189–193
  future outlook, 174–175
  issues in, 204
  jobs, 178–183
  trends, 201–206
  working conditions, 196–200
Airline pilots, 350–351
Alternative fuels, 371
Alternative sentencing, 549
American Society of Travel Agents (ASTA), 397
Amusement, 377
  Arts & Media industry, 112
  technology, 406–407
Animal trainers, 383
Applied mathematicians, 14
Apprenticeships, 6
Architecture & Construction industry
  building career, 151–153
  career path, 137–140
  education and training, 154–158
  future outlook, 141–142
  jobs, 145–149
  technology in, 165–168
  working conditions, 160–164
Artificial Intelligence (AI), 40, 100–101, 334
Arts & Media industry
  building career, 120–121
  career path, 105–109
  contemporary issues in, 133–134
  economy and, 134–135
  education and training, 122–126
  future outlook, 109–110
  jobs, 112–118

  skill standards, 124–125
  technology in, 132–133
  working conditions in, 129–131
Assistive Technology, 474
Associate degree, 7
  aerospace engineering technicians, 22
  agriculture, food, & natural resource jobs, 190
  business management & administration jobs, 258, 259
  climate change analysts, 218–219
  computer network support specialists, 84
  drafters, 52
  environmental engineering technologists and technicians, 146
  graphic designers, 112
  Health Science industry, 429
  hospitality & tourism fields, 393
  Human Services, 464
  morticians, undertakers, and funeral arrangers, 454–455
  paralegals and legal assistants, 216, 523
  preschool teachers, 487
  radiation therapists, 419
  STEM jobs, 22
  support services, 412
  tour guides, 385
Athletes, 114
Attractions, 377
  technology, 406–407
  work hours, 402
Audio and Video Technology and Film
  Arts & Media industry, 107
Auditors, 281
Automated Case Management Systems, 475
Automation, manufacturing, 71

B

Bachelor's degree, 8
   accountants and auditors, 281
   accounting job, 275
   actuaries, 281
   advertising, promotions, and marketing managers, 316
   agriculture, food, & natural resource jobs, 190
   airline pilots, copilots, and flight engineers, 351
   architecture & construction jobs, 155
   arts & media jobs, 123
   audiologists, 429
   coaches and scouts, 487
   computer and information systems managers, 282
   corporate trainers, 499
   entry-level jobs, 310
   financial analysts, 291
   financial managers, 279
   flight attendants, 350
   forestry, 191
   fundraisers, 282
   graphic designers, 112
   health care social workers, 418
   Health Science industry, 429–430
   information security analysts, 217
   interpreters and translators, 385
   IT jobs, 92
   journalism and broadcasting, 106
   management analysts/consultants, 218
   manufacturing jobs, 61, 62
   market research analysts, 279
   occupational therapists, 465
   paralegals and legal assistants, 523
   printing technology, 109
   private detectives and investigators, 524
   programmers, 78
   project management specialists, 247
   public relations specialists, 315
   registered nurses, 417
   securities and investments job, 275
   social media marketing specialists, 318
   software developers, 82
   software quality assurance analysts and testers, 83
   STEM jobs, 30, 31
   telecommunications engineers, 124
   training and development specialist, 250

Baggage porters, 382
Banking services, 273–274, 301
Bank tellers, 273, 280
Bell hops, 382
Bill collectors, 273, 280–281
Biofuels, 42
Biotechnology, 41
Biotechnology research and development, 413, 432
Blockchain, 102–103
Bookkeeping, 241
Botanists, 13–14
Broadcasting, 105–106
Building construction, 139
Bureau of Labor Statistics (BLS), 243
Business Finance, 274, 302
Business Information Management, 241–242, 268
Business Management & Administration
   building career, 255–257
   career path, 240–243
   education and training, 258–262
   future outlook, 243–244
   jobs, 247–252
   market trends, 269
   skill standards, 260
   technology, 267–268
   working conditions, 264–266
   workplace trends, 269–270
Business travel planning, 378

C

Campaigning and Voting, 235
Career
   building, 5
   choices, evaluation of, 4
   education and training, 6–8
   exploring, 3–4
   preparation, 3
Career schools, 7
Certification, 29–30
Civil engineering construction, 139
Civil engineers, 14
Claims Adjusters, Examiners, 250
Clean manufacturing, 70
Climate Change Analysts, 218–219
Cloud computing, 101
Coaches and scouts, 486–487
Commercial banks, 273
Communications, 310
Communication skills
   Agriculture, Food, & Natural Resource jobs, 192
   Architecture & Construction job, 157
   Arts & Media job, 125
   Business Management & Administration job, 261
   Education and Training Industry, 502
   Finance jobs, 293
   Government & Public Administration job, 228
   Hospitality & Tourism industry, 397
   Human Services, 467
   Information Technology job, 93
   Law, Public Safety, Corrections, & Security, 536
   Manufacturing job, 62
   Marketing jobs, 330
   STEM jobs, 32
   Transportation, Distribution, & Logistics industry, 362

Community association manager, 317
Compliance Officers, 216
Computer and information research scientists, 83
Computer and information systems managers, 281–282
Computer hardware, 76
Computer network support specialists, 84
Computer Numerically Controlled (CNC)
  manufacturing, 70
  programmers, 54–55
Computers, Agriculture, Food, & Natural Resource industry, 201
Computer support specialists, 84
Concierges, 384
Construction, 139–140
Construction equipment operators, 146
Construction Workers, 145
Consultants, 340, 442
  Government & Public Administration, 238
  Transportation, Distribution, & Logistics industry, 373
Consumer services, 448, 477
Contract work, 9
Contract workers, 168
Controllers, 274
Conveyor Systems, 369
Copilots, 350–351
Correction services, 516
  technology, 547
  work hours, 541
Cosmetologists, 453
Counseling and mental health services, 446–447, 476
COVID-19 pandemic
  Arts & Media industry, 133
  Business Management & Administration, 265
  and economic fallout, 305
  Information Technology, 95

Credit counselors, 452–453
Credit unions, 273
Cybersecurity, 269

D

Decision-making skills
  Agriculture, Food, & Natural Resource jobs, 193
  Architecture & Construction job, 157
  Arts & Media job, 126
  Education and Training Industry, 503
  Finance jobs, 294
  Government & Public Administration job, 229
  Hospitality & Tourism industry, 397
  Human Services, 467–468
  Information Technology job, 94
  Law, Public Safety, Corrections, & Security, 536
  Manufacturing job, 63
  Marketing jobs, 330
  STEM jobs, 32–33
  Transportation, Distribution, & Logistics industry, 363
Demographics
  Architecture & Construction industry, 166
  Education and Training Industry, 512
  Finance industry, 304
  Human Services, 477
Dental technologies, 441–442
Department of Defense (DOD), 209
Design/Pre-Construction, 138
Diagnostic services, Health Science industry, 411, 431
Distance learning, Education and Training Industry, 510
Distributors, 45
Diversity, equity, and inclusion (DE&I) initiatives, 304
DNA profiling, 230
Downsizing, Arts & Media industry, 134–135
Drafters, manufacturing, 52

E

Early childhood development and services, 445–446, 476
Economy
  Agriculture, Food, & Natural Resource industry, 205–206
  Architecture & Construction industry, 167–168
  Arts & Media industry, 134–135
  and Finance industry, 305
  Government & Public Administration, 237
  Hospitality & Tourism industry, 408
  and Marketing industry, 339–340
  Transportation, Distribution, & Logistics industry, 372–373
Education
  Architecture & Construction industry, 155–156
  Government & Public Administration, 226–228
  for Marketing jobs, 326–328
Education and Training Industry, 6–8
  administration and administrative support, 482
  Agriculture, Food, & Natural Resource industry, 189–193
  career building, 495–497
  career paths, 479–480
  coaches and scouts, 486–487
  demographics, 512
  Education & Training, 498–503
  elementary, middle, and high school principals, 488
  Finance opportunities, 290–294
  future outlook, 482
  Health Science industry, 428–433
  Hospitality & Tourism industry, 393–398
  Human Services, 463–468
  instructional coordinators, 487
  law, 511–512
  Law, Public Safety, Corrections, & Security, 532–537

Index 553

for Marketing opportunities, 326–331
paraeducators or teaching assistants, 488–489
preschool teachers, 487
professional support services, 481
program advisors, 481
STEM jobs, 29–33
student support professionals, 481
support administrators, 481–482
teaching, 480–481
Transportation, Distribution, & Logistics industry, 359–363
trends, 509–512
working conditions, 506–508

Electronic commerce
Information Technology, 102
Transportation, Distribution, & Logistics industry, 372–373

Elementary, middle, and high school principals, 488

Email, 338

Emergency and fire management services, 516–517
technology, 547
work hours, 541

Engine analyzers, 369

Engineering, 13–15

Engineers in advanced systems, 20

Entrepreneurs, 310

Entrepreneurship, Marketing management and, 310

Environmental dangers
Agriculture, Food, & Natural Resource industry workers, 199–200
Architecture & Construction industry, 163–164
Arts & Media industry, 131
Education and Training Industry, 508
Health Science industry, 437–438
Hospitality & Tourism industry, injuries and illnesses, 403–404
Human Services, 472
Law, Public Safety, Corrections, & Security, 542–543
manufacturing, 69
Marketing industry workers, 335
STEM workers, 39
Transportation, Distribution, & Logistics industry, 367

Environmental engineering technologists, 146

Environmental issues, 370–372

Environmental regulation, 236

Environmental science & protection technicians, 23–24

Ergonomics
Architecture & Construction industry, 164
Information Technology, 99

Ethics, 432

E-ticketing, 369

Exercise trainers, Arts & Media industry, 113

F

Facility and Mobile Equipment Maintenance, 344

Family and community services, 447

Fastest-growing occupation, 418

Federal Aviation Administration (FAA), 361

Federal Reserve Banks, 273–274

Finance
career building, 287–289
career paths, 272–276
education and training, 290–294
future outlook, 276
jobs, 279–284
trends, 301–305
working conditions in, 297–300

Financial analysts, 274

Financial managers, 279

First-line managers, 241

First-line supervisors (managers) of retail sales workers, 317

Flextime
Agriculture, Food, & Natural Resource jobs, 198
Marketing jobs, 334
STEM jobs, 37

Flight attendants, 349–350

Flight engineers, 350–351

Food/Beverage Services, 377

Food/beverage services
technology, 406
work hours, 401–402

Food preparation workers, 382

Food skill standards, 396

Foreign Service, 210

Foreign Service officers, 210

Foreign Service specialists, 210

Forest fire inspectors & prevention specialists, 522

Formal training and education options
associate degree, 7
bachelor's degree, 8
graduate degree, 8
on-the-job training, 8
technical and career schools, 7

Fraternal Order of Police (FOP), 544

Freight, stock, and material movers, 349

Fundraisers, 282

Fundraising managers, 316

Funeral arrangers, 454–455

Future career. *See also* Career
exploring, 3–4
formal training and education for, 7–8
intoduction to, 2–4
preparation, 2–3
trends, 9

G

General management, Business Management & Administration, 241

General workplace skills, 292

Genetic engineering, 41

Gig work, 9

Global economy
    and Marketing industry, 340
    Transportation, Distribution, & Logistics industry, 372–373

Global Positioning System (GPS), 370

Governance, Government & Public Administration, 209

Government & Public Administration
    building career, 224–225
    career path, 208–212
    education and training, 226–229
    future outlook, 212–213
    jobs, 216–221
    skill standards, 228
    trends in, 235–238
    working conditions, 232–234

Graduate degree, 8, 124, 501

Graphic designers, 112

Green chemistry, 43

Green energy, Government & Public Administration, 237

Greener transportation systems, 371–372

Green manufacturing, 72–73

Group fitness instructors, Arts & Media industry, 113

H

Hairdressers, hairstylists, 453

Hand laborers, 349

Hardware, Information Technology, 100

Hazards
    Agriculture, Food, & Natural Resource industry workers, 199–200
    Architecture & Construction industry workers, 163–164
    Arts & Media, 131
    Education and Training Industry, 508
    Health Science industry, 437–438
    Hospitality & Tourism industry, injuries and illnesses, 403–404
    Human Services, 472
    Law, Public Safety, Corrections, & Security, 542–543
    Manufacturing industry workers, 69
    Marketing industry workers, 335
    STEM workers, 39
    Transportation, Distribution, & Logistics industry, 367

Health care social workers, 418
    Human Services, 454

Health informatics, 412–413, 431

Health maintenance practices, 432–433

Health, Safety, and Environmental Assurance, 48, 67

Health, Safety, and Environmental Management, 344

Health Science Industry
    biotechnology research and development, 413
    career building, 425–427
    career paths, 410–411
    diagnostic services, 411
    education and training, 428–433
    fastest-growing occupation, 418
    future outlook, 413–414
    health informatics, 412–413
    highest-wage occupation, 419
    opticians, 418
    radiation therapists, 419
    registered nurses, 417
    services, 410
    skill standards, 431–432
    support services, 412
    therapeutic services, 411–412
    trends, 439–443
    working conditions, 436–438

Heavy truck drivers, 352–353

Highest-wage occupation
    accountants and auditors, 281
    actuaries, 281
    advertising, promotions, and Marketing managers, 315–316
    airline pilots, copilots, and flight engineers, 350–351
    fundraising managers, 316
    Health Science industry, 419
    physicists, 21

Hospitality & Tourism Industry
    career building, 390–392
    career paths, 375
    education and training, 393–398
    future outlook, 378
    jobs, 382–387
    opportunities, 379
    trends, 405–408
    working conditions, 401–404

Hostels, 376

Hotels, 376

Human Resources Management, 242

Human Services
    career building, 460–462
    career paths, 445
    consumer services, 448, 477
    counseling and mental health services, 446–447, 476
    credit counselors, 452–453
    demographic trends, 477
    early childhood development and services, 445–446, 476
    education and training, 463–468
    family and community services, 447
    future outlook, 448–449
    hairdressers, hairstylists, and cosmetologists, 453
    health-care social workers, 454
    mental health and substance abuse social workers, 453
    morticians, undertakers, and funeral arrangers, 454–455
    personal care services, 448, 476
    residential advisors, 455
    skill standards, 466–467
    trends, 474–475
    working conditions, 471–473

I

Industrial engineers, 15

Information Security Analyst, 85–86, 217

Information Support and Services, IT, 77
Information Technology (IT)
    building career, 89–90
    career paths, 75
    education and training, 91–94
    future outlook, 78–79
    Health Science industry, 433
    jobs, 82–86
    products and services, 76–78
    technology in, 100–103
    working conditions, 95–99
Injuries and Illnesses
    Architecture & Construction industry workers, 163
    Business Management & Administration workers, 266
    Education & Training Industry, 508
    Finance industry workers, 300
    Government & Public Administration workers, 234
    Health Science Industry, 436
    Hospitality & Tourism workers, 403–404
    Human Services, 472–473
    Information Technology workers, 97
    Law, Public Safety, Corrections, & Security Industry, 542–543
    Manufacturing Industry workers, 69
Inns, 376
Installation job, 47, 67
Institute of Certified Bankers (ICB), 292
Instructional coordinators, Education and Training Industry, 487
Insurance
    Finance companies, **275**
    Marketing industry, 309
    sales agents, **280**
    technology, 303
Intelligent Transportation System (ITS) program, 370
Intercity bus drivers, 351
Intermodal transportation, 372
Internal Revenue Service (IRS), 211

International Association of Fire Fighters (IAFF), 543
Internet, 76
Internet advertising, 338
Internet and Computers in Classroom, 509–510
Internet of Things, 103
Internships, 6
Interpreters, Hospitality & Tourism Industry, 385
Inventory control, 48, 67
Investigators, Business Management & Administration, 250
Investment underwriters, 275
IT services, 76

J
Jobs, changing, 5
Job-specific skills, 292
Journalism, 105–106
Just-in-time (JIT) inventory systems, 336
Just-in-time (JIT) production, 72

K
Knowledge workers, 266

L
Laser surgery, 441
Law enforcement services, 515
    technology, 545–546
    work hours, 541
Law, Public Safety, Corrections, & Security
    career building, 529–531
    correction services, 516
    education and training, 532–537
    emergency and fire management services, 516–517
    forest fire inspectors & prevention specialists, 522
    future outlook, 517–518
    law enforcement services, 515
    legal services, 515–516

    Lifeguards and Ski Patrol Officers, 521–522
    paralegals and legal assistants, 523
    paramedics, 522
    paths, 514
    private detectives and investigators, 524
    security and protective services, 517
    security guards, 522–523
    trends, 545–549
    unions, 543–544
    working, 540–543
Lawyers, 217
Legal assistants, 523
Legal responsibilities, 432
Legal services, 515–516
    technology, 546
    work hours, 541
Less-than-Lethal Force, 548–549
Licensing, Education and Training Industry, 501–502
Lifeguards and Ski Patrol Officers, 521–522
Life science, 12
Listening skills
    Agriculture, Food, & Natural Resource jobs, 192
    Architecture & Construction job, 157
    Arts & Media job, 125
    Business Management & Administration job, 261
    Education and Training Industry, 502
    Finance jobs, 293
    Government & Public Administration job, 228
    Hospitality & Tourism industry, 397
    Human Services, 467
    Information Technology job, 93
    Law, Public Safety, Corrections, & Security, 536
    Manufacturing job, 62
    Marketing jobs, 330
    STEM jobs, 32
Lobby attendants, 114–115
Local area network (LAN), 76

Lodging, 376
   Hospitality & Tourism industry, 396
   technology, 405–406
   work hours, 401

Logistics, 48, 67

Logistics Planning and Management Services, 343

Lower fuel consumptions, 371

M

Machine learning, 100–101

Maintenance and repair workers, 19

Maintenance job, 47, 67

Maintenance/Operations, 140

Management Analysts/Consultants, 218

Manufacturing 4.0., 70

Manufacturing industry
   career building, 58–59
   career path, 45–48
   categories, 45
   contemporary issues in, 72–73
   education and training, 60–64
   future outlook, 48–49
   jobs, 52–53
   technology in, 70–72
   working conditions, 68–69

Manufacturing Skill Standards Council (MSSC), 62

Mapping Technicians, 53

Market analyst, 319–320

Marketing, 307
   career building, 323–325
   career paths, 308–311
   communications, 310
   future outlook, 311
   jobs, 314–320
   management and entrepreneurship, 310
   research, 310–311
   skills, 314
   trends, 336–340
   working conditions, 333–335

Marketing managers, 315–316

Marketing specialists, 319–320

Market research analysts, 279, 311, 319–320

Market research consultant, 319–320

Market research specialist, 319–320

Mathematics, 13–14

Mechanical engineers, 14–15

Medical consultations, 442–443

Medical informatics, 440

Medical Secretaries, 248–249

Megastores, 340

Mental health and substance abuse social workers, 453

Merchandising, 308–309

Metaverse, Information Technology, 101

Meteorologists, 14

Mid-level managers, 241

Military technology, 235

Minimally invasive surgical techniques, 441

Morticians, 454–455

Motels, 376

Musculoskeletal disorder (MSD), 39, 300

N

Nanotechnology, 41

National Association of Securities Dealers (NASD), 292

National Automotive Technicians Education Foundation (NATEF), 362

National Business Education Association (NBEA), 292

National Council on Economic Education (NCEE), 292

National Security, 209

Natural language processing (NLP), 41

Natural scientists, 13

Network Systems, IT, 76–77

Neuromorphic engineering, 40

Nuclear power reactor operators, 22

Nurse practitioners, 418

O

Occupational injuries, 98

Occupational Safety and Health Administration (OSHA), 69

Occupations, 2. *see also* Highest-wage occupations
   Agriculture, Food, & Natural Resource jobs, 175
   Arts & Media, 109
   Business Management & Administration, 244
   Finance industry, 276
   manufacturing, 49
   Marketing industry, 312
   STEM jobs, 15, 16
   Transportation, Distribution, & Logistics industry, 346

Office Technology, 267

Online Marketing technology, 337–338

On-the-job training, 8

Operations Management, 242–243

Opticians, 418
   Health Science industry, 418

Organic chemists, 14

Organizing and Planning skills
   Architecture & Construction job, 158
   Government & Public Administration job, 229

Organizing and planning skills
   Agriculture, Food, & Natural Resource jobs, 193
   Arts & Media job, 126
   Education and Training Industry, 503
   Finance jobs, 294
   Hospitality & Tourism industry, 398
   Human Services, 468
   Information Technology job, 94
   Law, Public Safety, Corrections, & Security, 536
   Manufacturing job, 63
   Marketing jobs, 330
   STEM jobs, 33
   Transportation, Distribution, & Logistics industry, 363

Outsourcing
    Arts & Media industry, 134–135
    in manufacturing, 73
    Transportation, Distribution, & Logistics industry, 373

P

Paraeducators or teaching assistants, 488–489

Paralegals, 523

Paralegals and Legal Assistants, 216–217

Paramedics, 522

Passenger information display system (PIDS), 369

Performing Arts, 106–107

Personal care services, 448, 476

Personal financial advisors, 274–275, 283–284

Personal Service Workers, 249

Physical activities
    Agriculture, Food, & Natural Resource industry workers, 199
    Architecture & Construction industry, 162
    Arts & Media industry, 130
    Business Management & Administration, 265–266
    Education and Training Industry, 507–508
    Finance industry workers, 299
    Government & Public Administration, 233–234
    Health Science industry, 437
    Hospitality & Tourism industry, 403
    Human Services, 472
    Information Technology, 96–97
    Law, Public Safety, Corrections, & Security, 541
    Manufacturing industry, 68
    Marketing industry workers, 334–335
    STEM industry workers, 37–39
    Transportation, Distribution, & Logistics industry, 367

Physical environment
    Agriculture, Food, & Natural Resource industry, 196
    Architecture & Construction industry, 161–162
    Arts & Media industry, 129–130
    Business Management & Administration, 264–265
    Education and Training Industry, 506
    Finance industry, 297
    Government & Public Administration, 232
    Health Science industry, 436
    Hospitality & Tourism industry, 401
    Human Services, 471
    Information Technology, 95
    Law, Public Safety, Corrections, & Security, 540
    Manufacturing industry, 66–67
    STEM industry, 36–37
    Transportation, Distribution, & Logistics industry, 366

Physical science, 12

Physical work environment, 333

Physicians, 419

Physicists, 21

Planning skills
    Agriculture, Food, & Natural Resource jobs, 193
    Finance jobs, 294
    Government & Public Administration, 210–211
    Marketing jobs, 330
    STEM jobs, 33
    Transportation, Distribution, & Logistics industry, 363

Police and Detectives, 219

Police and patrol officers, 515

Police detectives, 515

Postgraduate education, 8

Preemployment job training, 6

Preschool teachers, 487

Printing technology, 108–109

Private detectives and investigators, 524

Privatization, 236

Problem-solving skills
    Agriculture, Food, & Natural Resource jobs, 193
    Architecture & Construction job, 157
    Arts & Media job, 126
    Business Management & Administration job, 261
    Education and Training Industry, 502
    Finance jobs, 293
    Government & Public Administration job, 228
    Hospitality & Tourism industry, 397
    Human Services, 467
    Information Technology job, 93
    Law, Public Safety, Corrections, & Security, 536
    Manufacturing job, 62
    Marketing jobs, 330
    STEM jobs, 32
    Transportation, Distribution, & Logistics industry, 362

Producers, 45

Production process development, 46–47, 66

Professional models, 316

Professional sales, 309

Professional skills
    Agriculture, Food, & Natural Resource jobs, 192–193
    Architecture & Construction industry, 157–158
    Arts & Media job, 125–126
    Business Management & Administration job, 261–262
    Government & Public Administration job, 228–229
    Information Technology job, 93–94
    Manufacturing job, 62–72
    Marketing jobs, 330–331
    STEM jobs, 32–33
    Transportation, Distribution, & Logistics industry, 362–363

Professional support services, 481

Program advisors, 481

Programming and software development, IT, 78

Project Management Specialists, 247

Promotions managers, 315–316

Property or real estate manager, 317

Public Management & Administration, 212

Public relations specialists, 315

Q

Quality assurance, 47–48, 67

R

Radiation therapists, 419

Rebuilding infrastructure, 168

Recreation, 377
- Arts & Media industry, 112
- Hospitality & Tourism industry, 383–384
- technology, 406–407
- work hours, 402

Registered nurses, 417

Regulation, Government & Public Administration, 211–212

Remote work, 9

Remote Work, Arts & Media industry, 134

Renewable energy, 42

Repair job, manufacturing, 47, 67

Repetitive stress injuries (RSIs), 300

Repetitive stress injury (RSI), 39

Research, Marketing, 310–311

Residential advisors, 455

Resort hotels, 376

Restaurant, 377
- technology, 406
- work hours, 401–402

Revenue, 211

Robotics, 441
- STEM industry, 40
- Transportation, Distribution, & Logistics industry, 369

S

Safety practices, 432

Sales and Marketing Executives International (SMEI), 326

Sales and service, of transportation, 344

Savings banks, 273

Science occupations, 11–14

Science, Technology, Engineering & Mathematics (STEM), 11–13
- career building, 27–28
- career paths, 13–15
- education and training, 29–33
- future outlook, 15–16
- jobs, 19–24
- trends, 40–43
- working conditions, 36–39

Search engine optimization, 338

Searchers, Government & Public Administration, 219

Securities and commodities traders, 275

Securities and Investments
- career, 274–275
- technology, 302

Security and protective services, 517
- technology, 548
- work hours, 541

Security guards, 522–523

Self-knowledge, 4

Sensor technology, 40

Sheet metal workers, 146

Sheriffs, 515

Shift work
- Agriculture, Food, & Natural Resource jobs, 198
- Marketing jobs, **334**
- STEM jobs, 37
- Transportation, Distribution, & Logistics industry, 366

Skill Standards
- Agriculture, Food, & Natural Resource jobs, 192
- Finance, 292
- Health Science, 431–432
- Hospitality & Tourism, 396
- Human Service, 466
- Law, Public Safety, Corrections, & Security, 535–536
- Marketing jobs, 329
- STEM, 31–32
- Transportation, Distribution, & Logistics industry, 361–362

Smartphones, 132, 369
- Education and Training Industry, 510
- Health Science industry, 439–440

Social and Human Service Assistants, 220–221

Social media, 338

Social media Marketing specialists, 318

Social science, 12

Social scientists, 14

Social skills
- Agriculture, Food, & Natural Resource jobs, 193
- Architecture & Construction job, 158
- Arts & Media job, 126
- Business Management & Administration job, 262
- Education and Training Industry, 503
- Finance jobs, 294
- Government & Public Administration job, 229
- Hospitality & Tourism industry, 398
- Human Services, 468
- Information Technology job, 94
- Law, Public Safety, Corrections, & Security, 537
- Manufacturing job, 63
- Marketing jobs, 330
- STEM jobs, 33
- Transportation, Distribution, & Logistics industry, 363

Software, 76
- Information Technology, 9100

Software developers, 82

Software quality assurance analysts and testers, 83

Solar cell installers, 20–21

Solar Photovoltaic Installers, 148–149

Sound engineering technicians, 116–117
Specialty trade construction, 139
Sports competitors, 114
Statement clerks, 273
Stress, 266
Student support professionals, 481
Supervisors, 52
Suppliers, 45
Support administrators, Education and Training Industry, 481–482
Support services, Health Science industry, 412, 432
Surgeons, 419
Surveying and mapping technicians, 147
Sustainability
    Agriculture, Food, & Natural Resource industry, 204–205
    Architecture & Construction industry, 166–167
    Finance industry, 305
    Hospitality & Tourism industry, 407
    Marketing industry, 339
    STEM industry, 42–43
    Transportation, Distribution, & Logistics industry, 370
Sustainable design, 43

T

Tablets, 510
Taxation, 211
Tax preparers, 251–252
Teaching, 480–481
Teamwork skills
    Agriculture, Food, & Natural Resource jobs, 193
    Architecture & Construction job, 158
    Arts & Media job, 126
    Business Management & Administration job, 261
    Education and Training Industry, 503
    Finance jobs, 294
    Government & Public Administration job, 229
    Hospitality & Tourism industry, 398
    Human Services, 468
    Information Technology job, 94
    Law, Public Safety, Corrections, & Security, 537
    Manufacturing job, 63
    Marketing jobs, 330
    STEM jobs, 33
    Transportation, Distribution, & Logistics industry, 363
Technical schools, 7
Technical skills, 433
Technology, 9
    Agriculture, Food, & Natural Resource industry, 193, 201–203
    Architecture & Construction industry, 157, 165–166
    Arts & Media industry, 126, 132–133
    Business Management & Administration, 261, 267–268
    Education and Training Industry, 502, 509–512
    Finance industry, 293, 301–304
    Government & Public Administration, 228
    Health Science industry, 439–442
    Hospitality & Tourism industry, 397
    Human Services, 467
    Information Technology, 94
    Law, Public Safety, Corrections, & Security, 536
    lodging, 405–406
    Manufacturing industry, 62, 70–72
    Marketing industry, 330, 336–337
    online Marketing, 337–338
    online sales and service, 337
    recreation, amusements, and attractions, 406–407
    restaurant and food/beverage services, 406
    STEM industry, 13–15, 32, 40–41
    Transportation, Distribution, & Logistics industry, 362–363, 368–370
    travel and tourism, 407
Telecommunications, 108
Telecommunications advances, 132
Telemedicine, 440–441
Temporary workers
    Government & Public Administration, 238
    Health Science industry, 443
Therapeutic services, 411–412, 431
3D printing
    Health Science industry, 442
    manufacturing, 70–71
Ticket takers, 114–115
Time-share arrangements, 376
Title Examiners, Government & Public Administration, 219
Top-level managers, 241
Tour guides, 385
Tractor-trailer truck drivers, 352–353
Training. *see also* **Education and training**
    Agriculture, Food, & Natural Resources jobs, 189–191
    Architecture & Construction industry, 155–156
    Arts & Media jobs, 124
    Business Management & Administration, 250, 258–262
    Education and Training Industry, 499–500
    Finance jobs, 290–292
    Government & Public Administration, 226–228
    Human Services, 464
    Information Technology, 93
    Law, Public Safety, Corrections, & Security, 533
    Manufacturing jobs, 61
    STEM jobs, 29–30
    Transportation, Distribution, & Logistics industry, 359–361
Transit bus drivers, 351
Translators, 385

Transportation, Distribution, & Logistics
   career building, 356–358
   career paths, 342–345
   education and training, 359–363
   future outlook, 345–346
   jobs, 349–353
   trends, 368–373
   working conditions, 366–367

Transportation/infrastructure planning, 345

Transportation Operations, 343

Travel Agent skill standards, 397

Travel and Tourism, 378

Treasurers, 274

U

Undertakers, 454–455

Ushers, 114–115

U.S. Intelligence Community, 209

US marshals, 515

V

Vacation travel planning, 378

Values, 4

Videoconferencing, 475
   Business Management & Administration, 267–268

Viral Marketing, 339

Virtual private networks (VPNs), 132

Visual Arts, 108

W

Warehouses and distribution centers, 344

Web and digital communications, IT, 77–78

Web and digital programming, IT, 76

Wi-Fi, 369

Wind turbine service technicians, 19–20

Work environment
   Agriculture, Food, & Natural Resource industry, 196
   Architecture & Construction industry, 161
   Arts & Media industry, 129
   Business Management & Administration, 265
   Finance industry, 297
   Information Technology, 95
   Manufacturing industry, 66
   STEM industry, 36

Work hours
   Agriculture, Food, & Natural Resource jobs, 198
   Architecture & Construction industry job, 162
   Arts & Media industry job, 130
   Business Management & Administration job, 265
   corporate trainers, 507
   correction services, 541
   distance-learning coordinator, 507
   emergency and fire management services, 541
   Finance jobs, 298–299
   Government & Public Administration job, 232–233
   Health Science industry, 436–437
   human resources, 507
   Human Services, 471–472
   Information Technology job, 95–96
   law enforcement services, 541
   legal services, 541
   lodging, 401
   Manufacturing industry job, 67–68
   Marketing industry, 334
   public school teachers, 506–507
   recreation, amusements, and attractions, 402
   restaurants and food/beverage services, 401–402
   security and protective services, 541
   STEM jobs, 37
   Transportation, Distribution, & Logistics industry, 366–367
   travel and tourism, 402

Working conditions
   Agriculture, Food, & Natural Resource industry, 196–200
   Education and Training Industry, 506–508
   Finance industry, 297–300
   Health Science industry, 436–438
   Hospitality & Tourism industry, 401–404
   Human Services, 471–473
   Marketing industry, 333–335
   STEM industry, 36–39

Working With Data
   Agriculture, Food, & Natural Resource career, 187
   Architecture & Construction, 151
   Arts & Media, 120
   Business Management & Administration, 255–256
   Education and Training Industry, 496
   Finance career, 288
   Government & Public Administration, 224
   Health Science industry, 426
   Hospitality & Tourism industry, 391
   Human Services, 460–461
   Information Technology, 89
   Law, Public Safety, Corrections, & Security, 529–530
   Manufacturing industry, 58
   Marketing industry, 323
   STEM career, 27
   Transportation, Distribution, & Logistics industry, 357

Working With People
   Agriculture, Food, & Natural Resource career, 187–188
   Architecture & Construction industry, 152
   Arts & Media industry, 121
   Business Management & Administration, 256
   Education and Training Industry, 496
   Finance career, 288
   Government & Public Administration industry, 224–225

Health Science industry, 426–427
Hospitality & Tourism industry, 391–392
Human Services, 461
Information Technology, 89–90
Law, Public Safety, Corrections, & Security, 530
Manufacturing industry, 58–59
Marketing industry, 324
STEM career, 28
Transportation, Distribution, & Logistics industry, 358

Working With Things
Agriculture, Food, & Natural Resource career, 188
Architecture & Construction industry, 153
Arts & Media industry, 121
Business Management & Administration, 256–257
Education and Training Industry, 497
Finance career, 289
Government & Public Administration, 225
Health Science industry, 427
Hospitality & Tourism industry, 392
Human Services, 462
Information Technology, 90
Law, Public Safety, Corrections, & Security, 531
Manufacturing industry, 59
Marketing industry, 324–325
STEM career, 28
Transportation, Distribution, & Logistics industry, 358

Workplace diversity, 304

Workplace skills
Architecture & Construction job, 156–158
Finance jobs, 292–294
Marketing jobs, 329–331

Workplace trends, 237–238

Z
Zoologists, 14